The Reception of Ḥāfiẓ

I0880047

IRANIAN STUDIES SERIES

The Iranian Studies Series publishes high-quality scholarship on various aspects of Iranian civilisation, covering both contemporary and classical cultures of the Persian cultural area. The contemporary Persian-speaking area includes Iran, Afghanistan, Tajikistan, and Central Asia, while classical societies using Persian as a literary and cultural language were located in Anatolia, Caucasus, Central Asia and the Indo-Pakistani subcontinent. The objective of the series is to foster studies of the literary, historical, religious and linguistic products in Iranian languages. In addition to research monographs and reference works, the series publishes English-Persian critical text-editions of important texts. The series intends to publish resources and original research and make them accessible to a wide audience.

CHIEF EDITOR
A.A. Seyed-Gohrab (Leiden University)

ADVISORY BOARD OF ISS
F. Abdullaeva (University of Cambridge)
G.R. van den Berg (Leiden University)
J.T.P. de Bruijn (Leiden University)
D.P. Brookshaw (University of Oxford)
N. Chalisova (Russian State University of Moscow)
D. Davis (Ohio State University)
F.D. Lewis (University of Chicago)
L. Lewisohn (University of Exeter)
S. McGlinn (unaffiliated)
Ch. Melville (University of Cambridge)
D. Meneghini (University of Venice)
N. Pourjavady (University of Tehran)
Ch. van Ruymbeke (University of Cambridge)
S. Sharma (Boston University)
K. Talattof (University of Arizona)
Z. Vesel (CNRS, Paris)
R. Zipoli (University of Venice)

THE RECEPTION OF ḤĀFIẒ

THE SWEET POETIC LANGUAGE OF ḤĀFIẒ IN NINETEENTH AND TWENTIETH CENTURY PERSIA

Bahman Solati

Leiden University Press

Cover design: Tarek Atrissi Design
Lay out: TAT Zetwerk, Utrecht

Amsterdam University Press English-language titles are distributed in the US and Canada by the University of Chicago Press.

ISBN 978 90 8728 197 7
e-ISBN 978 94 0060 154 3 (pdf)
e-ISBN 978 94 0060 155 0 (ePub)
NUR 630

© B. Solati / Leiden University Press, 2013

All rights reserved. Without limiting the rights under copyright reserved above, no part of this book may be reproduced, stored in or introduced into a retrieval system, or transmitted, in any form or by any means (electronic, mechanical, photocopying, recording or otherwise) without the written permission of both the copyright owner and the author of the book.

Contents

System of Transliteration

CONSONANTS

ء	ʾ	غ	gh
ب	b	ف	f
پ	p	ق	q
ت	t	ک	k
ث	th	گ	g
ج	j	ل	l
چ	ch	م	m
ح	ḥ	ن	n
خ	kh	ه	h
د	d	و	v
ذ	dh	ی	y
ر	r		
ز	z		
ژ	zh		
س	s		
ش	sh		
ص	ṣ		
ض	ḍ		
ط	ṭ		
ظ	ẓ		
ع	ʿ		

VOWELS

Long	ا ی	ā
	و	ū
	ِ ي	Final form ī
Doubled	ِ يّ	iyy Final form ī
	ُ وّ	uww Final form ū
Diphthongs	وَ	au
	یَ	ay
Short	َ	a
	ُ	u
	ِ	i

Acknowledgements

Many scholars and friends have contributed in a number of ways to this study; but, without a shadow of a doubt, the most assistance has come from one of the greatest western scholars on Sufism and the subject of Ḥāfiẓology, Dr. Leonard Lewisohn. As my dearest friend and supervisor, he has patiently made comments on all the chapters, and has guided me with care through this very difficult task. I shall never be able to repay his generosity and kindness.

It has taken, in total, about five years to complete my task, (the first year working part-time, and the subsequent four years full-time). Most research requires some degree of funding. I was fortunate to receive a travel grant from the British Institute of Persian Studies (BIPS). The grant enabled me to travel to Iran, to spend time in Tehran in the summer of 2010, where I was able to meet a number of notable scholars and specialists on Ḥāfiẓ. This fieldwork greatly facilitated my research.

Many friends have assisted me in a variety of ways. Thanks are due to them all, and I can only apologise for not mentioning their names here. The interpretation of the poems and most of the translations are my own and, therefore, I am responsible for all inaccuracies and errors.

حافظم در مجلسی دردی کشم در محفلی
بنگر این شوخی که چون با خلق صنعت می کنم

I am the Qurʾān-reciting Ḥāfiẓ in the congregation: the drainer of dregs at a party.
See the mischief! How I am playing verbal tricks on people.[1]

Preface

Ḥāfiẓ may certainly lay claim to being one of the world's great poets of erotic love whose verse expresses *par excellence* the 'Religion of Love' of Persia.[1] Yet his genius still goes further. His verse features a lyricism unequalled amongst the giants of Persian poetry throughout the ages. At the same time, as Bahman Solati shows in his Introduction, his verses are quoted day in and day out, furnishing Persian speakers of all ranks of society, both literate and humbly unschooled, with timeless verse epigrams and aphorisms of a universal nature, which serve as a ready hermeneutic in verse for every circumstance. His *bon mot*s provide a seemingly irrefutable poetic logic suitable for every argument, bringing joy to the despondent and inspired wisdom to those seeking guidance.

Ḥāfiẓ's erotic spirituality, his anti-clericalism, and his doctrine of God's mercy are amongst the most important legacies bequeathed by the poet to Persianate civilization.

As a theoretician of the erotic – and Ḥāfiẓ celebrates both Uranian and the Pandemian Venuses – he is singularly bold and brash:

> I broadcast it out loud and in this boast take delight:
> I'm the bond slave of love, free of earth and heaven both.[2]

> I am Adam come down from heaven
> Yet, here and now, in this journey, remain
> Bewitched – ensnared in love
> With youths with faces like the moon.[3]

Eros is his Muse:

> Once Eros in the Art of Rhetoric instructed me,
> All my words became key postulates of debate in every coterie.[4]

He is a votary of the Sufi philosophy that practises the adoration of beauty (*jamāl-parastī*),[5] contemplating God's appearances as the Beautiful (*al-Jamīl*) through His theophanic human forms (*shāhid*):

> I am a lover and a libertine, a player of
> The game of glances with eyes that gaze in love.
> A myriad arts and skills are my instruments:
> I say it plain – in fact, I show it off.[6]
>
> I'm well known throughout the whole city
> For being a wild-haired lover; and I'm that man who has
> Never darkened his vision by seeing evil.[7]

Among the world's great poets, Ḥāfiẓ is the foremost opponent of religious fundamentalism, his *Dīvān* a veritable manifesto of anti-clericalism:[8]

> Go into town where all the taverns are
> And let the winesellers have this news:
> Say: "Ḥāfiẓ is born again and forswears
> The cozenage of abstinence
> And quackery of austerity.[9]

'No vice worse than hypocrisy' is the main maxim of Ḥāfiẓ's gospel;[10] his moral teaching subverts all pious homily:

> Heart-friend, I guide you well along salvation's way:
> Neither by sin vaunt iniquity nor hawk austerity.[11]

Like Shakespeare[12] and Milton,[13] Ḥāfiẓ teaches that there is no greater sin than severity towards faults of others for offences of one's own liking, to which he adds that the quintessence of all sin lies in aggrieving and distressing others:[14]

> Cause no distress and grief to another,
> Then go and do as you wish – for in
> Our Holy Law no other sin than this exists.[15]

The arch-heretic in Ḥāfiẓ's religion of love is ill-starred pharisaic Muslim (*zāhid*), the motions of whose spirit are dull as night, and whose affections dark as Erebus, yet such a one receives the pardon of the generous poet:

> If the zealous puritan never found the way
> To penetrate into romance's universe, well,
> He's forgiven – since Love's a business that hinges
> On inculcation and tutelage.[16]

As Bahman Solati's study demonstrates, Ḥāfiẓ's abhorrence of Muslim puritanism had a huge impact on later Persian poetry. Throughout the Persian-speaking world today, but mainly in Tajikistan, Afghanistan and Iran, his poems fiercely critical of fundamentalist puritans (*shaykh, zāhid, faqīh, qāḍī*, or *wāʿiẓ*, etc.) there are the most commonly used sidearm in the rhetorical arsenal of artists and writers struggling against Muslim theocratic totalitarianism. Verses such as these still deliver the best riposte to those poor decayed formalists of law and order, the *sharīʿa*-oriented mullahocrats in these regions:

> I know this sort of talk won't
> be easy for the city preacher to take –
> But as long as he plays the hypocrite
> and plies the craft of his mummery
> A 'Muslim' is what he'll never be.[17]

> Don't kiss anything except the sweetheart's lip
> And the cup of wine, Ḥāfiẓ; friends, it is a grave mistake
> To kiss the hand held out to you by a Puritan.[18]

> When Paradise is mine today as cash in hand,
> Why then should I be taken in and count upon
> The Puritan's pledge of tomorrow's kingdom?[19]

The poet's vigorous anti-clericalism is complemented by the balm of broad-minded religious tolerance and pluralistic ecumenism:

> Let's forgive the seventy-two sects for their ridiculous
> Wars and misbehaviours. Because they couldn't take in
> The path of truth, they took the road of moonshine.[20]

Whether we are drunk or sober, each of us is making
For the street of the Friend. The temple, synagogue,
The church and the mosque are all houses of love.[21]

The best-beloved legacy of Ḥāfiẓ's poetry lies in his theology of religious tolerance and mercy; his view of God provides for leniency and generosity, while portraying Him as the sinner's best friend:

For sinners in their iniquity
Deserve God's grace and generosity.[22]

God's grace and favour is supreme,
His grace is there although we err;
God's benison is greater than our sin.[23]

Heaven is ordained for us. Paradise our destiny.
Oh theologian, go away!
It's erring sinners who deserve God's generosity.[24]

For Ḥāfiẓ's enlightened libertine (*rind*), although *Adam sinned and disobeyed his Lord* (Qur'ān, xx: 121), the pyrotechnics of hellfire are transmuted into a glowing lamp of love by Divine Mercy:

However much I am steeped in sin in a hundred different ways
Since I've become acquainted with love, I number myself
Among the company of those who enjoy God's mercy.[25]

Ḥāfiẓ figures as the last member of the trinity of three sacred poets in the pantheon Persian literature, the first two being Rūmī (d. 672/1273) and Shabistarī (d. after 741/1340). It is these three poets alone, above all others over the past six hundred years, who have been most frequently commented upon by the greatest philosophers and mystics of Islam in Iran, Turkey and India. Dr. Solati's chapter five – 'From Medieval to Modern Ḥāfiẓology' – highlights the process of the literary consecration of his *Dīvān*, that is, the elevation of it to virtually a sacred text, delineating the historical role played by some of the key commentaries penned on it over the past few centuries down to today. This chapter provides insight into how important these commentaries are to his legacy. Similar to Rumi's *Mathnawī* and Shabistari's *Gulshan-i rāz*, Ḥāfiẓ's *Dīvān* is a repository of wisdom which all Persian speakers, regardless of ideology or creed, consider sacred. One can hardly know Persian without becoming Ḥāfiẓophile by nature, that is, a lover of the Sophianic wisdom (*ḥikmat* = *philo-sophia*) which animates his verse:

> Each verse that Hafiz pens is a masterpiece
> of gnostic lore and sapience.
> Let's praise his fetching turn of phrase
> and his stunning power of speech.[26]

Throughout Persosphone countries in the Middle East, Central Asia, as well as literary circles of the Indian Subcontinent where Persian is known and cultivated, Ḥāfiẓ's *Dīvān* is the vade-mecum of the intelligentsia. Such bardic cultures tend to be utterly Ḥāfiẓocentric,[27] in which conventional Muslims, not to mention Ismāʿīlīs, secular humanists,[28] chauvinist Iranian nationalists,[29] free-thinking philosophers,[30] Zoroastrians,[31] oriental Christians, Jews, not to mention mystics of every hue, confidently assert that Ḥāfiẓ's mythopoetic vision perfectly expresses their own beliefs, finding evidence for their particular doctrines in his verse.[32] The great nineteenth-century *homme de lettres* Riḍā Qulī Khān Hidāyat (d. 1871) thus wisely quipped:

> Ḥāfiẓ was a sage philosopher of great substance, a theosopher of the highest degree... His philosophical works in verse so touches the hearts of the adherents to each sect that all these schools consider him to belong to their own denomination.[33]

In early twentieth-century Iran, with the rise of the cult of Iranian nationalism under the Pahlavi monarchy, Ḥāfiẓ became a virtual patron saint of the land.[34] Bahā al-Dīn Khurramshāhī, the great doyen of Ḥāfiẓ Studies in contemporary Iran, thus refers to the poet as the veritable "spokesman of the Collective Unconscious of the Persian race..."[35]

After Firdawsī and Rūmī, Ḥāfiẓ is our third national poet. Whereas our *national heroic poem* epitomizing the mythological history of the Persians can be found in Firdawsī's *Book of Kings*, while Rūmī's *Mathnawī* and the *Dīvān-i Kabīr* [*Shams*] represent the *national poetic chronicle of the Persian Sufi tradition*, Ḥāfiẓ's *Dīvān* constitutes Persia's *national lyrical epic*, expressive of the Persian people's refined wit, beauty, satire, joy and struggle for social reformation.[36]

Ḥāfiẓ enjoyed an international reputation during his own lifetime; his poetry was feted as far away as Central Asia and India, as the poet himself boasts:

> This itinerant Persian verse
> sent errant on Bengal ways
> is delicious and rich enough
> for Indian parrots to crunch
> its luscious, sugary lumps.[37]

And:

> Those Samarqandi Turks
> and black-eyed girls of Kashmir
> All dance and flaunt their charms
> to Ḥāfiẓ of Shiraz's verse.[38]

Introducing Ḥāfiẓ's *Dīvān* a few decades after his death, Muḥammad Gulandām describes the earliest beginnings of the reception history of Ḥāfiẓ's verse as follows:

It took but a very short time for the literary empire over which his ghazals reigned to stretch from the outermost borders of Khurāsān up into Turkistān and down into India. It took but a brief instant for the convoys of his enchanting speech to reach the outskirts of the lands of Iraq and Azerbayjan. The musical séances of the Sufis (*samāʿ-i ṣūfiyān*) without his passionate poems soon came to lack warmth; likewise, they were a *sine qua non* for the convivial banquets of kings to provide relish, savour and pleasing delectation.[39]

When one combs through the *tadhkira*s and chronicles about Persian poets written during the fifteenth through seventeenth centuries, the name of Ḥāfiẓ as a pre-eminent Persian poet-of-genius resounds. Only a few years after his death, we find scores of poets emulating his style. It would be useful to cite a few here:

- Kamāl Khujandī (d. 803/1400), a first-class *ghazal* poet himself, composed numerous lyrics both in emulation (*naẓīra*) of and response to (*javāb*) to Ḥāfiẓ.[40]
- The Persian gourmet poet, Busḥaq Aṭʿama-yi Shīrāzī (d. 827/1423 or 831/1427), famed for his brilliant parodies of the metaphysical musings of other poets' *ghazal*s, which he lampooned using culinary terminology, wrote parodies of twenty-five *ghazal*s of Ḥāfiẓ.[41]

- Shāh Qāsim-i Anwār (d. 837/1433) and Shāh Ni'matu'llāh Walī (d. 835/ 1431), the two foremost fifteenth-century Persian poets of the school of the Ibn 'Arabī, both wrote several responses to the *ghazal*s of Ḥāfiẓ,[42] while Shāh Dā'ī Shīrāzī (d. 870/1464-1465), another poet of this school, composed numerous imitations of Ḥāfiẓ's *ghazals*.[43]
- Sharaf al-Dīn 'Alī Yazdī (d. 858/1454) wrote several ghazals in imitation of Ḥāfiẓ.[44]
- Kamāl Turbatī (fl. 15th century) wrote responses to most of the *ghazal*s of Ḥāfiẓ using the quintet form (*mukhammas*).[45]
- Ādharī Isfarāyinī (784/1382-866/1462), an expert in the art of lyrical riposte (*javāb-gū'ī*) to the poems of past masters,[46] composed imitations of ten *ghazal*s of Ḥāfiẓ.[47]

Throughout the sixteenth century, this process of poetic emulation of Ḥāfiẓ intensified.

Many of the *ghazal*s of Ghazālī Mashhadī (d. 980/1572) were modelled after (*istiqbāl*) those of Ḥāfiẓ, such that it has been said that "the mindset of his entire *Dīvān* is permeated by the thought of Ḥāfiẓ."[48]

Lisānī Shīrāzī (d. 942/1535) was renowned as a follower of Ḥāfiẓ,[49] and Ḍamīrī Iṣfahānī (d. 987/1579) composed an entire series of poems in honour and imitation of Ḥāfiẓ.[50] Faḍlī (d. 971/1563) and Abū Faḍl Daftarī (d. 983/ 1575) were renowned to have imitated the *Dīvān* of Ḥāfiẓ so thoroughly that they wrote separate *ghazal*s in the same meters and rhymes of all of his poems...[51]

From this cursory list, the catholic impact of Ḥāfiẓ on Persian poets of the fifteenth and sixteenth centuries, which to date has not been properly chronicled, may be assessed. In this respect, Dr. Solati offers in chapter two an interesting overview of the influence of Ḥāfiẓ's verse on the four major Persian poets who flourished between the sixteenth to seventeenth centuries – Jāmī, Fighānī, 'Urfī and Sā'ib. My own preliminary survey indicates that the number of poets affected by his style, imagery and ideas over the fifteenth-seventeenth-century period amounts to as many as several hundred poets, both major and minor. Outside the lands of Greater Persia, particularly in Ottoman Turkey[52] and Mughal India, where the most important and largest amount of commentaries on his *Dīvān* were written, Ḥāfiẓ's undisputable conquest of his readers' heart and minds is also attested by medieval Persian literary histories.

The Reception of Ḥāfiẓ in Nineteenth and Twentieth-Century Persia is the first study of the impact of Ḥāfiẓ in Iran during the period in question. Ḥāfiẓ's influence affected poets of all persuasions and schools – as Bahman Solati shows here for the first time – from compilers of anthologies such as the neoclassical poet Ādhar Bigdilī (d. 1195/1778), to founders of Sufi orders such as the Niʿmatu'llāhī poet Ṣafī 'Alī Shāh' (d. 1316/1898), to great mystical philosophers like Ḥājj Mullā Hādī Sabzivārī (d. 1289/1872). Ḥāfiẓ figures as the dominant influence on Sabzavārī's poetry, such that his verse is permeated with Ḥāfiẓ's imagery and terminology. The *ghazal* poetry of the two greatest panegyrists of nineteenth-century Qājār Persia, namely: Viṣāl Shīrāzī (d. 1262/1845) and Qā'ānī Shīrāzī (d. 1270/1853), as Solati reveals, were steeped in Ḥāfiẓian compounds, images, lyrical coinages, diction and style.

In chapter three, 'The Influence of Ḥāfiẓ on the Poets of Zand and Qājār Persia' and chapter four, 'Ḥāfiẓ and the Poets of Pahlavi Iran', Ḥāfiẓ's influence on nineteenth- and twentieth-century Persian poets is highlighted. The appendix devoted to 'The Influence of Ḥāfiẓ on Eight Persian Poets of the Zand and Qājār Period', contains much valuable and original research, revisiting the works of minor poets who have been largely written out of the textbooks of Persian literature today.

Amongst poets of the twentieth century, the resonance of Ḥāfiẓ's speech is omnipresent; as Solati demonstrates, there have been practically no important Persian poets whose diction has not been influenced by Ḥāfiẓ to a greater or lesser extent. This is the first time in the history of the study of Ḥāfiẓ that we have had any proper scientific study and assessment of his impact on late pre-modern and modern Persian literary history. All students and lovers of the poet are truly indebted to Dr. Solati's thorough-going work of scholarship in this field. This bears out fittingly that the poet's prediction of his own posthumous fame was of course correct:

> Should you pass by my shrine when I am gone,
> Ask for soul-power, spirit-force and *esprit*,
> For all the world's pious rakes and holy reprobates
> Will be pilgrims to my tomb.[53]

– *Leonard Lewisohn*
University of Exeter, 22 May 2013

Introduction

The introduction of the citation of Ḥāfiẓ in a contextualizing manner in the tradition of 'poetic boasting' (*fakhriyya*) in Persian poetry, can best be presented by a verse from the tongue of the poet himself.

شعر حافظ در زمان آدم اندر باغ خلد　　دفتر نسرین و گل را زینت اوراق بود[1]

The poetry of Ḥāfiẓ in the time of Adam, within the Garden of Paradise,
Was the adornment of the pages of the book of the white and red rose.[2]

This study examines the reception of the medieval Persian poet Ḥāfiẓ Shīrāzī (d. 791/1389) during the eighteenth, nineteenth and twentieth centuries; the Zand, Qājār and Pahlavi periods, respectively. By undertaking a critical engagement with Ḥāfiẓ through an analysis of his influence on other poets and critics, I hope to cast new light on this supreme figure of classical Persian poetry for both western and eastern readers and his many admirers.

The importance of Ḥāfiẓ cannot be underestimated. Before the establishment of the modern system of colleges and universities, Ḥāfiẓ's *Dīvān* was studied as a subject of literary research (*Ḥāfiẓ-shināsī*), along with Sa'dī's *Gulistān* (Rose Garden) and the Qur'ān.[3] Ḥāfiẓ is seen as more than merely a poet; indeed, he is viewed by some as an incarnation of the spirit of the nation of Iran.[4] His poetry is so deeply interwoven into the psyche of Iranians that it might be said that to know Persians, one must know Ḥāfiẓ; likewise, it could be said that an in-depth understanding of the Persian character is impossible without understanding Ḥāfiẓ. His work is widely and commonly considered to be unparalleled; over the past seven centuries in Persia, no poet has matched his poetic skill, though many have tried. Ḥāfiẓ himself stated that he had no equal, that his verses are as valuable as gold:

حافظ تو این سخن ازکه آموختی؟ که یار　　تعویذ کرد شعر تورا و به زر گرفت[5]

> Ḥāfiẓ! From who have you learned this fluency? That the beloved
> Made your verse an amulet and gilded it with gold.

In addition to the almost universal acclaim for Ḥāfiẓ's work, it should be noted that exposure to and love of his verse is ubiquitous. Thābitī points out that as soon as any Iranian child learns to read and write, he or she becomes familiar with Saʿdī and Ḥāfiẓ. These two great poets of Persia are the friends and companions of every sad and lonely heart; they form a very special relationship with their fellow countrymen.[6] Even in ordinary written and verbal communication among friends and family, Ḥāfiẓ's verses are cited to express moods of joy or sadness, to poetically contextualize and summarize ideas.

One of the most important elements of Ḥāfiẓ's poetry is the independence of his verses within the body of the *ghazal*.[7] Many lines can be used as individual hemistichs on their own, thus contributing to their usage as proverbs. Saʿdī is the only other poet similar to Ḥāfiẓ in terms of the independence of themes. The following table shows a comparison of wisdom poetry by three first-class Persian poets: Nizāmī (d. 614/1213), Saʿdī (d. c. 691/1292) and Ḥāfiẓ. Wisdom literature (*andarz*) is a field of literature frequently employed in the Ancient Near East. This writing style is characterized by sayings of wisdom (*mithāl*) intended to teach about spirituality and virtue.

The key principle of wisdom literature is that while techniques of traditional storytelling are used, books also present insight and perception about nature and reality. The most famous examples of wisdom literature are found in the Bible. In Persian literature, wisdom verses are almost always rhythmic; one of the primary reasons for this is that a musical verse is more easily remembered than a non-musical verse. Thus, there are an immense number of couplets conveying many teachings in respect of humanity and moral conduct.

This is neither an assessment of the quality of poetry, nor a judgement of talent and skill; rather, it illustrates the ways in which Ḥāfiẓ's verses, like those of Saʿdī and Nizāmī, are full of delightfully composed proverbs and wise *bon mots*.[8]

Fear not the sin that benefits others.	(Ḥāfiẓ)	(حافظ)[9]	از آن گناه که نفعی رسد به غیر چه باک
It matters not if I am good or ugly. You correct yourself.	(Ḥāfiẓ)	(حافظ)[10]	من اگر نیکم اگر بد تو برو خود را باش
O Light of my eyes, peace surpasses war and is better than hostility.	(Ḥāfiẓ)	(حافظ)[11]	ای نور دیده صلح به ازجنگ و داوری
Cut short your speech before you are told it is enough.	(Saʿdī)	(سعدی)[12]	از آن پیش بس کن که گویند بس
Virtue from the malevolent cannot be learned.	(Saʿdī)	(سعدی)[13]	از بدان نیکویی نیاموزی
Speak sweetly to all God's creatures.	(Saʿdī)	(سعدی)[14]	با خلق خدا سخن به شیرینی کن
One must not speak ill of the dead.	(Nizāmī)	(نظامی)[15]	از پس مرده بد نباید گفت
Seek hardship for yourself and comfort for your friends.	(Nizāmī)	(نظامی)[16]	رنج خود و راحت یاران طلب
To the blind man's eye, the Tigris river appears a drop.	(Nizāmī)	(نظامی)[17]	دجله بود قطره از چشم کور
Become a man of God and live safely amongst foes.	(Ḥāfiẓ)	(حافظ)[18]	مرد یزدان شو و ایمن گذر از اهرمنان
Help the needy if you have the means.	(Ḥāfiẓ)	(حافظ)[19]	دریاب ضعیفان را در وقت توانایی
Every good deed brings a reward and each misdeed, a consequence.	(Ḥāfiẓ)	(حافظ)[20]	هر عمل اجری و هر کرده جزائی دارد
Great masters never praise themselves.	(Saʿdī)	(سعدی)[21]	بزرگان نکردند در خود نگاه
Do not crave appreciation for yourself.	(Saʿdī)	(سعدی)[22]	از کبر مدار هیچ در دل هوسی
Do not pass your time with base folk.	(Saʿdī)	(سعدی)[23]	مبر با فرومایه روزگار
Listen, because the advice of the sage will do you no harm.	(Ḥāfiẓ)	(حافظ)[24]	بشنو که پند پیران هیچت زیان ندارد
It is better not to associate with bad people.	(Ḥāfiẓ)	(حافظ)[25]	بهتر آن است که با مردم بد ننشینی
By pretence one cannot seat oneself in the chair of masters.	(Ḥāfiẓ)	(حافظ)[26]	تکیه بر جای بزرگان نتوان زد به گزاف

An additional praiseworthy characteristic of Ḥāfiẓ, as noted by ʿAlī Dashtī, is the scope of his imagination and his disinterest in the material world, particularly the trappings of place, greatness and power.[27] Dashtī presents the following verse as an example:

در این بازار اگر سودیست با درویش خرسند است   خدایا منعمم گردان به درویشی وخرسندی[28]

If in this marketplace there is any profit, it is to the contented dervish,
O God, make me the beneficiary of dervishism and blessed contentment![29]

This book is divided into five chapters, a conclusion, an appendix and a bibliography. In chapter I, I offer an overview of the life of Ḥāfiẓ and his political connections with the princes of the Muẓaffarīd court, his somewhat controversial relations with the various classes of the men of learning and clerics (*ʿulamāʾ*) and his conflict with Mubāriz al-Dīn (Shāh Shujāʿ's father), as these are some of the necessary components of his later reception in history. In addition, I analyze the presence or lack of political themes in Ḥāfiẓ's poetry and some key aspects of his poetic style.

Chapter II focuses on Ḥāfiẓ from a historical and sociopolitical perspective, covering the late Tīmūrīd period (771/1365-913/1507) through to the late Qājār era (1193/1779-1339/1925). I then discuss the reception of Ḥāfiẓ's poetry after his death and the effect his work had on key poets of the Ṣafavid era, such as Jāmī (d. 898/1492), Bābā Fighānī (d. 925/1519), Ahlī Shīrāzī (d. 942/1535-1536), ʿUrfī Shīrāzī (d. 999/1596) and Ṣāʾib Tabrizī (d. 1080/1669-1670 or 1088/1677). From the Qājār period, I explore the thought of seven critics and writers; namely, Mīrzā Āqā Khān Kirmānī (d. 1274/1896); Riḍā Qulī Hidāyat (d. 1288/1871); Mīrzā Fatḥ-ʿAlī Ākhūndzāda (d. 1295/1878); Mīrzā Malkam/Malkum Khān (d. 1315/1898); Muḥammad ʿAlī Furūghī Dhakāʾ al-Mulk (d. 1321/1942), ʿAbdul Raḥīm Ṭālibuf (d. 1329/1911) and Zayn al-ʿĀbidin Marāghaʾī (d. 1329/1911).

In chapter III, I introduce the lives of seven poets (listed below) of the Zand and Qājār period, then draw comparisons between their work and that of Ḥāfiẓ:

1. Ādhar Bigdilī (d. 1195/1778)
2. Viṣāl Shīrāzī (d. 1262/1845)
3. Qāʾānī Shīrāzī (d. 1270/1853)
4. Furūghī Basṭāmī (d. 1274/1857)
5. Yaghmā Jandaqī (d. 1276/1859)
6. Ḥājj Mullā Hādī Sabzivārī (d. 1289/1872)
7. Ḥājj Mīrzā Ḥasan Iṣfahānī ʿṢafī ʿAlī Shāhʾ (d. 1316/1898)

In this way, I offer evidence to support my research that Ḥāfiẓ's language, and in some cases his school of thought, greatly influenced the work of these poets. After undertaking a careful study of the *ghazal* collections of each of the selected poets, I then juxtapose their verses with those of Ḥāfiẓ and draw conclusions about the latter's influence.

Chapter IV examines Ḥāfiẓ's influence on a selection of poets and on the politics and literature of Pahlavi Persia. I consider the following poets:

1. Muḥammad-Taqī Bahār (d. 1330/1951)
2. Nimā Yūshij (d. 1338/1960)
3. Suhrāb Sipihrī (d. 1358/1980)
4. Shahriyār (d. 1366/1988)
5. Aḥmad Shāmlū (d. 1379/2000)

I provide a brief biography of each poet in order to historically contextualize their work before examining Ḥāfiẓ's influence on each of them. Although they were all influenced by Ḥāfiẓ's poetic style in greater and lesser degrees, my analysis underlines that each of the poets selected was clearly affected by his symbolism, imagery and ideas.

In chapter V, I concentrate on the field of Ḥāfiẓology from the medieval to the modern period, covering almost 450 years (1500-1942) of editions and compilations of his *Dīvān*, from Sulṭān Ḥusayn Mīrzā to Ghanī and Qazvīnī. I examine key studies and commentaries on the *Dīvān*, focusing on the most significant works produced over the past two hundred years. I analyze the recent editions of and commentaries on Ḥāfiẓ's *Dīvān* from the period from 1942 to 2010, concentrating on the works of the following scholars:

1. Bahā' al-Dīn Khurramshāhī
2. Ḥusayn Hiravī
3. Manūchihr Murtaḍavī
4. Muḥammad Istiʿlāmī
5. Muḥammad Riḍā Barzigar Khāliqī
6. Raḥīm Dhū'l-Nūr
7. Saʿīd Niāz Kirmānī
8. Sayyid Yaḥyā Yathrabī

Lastly, I consider two important commentaries on Ḥāfiẓ produced outside Persia, briefly discussing the seventeenth-century works of Sūdī in Ottoman Turkey and Lāhūrī in Mughal India.

The conclusion (VI) addresses and attempts to answer seven key questions raised by this study concerning the reception of Ḥāfiẓ's poetry during the nineteenth and twentieth centuries. This is followed by a lengthy appendix on eight Persian poets of the Qājār period whose language and thoughts have, in one way or another, been influenced and inspired by Ḥāfiẓ.

In the course of my research on this book, I have greatly benefited from interviews with a number of eminent scholars of Persian literature whose personal communications are recorded as and when necessary. These scholars include: Bahā' al-Dīn Khurramshāhī (Tehran), Dr. Shahram Pazouki (Tehran), Dr. Mohamad Movahedi (Tehran), Prof. Kavoos Ḥasanli (Shīrāz University), Dr. Homayoon Katouzian (Oxford), Dr. Julie Meisami (Berkeley), Mr. Hushang Ibtihāj *Sāya* (Germany) and Prof. ʻAlī Ferdowsi (Notre Dame de Namur University, Belmont, California). I have also made ample use of various libraries in Iran, the United Kingdom and the United States while researching the dissertation, including:

1. The John Ryland Library of the University of Manchester
2. The School of Oriental and African Studies, London
3. The Green Library at Stanford University, California
4. The Library of the University of Berkeley
5. The Library of Congress, Washington, D.C.
6. The Library of the Defense Language Institute, Monterey, California
7. The Library of the University of Tehran, Iran
8. The Iranian National Library (*Kitābkhāni-yi Millī-yi Iran*)

Note on translation

It is my belief that the aim of the translator is to present the original as accurately as possible; thus, I translate Persian poetry into prose, which does not impose any restrictions with regard to rhyme or metre. All translations of poetry and text in this study, unless otherwise stated, are my own.

Note on dates

Dates in the book referring to the Islamic lunar *hijrī* calendar (A.H.) are cited to the end of the Qājār period. Dates following 1330/1911 are written according to the solar (*shamsī*) Iranian calendar (A.Hsh.). Following the A.H. or A.Hsh. years, dates according to the Common Era (CE) are cited. Shāhānshāhī dates are noted as such.

CHAPTER I

The Life and Times of Ḥāfiẓ

The central focus of this Chapter is an examination of the historic and sociopolitical milieu of Shīrāz, the poet's hometown. This detailed analysis of the conditions and surroundings in which Ḥāfiẓ grew up and spent his life provides the reader with a broad understanding of Ḥāfiẓ's character while exploring his poetic persona. In addition, this chapter sheds light on examination and analysis of the reception of Ḥāfiẓ since his death and during the later periods in the literary history of Persia. Subsequent chapters gradually explore, examine, and analyze many different factors, such as Ḥāfiẓ's contemporaries from kings to poets, to support my argument that Ḥāfiẓ's reception has been significant since his death and, in some cases, throughout his lifetime.

The following chapters, in particular Chapter III, examine and compare the works of some selected poets of the Zand and Qājār periods and juxtapose their poetry with the poetry and poetic language of Ḥāfiẓ. In some cases, I have compared Ḥāfiẓ's school of thought with some of the selected poets of the periods mentioned above.

The Life and Times of Ḥāfiẓ

Ḥāfiẓ is one of the poets of medieval Persian literature whose life story is not very well documented by his contemporaries.[1] Dabāshī asserts:

> There is a historical Ḥāfiẓ, whom we know through scattered biographical references in a few hagiographical sources. Our actual knowledge of the historical Ḥāfiẓ is limited, not totally reliable, and leaves much to be desired. But there is also a mythical Ḥāfiẓ created in and by the collective imagination of generations of admirers who have fashioned 'their Ḥāfiẓ' according to their set of pride and prejudices.[2]

Lewisohn concisely sums up the biographies of many of the Sufi poets of this period, such as Ḥāfiẓ, Sāvajī, Khujandī and Maghribī and shows how they are filled with baffling stories, puzzling occurrences and delicately presented witticisms, demonstrating literary history itself as one of the many levels of Sufi emblematic poetry.[3]

The most reliable account about Ḥāfiẓ was written by one of his disciples, Muḥammad Gulandām, shortly after Ḥāfiẓ's death. Many stories, some greatly exaggerated, have been written about Ḥāfiẓ's life.[4] Shams al-Dīn Muḥammad Ḥāfiẓ Shīrāzī was born in 715/1315 in Shīrāz, Persia.[5] His father, a merchant called Bahā' al-Dīn, or Kamāl al-Dīn, was from Iṣfahān and died when Ḥāfiẓ was a child.[6] During Ḥāfiẓ's life, seven rulers rose and fell from power. During the Īnjū'īd period (r. 743/1343-753/1352), Shīrāz enjoyed a comfortable and peaceful time during which the treasury's wealth reached its peak. Such material comfort and luxurious living attracted many of the elite members of the intelligentsia and poets of the time; Ḥāfiẓ was no exception. Ḥāfiẓ may also have been attached to the court, being almost the same age as the young king of Īnjū.[7] Some scholars believe that one of the reasons Ḥāfiẓ was involved with the court and the young king Abū Isḥāq Īnjū must have been his need for financial assistance in order to continue with his scholarly works, because his studies were his first priority.[8] However, I believe Ḥāfiẓ's attachment to the young Īnjū'īd king, Abū Isḥāq, was not for financial support alone. Indeed, Ḥāfiẓ clearly states his beliefs in the following verse:

درویش را نباشد برگ سرای سلطان   مایيم و کهنه دلقی کآتش در آن توان زد[9]

> The dervish may not have the delicacies of the Sulṭān's palace;
> It is a case of us and a worn-out gown from which a fire might be lit.[10]

The poet Shams al-Dīn Muḥammad Ḥāfiẓ grew up in Shīrāz and was a young man in his late twenties during the Īnjū'īd dynasty. Abū Isḥāq Īnjū had an unstable side; he initiated dreadful conflicts and intensely mistrusted the people of Shīrāz, who had long defended his kin against various challengers.[11] Nonetheless, during his reign the city of Shīrāz thrived. Political instability and military disturbances did not interrupt the flourishing cultural life of the city and education, literature and poetry were greatly promoted.

Abū Isḥāq Īnjū (r. 743/1343-753/1352)

In 743/1343, Abū Isḥāq gained control of the provinces of Fārs and Iṣfahān, and maintained them for eleven years. Contemporary poets and historians, such as Shihāb al-Dīn 'Abdullāh ibn 'Abdul Rashīd, otherwise known as Ḥāfiẓ Abrū (d. 834/1432), as well as Ḥāfiẓ Shīrāzī, praised Abū Isḥāq for his intellect, heroism, bravery and open heartedness.[12] Ḥāfiẓ must have been close to his thirties when Abū Isḥāq came to power.[13] Poets and historians have mentioned Abū Isḥāq as an admirer of art, literature and religious learning; indeed, his short sovereignty saw sparkling accomplishments in all those areas.[14]

راستی خاتم فیروزهٔ بواسحاقی   خوش درخشید ولی دولت مستعجل بود[15]

Truly, the Abū Isḥāq turquoise ring
Dazzled, but with only ephemeral shine.[16]

The Īnjū'īd dynasty was ended by Amīr Mubāriz al-Dīn Muḥammad, who is considered the first ruler of the Muẓaffarīd dynasty, which lasted eighty years, from his succession in 715/1313 to the removal of the dynasty by Tīmūr in 795/1393. His initial rule started from the small town of Maybud near Yazd. However, in 742/1340, Kirmān also fell under his control. Thirteen years later, in 755/1353, the province of Fārs and the city of Shīrāz, despite a lengthy resistance, fell under his jurisdiction as well.[17] During the siege of Shīrāz by Mubāriz al-Dīn, Abū Isḥāq lost a number of his key advisers and patrons, such as Ḥājj Qavām al-Dīn Ḥasan Tamghachī (d. 755/1354), who had served the Īnjū families for twenty-five years. As a result of his generosity and morality he was frequently praised by Ḥāfiẓ.[18]

به رندی شهره شد حافظ میان همدمان لیکن   چه غم دارم که در عالم قوام الدین حسن دارم[19]

Ḥāfiẓ is notorious among his companions for *rindī*,
But what do I care? In this world I have Qavām al-Dīn Ḥasan?[20]

During the siege, the people of Shīrāz put up considerable resistance, but were finally forced to surrender to the invader. A final appeal to end the hostility was made by Qāḍī Majd al-Dīn (d. 756/1355), a reputable ascetic of the time who composed and sent Amīr Mubāriz al-Dīn this verse:[21]

مبارزان جهان قلب دشمنان شکنند　　　تورا چه شد که همه قلب دوستان شکنی؟[22]

The warriors of the world break the hearts of their enemies,
What has become of you, that you break the hearts of your friends?

Qāḍī Majd al-Dīn is one of five personages who appear in a *qiṭ'a* by Ḥāfiẓ, beginning with this verse:

به عهد سلطنت شاه شیخ ابو اسحق　　　به پنج شخص عجب ملک فارس بود آباد[23]

During the leadership of the Shāh Abū Isḥāq,
The province of Fārs prospered, due to five people.

In this short poem, Ḥāfiẓ describes the city's structure of authority throughout the reign of Abū Isḥāq, mentioning, in addition to the ruler himself, a minister, two judges, and a Sufi Shaykh who possessed great power and added lustre to the city during his reign in Shīrāz.[24] The besieging forces were eventually led into the city. Abū Isḥāq, realizing his imminent defeat, fled west with a few of his associates and took refuge in the Qal'i-i sifid.[25] In 774/1373, Muẓaffarīd armies captured Abū Isḥāq in Iṣfahān and delivered him to Mubāriz al-Dīn Muḥammad at Shīrāz, where, during the final moments before he was executed, it is said that he recited the following verse in front of the judges and some nobles of the court:

افسوس که مرغ عمر را دانه نماند　　　و امید به هیچ خویش و بیگانه نماند
دردا و دریغ که در این مدت عمر　　　از هرچه بگفتیم جز افسانه نماند

Alas no grain remains for the bird of life!
Alas no hope is left for family or stranger!

Alas from this span of our life,
Nothing I have said remains, but stories![26]

The cultural environment of Shīrāz allowed Ḥāfiẓ a good education, the high standard of which is evident from his pen name (*takhalluṣ*), 'Ḥāfiẓ', a title that was only given to those who had memorized the Qur'ān by heart, a feat he had accomplished even before he was a grown man.[27] By all accounts he wrote in prose about scholarly Arabic literature and theological works.[28] It is evident from some verses in his *Dīvān*, which can be used for reliable biographical clues, that he spent most of his time studying and took great pleasure in learning.[29]

In one of his verses, Ḥāfiẓ indicates that he pursued knowledge for forty years.[30]

علم و فضلی که به چل سال دلم جمع آورد　　　ترسم آن نرگس مستانه به یغما ببرد[31]

The science and learning, that in forty years my heart acquired,
I fear that drunken eye may take as plunder.

طاق و رواق مدرسه و قال قیل علم　　　در راه جام و ساقی مهرو نهاده ایم[32]

We have placed the arch and corridor of the school, and scientific disputation,
On the path of both the cup and Sāqī, whose face is like the moon.

In another verse, we see that he wishes for a companion and complains of loneliness.

جویها بسته ام از دیده به دامان که مگر　　　در کنارم بنشانند سهی بالایی[33]

From my eye to my skirt I have poured streams, hoping that, perchance,
By my side, there may sit, a tall idol.

Further evidence indicates that he married and enjoyed a happy family life, at least for a while.

مرا در خانه سروی هست کاندر سایهٔ قدش　　　فراغ از سرو بستانی و شمشاد چمن دارم[34]

In the house, mine is a cypress, in the shade of whose stature,
I am free of the cypress in the garden and the boxwood of the field.

The final verse of this *ghazal* mentions the name of the court minister, Qavām al-Dīn Ḥasan. It is therefore safe to assume that it was composed during the office of Ḥasan, between 743/1343 and 753/1352, when Abū Isḥāq was the ruler of Shīrāz. However, his family life did not last long, for in the following verse, Ḥāfiẓ directs the attention of the reader to his loss of a loved one. Although there are no indications about her date of death, there are unmistakable suggestions that he may well be referring to his wife.[35]

آن یار کز او خانهٔ ما جای پری بود　　سر تا قدمش چون پری از عیب بری بود
دل گفت فروکش کنم این شهر ببویش　　بیچاره ندانست که یارش سفری بود[36]

That friend, because of whom our house was the dwelling of the angels,
Was an angel, free from defect.

Heart said: With her scent, this town I shall fill,
Helpless, it knew not that its friend was a traveller.

Ḥāfiẓ also alludes to the death of his son. In the following verse, he mentions the word 'son' and refers to the death, but similarly, the date of his death is unclear.[37]

از آن دمی که ز چشمم برفت رودِ عزیز　　کنار دامن من همچو رود جیحونست[38]

From that time, when my precious son slipped from my grasp,
My skirt's border is like the Oxus River.

Ḥāfiẓ admired Abū Isḥāq's character and personality to such an extent that when the king was killed by Amīr Mubāriz al-Dīn in 757/1357, the young poet sank into a state of depression.[39]

Amīr Mubāriz al-Dīn Muḥammad Muẓaffarī (r. 754/1353-759/1357)

Amīr Mubāriz, who succeeded Abū Isḥāq, was ruthless and firm, very much like his father who had been courageous and determined.[40] Amīr Mubāriz al-Dīn Muḥammad Muẓaffar lived in the city of Maybud in Yazd until his father's death, when he was just thirteen years of age. By 718/1318, he had gained the governorship of Yazd and thirty-six years later, in 754/1353, he took full control of Fārs, Shabānkārān, Kirmān, Luristān and Iṣfahān.[41]

Amīr Mubāriz is considered to be the first ruler of the Muẓaffarīd dynasty.[42] One of Mubāriz al-Dīn's initial steps was to implement strict laws against wine-drinking and other religious irregularities found amongst the fun-loving Shīrāzīs.[43] He secured his name in literature and poetry through several panegyrical poets such as Imād Faqīh Kirmānī. Due to his fanatical religious ideas, he made life hard for literary men such as Ḥāfiẓ.[44] The happy period of social freedom was nearing an end.[45] The taverns were closed and serving wine was forbidden according to Islamic rules. This annoyed Ḥāfiẓ and his frustration and the tense atmosphere can be identified in some of his verses.[46]

در میخانه ببستند خدایا مپسند   که در خانهٔ تزویر و ریا بگشایند[47]

They have closed the tavern doors. O God, sanction not,
For, they will open the doors of the house of deceit and hypocrisy.[48]

It was during this period that both social and public life came under the close watch of assigned sheriffs (*muḥtasib*).[49] According to Ghanī, the name *muḥtasib* was given to Amīr Mubāriz as a satirical jibe about the artificial orthodoxy of his rule.[50] Nevertheless, Ḥāfiẓ continued to compose beautiful, ironic and profound verses using dynamic metaphors and images, despite the ruler's imposition of harsh religious rules and regulations.[51]

خدارا محتسب مارا به فریاد می و دف بخش   که ساز شرع از این افسانه بی قانون نخواهد شد[52]

O *muḥtasib*! For God's sake, let us enjoy the clamour of drum and reed,
For the instrument of the divine law will not go out of tune because of this tale.

محتسب شیخ شد و فسق خود از یاد ببرد   قصهٔ ماست که در هر سر بازار بماند[53]

The *muḥtasib* became a Shaykh and forgot his sins,
It is our tale that has remained in every market place!

Amīr Mubāriz al-Dīn killed his enemies without reason. It has been reported that on one occasion, whilst reciting the Qurʾān, he paused to kill some convicts and then resumed his recital.[54] Ḥāfiẓ, however, did not agree with Amīr Mubāriz's behaviour, and he began criticizing the hypocrisy that was introduced during Amīr Mubāriz's reign.

ناموس عشق و رونق عشّاق می برند   عیب جوان و سرزنش پیر می کنند[55]

The honour of love and splendour of lovers, they take;
The censure of the young and reproof of the old, they make.

During the reign of Mubāriz, traces of longing for Abū Isḥāq and expressions of nostalgia are evident in some verses of the *Dīvān*. Ḥāfiẓ is mournful for the lost days of joy and comfort.[56]

یاد باد آن صحبت شبها که با نوشین لبان   بحث سرّ عشق و ذکر حلقهٔ عشاق بود[57]

May those night talks be remembered, when, with sweet lips
There were discussions of love's mystery and the lovers' circle.

یاد باد آنکه نگارم چو کمر بر بستی   در رکابش مه نو پیک جهان پیما بود[58]

May the time be remembered, when my beloved would fasten on his belt,[59]
And at his stirrup, the new moon was the herald all around the world.[60]

In addition to his bad temper and fanatical ideas, Mubāriz was a greedy ruler who continued to look further afield for future conquests. In 759/1357, he marched on Azerbaijan and by 760/1358 he had occupied Tabriz, though he left it after just two months of occupation and returned to Iṣfahān.[61] Mubāriz al-Din's sons and immediate relatives feared his harsh temper and suspicious nature; he threatened them with arrest and execution.[62] In 760/1358, while he was returning from Tabriz to Iṣfahān, his son (Shāh Shujāʿ) and nephew arrested him and killed his minister; Shujāʿ then blinded his own father (Amīr Mubāriz) and confined him in the Qalʿi-i sifid.[63] The *Dīvān* includes an account of this event.

آنکه روشن بود جهان بینش بدو   میل در چشم جهان بینش کشید[64]

The son was the light of his father's eye,
That very son blinded his father.

Although Mubāriz soon reconciled himself to his son Shāh Shujāʿ and was eventually released from the Qalʿi-i sifid, he still wanted revenge. He joined forces with another of his sons to plot the death of Shāh Shujāʿ. Their conspiracy was detected and Shāh Shujāʿ killed the conspirators, except for his father, who he imprisoned once more, this time in the Qalʿi-i tabar, where he died in 766/1364.[65] It is believed that upon his death, Ḥāfiẓ composed this verse:

دل منه بر دنیی و اسباب او   زانکه از وی کس وفاداری ندید[66]

Do not fall in love with this material world,
For no one has seen any fidelity from her.

Shāh Shujāʿ Muẓaffarī (r. 759/1358-786/1384)

After the death of Amīr Mubāriz al-Dīn, his eldest living son Shāh Shujāʿ,[67] who was seventeen at the time, succeeded to the throne.[68] Amīr Mubāriz's prime minister and chief adviser to Shujāʿ, Khawja Qavām al-Dīn Muḥammad 'Ṣāḥib ʿAyyār' ('Master Assessor'), whose name also appears in Ḥāfiẓ's verses, was tortured and killed by Shāh Shujāʿ in 764/1362.[69]

هزار نقد به بازار کاینات آرند　　یکی به سکّهٔ صاحب عیار ما نرسد[70]

> Through a myriad coins' ready cash in the universe's marketplace be made to circulate
> The alloy of none of them matches our Master Assessor's coin.

In 760/1358, Shāh Shujāʿ made Shīrāz his capital and appointed his brother Shāh Maḥmūd ruler of Iṣfahān and Abarqūh, and his other brother, Aḥmad, ruler of Kirmān.[71] Shāh Shujāʿ imprisoned his nephew Shāh Yaḥyā, but reconciled in 764/1362 when Shāh Yaḥyā swore allegiance to his uncle. He was subsequently given the governorship of Yazd. During the period 765/1363-767/1365, Shāh Shujāʿ had numerous confrontations with his brother Shāh Maḥmūd.[72] Both made many agreements to live in peace but broke them all. During this time, it is said that Shāh Shujāʿ had illicit communications with his brother's wife (Khān-i Sulṭān) and in 768/1366, when Shāh Maḥmūd learned about their impropriety, he killed his wife.[73] After the death of Maḥmūd, Shāh Shujāʿ continued to fight with his nephew Shāh Yaḥyā.[74]

From the beginning of Shujāʿ's reign, Ḥāfiẓ was greatly valued and rightfully respected in the court. It is likely that the friendship between Ḥāfiẓ and the Shāh started as a result of their common interest in poetry, since Shujāʿ was a reliable patron of the arts and education and was himself something of a poet. He composed poetry in Persian and Arabic and encouraged the practice of poetry and the cultivation of the fine arts in the province of Fārs during his rule.[75] Ḥāfiẓ's own poetry flourished most recognizably during Shāh Shujāʿ's reign.[76] Ḥāfiẓ frequently praises Shāh Shujāʿ in his poems and it seems that his intentions were sincerely based on his personal admiration of Shujāʿ.[77]

Although Shāh Shujāʿ inherited his father's hot temperament and suspicious nature, and perhaps even his ruthlessness, he also had a poetic spirit and substantially improved the city of Shīrāz. He enjoyed considerable popularity with the people of Shīrāz; many contemporary poets besides Ḥāfiẓ praised him frequently.[78] Ḥāfiẓ emphasizes that during the period of Shujāʿ's reign, the city of Shīrāz experienced a period of peace and that the citizens enjoyed social freedom.

زمان شاه شجاع است و دور حکمت و شرع   به راحت ای دل و جان کوش در مسا و صباح[79]

It is the period of Shāh Shujāʿ and the time of wisdom and piety,
O heart and spirit strive for peace, dawn and dusk.

However, after a long senseless disagreement with his nephew Yaḥyā, Shāh Shujāʿ engaged in conflicts with another nephew, Yaḥyā's brother. One night, in a state of intoxication, he ordered one of his men to blind Yaḥyā's son.[80] The following morning, once sober, he repented for his action, but by then it was too late, such brutality could not be reversed. Shāh Shujāʿ died in 786/1386.[81]

Zayn al-ʿĀbidin (son of Shāh Shujāʿ) (r. 786/1384-789/1387)

Shāh Shujāʿ's fatal illness was caused by heavy drinking. On his deathbed, he appointed his son Zayn al-ʿĀbidin as successor and advised him not to repeat his father's mistakes, asking him to avoid conflict with family members and maintain unity instead of war.[82] Zayn al-ʿĀbidin appointed his brother Abū Yazīd ruler of Iṣfahān, his nephew Shāh Yaḥyā ruler of Yazd, and another brother, Sulṭān Imād al-Dīn Aḥmad, ruler of Kirmān. Tīmūr allowed Zayn al-ʿĀbidin to rule Shīrāz for three years to fulfil a request from his dying father to Tīmūr and to the Jalāyirīd family, entrusting the fate of his heir to their hands.[83] Despite the advice of Shāh Shujāʿ to his family members to stay united, the family involved themselves in myriad quarrels and conflicts.[84]

Shāh Manṣūr b. Shāh Muẓaffarī (r. 790/1388-795/1392)

Four years after the death of Shāh Shujāʿ, Shāh Manṣūr b. Shāh Muẓaffarī took control of Shīrāz. Shortly after settling in Shīrāz, he moved to Iṣfahān to gain control of the city, wresting it back from Shāh Shujāʿ's son, Zayn al-ʿĀbidīn. After occupying the city, he captured and blinded Zayn al-

ʿĀbidin and imprisoned him in the Qalʿi- i sifid. In the meantime, Tīmūr was growing increasingly frustrated with Manṣūr's frequent occupations of one city after another, and so decided to rescue Zayn al-ʿĀbidīn, promising him that he would be avenged.[85] During these turbulent times, Ḥāfiẓ remained very fond of Shāh Manṣūr, an attraction that is clearly evident in the *Dīvān*.

بیا که رایت منصور پادشاه رسید نوید فتح و بشارت به مهر و ماه رسید[86]

Come, because the conquering flag of Shāh Manṣūr has arrived,
News of victory and glad tidings have reached the sun and the moon.

شهنشاه مظفّر فر، شجاع ملک و دین منصور که جود بی دریغش خنده بر ابر بهاران زد[87]

The King of Kings, the Glorious Muẓaffar, fearless one of sovereignty and religion, 'Manṣūr',
Whose continuous kindness smiled at the clouds of spring.

Ḥāfiẓ admired the courage and conduct of this king and, according to certain Iranian historians, praised him in the following verse:[88]

نکتهٔ دلکش بگویم خال آن مهرو ببین عقل و جان را بستهٔ زنجیر آن گیسو ببین[89]

Let me speak of a joyous point: Look at the mole on the beautiful, radiant face,
Look how the soul and reason are entangled in those tresses!

Shāh Manṣūr was killed by Tīmūr on the battlefield outside Shīrāz in 795/1393.

According to most authorities, Ḥāfiẓ died in Shīrāz, in 792/1389-1390.[90]

بر سر تربت ما چون گذ ری همّت خواه که زیارتگه رندان جهان خواهد بود[91]

When you pass by the head of my tomb, ask for benediction,
Because to the *rind*s of the world, it will become a place of pilgrimage.[92]

Tamerlane (r. 771/1370-807/1405)

Tīmūr, a Mongol born in 736/1336, was the architect of the Tīmūrīd empire. He governed from 771/1370 to 807/1405, during which time he conquered western, southern and Central Asia. As an adult he was better known as Tīmūr Gūrkānī, Gūrkān being the personalized form of the original Mongolian word, *kürügän* (son-in-law). One of Tīmūr's ancestors converted to Islam and married the daughter of Chagataī Khān (son of Genghis Khān). Thus, Tīmūr was addressed as the son-in-law of Chagataī Khān. Various Persian sources use a byname, Tīmūr-i Lang (or Tamerlane as he is generally referred to in English), which translates to 'Tīmūr the Lame', a name given to him when he sustained an injury to his foot in battle.[93]

Tīmūr was a contentious man who strove to rebuild the Mongol empire and, in doing so, became embroiled in conflicts that devastated many Muslim lands, including Persia, northern India, as well as large parts of Central Asia and the Ottoman empire. He was a great sponsor of the arts, but, paradoxically, his battles caused vast destruction.[94] He knew very little Arabic and frequently had Persian books read to him; he was, evidently, illiterate.[95]

Nominally speaking, Tīmūr was a Muslim who, for purely political motives, behaved obsequiously towards theologians and Sufis. According to Browne, Tīmūr's prime objectives were to gain popularity and to conquer; to this end, fine cities were laid to ashes and citizens of many provinces were slaughtered. Tīmūr assumed, coldly and selfishly, that the end result would justify the means.[96] It is possible that Ḥāfiẓ had Tīmūr in mind when he used the phrase 'Sufi anti-Christ' (*Sufi-i dajjāl*),[97] for, by excessive brutality, Tīmūr managed to surpass even the dreadful devastation and massacres of the Mongols.[98] In a *ghazal* penned in praise of Shāh Manṣūr, referring to Tīmūr as a false Sufi, Ḥāfiẓ entreats:

کجاست صوفی دجال فعل ملحد شکل   بگو بسوز که مهدی دین پناه رسید[99]

> Where's the Sufi of false pretentions and impious mien?
> Say, 'Burn, because the rightly guided refuge of the Faith has come.'[100]

Before invading Persia, Tīmūr established himself in Samarqand, which he made his capital city. Soon the whole of Iran fell under his control; as he marched through the Persian territories, pillars of impaled human heads were erected.[101] Cities were demolished, citizens slaughtered and prized possessions sent back to Samarqand. The glory of Samarqand and Bukhārā is apparent in Ḥāfiẓ's poetry.[102] Although Tīmūr was commended by some of the poets of his era, Browne asserts (and here Rypka is in agreement with him) that we must not forget Tīmūr's acts of mass murder and massacre:

> As specimens of those acts, mention may be made of his massacre of the people of Sistān in 785/1383-1384, when he caused some two thousand prisoners to be built up in a wall; his cold-blooded slaughter of a hundred thousand captive Indians near Delhi in 801 (December, 1389); his burying alive of four thousand Armenians in 803/1400-1401, and the twenty towers of skulls erected by him at Aleppo and Damascus in the same year; and his massacre of 70,000 of the inhabitants of Iṣfahān in 789 (November, 1387).[103]

In 795/1393, during his first occupation of Fārs, Tīmūr overthrew the last member of the Muẓaffarīd family, Shāh Manṣūr, and divided the province of Fārs between his own family members.

During the second occupation of Shīrāz, Tīmūr called all surviving Muẓaffarīd princes to Shīrāz and, after treating them well for a time, executed them, thus ending the Muẓaffarīd dynasty.[104] Ḥāfiẓ seems to have been well aware of Tīmūr's brutality, as the following verse demonstrates:

به خوبان دل منه حافظ ببین آن بی وفاییها   که با خوارزمیان کردند آن ترکان سمرقندی[105]

> Ḥāfiẓ, to the fair ones give not your heart. Behold those deeds of unfaithfulness
> That the Turks of Samarqand visited on the men of Khārazm!

The Muẓaffarīds earned long-lasting fame through commendation by contemporary poets such as Ḥāfiẓ, 'Ubayd Zākānī (d. 772/1371),[106] Khājū Kirmānī (d. 753/1352)[107] and others. In Shīrāz, however, there remains little trace of their rule, rather their presence was more apparent in the cities of Kirmān, Yazd and Iṣfahān.

A Note on Ḥāfiẓ's Poetic Style

This section of the chapter examines Ḥāfiẓ's poetic style and explores different poetic devices that Ḥāfiẓ uses in his poetry. I will address in detail one very important technique used by Ḥāfiẓ, which is allegoric and metonymic language. Every time a literary work is prevailed with its idea and base – its theme – it is probably addressed as an allegory, for the simple reason that thematic content is not generally so free of rational control that it could be there by chance.[108] The opposite assumption that imitative art resists thematic surplus follows Aristotle's method of defining mimesis, *viz*, imitation of an action. 'Action' (*praxis*) in Aristotle's logic can and does exist without any extra help from secondary systematizations, the secondary level that he called 'thought' (*dianoia*).

Allegory, however, presents a different case. The secondary meaning arises immediately from the primary surface of literal narration of drama, or in our case the *ghazal*, and constitutes the raison d'être of the original fascia.[109] Specifically, this does not apply to some of Ḥāfiẓ's poems, because, from then on, the ambiguity of his verses takes over and, in some cases, the meaning remains unclear indefinitely. Some scholars have attempted to interpret the meaning of his most ambiguous poems, and some have come close; however, the true reality of the poet's intention in his various *ghazal*s has remained ambiguous for almost seven hundred years and, in my opinion, they always will be ambiguous.

As Fletcher explains, allegorical stories exist, as it were, to put secondary meaning into orbit around them; the primary meaning is then valued for its orbiters.[110] The other device Ḥāfiẓ often employs in his poetry is dualism, but dualism in its theological sense, where it implies the radical opposition of two independent, mutually irreducible, mutually aggressive substances – in short, the conflict of Absolute Good and Absolute Evil, such as one finds in a variety of Manichaean philosophies. Dualism is found in all allegories and the thematic antagonism of absolutes (Good an Evil) is articulated by an ordering of imagery and factors that are likewise dualistic.[111] For example, if either *L'Allegro* or *Il Penseroso* was lost, we could make a good guess from the one residual poem what the other was about, and possibly even distinguish what the form of the lost poem would be.[112]

What are the proportion and symmetry of the two poems based upon? Surely both refer, though in sharply contrasted terms, to a single, comprehensive tradition; the principle that the powers of darkness are forever at war with the powers of light? This ultimately Zoroastrian doctrine carries with it a host of subdivisions of the light /dark duality and is ever apparent in the poetry of Ḥāfiẓ.

My analysis examines the two most important styles of poetry used by Ḥāfiẓ; that is, the Khurāsānī and 'Irāqī styles. The mixture of these two language styles employed by Ḥāfiẓ is carefully examined and illustrated in a chart. This section is focused on exploring the poet's style in order to better understand the reason behind his wide reception throughout the literary history of Persia since his death, why the Ḥāfiẓian style is so popular, and what the components of this style are.

Ḥāfiẓ was a well-known poet during his own time; in fact, he was legendary among his peers and contemporaries, such as 'Ubayd Zākānī, Khājū Kirmānī, Salmān Sāvajī (d. 778/1377),[113] Imād Kirmānī (d. 773/1371),[114] Kamāl Khujandī (d. 807/1404),[115] Jahān Malik Khātūn (d. 795/1393),[116] Shāh Ni'matullāh Valī (d. 834/1433)[117] and Nāṣir Bukhārā'ī (d. 772/1371).[118] Whilst most of these poets were masters in their own right, Ḥāfiẓ's artfulness stood out. Ḥāfiẓ was aware of his stature and conscious of his ability; in many verses, he repeatedly refers to his uniqueness in the art of poetry.

عراق و فارس گرفتی به شعر خوش حافظ　　　بیا که نوبت بغداد و وقت تبریز است[119]

O Ḥāfiẓ, Iraq and Fārs you captured with your sweet verse,
Come now, it is the turn of Baghdad and Tabriz!

Ḥāfiẓ further confirms that he followed Khājū Kirmānī in *ghazal* writing and in the same verse asserts that Sa'dī is the master of lyrical poetry.

استاد غزل سعدی است پیش همه کس اما　　　دارد غزل حافظ طرز و روش خواجو[120]

Sa'dī is the master of lyrics above all. However,
Ḥāfiẓ's lyrics follow the style and form of Khājū!

Another of Ḥāfiẓ's talented contemporaries was a young poetess called Jahān Malik Khātūn. She was the daughter of Maṣ'ūd Shāh Īnjū.[121] Numerous verses in her collection bear great similarities to those of Ḥāfiẓ. The mastery and skill of Ḥāfiẓ's poetry, however, make the works of other poets, whether his contemporaries or modern day poets, pale by comparison.

In Persian, poetry plays a prominent role; indeed, it is the prevalent branch of literature since Persian verse is acknowledged as superior to Persian prose. Understanding Ḥāfiẓ and determining his legacy is not a question of writing a better and more complete biography – it is a matter of knowing how his genius reformulated and restructured the conventional voices of the *ghazal* to make them his own.[122]

Ḥāfiz's style of poetry is partly a result of his poetic persona as well as other factors that will be discussed later.[123]Many aspects of Ḥāfiẓ's *ghazal*s seem to originate from earlier poets. By Ḥāfiẓ's time, the *ghazal* already had a long history going back for almost two centuries. It would be difficult to point to any single factor of Ḥāfiẓ's *ghazal*, either formal or thematic, that is not visible in the works of his predecessors.[124]

> In order to assess Ḥāfiẓ's personal contribution to the development of the *ghazal*, his debt to his predecessors, and even to his contemporaries who cultivated the same genre, must be taken into proper account. A proper assessment of his originality can only be attempted when all possible influences on his work have been examined.[125]

In this regard, Kadkanī argues that the clarity and fluency of Ḥāfiẓ's verse is due to his vast knowledge of the Persian language and the poems of his predecessors and master poets.

He further claims that Ḥāfiẓ comprehended the mystery of the culture embedded in the Persian language itself.[126] Ḥāfiẓ's style of poetry was derived from the 'Irāqī style, together with some aspects of the Khurāsānī style. However, some contemporary scholars believe that a style of poetry is merely a vehicle by which the poet chooses to deliver his message. Maḥjūb was of the opinion that poets compose poetry according to their own sociopolitical perspective; he viewed the environment in which the poet lives as having the greatest impact on his style of delivering his message.[127]

In Shamīsā's view, Ḥāfiẓ's *ghazal*s echo the 'Irāqī style. He also asserts that this style of poetry should have ceased to exist in the fourteenth century, but, as a result of the socio-economic conditions of the fifteenth-century, no new master poets emerged and hence, the 'Irāqī style continued. In the fourteenth century, Tīmūr's attack on Persia brought about a cultural and social decline. The literary decline continued into the first half of the fifteenth century, which is sometimes known as the Age of Shāhrukh (the fourth son of Tīmūr, r. 807-850/1400-1443).[128] Since literary works of high quality could not thrive, the customary creative practice was the imitation of the works of old masters.[129] Yarshater asserts that during the latter half of the fifteenth century many poets imitated master poets such as Sa'dī and Ḥāfiẓ.[130]

One such poet of the period was Ḥāfiẓ Halvā'ī, who stated openly that he followed Ḥāfiẓ:[131]

حافظ حلوائیم و از کمال معتقد حافظ شیرازیم[132]

I am Ḥāfiẓ Halvā'ī, and due to my wisdom,
I believe in Ḥāfiẓ of Shīrāz.

One of the last great poets of this period was Jāmī who followed the 'Irāqī style; he flourished shortly before the Indian style emerged.[133] According to Shamīsā, the 'Irāqī style was more or less the same as the Khurāsānī, though it had lost most of its unique features by allowing too many Arabic words to infiltrate its language, which became more mystical and romantic in style. The 'Irāqī style lasted in Persia for over three hundred years.[134] The table below illustrates the thematic elements of both styles used by Ḥāfiẓ in his *ghazals*.

'Irāqī Style	**Khurāsānī Style**	**Ḥāfiẓ's Usage 'Irāqī Style**	**Ḥāfiẓ's Usage Khurāsānī Style**
Praise of love	Praise of wisdom	✓	✓
Exaggeration	Modesty	–	✓
Promotion of mysticism	Neglect of mysticism	✓	–
Divine philosophy	Nativism/chauvinism	✓	–
Separation	Union	✓	✓
Despair	Joyfulness	✓	✓
Humbleness	Pride	✓	–
Focus on Islamic science	Focus on nativism	✓	✓
Spiritualism	Materialism	✓	–

✓ Indicates themes used by Ḥāfiẓ.
– Indicates themes not used by Ḥāfiẓ.

Shamīsā points out that, unfortunately, no credible book is available to help students evaluate the 'Irāqī style in depth or even to compare it with the work of Ḥāfiẓ.[135] However, I believe that Ḥāfiẓ's poetry is a balanced mixture of both styles, the 'Irāqī and the Khurāsānī. As the table above illustrates, he uses themes from the two styles mentioned, though he leans more towards the ʿIrāqī style. Shamīsā claims that mysticism is one of the most outstanding elements of the ʿIrāqī style, because it provides the poet with an efficient tool to compose mystical poems. Shamīsā believes Ḥāfiẓ's genius is partly a result of this Sufi element in his ʿIrāqī-style poetry.[136]

In an introduction to Bahār and Persian literature (*Bahār va adab-i fārsī*), Bahār asserts that poetry is only recognized as good when the imagination of the poet instigates its composition.[137] In Bahār's opinion, it is impossible for a villain or an individual of bad character to compose verses that please people of all classes. This kind of poetry must, without a doubt, come from a righteousness of spirit.[138] Bahār further asserts that some poets develop the ability to write fluent *ghazal*s, and become the finest poets of their time because they devote themselves to Ḥāfiẓ, following his style in great detail.[139]

Conclusion

Although Ḥāfiẓ is generally not considered to be primarily a political poet, as we can see from the few verses cited above, it is clear that his satirical language and use of irony, at least with regard to religious hypocrisy and sociopolitical pretence, did have serious political implications. Verses cited throughout this chapter illustrate how his penetrating and censorious tongue was, in some instances, directed at the rulers of the period, in particular at Mubāriz al-Dīn Muḥammad and Tīmūr. It can thus be seen that there is a strong political and anticlerical dimension to his poetry, in which he expresses, through satire and irony, his opposition to political injustice and religious hypocrisy of all shades. The following verse, which is just one instance out of hundreds like it, illustrates this:

خدای را به میم شستشوی خرقه کنید   که من نمی شنوم بوی خیر از این اوضاع[140]

For God's sake, in wine wash my tattered robe,
Because in that posturing, I sense no hope of good.[141]

Ḥāfiẓ lived in the turbulent interlude between Genghis Khān and Tīmūr; a period of volatility, in which minor dynasties rose and fell, creating social chaos and political insecurity. Yarshater observes, I believe correctly, that the panegyric lines in the *Dīvān* echo the political instability of the time, and the dominance and fall of dynasties such as the Īnjū, the Muẓaffarīd and the Jalāyirīd. However, it was at the same time an era of immense cultural and literary advancement; a period when masterpieces were produced in various fields, as illustrated not only by the splendour of Ḥāfiẓ's language, but also by the appreciation of his contemporaries.[142]

Khurramshāhī reminds us that there has been much debate about whether Ḥāfiẓ was simply doing his job as a court poet, or if perhaps he was using his outstanding talent for irony to deceive his naïve medieval patrons and appeal to his more intelligent admirers.[143] Scholars also debate whether or not Ḥāfiẓ was a court poet who composed poetry merely for financial benefits. Most of Ḥāfiẓ's life as a poet was spent in the era of Shāh Shujāʿ and many of the references from this time are *pas seuls* on the theme of happiness or salvation from tyranny and adversity, giving the researcher ample evidence to believe that his appearances at the court and his frequent praise of Shujāʿ and Shāh Manṣūr were based simply on his personal admiration for them. This view is contrary to the opinions of those who consider Ḥāfiẓ a court poet by profession. We know that Ḥāfiẓ developed a sincere admiration for these kings, and that the verses he composed in praise of them were nothing less than statements of his opinion. With regard to Ḥāfiẓ's style, Shamīsā claims that the ʿIrāqī style of poetry was partly responsible for Ḥāfiẓ's genius, insofar as it provided him with the tools necessary to compose consummate verses. The table above illustrates that Ḥāfiẓ's poetry was influenced by both the ʿIrāqī and, to a lesser degree, the Khurāsānī style. In my opinion, Ḥāfiẓ took advantage of both styles, but added a number of original elements and themes, thereby improving the quality of both styles and laying the foundation for the forthcoming Indian style. Ḥāfiẓ can thus be classified as a poet whose talent in the art of rhetoric and lyricism exceeds that of other poets.[144] Ḥāfiẓ's achievements won him a vast number of followers, but their perpetual and consistently inferior repetition of his ideas and images appear pale in the light of his excellence. Any poet wishing to replace Ḥāfiẓ will have to surpass his bequest and create a new dimension in poetry.[145] However, few poets are able to ignore that which is defined as poetic utterance by the masters of classical poetry.[146] Ḥāfiẓ is absent in body and his living voice can never be recaptured, but his legacy has set the standard from which poets must derive their inspiration and the echo of his voice continues to be heard through the work of his followers.

CHAPTER II

Ḥāfiẓ in Historical Perspective, from the Late Tīmūrīds to the Qājārs

A Short Summary of the Literary History of Persia from the Death of Tamerlane to the Rise of the Ṣafavids

This chapter concentrates on Ḥāfiẓ from an historical perspective, from the late Tīmūrīd to the Qājār era. I examine the reception of Ḥāfiẓ's poetry from the time of his death through to the Qājār period, including his influence on selected Ṣafavid poets, such as Jāmī, Bābā Fighānī, 'Urfī Shīrāzī and Ṣā'ib Tabrīzī, and the impact of the first of these five figures on the resurgence of Persian literature during the ninth/fifteenth century.[1] The chapter also presents a short summary of the literary history of Persia, from the death of Tīmūr to the rise of the Ṣafavids, followed by a brief introduction into the Zand dynasty. I follow this with a short summary of the political and dynastic history of Persia from 1400 to 1800 and a general literary overview of the Ṣafavid period, together with the sociopolitical conditions in late Qājār Persia between 1848 and 1923, assessing the reception of Ḥāfiẓ during this period.

In order to further expand on the reception of Ḥāfiẓ during the Qājār period, I have selected seven writers and critics to examine in this regard. This has proven useful to show the effect of Ḥāfiẓ on these important writers and critics of Iran. This examination helps to illustrate the importance of Ḥāfiẓ's language in different historical and sociopolitical eras and aims to prove that his multidimensional diction knows no frontier or limitation. The scrutiny of Ḥāfiẓ's influence is necessary to demonstrate the vast impact of Ḥāfiẓ's language on all the poets of Persia.

Jāmī and Ḥāfiẓ

'One of the most remarkable geniuses whom Persia ever produced,' in the words of E.G. Browne, was Mullā Nūr al-Dīn 'Abdul Raḥmān Jāmī, who was born in the town of Jām in Khurāsān in 817/1414 and died in 898/1492.[2] Jāmī is believed to be the last of the great classical Sufi poets.[3] During Jāmī's lifetime, his hometown of Herat became the centre of the newly-revived

Persian culture and, for almost the entire ninth/fifteenth century, it was considered the centre of knowledge, literature and arts for Iran, and also, partly, for India and Turkey. Jāmī produced a number of masterpieces in poetry and literature over nearly half a century,[4] and his mystical writings and poetry were known across a large part of the territory of the Muslim world and he was revered and admired by his countrymen.[5]

Ḥāfiẓ's influence on the poets of Persia began immediately after his death, if not during his life. Most of the poets of the ninth/fifteenth century followed the master poets of the previous century, particularly poets such as Saʿdī and Ḥāfiẓ. Jāmī was no exception in this respect and there is much evidence that he took inspiration from Ḥāfiẓ. Indeed, Arberry asserts that Jāmī was considered a shining star, similar to Ḥāfiẓ of Shīrāz: 'It was thirty-one years since the shining star Ḥāfiẓ had set, and now the hand of destiny placed another candle in the lamp-stand of Persian literature.'[6] Jāmī expressed his opinion about Ḥāfiẓ in the following verse, in which he states that no one is able to understand Ḥāfiẓ adequately:

هیچ کس سر دهانت به حقیقت نشناخت　　　هرکسی بهر دل خود سخنی می گوید[7]

No one could truly unveil the secret of your tongue,
Everyone speaks according to their heart's desire.

The following verse is comparable to a similar verse by Ḥāfiẓ in terms of rhyme and metre:

Jāmī	سر به راه تو خفتنم هوس است[8]	راهت از دیدن رفتنم هوس است
Ḥāfiẓ	سخن دل شنفتنم هوس است[9]	حال دل با تو گفتنم هوس است

Haravī asserts that Jāmī was so familiar with the poems of Ḥāfiẓ and his poetry displayed such an intimacy with that of the great poet, that it seemed he had almost memorized most of Ḥāfiẓ's *Dīvān* by heart.[10] Haravī further claims that if one searched the entire *Dīvān* of Jāmī, one would undoubtedly find many examples of similarities with the *ghazal*s of Ḥāfiẓ; he gives the following examples:[11]

Jāmī	ز مَی مشکل بوَد توبه اَدِر کاسَاً وَناوِلها[12]	الا یا ایّها الساقی مَی آمد حَلّ مشکلها

O Sāqī, the wine is the key to all problems,
It is hard to repent from wine, pass the bowl around and offer it.

الا یا ایّها ساقی آدِر کاساً ونا ولها	که عشق آسان نمود اوّل ولی افتاد مشکلها[13]	Ḥāfiẓ

O Sāqī, pass the bowl round and offer it;
At first love seemed easy, but snags have cropped up.[14]

Haravī adds that Jāmī was so enthralled and influenced by the captivating *ghazal*s of Ḥāfiẓ that most of his poetry is imbued with the scent of Ḥāfiẓ's verse. Haravī cites the following two verses as a further example of this fact:

معاشران گره از زلف یار باز کنید	شبی خوش است بدین قصه اش دراز کنید[15]	Ḥāfiẓ
معاشران چو می لعل در پیاله کنند	ز جم حکایت حال هزار ساله کنند[16]	Jāmī

Although Jāmī made every effort to employ different metres than those of Ḥāfiẓ, he did not succeed in developing an independent style.[17] According to Muʿīn, who quotes Bahār, Jāmī was the greatest poet of the Tīmūrīd era and, although in terms of speech he comes somewhat close to Ḥāfiẓ, in terms of profundity and meaning we cannot see much original work in his lyrical verse, but mostly imitation of Ḥāfiẓ.[18]

Fighānī and Ḥāfiẓ

Bābā Fighānī was another genius in the annals of classical Persian poetry and a contemporary of Jāmī.[19] He was born in Shīrāz and was very much inspired by Ḥāfiẓ; thus, Rypka refers to him as 'little Ḥāfiẓ'.[20] He flourished during the reign of Sulṭān Ḥusayn Bāyaqrā and was known as a sensitive, kind-hearted man; he was also a drinker and an impassioned lover.[21] He was brought up in Shīrāz where he began work as a trader in his father's shop. At first, he chose the pen name 'Sakkākī' (the 'Knife Maker'), but later changed it to Fighānī.[22] After Sulṭān Yaʿqūb Bāyundurī had given him the title 'Bābā' (a denomination of leading dervishes and *qalandar*s), he was widely known as Bābā Fighānī.[23]

Fighānī's character was very much like that of Ḥāfiẓ's inspired libertine (*rind*), at least if the term is understood in a non-mystical sense. He spent some time in Tabriz and Herat, later returning to his hometown, Shīrāz. He stayed there for some time before travelling to Khurāsān, where he remained for the rest of his life. The end of Fighānī's life heralded the reign of Shāh Ismāʿīl Safavī (r. 901/1501-924/1524).[24] Losensky states that in India and Pakistan, Fighānī is recognized as the founder of a new poetic school.[25] In his brief notice on Fighānī, Browne states:

> Fighānī appears to be one of those poets who are much more highly esteemed in India than in their own country, for while Shiblī in his *Shi'r al-'Ajam*, like Wālih in his *Rīāḍ al-Shu'arā*, deems him the creator of a new style of poetry, Riḍā Qulī Khān only accords him a brief mention in his *Rīāḍ al-'Ārifīn* and entirely omits him in his larger *Majma' al-Fuṣahā*, while the notices of him in the *Ātashkada* and the *Tuhfi-i Sāmī* are very brief.[26]

However, Ehsan Yarshater dismisses this statement, and believes that Fighānī was a follower of the earlier 'Irāqī school, rather than the founder of the Indian one.[27] In disagreement with Yarshater, Razīya Akbar states that considerable evidence of the Indian style is apparent in Fighānī's poetic language.[28] Safā agrees with Browne (and Losensky) and believes that Fighānī must definitely be the founder of a new style.[29] Shiblī Nu'mānī confirms that Fighānī initiated a new style that transformed the *ghazal* in Iran and India at the end of tenth/sixteenth century.[30] Despite the difference of opinion mentioned above, it is clear that Fighānī took inspiration from Ḥāfiẓ, to some extent, when writing *ghazals*.[31] The following examples demonstrate similarities in meaning and rhyme, and convey the same philosophy to the reader:

Fighānī گرچه صد نامه سیه کرد فغانی ز گناه نظرش بر کرم و رحمت درویشان است[32]

Although Fighānī has stained many letters black in sin,
He is optimistic he will receive kindness and compassion from the dervishes.

Ḥāfiẓ گنج عزلت که طلسمات عجایب دارد فتح آن در نظر رحمت درویشان است[33]

The compassionate vision of dervishes holds the key,
To the treasure of solitude and the talismanic mysteries.

Ḥāfiẓ was considered by his followers to be the last prophet of *ghazal* writers. His diction and phraseology reflected his romantic attitude and his love songs were so filled with mystical thought that the beloved was considered something of a divinity, unearthly and unreal; at times ethereal and celestial, but at other times, like a mortal being. It was sometimes difficult to determine the subject's celestial or earthly character, its divine or human nature. Kausar believes, however, that Fighānī separated himself from this sort of Ḥāfiẓian mysticism and restored the subject of ideal love of the great master mystic poets to its human form.[34] With regard to the subject of mysticism, Losensky claims that Kausar exaggerates when mentioning that Fighānī was against mysticism;[35] by contrast, Losensky believes that mystical and philosophical themes are rarely found in Fighānī's work, but he was not opposed to them.[36]

ʿUrfī and Ḥāfiẓ

ʿUrfī was a major first-class Persian poet of the latter half of the tenth/sixteenth century. He was born in Shīrāz in 957/1555 and died in Lahore in 999/1596.[37] His name is given as Jamāl al-Dīn Muḥammad Sayyidī in early references.[38] His father, Zayn al-Dīn ʿAlī Balawī, was a well-known official of the regional administration whose connections with customary or civil law (*ʿUrf*) in the course of his profession resulted in his son's choice of "ʿUrfī' as his pen name (*takhalluṣ*).[39] The young ʿUrfī soon became a leading figure in the literary salons of Shīrāz, being a contemporary of Bābā Fighānī, among others.[40]

In spite of the expanding and highly competitive literary world of tenth/sixteenth-century Shīrāz, ʿUrfī made his mark and his talents were soon recognized. ʿUrfī travelled to India to benefit from the generous patronage of the Mughul courts, like many other poets of the period had done.[41] He became famous throughout the Ottoman empire, India and Iran. His panegyric style followed Nizāmī, though in *ghazal* writing he followed Saʿdī and Ḥāfiẓ.[42] He mainly composed in the Indian style, for he lived most of his life in India. The following verses exemplify the impact of Ḥāfiẓ's *ghazal*s on those of ʿUrfī.

ʿUrfī — در مذهب ما تشنه لب شربت کوثر — بی چاشنی آن لب چون قند حرامست[43]

In our faith, the thirsty one is forbidden to drink of the celestial nectar
Without the presence of the sweet lips of the beloved.

Ḥāfiẓ — در مذهب ما باده حلال است ولیکن — بی روی تو ای سرو گل اندام حرامست[44]

In our order the wine is lawful, but O Cypress Roselike Stature,
Without your face it would be unlawful.

ʿUrfī عشق اگر حکم کند کز سر جان برخیزم همچو عرفی نه، چو مردان جهان برخیزم[45]

Should love command me to rise from desiring life,
I shall do so, not like ʿUrfī, but in such a manner that real men would act.

Ḥāfiẓ مژدهٔ وصل تو کو کاز سر جان برخیزم طایر قدسم و از دام جهان برخیزم[46]

Where is the good news of union with you, for me to rise from desiring life?
I am the holy bird and would rise from the snare which the world sets.[47]

ʿUrfī شراب بیغش و ساقی بکام و بخت شفیق اگر اجل نبود در کمین، زهی توفیق[48]

Pure wine; agreeable Sāqī and kind fate,
Then bravo to success, if only death wasn't in pursuit.

Ḥāfiẓ مقام امن و می بیغش و رفیق شفیق گرت مدام میسر شود زهی توفیق[49]

The abode of security, unadulterated wine, the kind companion,
Were they to be available to you, O what a blessing![50]

Ṣā'ib and Ḥāfiẓ

During the rise of the Ṣafavids, a remarkable poet and master of Persian poetry writing in the Indian style emerged. His name was Mīrzā Muḥammad ʿAlī Ṣā'ib Tabrizī (d. 1087/1678), often known as 'Iṣfahānī', in reference to the place where he was educated.[51] He travelled to India around 1036/1626 and was recognized as an exceptional poet in the court of Shāh Jahān.[52] At the request of his elderly father, he finally returned to his homeland after some six years.[53] He was granted the favour of Shāh ʿAbbās II and was given the honour of the title, 'Amīr al-Shuʿarā'' ('King of Poets'). His fame was based on his *ghazals*; Ṣā'ib greatly admired Ḥāfiẓ and was well versed in all aspects of Persian poetry.[54] His works, composed in the Indian style, led some to accuse him of excessive verbosity; hence, the following verse:

Sā'ib نفس درازی من نیست صائب از غفلت دلم گشاده ز گفتار می شود چه کنم ؟![55]

My excessive utterance is not due to ignorance 'Sā'ib',
What can I do? Through speech my heart opens up!

Another of his habits was to imitate other master poets, mainly Ḥāfiẓ:

Sā'ib   هر مصرعی که گوشهٔ ابرو کند بلند   افسر به فرقش از رقم انتخاب ماست[56]

Every hemistich that lifts an eyebrow to us,
Has a crown placed on its head due to our good choosing.

Sā'ib   فدای حسن خداداد او شوم که سرا پا   چو شعر حافظ شیراز انتخاب ندارد[57]

May my life be sacrificed for him,
For one cannot be selective in Ḥāfiẓ's verses.

In the verse above, Ṣā'ib says that all of Ḥāfiẓ's verses are so good that it would be difficult to choose between them. It is said that Ṣā'ib was a cheerful, polite and well-mannered poet; even Ādhar Bigdilī, who frequently criticized him in his *Ātashkada*, confirms this.[58] It is also claimed that most of the poets of the Ṣafavid period were involved in taking drugs, mainly opium.[59] Ṣā'ib was no exception; we can see indications of this in some of his verses:

Sā'ib   صائب آن فیضی که مخموریان نیابند از شراب   در طلوع نشأهٔ تریاک می یابیم ما[60]

Sā'ib, the state of intoxication not found in wine,
We find in the dawn of opium's influence.

Below are some examples of similarities between Sā'ib's poetry and that of Ḥāfiẓ:

Sā'ib   نمک عشق در آب و گل درویشان است   حاصل روی زمین دردل درویشان است[61]

The sweetness of love lies within the bricks and mortar of the dervishes;
What lies in their hearts is the profound meaning of this earth.

Ḥāfiẓ   آنچه زر می شود از پرتو آن قلب سیاه   کیمیاییست که در صحبت درویشانست[62]

By the light of that through which counterfeited alloy turns to gold,
Is an alchemy that reposes in the company of dervishes.[63]

هیچ جوینده ندانست که جای تو کجاست   آخر ای خانه برانداز سرای تو کجاست؟[64]   Sā'ib

No seeker found your place of abode,
O demolisher of heart and home, where is your place of abode?

ای نسیم سحر آرمگه یار کجاست   منزل آن مه عاشق کش عیار کجاست؟[65]   Ḥāfiẓ

O breeze of the morning, where is the resting place of the friend;
Where is the setting place of that vagabond, lover-slaying moon?[66]

Although the Tīmūrīd period witnessed a decline in literature and poetry, some poets of the late Tīmūrīd era, for example, Jāmī, Fighānī, ʿUrfī and Sā'ib, managed to leave their mark purely because they took their inspiration from master poets, such as Saʿdī and Ḥāfiẓ. Regardless of the political and economic decline of dynasties throughout history, Persian literature and poetry has continued to survive and has even recovered its former glory, not least because of the high standards set by such master poets.

A Short Summary of the Political and Dynamic History of Persia from 1400 to 1800

Literary and Political Overview of the Ṣafavid Period

This section of the chapter summarizes the period from 1400 to 1800, one of the most important eras in the history of Persia. The Ṣafavids witnessed a political, religious and military reformation and unification from which Iran still benefits today. Socially, the Ṣafavids unified the Iranian people and gained them recognition as an entity of importance in world affairs; this distinguished the period from the distruction and mayhem that preceded it. In addition, Islamic philosophy flourished during the Ṣafavid era, in what scholars generally refer to as the 'school of Iṣfahān'.

The era of the Tīmūrīds witnessed a disparity between the quantity of literary works produced and the quality achieved. It was almost inconceivable that in such a tempestuous time the wounds visited by the Mongols and further inflicted by Tīmūr would heal apace.[67] However, the emergence of the Ṣafavids heralded a new era. The establishment of the Ṣafavid state constituted, once again, a strong, powerful central government in Iran after centuries of foreign domination and an extended period of political disintegration.[68]The Ṣafavid kingdom prolonged the old-style political and cultural traditions of Persia and provided the country with a distinctive character of historic importance, which has lasted, in part, up to the present day.[69]

One of the most peculiar and, at first sight, incomprehensible changes of the Ṣafavid period is the extraordinary dearth of noteworthy poets in Persia during the two hundred years of its continuing domination. Although numerous poets appeared during this period, there are only a few worthy of mention, apart from Jāmī, Hātifī (d. 927/1525), Hilālī (d. 908/1506) and some other poets of Khurāsān, who were really the last of the school of Herat.[70] Besides Ḥāfiẓ, there were at least eight to ten poets who outshone the rest during the seventy years of Tīmūr's life, and whose influence on Persian literature cannot be ignored. Two of the most notable figures worthy of mention are 'Urfī Shīrāzī and Ṣā'ib Iṣfahānī.[71]

The main political accomplishment of the Ṣafavids was the formation of a self-sufficient, firm and lasting state in Iran after centuries of foreign rule and a prolonged period of political disorder. Although the previous Turkmen dynasties, the Qarā Quyūnlū and the Āq Quyūnlū, had created some of the conditions necessary for this achievement, and had followed similar goals for a short time, their success was transient.[72] It was only after the rise of the Ṣafavids that Iran witnessed the emergence of a state equal in importance to the Ottoman empire or the empire of the Egyptian Mamlūks.[73]

During the Ṣafavid dynasty, which lasted nearly two and a half centuries, Shi'ism, as the official religion of the state and as a faction of secondary importance, controlled the nation. This faith offered a solid expression for Iran's identity – 'it might even be said, of Iranian nationalism in face of the challenge presented by the Sunni Ottoman Empire, the Sunni Central Asian Turkish states and the Mongol Empire of India'.[74] According to Ṣafā, this concerns the literary historian because the official recognition of Shi'ism, with its active promotion by the Ṣafavid rulers, spread the faith, resulting in the composition of large volumes of works in the Persian and Arabic languages.[75]

Zand Dynasty (r. 1163/1751-1193/1779)

The Zand period was, to some extent, a period of stability in sociopolitical and economic terms.[76] Throughout the period, the inhabitants of Shīrāz enjoyed a period of placidity and felicity.[77] Bahār describes it in poetic terms, as a society of moon-faced young women, who passed their leisure hours with a sparkling chalice circulating, love and pleasure reigning in every bosom.[78]

Karīm Khān gave fatigued Iran over two decades of much needed rest. The political turmoil of the period immediately preceding the Zand, with its numerous battles and conflicts, had left little time for scholars and poets to thrive or concentrate on literature and arts. His reign lasted twenty-nine years, and for over twenty of those he was the unchallenged ruler of Persia. The Zand family's focus on scholars and men of letters was substantial.

This concentration was the reason behind the progress of literature and poetry in this period, although the Indian style, which had been popular during the Ṣafavid period, rapidly declined. Poetry entered a new phase and neoclassical poetry began its emergence during the latter half of the eighteenth century.[79] The poets of the period aimed to rescue the poetry and literature of Persia from the literary fashions of the Ṣafavid period, mainly the Indian style. They believed that the only way forward was to return to the style of medieval masters such as Saʿdī and Ḥāfiẓ. The neoclassical movement thus evolved purely to eliminate the Indian style and to revive the ʿIrāqī and Khurāsānī styles of poetry.

Sociopolitical Conditions in Late Qājār Persia and the Reception of Ḥāfiẓ

The early modernization of Persia is related to the emergence of Qājār dynasty (1848-1923) and the role of Ḥāfiẓ in Iranian national consciousness during this period must be interpreted in light (or rather, under the shadow) of the sociopolitical, economic and religious conditions then prevailing in Persia. During the period from 1722 to 1848, between the demise of the Ṣafavid state and the rise of Nāṣir al-Dīn Shāh (r. 1848-1898), the Qājārs evolved from a minor tribe with significant influence in northern Persia, into a national Persian dynasty with Islamic roots and ideas.

The Qājār dynasty ruled Persia until 1923, when the forces of a nationalist and reformist movement overcame it. During the greater part of Qājār rule, the country continued the political, social and religious traditions of Ṣafavid Persia. Literature and poetry, however, continued to revive and move towards the style of classical poets, such as Saʿdī and Ḥāfiẓ, who had established such solid foundations for the poetry of Persia that disregarding it would have been, and still is, an impossible task. Furthermore, at this time, Persia was isolated from most of the Muslim world and the West, and the country found itself lacking hope and energy. It suffered from a weak political and cultural climate, a circumstance that, on its own, would have been enough to prompt the decline of poetry and literature.[80] Credit for innovation and the creation of valuable works is due to poets such as Īraj Mīrzā (d. 1344/1926) and Muḥammad Taqī Bahār (d. 1330/1952), who produced more valuable work during the Pahlavi period than during the Qājār era.

Ample research undertaken on this period for the purpose of this study, reveals that the evolution of neoclassical literature in Iran started during the late Zand dynasty (1750-1794) and continued into the early Qājār period.[81]

Moreover, it was during this period that poets like Ṣabā Kāshānī (d. 1238/1822) and Surūsh Iṣfahānī (d. 1285/1868) began to follow the style of poets of the Ghaznavid and Saljūq period, such as ʿUnṣurī, Khāqānī, Anvarī and so on. In their lyrical *ghazal* writings, Basṭāmī (d. 1274/1857) and Nishāṭ (d. 1244/1827) also took their inspiration from Saʿdī and Ḥāfiẓ.[82] During the Qājār period, elegy writing took precedence over *ghazals*.[83] *Mathnawī* writings were also favoured and, as is evident, the *Shāhanshāh-nāma* of Ṣabā is an incomplete reproduction of Firdawsī's *Shāh-nāma*.[84] The neoclassical movement, which had begun during the Zand era, greatly progressed during this period and, in fact, gradually escalated into being the major literary movement of the day.[85]

As previously mentioned, the latter part of the Zand era saw poets reviving the style of the classical masters, such as Saʿdī and Ḥāfiẓ, thus creating the neoclassical movement. This movement was designed to return from the Indian style back to the ʿIrāqī style. Soon after the reign of Fatḥ-ʿAlī Shāh Qājār (r. 1797-1834), poets such as Qāʾānī and Mijmar (d. 1225/1810-1811) gradually improved upon what Ṣabā had aimed to achieve, creating a style closer to those of Khāqānī (d. 582/1165),[86] Manūchihrī (d. 442/1040),[87] ʿUnsurī (d. 431/1029)[88] and Farrukhī (d. 424/1007).[89] This movement continued through the period of Nāṣir al-Dīn, aiming to revive *ghazal* writing in the style of classical poets such as Saʿdī and Ḥāfiẓ. The main poets responsible for this improvement in style were Surūsh Iṣfahānī and Shahāb Iṣfahānī (d. 1291/1874). Other writers and intellectuals of note include Riḍā

Qulī Khān Hidāyat, Muḥammad Taqī Sipihr (d. 1297/1895), Jamāl al-Dīn Asadābādī (d. 1275/1873), Ākhūndzāda (d. 1295/1878) and 'Abdul Raḥīm Ṭālibuf, some of whom are discussed later in this chapter.

Conclusion

The Iranian social classes were generally dependent on the state, and the higher the social class, the greater its dependence. I concur with Katouzian's belief, that during the Qājār period the state experimented with the social classes. In Europe, the social classes influenced the state.[90] This explains the great differences in social mobility between the two societies. In Iran, there was no private ownership amongst the social classes and this, together with the state's monopoly of all independent power, meant that any individual or family, however poor, could rise to high position and great wealth, even within their own lifetime; the most prosperous people could likewise lose everything. Rulers almost always benefited from absolute power; hence, the sanctioning of any law or change in society was generally subject to royal decree. Iran had no laws regarding the limitation of state power, and it is commonly known that in societies in which individuals do not have rights, laws cannot be just. Women's rights were almost non-existent in the Qājār period. Religion and politics were almost inseparable, to the extent that even the establishment of the parliament (*majlis*) had to meet the approval of the clergy. There were other problems as well, for the state was independent of the social classes – being above society – and it did not enjoy legitimacy comparable to European states. It is clear that the Qājār dynasty imposed economic, financial and human suffering on Iran and the extent of such damages brought the country to breaking point. In the words of 'Ārif-i Qazvīnī:

چه ظلمها که از گردش آسمان ندیدیم　　به غیر مشتی دزد همره کاروان ندیدیم
درین رمه به جز گرگ دگر شبان ندیدیم　　به پای گل بجز زحمت باغبان ندیدیم[91]

> Under the sky, such cruelty we saw,
> Except for a handful of thieves alongside this caravan, we saw nothing!
>
> Amongst this herd of sheep, we saw no other shepherds, except wolves!
> In longing for the rose, we saw nothing, except the gardener's hardship!

During the reign of Aḥmad Shāh, literature and poetry continued their previous course towards cultivation and development of the neoclassical style. The poets and writers of note in this period are Parvin I'tisāmī (d. 1320/1942), Malik al-Shu'arā' Bahār, and Mīrzā Abū'l Qāsim 'Ārif Qazvīnī (d. 1349/1930). Other intellectuals worthy of mention are Ḥusayn Khān Sipahsālār (d. 1309/1892) and Mīrzā 'Alī Khān Amīn al-Dawla (d. 1322/1905).[92]

Ḥāfiẓ and the Scholars of Qājār Persia

Preliminary Conclusions on Literary Critics and Criticism in Iran (1848-1923)

This section draws some preliminary conclusions about a number of important issues surrounding Ḥāfiẓ and the scholars of Qājār Persia in an effort to analyze the following questions:

- Were the critics a positive or a negative force? Did they encourage decadence or advancement?
- In what way did literary criticism contribute to the advancement of Ḥāfiẓology in Iran?
- How did these critics view Ḥāfiẓ in relation to important issues in the neoclassical period and in relation to Iranian nationalism more generally?

Mīrzā Āqā Khān Kirmānī (d. 1274/1896)

Mīrzā Āqā Khān Kirmānī was an Iranian writer and scholar. He was a spiritual nationalist, remembered as one of the great intellectuals of his time.[93] He was born in 1270/1854 in a village on the outskirts of Kirmān to a wealthy family whose traditions blended with mysticism.[94] He was educated in the Persian and Arabic languages, literature and grammar, rhetoric, logic, mathematics, philosophy, history and religion. He continued his studies in philosophy, a field considered to be the summit of wisdom and knowledge. He later discovered Babism and apparently converted, but he continued to search for new ideologies and new faiths.[95] In 1301/1883, he was assigned as a tax collector in his hometown, a responsibility that ended after an intense argument with the governor, who held him responsible for the shortfall in payments. At the age of thirty, he decided to leave Kirmān.[96] He moved to Iṣfahān and stayed there for two years. He found a job in the service of Nāṣir al-Dīn Shāh and joined a literary community that focused on 'progressive ideas'. He spent a few months in Tehran and in 1303/1886 travelled to Mashhad and Istanbul to escape the constant attempts by Kirmānī officials to have him extradited to Kirmān. In the same year, he made a short journey to Cyprus, where he married, before returning to Istanbul where he stayed for the remainder of his life.[97] Kirmānī believed that poetry orchestrates the style and nature of a particular period.

It can be impressive when it illustrates the mood of a society or expresses parallels between objects and nature. He records in one of his letters: 'The poet should be like an artist who pictures flowers, men, animals, the sea, forests, mountains and deserts as they are, in such a way that the nature and traditions of a community take shape in the reader's perception.'[98]

As a writer and a poet, and in his confrontation with fanaticism, Kirmānī was a precursor of Kasravī. He favoured liberty and neoclassical literature, and disliked panegyrists, finding their works of little literary value.[99] He was a Muslim and expressed interest in mystical language and mysticism, but despised fanaticism and believed that incorrect religious beliefs and superstitions impede progress.[100] According to Ferdowsi, Kirmānī believed that poetry is nothing but an ethical and scholarly blight on rulers and people alike.[101] Hakkak informs us that Kirmānī had a low opinion of the Persian poetry of his time, but his views on classical poetry were somewhat different.

Ferdowsi asserts that Kirmanī likened poetry to trees, and thus measured its value according to the fruit it produced.[102]

> [...] Trees ought to be known by their fruits, and [human] undertakings by their results. None can question the effectiveness and creativity of Iran's ancient men of eloquent speech. Nor do I doubt the tenderness and delicacy of their poems. [...] It ought, however, to be seen what the work of our litterateurs has thus far brought about, what fruit has been produced by the saplings they planted in the garden of speech (*bāq-i sukhanvarī*), and what harvest has cropped up from the seed they have sewn.[103]

Parsinejad informs us that Kirmānī's early works completed in 1887 in Istanbul give clear evidence of works written in the style of the fourteenth-century poets, in particular Saʿdī and ʿUbeyd Zākānī. Parsinejad further asserts that apart from his adaptation from Sa'dī's *Gulistān* and Zākānī's satirical and witty narratives, Kirmānī at times took his inspiration from Rūmī's *Mathnawī* and the poetry of Ḥāfiẓ.[104] However, in general, Kirmānī was a virulent modernist and a radical pro-European who looked contemptuously upon classical Persian poetry, poets and their ideas.

Riḍā Qulī Hidāyat (d. 1288/1871)

Hidāyat had somewhat different views to Kirmānī's and was a firm believer in the classical literature while favouring innovation in poetry. He was introduced to Fatḥ-'Alī Shāh Qājār when Fatḥ-'Alī Shāh visited Shīrāz in 1829. He was granted the title of 'Amīr al-Shu'arā'' ('Kings of Poets') for a panegyric *qaṣīda* that he had composed for the Shāh. He served at the court of Tehran in various functions from 1254/1834 onwards, reaching the acme of his growth during the reign of Nāṣir al-Dīn Shāh, when he was selected as assistant to the minister of public education and principal of the newly established *Dār al-Funūn*.[105] Among his most interesting works are *Rīyāḍ al-'ārifīn* (*The Gardens of the Mystics*), *Majma' al-fuṣaḥā* (*The Meeting Place of the Eloquent*) and the *Gulistān-i Iram* (*Rose Garden of Iram*).[106]

Hidāyat believed that poets should, preferably, focus their attention on meaning rather than rhyme and wording. In the introduction to his diaries (*khāṭirāt*) he starts with the following verse, which clearly surmises his views:[107]

در سخن ترتیب و آدابی مجو   هر چه می خواهد دل تنگت بگو[108]

In speech, do not seek rules and regulations,
Whatever your fatigued heart desires, speak!

Indeed, Hidāyat valued the works of classical poets such as Ḥāfiẓ and Sa'dī; he was among the writers who refined the poetic work of Ṣabā to bring it closer to that of Manūchihrī, Anvarī and Khāqānī. According to Losensky, Hidāyat was among the second rank poets of the Qājār period and this ranking was recognized by Browne, Rypka and Āryānpūr.[109]

Mīrzā Fatḥ-ʿAlī Ākhūndzāda (d. 1295/1878)

Mīrzā Fatḥ-ʿAlī Ākhūndzāda was born in 1812 in the town of Nūkhā, in a part of Azerbaijan that later became Russian territory (1828).[110] His education was orthodox, with study of the Qurʾān and theology, as well as Arabic and Persian language and grammar. Indeed, he is considered an intellectual of the pre-constitutional revolution.[111] He learned Russian at a Russian school in Tiflis,[112] and had such an aptitude for the language that, in November 1834, he was selected as a trainee translator in the office of the Russian governor of the Caucasus.

Ākhūndzāda did not write any major work in Persian; all his writings were translated from Ādharī Turkish into Persian. He was an atheist and a materialist (intensely opposed to Islam), and was the founder of modern Iranian theatre. Ākhūndzāda was an extremist in his views of poetry, yet he believed that poetry, while simple in language, must reflect the natural surroundings and environment and be realistic.

In his interpretation of poetry, Ākhūndzāda asserts that good poetry should properly be of a realist nature, comprised of statements on the surroundings and the nature of people or groups precisely as they are, or it is a commentary on some query or characterisation of the condition of the natural world, which is flawless in its creativeness. He further points out that poetry should not be difficult to grasp, and that the words of a good poet should be effortlessly comprehensible to the public, not just scholars and men of literature.[113]

He insisted on classical poetry and the philosophy and styles of the classical masters, emphasizing that we must learn from them; indeed, he saw poetry as an essential element for the advancement of education in literature. Although his understanding of classical Persian literature was not vast, he favoured Saʿdī and Ḥāfiẓ and insisted that their style and expression were worthy of attention and preservation. Of all the Persian poets, he believed only five (Firdawsī, Nizāmī, Rūmī, Saʿdī and Ḥāfiẓ) to be worthy of acknowledgement.[114] Hakkak points out that all Ākhūndzāda's objections to Persian poetry arise from two main concerns. His main anxiety was that literature, as it was practised in his time, pondered little on its environment. Second, as a result of the first issue, Persian poetry had lost its primary purpose.[115] Hakkak further asserts that, as far as Ākhūndzāda was concerned, poets such as Firdawsī, Homer and Shakespeare were considered real poets because their language affects people of all times and all cultures.[116] Therefore, in light of his beliefs, it makes sense that he favoured the Persian poets named above, Ḥāfiẓ included.

In Ākhūndzāda's essay on literary criticism, we see that a reasonable perspective directs his assessments. He infers that people should gain insight from the ingredients of insightful poetry. It becomes clear that he does not differentiate between the role of moral values and wisdom, and that of poetry, or for that matter, art in general. He considered poetry and art as ways to propagate thoughtfulness and serve in an educational capacity. In this respect, Ākhūndzāda left an enduring impact on Iranian scholars such as Aḥmad Kasravī.[117]

Mīrzā Malkam Khān (d. 1315/1898)

Mīrzā Malkam Khān was an Iranian advocate of Freemasonry, active during the period leading up to the Constitutional Revolution.[118] A believer in social Darwinism, Malkam Khān advocated that Iran should become a state modelled on the values of the enlightenment and urged a return to a 'Persian' heritage. Malkam Khān was born to an Armenian Christian family in Persia.[119] He was educated at the Samuel Muradian School in Paris from 1843 to 1851. He later returned to Persia and, it is said, converted to Islam. However, such a statement was never proved and there is no credible evidence to support this claim.[120] He later entered government service and was elected as an instructor at the newly established Tehran polytechnic (*Dār al-Funūn*) in 1852. He went to Paris on a diplomatic assignment in 1857.[121]

Malkam Khān introduced societies, similar to the Freemasons, in Persia in 1859; for this Nāṣir al-Dīn Shāh exiled him in 1862. He was later pardoned and given a post at the embassy in Constantinople. He returned to Tehran in 1872, as assistant to the grand minister, Mīrzā Ḥasan Khān Pirnīā. He was given the title 'Mushir al-Dawla' the Prime Minister, and became chief of the Persian legation in London, and later ambassador in 1872. He remained in the same position until 1888.[122]

From London, Malkam Khān criticized both the Shāh and the Persian government.[123] He edited the newspaper, *Qānūn*, which was banned in Persia but read by the Shāh and his ministers.[124] Malkam Khān was eventually acknowledged as the most significant Persian modernizer of the century, and was later pardoned and reinstated as ambassador to Italy by Muẓaffar al-Dīn Shāh, with the title of 'Nizām al-Dawla'. He remained ambassador to Italy until his death in 1898.[125]

In line with Ākhūndzāda, Malkam condemned the unoriginal panegyric odes fashionable in his time. These generally began with glorification and finished by eulogizing the Shāh:[126]

> I saw ten thousand panegyric odes which all, in one manner and style, began with the spring. Then, racing back and forth between mountain and plain, sea and river, after a thousand adventures, the poets arrived in the patron's presence. Then from his eyelashes to his horse's tail, all would be praised in a flurry of rhyme. After limitless and unbounded extravagances, they would finally petition the cerulean vault to halt the course of time that the life of their patron might be eternal.[127]

Malkam was exceptionally judgemental about the hollowness of such eulogies, whichever oppressor they praised.[128] He was not impressed with the works of the poets of the Qājār period, believing their expressions had little literary value.[129]

He believed poetry was nothing but a waste of time.[130]However, Mukhbir al-Salṭana Hidāyat, who was the minister of sciences at the time, remarked that his works were imitations of Sa'dī's *Gulistān* and *Būstān*. In addition to this remark, Qazvīnī described him as 'an example of vulgarity and complete ignorance' and 'an illiterate and an Armenian crook and charlatan.'[131]

H. Aṣil informs us that Malkam thought of religion as an obstacle to progress.[132] Although Ḥāfiẓ opposed religious hypocrisy and combated hypocrisy of the ascetic, it remains unclear what Malkam as a modernist would have made of him. Furthermore, a detailed search of Malkam Khān's views on Ḥāfiẓ was made by reading all the key primary and secondary sources available in libraries and online, but I was unable to actually find any place where he specifically mentioned his views of the poet.

Muḥammad 'Alī Furūghī Dhakā' al-Mulk (d. 1321/1942)

An important scholar of the nineteenth century, Muḥammad 'Alī Furūghī, believed that the cultural wealth of Persia was a treasure to be explored and learnt from. He was very concerned that this national heritage, including Persian literature, was not fully appreciated. Furūghī admired the work of the classical masters, in particular those of the fifth/twelfth to seventh/fourteenth centuries. He had a high regard for the wisdom of their words, particularly those of Ḥāfiẓ. He emphasized that their advice to humanity was the key to orderly and decent social behaviour and human advancement.

Muḥammad 'Alī Furūghī was born in Tehran in 1294/1877 into a family of Iṣfahānī origin. Furūghī was the eldest child of Muḥammad Ḥusayn

Khān Dhakā' al-Mulk Furūghī, a Qājār writer, poet, translator and official.[133] Furūghī completed his early education under the direction of his father. He studied French and English before enrolling in medical school at the *Dār al-Funūn*. However, he developed a change of interest and redirected his studies to literature and philosophy.[134] According to Itiḥād, Furūghī was a prominent scholar and intellectual thinker of the time.[135] In 1312/1894, he was employed at the Translation Bureau (*Dār al-Tarjuma*), managed by his father. He also taught a variety of subjects in different schools, contributed to the literary newspaper (*tarbīat*) directed by his father and, in 1316/1899, began to teach at the College of Political Science (*Madrasa-i 'Ulūm-i Sīāsī*), where his father was a teacher and, later, director. Furūghī later considered education in its broad sense (*tarbīat*) to be a requirement not only of civilization (*tamaddun*), but also of the very endurance of nations in the contemporary world.[136]

Another distinguishing feature of Furūghī's learning was his readiness to work in partnership with other scholars, and to search for proficient guidance. Among the scholars of his time, Nāsrullāh Taqawī helped plan his anthology of selections from Ḥāfiẓ, the *Zubda-i Ḥāfiẓī* (Tehran, 1316/1937). He also collaborated with Qāsim Ghanī in editing the *Rubā'īyāt* of 'Umar Khayyām (Tehran, 1320/1941), and with Mujtabā Mīnuvī on the anthology of selections from the *Shāh-nāma*, the *Khulāsa-i Shāh-nāma* (Tehran, 1313/1934). Habīb Yağmā'ī worked with him for eight years on several literary projects, including selections from the *Shāh-nāma*, the *Muntakhab-i Shāh-nāma* (Tehran, 1320/1941), and his edition of the works on Sa'dī (Tehran, 1320/1941).[137] Muḥammad 'Alī Furūghī was one of the most important intellectual thinkers of the late nineteenth and early twentieth centuries.[138] His views were highly respected by contemporary scholars and experts in literature and literary criticism. He believed that the Iranian people possessed cultural wealth but did not appreciate its importance and value. In his essays, he mentioned that the work of the classical poets, in particular those of the pre-Tīmūrīd era, presented significant literary value to the national and cultural heritage of Iran and, as a consequence, should be considered as material of great importance.[139] Furūghī believed that the key to humane and decent social behaviour for the Iranian people (and indeed for the whole of mankind) was to observe and practise the profound and meaningful advice inherited from medieval masters; otherwise, one would remain in ignorance and lack any mental and moral improvement. In an ironic tale, he emphasizes his point of view:

> A passing pedestrian saw a person lying on his stomach, drinking water from a stream. Said the pedestrian to the man: My dear fellow, do not drink like this, drinking in this position will cloud your mind. Asked the man: What is a mind? The passing pedestrian said: Forgive me and never mind. I was in the wrong, carry on.[140]

Furūghī believed Ḥāfiẓ's poetry to be free from exaggeration and blandishment; in fact, he emphasized that the source of the profound words and poetry of this great classical poet was his vast knowledge and mystical wisdom.[141] He quotes the following verse from Ḥāfiẓ, a statement pertinent to the story above.

زحمتی می کشم از مردم نادان که مپرس...[142]

> Do not ask of the hardship I suffer from the ignorant!

Furūghī believed that this manner of encouragement by means of teasing or irony distinguished Ḥāfiẓ's work from that of the nineteenth and twentieth-century poets. As Milani asserts:

> [...] this rich cultural legacy is, in his opinion, based on the foundation of the works of Ferdowsi, Sa'di, Ḥāfiẓ, and Rumi. His masterful praise of Sa'di's prose is itself a masterpiece of modern Persian Prose.[143]

Furūghī further asserts that what makes Ḥāfiẓ so admirable is the vastness of his imagination; the depth of his vision; the greatness of his spirit; the profundity of his words; the sweetness in his mystical and divine wisdom; his ability to soothe the mind of his readers whilst giving them hope; the tenderness of his words; and finally, the precise balance that he employs

between the meaning and the words. However, in expressing his opinion of Sa'dī and Ḥāfiẓ, he states that, in his view, Sa'dī is an ocean and Ḥāfiẓ is a mountain; thus, how can one compare them?[144] With regard to the neoclassical movement, Furūghī asserts that he prefers the poets of the pre-Ṣafavid period, such as Ḥāfiẓ and Sa'dī, but this does not mean the works of other poets have no literary value or are less desirable; this is purely his personal preference.[145]

Furūghī's views on Ḥāfiẓ and literary criticism are fair and just. He greatly respected the poetry of Sa'dī and Ḥāfiẓ and declared that if anyone criticized them he would be deeply insulted; however, he welcomed valid criticism made with the aim of questioning true faults. As long as these views pertained to their literature, he considered them fair and acceptable.[146]

ʿAbdul Raḥīm Ṭālibuf (d. 1329/1911)

Mīrzā ʿAbdul Raḥīm Ṭālibuf was one of the modern literary critics of Iran in the nineteenth century.[147] According to Qazvīnī, he travelled to Georgia at the age of sixteen and stayed there to complete his studies.[148] While as a creative thinker Ṭalibuf's writings were mainly concerned with social and political ideas, this section of the chapter is concerned with his views on literature and particularly the language of Ḥāfiẓ. Ṭālibuf's literary thought is dispersed throughout his work, a fact that demands a somewhat thorough examination of a vast part of his writings, in order to reach a complete depiction of his critical philosophy. In pursuit of such an analysis, it can be determined that for Ṭālibuf, literary criticism is a substitute for critically handling the social and political tribulations of his time.[149] 'In institutions of his time, Ṭālibuf is also brought to address critically the literature which served and supported them.'[150] Ṭālibuf's main concern was social reform, and he did not apply himself specifically to literary criticism.[151]

However, references to literature are found in his work, especially when he felt the writing was unhelpful in its social implications. Some of his works that include literary criticism are *Nukhbi-i sipihrī* (*The Best of the Spheres*) (Istanbul, 1310/1892); and a brief biography of Islam's prophet, *Kitāb-i Aḥmad yā safina-i Ṭālibī* (*The Book of Aḥmad or the Ṭālibī Anthology*) (Istanbul, 1311/1893), in two volumes.[152]

This second book is a reflection of a discussion between Ṭālibuf and his imaginary son, Aḥmad, on physics, nature and the important issues of their time.[153] The *Masālik al-muḥsinīn* (*The Principles of the Beneficent*) (Cairo, 1323/1905), is a collection of philosophical deliberations and socio-literary criticism based on an imaginary travelogue.[154] *Ḥayāt-i jadīd* (*Modern Life*) (Istanbul, 1311/1893) is the translation from Russian to Persian of one of C. Flammarion's (1842-1925) works on astronomy, among other subjects.[155]

In addition to these works, Ṭālibuf published articles in the papers of the time, such as *Anjuman* and *Ḥabl al-matīn*. Moreover, he composed a number of poems dealing with the political and social ideas of Iranians.[156] It is often said that he was the first Iranian political poet. Ṭālibuf was interested in modernism and political issues of the period and was a supporter of the

Constitutional Revolution. As a nationalist who loved his country, he stated 'I am not a tycoon in Iran; I am a man who understands responsibility and believes in fairness and strongly oppose injustice; I neither seek power nor titles.'[157] Ṭālibuf's moral beliefs seem to parallel Ḥāfiẓ's social philosophy, as the following verse by Ḥāfiẓ clearly states:

من از بازوی خود دارم بسی شکر که زور مردم آزاری ندارم[158]

Very grateful am I to my arm,
Because I lack the strength of an injurer of men.[159]

With regard to literature, he favoured simplicity of prose and despised the classical style of poetry and writing.[160] We only come across literary criticism in three of his books; however, in one of these, *Masā'il al-hay'at*, Ṭālibuf stresses that we should learn from our forefathers and, in particular, from the 'poetry and literature' of the classical masters. He admired neoclassical poetry not only for its role in reviving the poetry of the classical masters, but also for its function in preserving the Persian language so that the messages of Persian poets such as Firdawsī, Sa'dī and Ḥāfiẓ could be understood. Ṭālibuf approved of neoclassical poetry mostly because it helped to revive the poetry of the master poets of the past. Moreover, he expressed some critical views about the purity of the Persian language because, for a short time, Prince Jalāl al-Dīn Mīrzā (d. 1289/1872) and Yaghmā Jandaqī set the task of writing in pure Persian, their aim being to extract all Arabic words that they deemed too difficult to grasp.[161] Ṭālibuf expressed his views on the issue, pointing out that the Arabic language, which had intermingled with the language of Persia for over fourteen hundred years, could not be extracted without causing irreversible harm to Persian.[162]

Zayn al-'Ābidin Marāgha'ī (d. 1329/1911)

Ḥājj Zayn al-'Ābidin Marāgha'ī was a remarkable nineteenth-century author and analyst of Iran, who, in the process of expressing his reformist and modernist social conceptions, also dealt with literary criticism.[163] Like Ṭālibuf, Marāgha'ī did not write any works specifically on literary criticism – his views about literature, past and present, can be found in the *Sīyāḥat-nāma* (*Travelogue*).[164] In his travelogue, Marāgha'ī says that so far Iranian writers have not written about love of their country, or offered words of any value to ordinary men. Whatever they have written about the passion of the nightingale's love towards the rose or that of the moth and the candle is only the author's praise of unworthy patrons.[165]

Marāgha'ī believed Iranian writers and poets should recognize other loves – besides that of the Laylī and Majnūn and Shirīn and Farhād. This erotic love dominates their work and they speak of nothing else in their books and poems. He further asserts that this is no time for masters of literature and intellectuals to waste their time with madness, nonsensical stories and meaningless words; like the writers of the past, they will learn nothing but fantasy.[166] Rather, they should educate the masses in humanism and culture, as do European and Japanese intellectuals, and teach them that the blessed name of the homeland is the source of all good fortune and that her protection is necessary for every Iranian.[167]

Clearly, patriotism is a central concern that Marāgha'ī highlights in his literary criticism.[168] In fact, allegiance to one's country was a primary aspect of the philosophy of Iran's reformist thinkers in the nineteenth century.[169] Although many of these writers, such as Hidāyat, Bahār and Malkam Khān, exhausted much of their energies outside Iran – or possibly because of this – they remained intensely patriotic. Identifying the Russian and British colonial authorities as sponsors of the Qājār state, and consequently as an impediment to legitimate government, they regarded it as their obligation to combat these powers. For them, nationalism was necessary to the project of assessing literary works.[170]

In an essay in the *Sīyāḥat-nāma*, Marāgha'ī stresses that the time has come for poets and authors who invested their lives in praising tyrants to write ballads glorifying the love of country. He argues that just as they used to mourn every hardship, they should now sing elegies for their native land and weep for her difficulties because without a country one would be denied the right to give service. Marāgha'ī felt that some poets of the period who used to disapprove of nationalists should now criticize the cruelties of those who betray their country in poetry and praise.[171] Marāgha'ī did not tolerate any form of exaggeration in prose and poetry. He believed that it is essential that writers of literature avoid fantasy and ostentation. The works of the Qājār writers provoked him because they were excessive and deceitful in their flattery of kings.[172]

Marāgha'ī goes so far as to establish the criteria for being a poet. He emphasizes that poetry is one of the more difficult arts, because it needs to be both traditional and logical. The poet must be eloquent and proficient in direct and indirect ways, in allegory and metaphor, orderly and disorderly speech, and in rhetoric, philosophy and astronomy. He must also be fluent with ease of expression, be unequalled in performing ethical deeds, be accurate in moral judgement and possess a powerful memory and love his country. He praises Saʿdī and Ḥāfiẓ for meeting these criteria.[173]

Marāghaʾī was a true patriot who spoke continually about the importance of allegiance to one's country. He frequently wondered why so few poets wrote patriotic poems and he considered Persian verses that spoke of a beloved, whether human or divine, a waste of time, or efforts that carried no literary value whatsoever. Marāghaʾī insisted that love of one's country is more important than any other love, because, he thought, without one's country all literary efforts would mean nothing. He admired Ḥāfiẓ as a patriotic poet whose verses stood against tyranny and deceit. Marāghaʾī believed that a poet should meet a certain criteria of eloquence and rhetoric.

Summary

The intellectuals considered in this chapter may not all have revered Ḥāfiẓ, but none of them dared to criticize, much less, condemn him. Ḥāfiẓ's influence has never been limited to ordinary people, rather it has even extended to kings, who used his verses in communications to other sovereigns and even to their own officials. It has been said that when Nīzām al-Salṭana, a government official during the reign of Nāṣir al-Dīn Shāh, wrote a letter asking the Shāh to grant him the governorship of the province of Fārs, Nāṣir al-Dīn Shāh responded with one of Ḥāfiẓ's verses:

ای مگس حضرت سیمرغ نه جولانگه توست   عرض خود می کنی و زحمت ما می داری[174]

> O fly! The realm of Sīmurgh[175] is not a place for display,
> You dishonour yourself and cause us trouble!

Many poets of the Qājār period attempted to imitate Ḥāfiẓ but all, without exception, failed to equal his lyricism. Ḥāfiẓ's conflict with ascetics, clerics and religious hypocrites came at a time when Iran was plagued by conservative religious extremists, and this was another reason that scholars, particularly the poets of the Qājār era, deemed him laudable. Ḥāfiẓ was the voice of his people and he battled the deceit and dishonesty of the clergy.

ʿAbdullāh Rāzī (d. 1334/1955), a scholar of the Qājār period, stated that Ḥāfiẓ's poetry benefited from the wisdom of Saʿdī's articulation, the beauty of Niẓāmī's words and the philosophy of Rūmī, yet there was always something extra to Ḥāfiẓ's poetry. He also said that no one had been able to equal him to this day.[176]

منم آن شاعر ساحر که به افسون سخن　　　از نی کلک همه شهد و شکر می بارم[177]

That poet-magician I am, who, with the sorcery of speech
From the reed-pen, all sweetness I pour.

I believe that the views of the critics named above enhanced the reputation of the classical masters, particularly Ḥāfiẓ. Somewhat surprisingly, even the adverse views held by Kasravī strengthened Ḥāfiẓ's status in the minds of his supporters and aroused curiosity in those who knew little about him. Literary criticism has helped the advancement of Ḥāfiẓology, as proven by the many improved commentaries and editions of Ḥāfiẓ's work, as explained in detail throughout this study. Ḥāfiẓ's philosophy is more popular today than ever before, particularly in the West. His verses are being translated into many languages and his popularity in Iran continues to increase.

It is clear that nineteenth-century Persian critics and poets held Ḥāfiẓ in high esteem. Throughout the turbulence of the constitutional era, a number of poets, such as ʿĀrif Qazvīnī, Bahār and many others composed nationalistic poems, all inspired by Ḥāfiẓ and other classical masters.

Moreover, as already observed in this study, Persia has suffered wars, political turmoil and economic disasters; and it has witnessed numerous dynasties emerge and disappear through the centuries. The one element that has remained constant is the language of the classical master poets, in particular Ḥāfiẓ, who has influenced the poets and writers of Persia. It has been demonstrated that poets like Bābā Fighānī and Muḥammad Taqī Bahār were inspired by, and have imitated Ḥāfiẓ in one way or another.

The intellectuals and modernizers of the Qājār period, as we have already observed, had different views on literature and poetry. For example, Kirmānī was a writer and a poet who opposed panegyric poetry, yet admired the works of master poets such as Saʿdī and Ḥāfiẓ. Kirmānī detested extremism and believed that erroneous religious attitudes and superstitions prevent progress. There are some indications that Kirmānī admired the poetry of a few classical poets, in particular Saʿdī and Ḥāfiẓ, for they held the same ideas.

ما شیخ و واعظ کمتر شناسیم   یا جام باده یا قصه کوتاه[178]

We know not the Shaykh or the ascetic,
Let us have the cup of wine; or cut the story short.

Hidāyat also admired the classical masters, in particular Sa'dī and Ḥāfiẓ. Although his views on the rhyme and regulation of classical poetry differed from those of the master poets, he was overwhelmed by their poetic diction. Hidāyat believed that a poet should focus on meaning rather than rhyme. Ḥāfiẓ's poetry in general impressed him, for the poet's utterance reflects day to day life and the problems society faced at the time.

یاری اندر کس نمی بینم یاران را چه شد   دوستی کی آخر آمد دوستداران را چه شد
شهریاران بود و خاک مهربانان این دیار   مهربانی کی سرآمد شهریاران را چه شد[179]

I see no friendship in anyone. What's become of friends?
When did friendship come to an end? What's happened to friends?

This land was 'the city of friends' and 'the dust of the kindly'.
When did kindness come to an end? What's happened to the city of friends?[180]

In contrast to the views of the two previously mentioned scholars, Ākhūndzāda points out that poetry should be easy to comprehend, and that the speech of a good poet should be easily understood by ordinary men, not just scholars.[181] However, his understanding of classical Persian literature was somewhat narrow. It is emblematic that, of all the Persian poets, he believed only five (Firdawsī, Nizāmī, Rūmī, Sa'dī and Ḥāfiẓ) to be praiseworthy and fit for recognition.[182] Malkam distinguishes between the quality of effectiveness, on the one hand, and the prerequisite requirement of clarity, on the other. Therefore, in a sense, Malkam establishes the need for transformation without directly involving himself in the task of effecting such a change, whereas Ākhūndzāda and Kirmānī thought involvement was essential.[183]

In sum, writings of men such as Ākhūndzāda, Kirmānī and Malkam exemplify the preliminary stages of an enduring cultural evolution by which the yearning to change Iranian culture has acceded to the notion of conventional Persian poetry undergoing continuous critical review and reassessment.

CHAPTER III

The Influence of Ḥāfiẓ on the Poets of Zand and Qājār Persia

In the first few pages of this chapter I offer a general overview of literary developments in Persian poetry from the earliest days through to the Qājār era, commenting briefly on the various Persian poetic styles. I also briefly discuss the literary revival that occurred during that period. Next, I focus on the views of modern critics and scholars of Persian literature and poetry concerning new developments that took place in poetry during the Qājār period and the impact of translations from European literature on the literary milieu of Qājār poets. I follow this with an examination of the influence of western literature, particularly French, on Persian poets. In the final and longest section of this chapter, I discuss the influence of Ḥāfiẓ's language on seven key poets of the Zand and Qājār era. It is not my intention, however, to provide an elaborate literary analysis of the poets' merits or to go into detail about their places in Persian *Belles Lettres*.

Key Developments in Persian Poetry during the Qājār Period

In order to familiarize the reader with the significant changes poetry underwent during this period, it is necessary to briefly discuss the different styles of poetry that poets were accustomed to in Persia from the earliest Islamic period and the reasons and extent to which these styles changed. The early poets of Islamic Persia based their poetry on the Turkish style (*sabk-i Turkistānī*), which was very similar to the Khurāsānī style (*sabk-i Khurāsānī*). The popularity of this style lies in the plain nature of its wording and the clarity of the subject and metaphors: the verse is easily understood by the reader.[1]

A further genre of poetry was written in the 'Irāqī style (*sabk-i 'Irāqī*). After the fifth/eleventh-century, Persian literature developed complexity in prose and poetry. This was due to the proximity of the Persian capital to Baghdad and the Islamic centres of the time, which also inspired the majority of the poets of the period to use mystical, theological and spiritual words in their poetry. As Arabic idioms and metaphors were also commonly used, this style of poetry was named *sabk-i ʿIrāqī*.

The third approach to poetry was that of the Indian style (*sabk-i Hindī*), which reached its peak during the Ṣafavid dynasty (1501-1722). The Indian style of poetry moved radically away from the styles of earlier Persian poetry. For the most part, poets working in the Indian style portrayed a notable truthfulness vis-à-vis their social environment.[2] As noted in the previous chapter, many scholars maintain that the foundation for the Indian style was laid by Ḥāfiẓ.

One of the significant transformations in the literary history of Persia took place during the Qājār period (1193/1779-1344/1925). Because almost all the poets of this period took their inspiration from the master poets of the third/ninth and the eighth/fourteenth centuries (those who wrote in the Khurāsānī and ʿIrāqī styles), this turning point is called the neoclassical period.[3] The new intellectuals of the Qājār period expressed a deep-seated passion with regard to the value of the poetic tradition of the Persian language.[4]

The poetry of the Qājār period took a turn towards something more demanding, in particular during the period before the Constitutional Revolution. Economic and cultural contact with the West, which had greatly increased from the middle of the nineteenth century, was a core element in bringing qualitative change to the way of life in many countries of the East, and Iran was no exception.

Literature was affected by a transformation that shaped its flow, transforming it into a literature that is controversial and belligerent, able to confront the nation as a whole, to educate and encourage people to awaken from their apathy. The best poets of the country, for as long as could be remembered, had composed *qaṣīdas* in praise of the kings and their courts. They now focused on limiting, and finally overthrowing, the monarchal dominance, and on the enlightenment and liberation of their fellow countrymen.[5]

Westernization, Modernization and Persian Poetry of the Late Qājār Period

During the Qājār period, elegy writing took precedence over *ghazals*,[6] and *Mathnawī* writings were favoured. The neoclassical movement slowly began its course and gradually broadened.[7] For this, we are indebted to poets such as Qā'ānī and Yaghmā Jandaqī, who are discussed below. The expansion of British and Russian imperialism in the nineteenth century brought about the beginning of modernization in Iran.[8] The polytechnic institute (*Dār al-Funūn*) catered to the new demand for foreign languages, in particular French; and thousands of other cultural, social and political changes all reflected the movement towards modernization and westernization.[9] It was close to the end of the Qājār dynasty that Iranian literature took a new turn towards the West.[10]

Hakkak asserts that, to a large degree, the consciousness of a European literature was also becoming understood in relation to an association between literary and political history. This was considered an exceptional occurrence in Iranian history and an enormous step towards the future. The Constitutional Revolution created an ambiance that saw poets akin to those in Europe flourish.[11] Many intellectuals were in agreement that poets should concentrate on patriotic poetry more than anything else and that they should free themselves from rhythmic rules and styles and concentrate more on politically meaningful themes.[12]

The role of literary prose in the contemporary literature of Iran is, Rypka believes, a fundamental and often-debated question among conservatives and modernists.[13] It was the modernists of the Qājār period who promoted prose as a literary genre. As observed in chapter II, Iranian scholars had already distinguished between the plainness and clarity of early Persian poetry and the elaborate rhetoric and perplexed character of poetry in later centuries.

In the aftermath of the Constitutional Revolution, this cultural decline that referred back to the decline during the Mongol invasions expanded to such an extent that it connected poetry to its social context. As these observations were new to poetry and prose, a new subject had to be found to match them; hence, the birth of the *Shi'r-i naw*, or New Poetry during the Pahlavi period, with influences unseen in the poetry of the classical poets.

Although it can be said that there was a substantial move away from traditional poetry, there were some who argued that there existed an implicit attachment to it. However, the debate on poetry quickly shifted to a concern with the characteristics of a new poetry and the scope and tempo of the poetic transformation. The greater the exposure to European poetry and poetic customs, the greater the tendency of a poet to employ general material to form the new poetry of Iran. Conversely, the more absorbed a poet or critic was in the classical tradition, the more he or she was prepared to depend on the terminology associated with the Persian poetry of the early classical period.[14]

Hakka asserts that we can witness the most fluent phase of a developing social discussion a decade after the Constitutional Revolution. Although the majority of the poets of this period followed in the footsteps of the classical poets, through their focus on the traditional principles of poetic neoclassicalism, they provided an invaluable contribution to the revival of forgotten words and themes, and in some cases expanded these expressions even further.

Ḥāfiẓ and the Poets of Zand and Qājār Persia

The purpose of this section is to give a short biographical sketch of seven important poets of the Zand and Qājār period and then to attempt to demonstrate the influence Ḥāfiẓ had on their work. The entire collections of *ghazal*s of each poet have been carefully studied and examined, and examples are offered to illustrate Ḥāfiẓ's influence. Although the poets analyzed here represent only a fraction of those of the Zand/Qājār period, they are some of the most important poets of nineteenth- and twentieth-century Persia. The poets whose work has been chosen for close examination are listed below:

1. Ādhar Bigdilī (d. 1195/1778)
2. Viṣāl Shīrāzī (d. 1262/1845)
3. Qā'ānī Shīrāzī (d. 1270/1853)
4. Furūghī Basṭāmī (d. 1274/1857)
5. Yaghmā Jandaqī (d. 1276/1859)
6. Ḥājj Mullā Hādī Sabzivārī (d. 1289/1872)
7. Ḥājj Mīrzā Ḥasan Iṣfahānī 'Ṣafī 'Alī Shāh' (d. 1316/1898)

In order to better understand the debate regarding the conflict between imitation and originality in Persian poetry, it is necessary to mention, briefly, the various terms related to literary imitation in the Persian poetic tradition. All the Persian poets imitated each other carefully, and did so by using some of the following devices: poetic imitation (*tattabu' va taqlīd*), which means following another poet's style (*sabk*);[15] verse parallelism (*naẓira*), which means poetic 'paraphrase' or imitation of a previous poet's poems;[16] verse insertion (*taḍmīn*), which means the quotation of a hemistich from original poetry in any verse of a poet's composition;[17] verse homage (*istiqbāl*), which means '*javāb*: composition of a poem of varying length and form in 'response' and direct reference, sometimes to refute, sometimes to emulate the ideas of the source poem,'[18] and poetic plagiary (*sirqat-i shiʿrī*), or the plagiarism of a verse by another poet. In my discussion of the seven poets below, I will draw attention to their usage of these devices in the act of imitation of and paying homage to Ḥāfiẓ.

Ādhar Bigdilī (d. 1195/1778)

Ādhar Bigdilī, the poet and author of the famous biographical anthology entitled *Ātashkada-yi Ādhar*, was born in 1134/1721. His biography (*tadhkira*), which provides the biographical details accompanied by citations from some 850 Persian poets, was compiled in 1174/1760 and dedicated to Karīm Khān Zand (r. 1163/1751-1193/1779).[19]

Ādhar allegedly lost 7,000 verses of his poetry during the plundering of Iṣfahān by ʿAlī-Mardān Khān Bakhtīyārī in 1074/1657, but a *Dīvān* consisting of *qaṣā'id*, *ghazalīyāt*, *qaṭiʿāt*, and a *Mathnawī* ('Yūsuf va Zuliykhā') has survived.[20] Influenced by his concerned uncle and the master poet Mīr Sayyid ʿAlī Mushtāq Iṣfahānī (d. 1192/1778), Ādhar thrived as a poet.[21]

Ādhar was one of the leaders of the movement against the so-called Indian style (*sabk-i Hindī*) and an exponent of neoclassical poetry; as such, he was bluntly critical of the poetry of Ṣā'ib and his followers. However, for those such as Mushtāq, who denied the Indian style and tried to revive the language of the early poets, he has nothing but commendation. For some poets, he gives detailed biographies; however, for the majority he finds two or three lines sufficient.

Ādhar and Ḥāfiẓ

In examining Ādhar's *Dīvān*, it is clear that only a small portion of his verses are similar to those of Ḥāfiẓ. In his *ghazal*s, we encounter different types of verse imitation (both *naẓira* and *tattabu'*) of Ḥāfiẓ.[22] He also follows Ḥāfiẓ's style of combating hypocrisy and deceitful ascetics. We witness further similarities between Ādhar's poetry and Ḥāfiẓ's language in terms of topoi, themes, imagery and symbolism. In the following poem, Ādhar's meaning matches that of Ḥāfiẓ in regard to religious questions, hypocrisy and the issues of the *sharīʿa*. It is necessary to present the whole poem, since the full meaning manifests itself only in the poem's entirety.

به شیخ شهر فقیری ز جوع برد پناه	بدین امید که از جود، خواهدش نان داد	Ādhar
هزار مسئله پرسیدش از مسائل و گفت:	"جواب ندادی، نبایدت نان داد"	
نداشت حال جدال آن فقیر و شیخ غیور	برد آبش و نانش نداد تا جان داد	
عجب که با همه دانایی این نمی دانست	به بنده نه روزی به شرط ایمان داد	
من و ملازمت آستان پیر مغان	که جام می به کف کافر و مسلمان داد[23]	

A starving man sought the help of the town's ascetic
Hoping that, out of decency, he would share his food.

The puritan asked him thousands of questions and said:
'If you do not give the correct answers, you do not deserve food.'

The poor destitute [man] had no strength to speak,
and the eminent ascetic denied him food and water,
and hence, the man died!

It is a marvel that, with all his wisdom, he did not know
That sustenance from the Lord is not conditional on faith.

Therefore, I seek the estate of the sage of Magi,
For he gave wine to Muslims and the faithless.

In the following verse by Ḥāfiẓ, one can see exactly the same topoi, which precisely echo the meaning and philosophy expressed by Ādhar in the above lines:

بندهٔ پیر خراباتم که لطفش دائم است	ورنه لطف شیخ و زاهد گاه هست و گاه نیست[24]	Ḥāfiẓ

I am the servant of the sage of Kharābāt,[25] whose generosity is constant,
While the generosity of the ascetic and the cleric, is not!

The following verses are examples of *naẓira*; the underlined words in the verse's rhyme and meter correspond to parallel or identical expressions found in Ḥāfiẓ's verses:

Ādhar

شب عید است در میخانه باید بستر اندازیم　　که پیش از صبح ساقی را نظر بر منظر اندازیم[26]

It is the time of celebration; we must make our bed at the door of the tavern
So we can gaze on the face of Sāqī at dawn.

Ḥāfiẓ

صبا خاک وجود ما بدان عالی جناب انداز　　بود کان شاه خوبان را نظر بر منظر اندازیم[27]

O breeze, to the majestic beloved, the dust of our existence cast,
So that we may glance at the king of fair ones.

Ādhar

حساب زاهدان در روز محشر مشکل است آذر!　　بیا تا ما حساب خود به روز دیگر اندازیم[28]

Ādhar, judgement of the ascetics will be arduous on the day of reckoning, come; let us delay our own judgements until another day.

Ḥāfiẓ

سخن دانی و خوش خوانی نمی ورزند در شیراز　　بیا حافظ که تا خود را به ملکی دیگر اندازیم[29]

In Shīrāz, they appreciate neither articulation nor verse,
Come Ḥāfiẓ, into another land we may cast ourselves!

Ādhar

تا تماشایی ز گلشن باز داند باغبان　　گر گشاید در و گر بندد تأمل بایدش[30]

If the gardener knows that one can gaze on the garden, whether the garden gate is opened or shut to him, he must have patience.

Ḥāfiẓ

رند عالم سوز را با مصلحت بینی چه کار؟　　کار ملک است آنکه تدبیر و تأمل بایدش[31]

The *rind*, with an all-consuming passion, has no business with prudence,
It is the business of sovereigns which requires heed and planning.

Ādhar

هرکه عشق کودک سنگین دلش دیوانه کرد　　گر زنندش کودکان سنگی تحمّل بایدش[32]

He who has become insane through loving a hardhearted youth,
Must bear it if kids throw stones at him.

ای دل اندر بند زلفش از پریشانی منال　　مرغ زیرک چون بدام افتد تحمّل بایدش[33]　　Ḥāfiẓ

O heart, entangled in her tresses, bewail not your state,
When the wise bird falls into the snare, resignation is required.

Viṣāl Shīrāzī (d. 1262/1845)

Mīrzā Shafīʿ Shīrāzī, known as Mīrzā Kūchak, with the pen name 'Mahjūr', and later 'Viṣāl', was born in Shīrāz in 1193/1791. He was one of the greatest poets during the reign of Fatḥ-ʿAlī Shāh Qājār (1798-1834). Due to his talent for poetry and also his pleasant voice, he was known throughout the city and when Fatḥ-ʿAlī Shāh Qājār learned of him, he invited him to the court. Viṣāl showed considerable interest in the subjects of mysticism, *ʿirfān* or Gnosticism and literature. He became blind at the age of sixty-nine, and died during the reign of Muḥammad Shāh.

His style of poetry is elegiac and laudatory of kings and various state officials. Most of his poetry is composed in the style of Saʿdī and Hāfiz and belongs to the neoclassical school. His style of *ghazal* composition leans more towards that of Ḥāfiẓ, and also inclines somewhat towards mystical concepts. Before his death, Viṣāl realized the unimportance of panegyrical poetry and had some feelings of remorse about his profession.[34] Viṣāl's *Dīvān* consists of approximately 22,000 couplets, including *ghazalīyāt*, *tarjīʿ-band*, *qaṣāʾid*, *qaṭaʿāt* and *Mathnawīhā*.[35] He had a major impact upon the development of Persian poetry.[36] Viṣāl died in Shīrāz in 1262/1845.

Viṣāl and Ḥāfiẓ

Viṣāl Shīrāzī was greatly influenced by Ḥāfiẓ in his lyric writing.[37] In some of his verses, we can see imitations of Ḥāfiẓ's rhyme and meaning. The verses quoted below are clearly imitations of Ḥāfiẓ's rhymes and metres, and demonstrate Viṣāl's similar use of symbolism, imagery and content.

از جفا ترسی و راه وصل میپرسی وصال　　هیچ کس بی نیش خاری زین گلستان گل نچید[38]　　Viṣāl

O Viṣāl, you fear cruelty, yet you search the path of union,
No one has picked a rose from this garden without the sting of a thorn.

Ḥāfiẓ

درین چمن گل بی خار کس نچید آری　　چراغ مصطفوی با شرار بولهبیست[39]

No one in this field has gathered a thornless rose. Yes,
The lamp of the Prophet with the sparks of an Abū Lahab![40]

The following verses are an example of *naẓira*; the rhyme and metre correspond to Ḥāfiẓ's style.

Viṣāl

حریفان را می باقی و ما را لعل ساقی بس　　چه باید عیش شیرین تلخ کردن زان شر و شورش[41]

For the rivals, the eternal wine is fit, but for us, the Sāqī's ruby lip is enough.
Why should we ruin a good time with their wickedness and noise?

Ḥāfiẓ

شراب تلخ میخواهم که مردافکن بود زورش　　که تا یکدم بیاسایم ز دنیا و شر و شورش[42]

I desire a bitter wine, whose power knocks men out,
Perchance, I may rest a moment from the world's wickedness and noise.

Viṣāl

گرچه دریای غمش را خطری نیست که نیست　　صبر ای دل، که در آنجا گهری نیست که نیست[43]

Although there is no danger not found in your ocean's grief,
Be patient, O Heart, for no treasure exists that is not there.

Ḥāfiẓ

روشن از پرتو رویت نظری نیست که نیست　　منّت خاک درت بر بصری نیست که نیست[44]

There is no glance not illuminated by the radiance of your face;
There is no eye not bound by the dust of your threshold.

Viṣāl

آمد از ناز رخش سیر ندیدیم و برفت　　شکوه کردیم و جوابی نشنیدیم و برفت[45]

She came, and we did not see enough of her coy countenance, and she left!
To our complaints, we heard no response, and she left!

Ḥāfiẓ	روی مه پیکر او سیر ندیدیم و برفت[46]	شربتی از لب لعلش نچشیدیم و برفت

From her ruby lips, a sip we tasted not, and she's gone!
Her beautiful face, we beheld not enough, and she's gone!

Qā'ānī Shīrāzī (d. 1270/1853)

Mīrzā Habībullāh Shīrāzī, who wrote under the pen name 'Qā'ānī', was born in 1223/1808 in Shīrāz.[47] Qā'ānī lost his father at the age of eleven and faced extreme poverty. He spent several years in Iṣfahān studying mathematics and Islamic studies, and later returned to Shīrāz, where he commenced teaching poetry. In the year 1239/1823, he became tutor to the son of Fatḥ-'Alī Shāh, 'Shujā' al-Salṭana'. After travelling extensively, he went to Tehran, where he became the court poet and spent the rest of his life. His style of poetry follows that of Sa'dī.[48]

Bahār affirms that since Qā'ānī followed Ṣabā's style, he should also be counted among the votaries of the neoclassical school. He eventually developed his own independent style, and the poets of Tehran followed his example for some time. Shiblī Nu'mānī claims that there was no innovation in Qā'ānī's poetry, saying 'he just awakened 700 years of forgotten poetry'.[49]

Qā'ānī's *Dīvān* has been published numerous times in Tehran, Tabriz, and India. According to Browne, Qā'ānī is one of the most melodious of all the Persian poets, but while his command of the language is vast, he lacked honour and moral standards. However, Qā'ānī made a significant contribution to the development of neoclassical Persian poetry in the nineteenth century.

Qā'ānī and Ḥāfiẓ

Qā'ānī's poetry is similar to that of Ḥāfiẓ in terms of symbolism and imagery, and exhibits some parallels with his in its use of similar themes and topoi. The following comparisons demonstrate these similarities. The first couplet is an example of poetic plagiarism or *sirqat-i shi'rī*.

Qā'ānī

گفتمش در عین وصل این ناله و فریاد چیست　　گفت مارا جلوهٔ معشوق در این کار داشت[50]

I asked: Why this crying and lament at the moment of union?
It replied: The manifestation of the Beloved has caused my disarray!

Ḥāfiẓ

گفتمش در عین وصل این ناله و فریاد چیست　　گفت مارا جلوهٔ معشوق در این کار داشت[51]

I asked: Why this crying and lament at the moment of union?
It replied: The manifestation of the Beloved has caused my disarray!

The example below demonstrates *taḍmīn*, the quotation of a hemistich of another poet's composition in one's own poem.[52]

Qā'ānī　　الغرض با آب غلمان چشمه سار حور را　　شیوهٔ جنات تجری تحتهاالانهار داشت[53]

In sum the fountain head of the maidens of paradise through the aqua vitae of the angelic heavenly men
Seemed to be like an apparition of paradise under which streams of water flowed

Ḥāfiẓ　　چشم حافظ زیر بام قصر آن حوری سرشت　　شیوهٔ جنات تجری تحتهاالانهار داشت[54]

Beneath the roof of the castle of the one whose nature is like that of an angel, Ḥāfiẓ's eyes
Seemed to be like an apparition of paradise under which streams of water flowed

The following verses are an example of *naẓira*; their rhyme and metre mimicking the style and methods used by Ḥāfiẓ.

Qā'ānī　　این پنج روز عمر گرامی عزیز دار　　با دوستان بهل که بصدق و صفا رود[55]

Treasure these five valuable days of life;
Humbly spend them with friends in honesty and purity.

Ḥāfiẓ حافظ بکوی میکده دایم بصدق دل چون صوفیان صومعه دار از صفا رود[56]

With wholeheartedness, Ḥāfiẓ always goes to streets of the wine-house, like the cloister-keeping Sufis, he goes out of sincerity.[57]

Qā'ānī چون کس خبر ندارد از اسرار علم غیب حیفست از آن نفس که به چون و چرا رود[58]

Because no one knows the mystical secrets,
It would be a shame if a breath was wasted in debate.

Ḥāfiẓ مارا به آب دیده شب و روز ماجراست زآن رهگذر که بر سر کویش چرا رود[59]

Day and night our obsession is crying,
As to reason why someone might walk on her street.

Qā'ānī رویی گشاده دار و لبی بسته تا ز در بیگانه آید ار بدرون آشنا رود[60]

Have a cheerful face and closed lips so that
If a stranger comes in, he leaves as a friend.

Ḥāfiẓ بر خاک راه یار نهادیم روی خویش بر روی ما رواست اگر آشنا رود[61]

Our face is placed on the dust of the friend's path,
It would be lawful if the friend were to walk all over us.[62]

Qā'ānī زلفت چو ما نگون و پریشان و درهمست آشفته روز آنکه ترا در قفا رود[63]

Your hair, like us, is dishevelled, forlorn and gloomy,
How gloomily pass the days in your absence.

Ḥāfiẓ خورشید خاوری کند از رشک جامه چاک گر ماه مهر پرور من در قبا رود[64]

From envy, the eastern sun splits her garment,
If under a gown my loving moon hides.

Qā'ānī دست در حلقهٔ آن طرهٔ پر چین دارم پنجه انداخته در پنجهٔ شاهین دارم[65]

My hands are curled in those wavy locks,
My fists are twisted in falcon claws.

Ḥāfiẓ دست در حلقهٔ آن زلف دوتا نتوان کرد تکیه بر عهد تو و باد صبا نتوان کرد[66]

There can be no reaching into that tangled lock,
There can be no depending on your promises and the eastern breeze!

Qā'ānī در هوای قد و اندام و خط و عارض یار عشق با سرو و گل و سنبل و نسرین دارم[67]

In yearning for the stature, tallness, dusky line and visage of the beloved, I have a love for the cypress, rose, hyacinth and jasmine.[68]

Ḥāfiẓ چو در گلزار اقبالش خرامانم بحمدالله نه میل لاله و نسرین نه برگ نسترن دارم[69]

When I am strolling in the rose bed of her acceptance, praise be to God, for I have no desire for tulips and roses, or the petals of the narcissus.[70]

The verses below demonstrate *tattabu'* because they imitate an original style and method of poetry, in this case, that written by Ḥāfiẓ.

Qā'ānī زخویشتن بجهان هر کسی خبر دارد خلاف من که نباشد خبر ز خویشتنم[71]

Everyone has some awareness of themselves in this world,
Except I who have no knowledge of myself!

Ḥāfiẓ عیان نشد که چرا آمدم کجا رفتم دریغ و درد که غافل ز کار خویشتنم[72]

It did not become clear why I came or where I went,
Alas, I am oblivious to my own affairs!

Qā'ānī پس از هلاک تنم گربه دجله غرق کنند زسوز آتش دل دود خیزد از کفنم[73]

If after death, my body in a Tigris they drown,
From the flames of the heart's fire, smoke shall rise from my shroud.

Ḥāfiẓ بگشای تربتم را بعد از وفات و بنگر کاز آتش درونم دود از کفن برآید[74]

After death, open my tomb and look,
For from the fire within, smoke shall rise from the shroud.[75]

Qā'ānī دوستی گفت عیب من با غیر   من خود از عیب خود ابا نکنم[76]

A friend spoke of my faults with a stranger,
I shall not hesitate to mention my own faults.

Ḥāfiẓ دی عزیزی گفت حافظ میخورد پنهان شراب   ای عزیز من نه عیب آن، به که پنهانی بود[77]

Last night a dear one said, Ḥāfiẓ drinks wine in secret,
O my dear, this is no crime, however, it is better done in secret.

Furūghī Basṭāmī (d. 1274/1857)

Mīrzā 'Abbās Furūghī was born in Iraq in 1213/1798. His father died when he was sixteen and, following his death, he travelled to Iran with his mother. The young Mīrzā 'Abbās Furūghī was determined to learn to read and write. He developed a talent for poetry and chose the pen name, 'Miskīn'.[78]

With the help of his uncle, 'Abbās Furūghī was introduced to Fatḥ-'Alī Shāh. He composed a *ghazal* for the Shāh, which the monarch found pleasant and, as a result, Furūghī was ordered to go to Khurāsān to serve one of the Shāh's sons. In 1249/1833, Furūghī accompanied Shujā' al-Salṭana to Tehran. He remained there during the reign of Fatḥ-'Alī Shāh and part of the reign of Muḥammad Shāh, then left Tehran for Iraq.

Furūghī familiarized himself with the works of mystics. His interest in their school of thought influenced his decision to spend time in solitude. The news of his solitary state reached Nāṣir al-Dīn Shāh, who summoned him to court. Although he wrote occasional panegyrics for the monarch, he never became a full-time court poet.

In his poetry, there is some evidence of the influence of Sa'dī's style of writing. His attraction to Sufism is reflected in most of his *ghazal*s, and a feeling of mysticism is also apparent. There is no evidence of innovation, novelty, or originality in his poetry, but because of his dynamic usage of the language of Sufism, this apparent unoriginality has been charged with fresh beauty and meaning. From his works, there remains only his *Dīvān*, consisting of approximately 6,500 couplets.[79]

Furūghī and Ḥāfiẓ

Furūghī Basṭāmī is one of the mystical poets of the Qājār period who emulates Ḥāfiẓ in the realm of meaning and rhyme. With regard to mysticism, he follows Ḥāfiẓ by using similar mystical terms and themes, including words such as separation, (desire for) union, sage, beloved, asceticism, compassion, and so on. In composing ironic verses, his imitation of Ḥāfiẓ is quite apparent.[80]

In examining his *Dīvān*, it is clear that his poetry was heavily influenced by Ḥāfiẓ. Literary plagiarism (*sirqat-i shiʿrī*) is also apparent in his poetry, with words or phrases used by Ḥāfiẓ being inserted into his poems to form the metre and rhyme. In terms of terminology and content, he also makes use of Ḥāfiẓ's lexicon of love mysticism, his anticlericalism, and his opposition to hypocrisy. Although numerous examples of these similarities exist, only a few examples can be provided here.

The following verse is an example of *naẓira*, its rhyme and metre imitate Ḥāfiẓ's style and methods:

Furūghī　　گر پس از مرگ قدم بر سر خاکم بنهی　　استخوانم/ ز لحد رقص کنان برخیز/د[81]

If after death, you come to pass my tomb,
My bones will rise from the grave, dancing!

Ḥāfiẓ　　بر سر تربت من با می و مطرب بنشین　　تا به به بویت/ ز لحد رقص کنان برخیز/م[82]

At the head of my tomb, with wine and minstrel sit,
So that by your scent, dancing, I may rise![83]

In the following verses, Furūghī follows Ḥāfiẓ's poetic rhyme and wording, referred to as *tattabu'*, in literary terms.

Furūghī　　تا خط سبز تو از یاسمن چهره دمید　　برق یاس آمد و بر کشت طلبکاران زد[84]

Since the dusky line sprung from the jasmine of your countenance,
The lilac stem [of despair] came out and dashed [the hopes of] the field of the seekers.

Ḥāfiẓ   مدعی خواست که آید به تماشاگه راز   دست غیب آمد و بر سینهٔ نامحرم زد[85]

The adversary sought to come to the spectacle of the mystery,
An invisible hand came out and struck the chest of the intruder!

Yaghmā Jandaqī (d. 1276/1859)

Mīrzā Raḥīm Yaghmā Jandaqī was born in 1196/1781 in the village of Jandaq. He worked as a camel driver to support his family. As a result of constant slander by jealous rivals, Yaghmā fell into the hands of a governor called Ja'far Sulṭān, who had him arrested, beaten, and subsequently thrown in jail. Sheriffs then sent soldiers to his place of residence to confiscate all his possessions.

After escaping from prison, Yaghmā changed his name to Abū'l Ḥasan and his pen name to 'Yaghmā' (meaning plundered, usurped). He moved to Baghdad, where he stayed until his innocence was proven. He eventually travelled to Tehran, where he met the prime minister, Ḥājj Mīrzā Āqāsī, who was an exponent of Sufi teachings. Āqāsī grew fond of Yaghmā and appointed him to a ministerial position in Kāshān. Yaghmā left Kāshān and travelled before returning to Jandaq, where he died at the age of eighty.

His style of poetry follows the path of the classical masters, though he showed a vision far beyond his time: Yaghmā is one of the few Persian poets who wrote only in Persian, free of foreign (Arabic) words.[86] He is most commonly remembered for his disdain of the Arabic language and his great effort to preserve his work independent of any foreign words.

A thorough examination of his *Dīvān*, however, dictates otherwise. I disagree with some scholars who believe that his work is free from foreign words, as there is considerable Arabic vocabulary in his poetic diction. Throughout the following examples, I present instances where Yaghmā uses foreign vocabulary.

Yaghmā and Ḥāfiẓ

In studying the poetry of Yaghmā, one can observe that in his battles with clerics, he often used Ḥāfiẓ's style to transmit his message. In his *ghazal*s there are many other similarities to those of Ḥāfiẓ – similarities both in meaning and rhyme, which the following comparisons demonstrate:

Yaghmā

سّر سالوس و ریا پرسیدن از یغما چه سود   واعظ از وی خوبتر می داند این افسانه را[87]

What good is it to ask Yaghmā the mysteries of hypocrisy and deceit?
The preacher knows this myth better than he!

Ḥāfiẓ   واعظ ما بوی حق نشنید بشنو کاین سخن   در حضورش نیز می گویم نه غیبت می کنم[88]

Perceived not the scent of truth our preacher, hear this word,
In his presence I also speak, no calumny I make.

Yaghmā

دوست دشمن، مدعی داور، وفا تقصیر ما   چیست غیر از جان سپاری در رهش تدبیر ما[89]

Friend is a foe, the adversary an arbiter, and our fault is fidelity.
What is our plan, other than leaving the soul on her path?

Ḥāfiẓ   دوش از مسجد سوی میخانه آمد پیر ما   چیست یاران طریقت بعد از این تدبیر ما[90]

Last night, our sage came out of the mosque and went to the
tavern, So now, peers of the way, what must be our plan?[91]

Yaghmā   شیخ و قاضی سر زدند از ملت اسلام عشق   تا چه خواهد کرد با جهال امت پیر ما[92]

The Shaykh and the judge have denied love for Muslims,
Let us see what Our Master has in mind for this ignorant tribe.

Ḥāfiẓ   ما مریدان روی سوی قبله چون آریم چون   روی سوی خانهٔ خمّار دارد پیر ما[93]

How can we, the disciples, turn our faces towards the Kaaba,
When Our Master has set his on the tavern?[94]

Yaghmā   دام نیرنگ تو نازم که به بند افتادست   گردن ما و به پای تو کمند افتادست[95]

I revel in your deceit, for it has enchained the neck,
And hence, a lasso has fallen at your feet!

Ḥāfiẓ تا سر زلف تو در دست نسیم افتادست دل سودا زده از غصّه دو نیم افتادست[96]

As soon as the end of your tresses fell into the hands of the breeze,
The devoted heart broke into two halves with sorrow.

Yaghmā گر به کوثر نبرم مستی می حشر کناد ایزدم در صف آن قوم که هوشیارانند[97]

May the Lord interrogate me in the line of the sober,
If I do not deliver the intoxicating wine to the river of paradise.

Ḥāfiẓ غلام نرگس مست تو تاجدارانند خراب بادهٔ لعل تو هشیارانند[98]

The captives of your drunken eye are the wearers of crowns;
Those wrecked on the wine of your ruby lips are the sober.

Yaghmā خون خلقی به تکلف بخوری ای لب یار گر تو ضحاکی و زلفین سیه مارانند[99]

O Beloved, your lips drink the blood of the whole of creation.
If you are Ḍahhāk,[100] your tresses are black snakes.

Ḥāfiẓ بیا به میکده و چهره ارغوانی کن مرو به صومعه کانجا سیه کارانند[101]

Come to the tavern and put some colour in your cheek,
Do not go to the cloister, where sinners abide.

The following are examples of *naẓira*:

Yaghmā گر غباری ز کف پای تو آرد سر چیست که نثار قدم پیک صبا نتوان کرد[102]

If the messenger of the eastern breeze brings the dust trodden under your feet,
What value has a head to be gifted to the messenger's feet?

Ḥāfiẓ دست در حلقهٔ آن زلف دوتا نتوان کرد تکیه بر عهد تو و باد صبا نتوان کرد[103]

There can be no reaching into that tangled lock,
There can be no relying on your pact and the eastern breeze!

Yaghmā زاهد از توبهٔ پیمانه مرا عذر بده کاین گناهی است که در مذهب ما نتوان کرد[104]

O ascetic, exempt me from repentance for drinking,
Because in our order, contrition for this would be a sin one cannot commit.

Ḥāfiẓ بجز ابروی تو محراب دل حافظ نیست طاعت غیر تو در مذهب ما نتوان کرد[105]

Aside from your eyebrow, there is no prayer niche for Ḥāfiẓ's heart;
In our sect, there can be no allegiance other than to you.

The following are examples of the poetic devisce of *tattabu'*:

Yaghmā تا کنم چاک به کوی تو گریبان‌ای چند روزگاری زده ام دست به دامان‌ای چند[106]

A few days have passed since I decided
To tear my clothes in your street.[107]

Ḥāfiẓ حسب حالی ننوشتی و شد ایّام‌ای چند محرمی کو که فرستم به تو پیغام‌ای چند[108]

You have not written how things are for a few days,
Where is a bosom friend that I may send you a message or two?[109]

Yaghmā فراز سرو تو یک نیزه آفتاب جمال هزار کوکب بخت است و کوکب مسعود[110]

The acclivity of your cypress-like stature is a spear of the sun,
It is a thousand lucky and prosperous stars.

Ḥāfiẓ شد از خروج ریاحین چو آسمان روشن زمین باختر میمون و طالع مسعود[111]

From the burgeoning of sweet basil, the earth became bright as shining heaven,
Blessed with lucky stars and auspicious ascendant.

Ḥājj Mullā Hādī Sabzivārī (d. 1289/1872)

Ḥājj Mullā Hādī Sabzivārī, the great Iranian philosopher and poet, was born in 1204/1797 in Sabzivār, in the province of Khurāsān, where he also died in

1289/1872. He wrote *Asrār al-ḥikmat* (*The Secrets of Philosophy*), which, together with his Arabic treatise, *Sharḥ manzūma-yi ḥikmat* (*A Commentary on the Poem on Philosophy*),[112] remain some of the most renowned works in the field of traditional philosophy in Iran today.

Not limited to philosophy, he also wrote poetry under the name Asrār and completed a commentary on the *Mathnawī* of Jalāl al-Dīn Mawlavī (Rūmī), the great mystic poet of Islam. His interpretations of Mullā Sadrā contributed to his becoming the 'Master Thinker' of Iranian philosophers.

In his poetry Ḥāfiẓ's influence is apparent and, hence, the language of *'irfān* can be seen throughout his *ghazals*.[113] His *Dīvān* suggests a predilection towards Sufism and Sufi thought, and though he never openly claimed to be a Sufi, his lifestyle is evidence that he was and research suggests that he was a *sālik*.[114]

Sabzivārī's significance in Persian literature lies in his mystical language and his neoclassical poetry. He frequently allowed the mysticism and ambiguity, which have always been part of classical poetry, to remain in his verses; hence, his pen name: 'Asrār' ('Mystery'). His *Dīvān* consists of *ghazalīyāt*, miscellaneous verses, *tarji'-band*, *Mathnawīhā*, *rubā'īyāt*, *du baytī* and *qaṭa'āt*. He wrote approximately 1,600 couplets.

Sabzivārī and Ḥāfiẓ

In studying Sabzivārī's collection of verses, it is evident that his *ghazals* closely parallel those of Ḥāfiẓ, in rhyme, meaning, metaphors, and even in the phonetic arrangement of syllables. Sabzivār's mystical language is also similar to that of Ḥāfiẓ and *sirqat-i shi'rī* is apparent in his poetry. The following comparisons are an illustration of Sabzivārī's poetry and its similarity to that of Ḥāfiẓ. He composed an entire *ghazal*, an example of *istiqbāl*, in praise of Ḥāfiẓ, the rhyme-word of which is 'Ḥāfiẓ', and the first verse of which is as follows:

هزاران آفرین بر جان حافظ　　همه غرقیم در احسان حافظ[115]　　Sabzivārī

A thousand praises upon the spirit of Ḥāfiẓ,
We are all drowned in the beneficence of Ḥāfiẓ!

The following are examples of *naẓira*:

Sabzivārī

شورش عشق تو در هیچ سری نیست که نیست   منظر روی تو زیب نظری نیست که نیست[116]

There is no head that is not full of the excitement of your love;
There is no eye that does not adore the beauty of your face.

Ḥāfiẓ

روشن از پرتوی رویت نظری نیست که نیست   منت خاک درت بر بصری نیست که نیست[117]

There is no glance that is not illuminated by the radiance of your face;
There is no eye not bound by the dust of your door.

Sabzivārī

چنان کارم ز عشق او به رسوایی کشید اسرار   که خوانند داستان ما به دستان در دبستان ها[118]

Because of her love, all my affairs have caused such disgrace, 'Asrār',
These tales will be read in every school.

Ḥāfiẓ   همه کارم ز خودکامی به بد نامی کشید آری   نهان کی ماند آن رازی کز آن سازند محفل‌ها[119]

By following my own fancy, all my affairs led to disrepute,
How do secrets remain secrets if spoken in every assembly?

Sabzivārī   نقد عالم همه قلب است، ولی نقد صحیح   کیمیای نظر کامل درویشان است[120]

The world's coinage is all counterfeit, but the true coin
Is the glance of the perfect dervishes!

Ḥāfiẓ   گنج عزلت که طلسمات عجایب دارد   فتح آن در نظر رحمت درویشان است[121]

The compassionate vision of dervishes holds the key
To the treasure of solitude, the talismanic mysteries.

Ḥājj Mīrzā Ḥasan Iṣfahānī 'Ṣafī 'Alī Shāh' (d. 1316/1898)

Ḥājj Mīrzā Muḥammad Ḥasan Iṣfahānī, also known by his Sufi title, Ṣafī 'Alī Shāh, was born in 1251/1835 in Iṣfahān. His grandfather was a trader who died in Yazd during one of his trips. Ṣafī 'Alī Shāh stayed in Yazd for twenty years to complete his education.[122]

In 1280/1863, he planned to travel to Mecca via India. Once in India, he met many dervishes and Sufi masters. During this time, he wrote his book, *Zubdat al-asrār* (Compendium of Mysteries) which he completed and published in Bombay. His two-volume versified interpretation of the Qur'ān is, according to Baraq and Lewisohn, a 'literary and spiritual masterpiece'.[123]

His collected poetical works include a number of interesting mystical *Mathnawī* poems as well as his immense versified Qur'ānic *tafsīr*, known as *Tafsīr-i Ṣafī 'Alī Shāh*. He was a neoclassical poet of the Khurāsānī and Turkistānī styles, and made a great literary contribution to classical Persian and Sufi poetry.

Many literary historians believe that Ṣafī, because of his religious, Sufi and philosophical beliefs, should not be classed as a poet. Other critics consider him a great mystical poet of Persia.[124]

Ṣafī 'Alī Shāh and Ḥāfiẓ

A close study of Ṣafī 'Alī Shāh's *Dīvān* reveals that his poetry follows that of Ḥāfiẓ in terms of rhyme, mystical themes, metaphors and metre. In his *ghazal*s, he adheres to the mystical language and style of Ḥāfiẓ. The themes used in his poetry resemble those of Ḥāfiẓ in terms of *tattabu'* and *naẓira*. The following examples show the resemblance between Ṣafī's poetry and that of Ḥāfiẓ:

Ṣafī 'Alī Shāh

دلبر امروز کمر بست و بقامت برخاست   مست از خانه برون رفت و قیامت برخاست[125]

Today, the beloved rose and dressed up,
Intoxicated, she left the house and stirred up the resurrection.

Ḥāfiẓ   مست بگذشتی و از خلوتیان ملکوت   بتماشای تو آشوب قیامت برخاست[126]

Intoxicated you passed by, and from the solitude of angels,
The tumult of resurrection arose at the sight of you!

Ṣafī 'Alī Shāh   راز عشق تو که از خلق نهان می کردم   گشت افسانه و بر هر سر بازار بماند[127]

The secret of your love that I tried to conceal,
Became a tale in every marketplace.

Ḥāfiẓ محتسب شیخ شد و فسق خود از یاد ببرد قصهٔ ماست که بر هر سر بازار بماند[128]

The sheriff became a cleric and forgot his sin,
Our tale remained in every marketplace.

Conclusion

As Iran experienced the turbulence of the constitutional era, poets joined the ranks of the overtly patriotic by composing nationalistic poems. Poets such as ʿĀrif Qazvīnī, Bahār and many others were inspired by Ḥāfiẓ and other classical masters. Ḥāfiẓ was considered a true Persian and a poet beyond compare. He was admired for many things, including his honesty, wit, and his stance against hypocrisy and deception, but perhaps the most important element in the reception of Ḥāfiẓ in nineteenth- and twentieth-century Persia is patriotism. We must bear in mind, when calling on Ḥāfiẓ as an Iranian nationalist, that the discourse of Iranian nationalism adopted in the Qājār period was particular to that day and age. Classical poets such as Saʿdī and Ḥāfiẓ did not share the concerns of constitutional nationalists. Nevertheless, these poets played a key role for them; the one poet that has been universally admired by nationalists and nationalist poets alike is Firdawsī. A brief reading through the *Dīvān* is enough to demonstrate that Ḥāfiẓ himself was influenced by Firdawsī – at least with regard to his love of Persia. We can find numerous examples of kings and heroes from the *Shāhnāma* of Firdawsī echoed in the verses of Ḥāfiẓ, including names such as Rustam, Tahamtan, Tūr, Bahman, Dārā, Zardusht, Jamshid, Afrāsīyāb, Bārbud, Bahrām Gūr, Sīyāmak, Shīda, Shirin, Fireydūn, Qubād, Kāvūs, Kasrā, Key, Kīyān, Key-qubād and KeyKhusru.[129]

The following are a few of Ḥāfiẓ's verses that refer to characters from Firdawsī's epic poem:

شاه ترکان سخن مدعیان می شنود شرمی از مظلمه خون سیاووشش باد![130]

The king of the Turks was listening to the word of caluminators;
May some shame be his for the wronging of Sīyāvūsh.[131]

The above verse is a reference to the story of Sīyāvūsh, who, in the *Shāhnāma*, is killed in Tūrān.

شاه ترکان چو پسندید و به چاهم انداخت　　　دستگیر ار نشود لطف تهمتن چه کنم؟[132]

When the king of the Turks approved and threw me into the pit,
If Tahamtan proves no rescue, what can I do?[133]

This is a reference to the story of Bizhan and Manizha.

سوختم درچاه صبر از بهر آن شمع چگل　　　شاه ترکان فارغ است از حال ما، کو رستمی؟[134]

In the well of patience I burned for the sake of that candle of Chigil.[135]
The king of the Turks disdains our condition. Where a Rustam?[136]

While many poets of the Qājār period imitated Ḥāfiẓ (as we have seen repeatedly throughout this chapter) and attempted to follow in his footsteps, none equalled him in the genre of lyric poetry. Ḥāfiẓ was also deemed worthy in the eyes of the elite and scholars, particularly the poets of the Qājār era, because of his opposition to ascetics, clerics and religious hypocrites. Ḥāfiẓ was the voice of his people, continuously battling deceit and dishonesty.

منم آن شاعر ساحر که به افسون سخن　　　از نی کلک همه شهد و شکر می بارم[137]

That poet-magician I am, who, with the sorcery of speech
From the reed-pen, all sweetness I pour.[138]

As Islāmī so rightly observes, 'Ḥāfiẓ has squeezed the essence of the entire history of Iran into a comparatively small collection – this is his miracle.'[139] This perception of Ḥāfiẓ is not limited to any particular group or philosophical trend. The concept of the close attachment between Ḥāfiẓ and the national spirit of Iran is shared, from the most zealous Aryan nationalists to the supreme leader of the Islamic Republic. Even in disagreements over the essence and sources of this connection, this strong bond of affection continues to grow stronger.[140] Ḥāfiẓ's poetry, though written in a Sunni Sufi language, has always been – and remains – relevant in both the Sufi (and, in certain instances, anti-Sufi) and the Shi'i contexts, because his language is based on Qur'ānic verses, the basis for both Sufi and Shi'i orders, as the following verse indicates:

حافظا می خور و رندی کن و خوش باش ولی　　دام تزویر مکن چون دگران قرآن را[141]

Ḥāfiẓ, drink wine, play the rapscallion and be joyful, but
Do not, as others do, falsify the Qur'ān.[142]

It should not go without mention that the sharp tongue of Ḥāfiẓ in criticizing the hypocrisy and deceit has in addition been always an area of interest to the poets, writers and scholars of Persian literature and poetry. As we can see from the examples from the seven selected poets of Persia featured in this chapter, the mystical turns of speech and the anti-clerical language of Ḥāfiẓ seems to have had a greater impact on their verse than any other factors found in his poetry. By choosing these seven poets of the Zand and Qājār period I have tried to make a case that in some remote cases even unconsciously some poets have implemented ambigious language and mystical terms to further promote their poetry, but whether this has been an intended act or merely a preference in composing poems remains to be discovered. However, my intention here has been to provide solid evidence that amongst all the various layers that exist in the poetic language of Ḥāfiẓ, the most popular dimensions of his expression remain his mystical language, anticlericalism and romanticism. The popularity of Ḥāfiẓ's brilliant poetization of these key themes, remains in my opinion the reason why so many of the *ghazal* writers of this period were inspired by Ḥāfiẓ and why their poetry is filled with similar mystical and romantic concepts and ambiguous poetic language that ultimately largely derive from him.

The reception of Ḥāfiẓ can also be observed in the period immediately after the end of the Zand era. For example, Ādhar Bigdilī condemned the Indian style of poetry and those who composed in that style merely because it lacked the necessary components of the 'Irāqī style, which was more commonly used during the Qājār period. Ādhar followed Ḥāfiẓ's style, thus we come across different types of verse imitation of Ḥāfiẓ.[143] He also followed Ḥāfiẓ's style of confronting hypocrisy and deceit. In terms of theme and symbolism, there are further similarities between Ādhar's poetry and Ḥāfiẓ's language. Two years after the death of Ādhar Bigdilī, a famous poet of the early Qājār period was born – Viṣāl Shīrāzī. He was also greatly influenced by Ḥāfiẓ, and, as demonstrated in this chapter, he clearly imitated Ḥāfiẓ's rhymes and metres; we see further examples of this imitation of Ḥāfiẓ in Viṣāl's similar use of imagery, similes and content. Another poet and contemporary to Viṣāl was Qā'ānī Shīrāzī, who also followed Ḥāfiẓ in terms of imagery, metaphor, themes and topoi, as has been demonstrated in some detail in this chapter.

The language of Ḥāfiẓ continued to inspire poets of this period. Furūghī Basṭāmī was greatly influenced by the mystical side of Ḥāfiẓ's poetic language, meaning and rhyme. He followed Ḥāfiẓ by using similar numinous terms. His ironic verses are imitations of Ḥāfiẓ's style and the terminology and content of his poetry matches Ḥāfiẓ's vocabulary of love mysticism and anticlericalism.

Yaghmā Jandaqī, not surprisingly, was another poet influenced by the magical poetic language of Ḥāfiẓ. In his collections we cannot find any trace of praise for monarchs or government officials, and we definitely do see clear similarities in his verse to Ḥāfiẓ's philosophy of inspired libertinism (*rindī*). His *ghazal*s are similar in style to Ḥāfiẓ's poetry, and he is particularly recognized for his disapproval of religious hypocrisy and for his anticlerical views, which are largely reflections of Ḥāfiẓ's school of thought. By studying the work of Ḥājj Mullā Hādī Sabzivārī, the great Iranian philosopher and poet, one can clearly see that his *Dīvān* suggests a fondness towards Sufism and Sufi reflection, and though he never overtly claimed to be a Sufi, his lifestyle indicates that he was. However, in the history of Persian poetry, as Lewishon asserts, 'Sabzivārī figures as only a very minor poet, he authored a number of memorable *ghazal*s which display not only extraordinary passion and feeling but great insight and depth.'[144]

Lewishon further asserts that Sabzivārī's *Dīvān* represents Ḥāfiẓ as the most dominant and influential figure on his poetry.[145] Sabzivārī's verse, being influenced by Ḥāfiẓ's imagery and expressions, offers examples of *naẓira*, or in some cases *istiqbāl*, which indicate that he often followed Ḥāfiẓ almost line by line in his poetry.[146]

Ḥājj Mīrzā Muḥammad Ḥasan Iṣfahānī, also known by his Sufi title, Ṣafī 'Alī Shāh, was another follower of Ḥāfiẓ. A rigorous examination of Ṣafī 'Alī Shāh's *Dīvān* reveals that his poetry follows that of Ḥāfiẓ in many aspects, including rhyme, mystical themes, metaphors and metre. In his *ghazal*s, he coheres with the mystical poetic language and style of Ḥāfiẓ. The themes used in his poetry bear a resemblance to those of Ḥāfiẓ in terms of *tattabu'* and *naẓira*.

To sum up, the above snapshot from the *Dīvān*s of seven of the most important poets of the late Zand and the Qājār period may not give a comprehensive summary of Ḥāfiẓ's impact on the poets of this period, but it does hopefully provide an impressive synopsis of the undeniable literary impact that this great fourteenth-century poet had upon the neoclassical poets and poetics of nineteenth-century Persia.

CHAPTER IV

Ḥāfiẓ and the Poets of Pahlavi Iran

This chapter examines Ḥāfiẓ's place among the poets of the Zand and Pahlavi eras. I begin with a brief summary of the sociopolitical situation in Iran from 1925 to 1978, followed by a glimpse at the literary milieu of Pahlavi Persia, in which I assess the work and thought of Aḥmad Kasravī, Ṣādiq Hidāyat (d. 1330/1951) and Muḥammad Taqī Bahār. I then undertake an overview of literary developments in Iran from 1925 to 1978, referring briefly to the late Qājār period but focusing mainly on the Pahlavi era. I assess five poets of the period and the influence of Ḥāfiẓ on their work. These poets are Malik al-Shuʿarāʾ Bahār, Nimā Yūshij, Suhrāb Sipihrī, Shahriyār and Aḥmad Shāmlū.

A Summary of the Sociopolitical Circumstances of Iran (1925-1978)

In the period prior to the rise of Riḍā Shāh (d. 1323/1944) in 1925, the sociopolitical situation in Iran was marked by chaos, particularly in the economic realm. Shuster (the former treasurer-general of Iran) observed that the constitutional government experienced such financial hardship that it was unable to pay a large number of pensions. Pension warrants, which were issued with substantial regularity at this time, were difficult to change into hard cash at the treasury.[1] Shuster further reports:

> Numbers of small shop-keepers, and, at times, wealthy merchants bought up these warrants for a song and put them into the hands of professional 'pension-collectors'. These men, having accumulated a number of warrants, would hire crowds of miserable-looking men and women to stand around the Treasury pay office and shout, moan, beat their breasts, tear their hair, and roll on the ground in well-feigned fits – all the while waving their pension warrants and calling on Allah to save them and their children from starving.[2]

During Riḍā Shāh's reign, a number of significant shifts took place, leading to a slow change of course in the sociopolitical and economic decline. These improvements came at a price, and in spite of the formal preservation of constitutional and parliamentary elections, decision making became increasingly and exclusively controlled by the Shāh himself. Political life was extremely restricted as a result of the Shāh's tyrannical control and censorship of political opponents.[3] The death of ʿIshqī (d. 1303/1924), a famous contemporary poet and a nationalist, was later blamed on Riḍā Shāh. The clerical opposition leader, Sayyid Ḥasan Mudarris (d. 1316/1938), a broadminded reformist, was imprisoned in 1929 and killed nine years later.[4] Muḥammad Musaddiq (d. 1345/1967), an eminent western-trained liberal, nationalist scholar, continued to attack Riḍā Shāh's programs in the *majlis*.[5] He was soon put out of office and confined to his estate.[6] Other important opponents were forced into silence; some were, for a time, tolerated by the regime. One of these was the former democratic leader of the Constitutional Revolution, Ḥasan Taqizāda (d. 1348/1970), who later became minister of finance.[7] He was a great scholar and a controversial cultural and political figure.[8]

More conspicuous was the fate of some of Riḍā Shāh's top advisers and aides-de-camp. ʿAbdul Ḥusayn Timūrtāsh, an able counselor on whom the Shāh relied a great deal, died in prison after the oil negotiations of 1933. The Shāh had assumed that he was dishonest in his dealings. Lesser men accused of betrayal were similarly treated; other politicians continued to serve Riḍā Shāh to the end of his reign.[9] In order to effectively suppress any opposition to his reign, the Shāh allowed only official nationalism accentuating national homogeneity, anticlericalism, modernity and strength to thrive.[10] The years 1925-1941 witnessed the partial accomplishment of a transformation programme far larger than had ever been attempted in Iran.[11] This was a period of secularism and modernization that clearly rejected religious extremism.[12] Ākhūndzāda stated that religion and fanaticism had ruled Iran for over a millennium and yet the country had not benefited from such beliefs.[13] He asserted that the people of Iran should change their ways to see if progress could be made by the rejection of religious extremism; if it failed, they could always return to earlier ways. He offered a verse, written by Ḥāfiẓ, in support of his statement:[14]

از قیل و قال مدرسه حالی دلم گرفت   یک چند نیز خدمت معشوق و می کنم[15]

Now I've sickened of the disputation of the schools
Let me awhile again take up attendance upon wine and the beloved.[16]

During Riḍā Shāh's reign, culture and the arts were promoted, and Persian literature was given special attention.[17] Abrahamian asserts that 'the contact with the West – through travel, translations, and educational establishments – created modern ideas'.[18] It was during this period that the cornerstones of a more comprehensive transformation were laid. Public education became more widely available and Iran's identity as a monarchy was firmly established.[19]

In 1941, when the Allied Forces invaded Iran, Riḍā Shāh renounced the throne, ushering in a new epoch of independence; along with it came the unrestrained criticism of previous policies. This was a period of fervid reaction, not only against the previous political regime, but also against the literary customs that had been imposed during Riḍā Shāh's sovereignty. The Soviet-supported Tuda Party furnished a Marxist political platform and membership of the Party was popular among those in artistic and academic circles.[20] This new era, if not advantageous to successful government, proved a strong motivation for the world of arts and scholarship. It was during this period that Ṣādiq Hidāyat began to attract notice and Jamālzāda resumed writing. In addition, a number of new scholars, notably Āl-i Aḥmad (d. 1348/1970)[21] and Ṣādiq Chūbak (d. 1377/1999),[22] all of whom promoted revolutionary principles, emerged.

At the same time, Nimā began to be more widely read and cherished by a new cohort of poets that included Nādirpūr, Shāmlū and Farrukhzād.[23] The sociopolitical situation and widespread rejuvenation programme under Riḍā Shāh led to the development of a new literary movement. The new style of poetry by Nimā and short stories by Jamālzāda and Ṣādiq Hidāyat helped bring about this new literary movement.[24] Nimā's New Poetry (*Shiʿr-i naw*) violated the rigid patterns of the division of syllables into short, long, and overlong, and disregarded earlier forms and styles. This move led to the emergence of Persian free verse.[25] Modernists contended that traditional styles could not meet the needs of contemporary society, and claimed that metre and other rudiments of classical poems obstructed the poetic phrasal idiom. This stream of New Poetry reached its zenith in the works of Nimā, who developed free verse. He substituted religious themes for social matters of interest by exploiting non-religious metaphors. Creative writing also began to profit from a straightforward and clear language that employed new styles and forms. It experienced a complete break with the earlier popular, but exaggerated neoclassical style. Like the poets, short story writers did not commend any Muslim public figures; rather they held Islam responsible for society's tribulations and regarded the West with admiration. They, too, encouraged good and accurate writing according to the new system that more closely resembled everyday language.[26]

The Literary Milieu of Pahlavi Persia

This section of the chapter analyzes the philosophical and literary discourses of nineteenth- and twentieth-century Iranian thought; that is, those articulated by Aḥmad Kasravī, Ṣādiq Hidāyat and Muḥammad Taqī Bahār. To prepare a purposeful analysis of the formation of literary criticism in twentieth-century Iran, it is necessary to briefly recapitulate some of the issues discussed in the last two chapters regarding the literary trends that occurred at the start of the nineteenth century.[27] The literature of Iran in this period (nineteenth century) must be described as one of replica and duplication. This loss of originality was even more apparent than in the Ṣafavid period. The aridity of a society whose artistry was in decline was exposed.[28] As a consequence of this decline, a new style emerged in late nineteenth-century Persian literary criticism, one that had little tolerance for complicated poetry ornamented with ambiguity. This new approach sought a literature that echoed the real life of the people, their aspirations, passions and difficulties.[29]

Some of the most important Qājār anthologists, such as Riḍā Qulī Hidāyat,[30] followed their predecessors and indulged in unnecessary word play and verbosity. Nonetheless, Hidāyat believed that the works of the poets of the period were spoiled by flattery and the biased favouritism they exhibited in their evaluation of literary works. According to Rypka, Hidāyat was a faithful follower of the classical poets and the old masters.[31] This was not the case for all the poets of this period; indeed some considered their work superior to the master poets, for example, Fatḥ-ʿAlī Khān Ṣabā vaunted his own work over Firdawsī's and was convinced of its superiority.[32] With the commencement of the reign of Fatḥ-ʿAlī Shāh, Persian poetry returned to the styles of the past (the Khurāsānī and ʿIrāqī styles). The composition of panegyric odes (*qaṣāʾid*) and lyrical odes (*ghazalīyāt*) continued as in the past among most of the poets. Scholars usually argue, I believe quite unfairly, that the poetry of this period, if not all insignificant panegyrics or satire, was superficially romantic in nature, boring and insincere in character. The conventional critique levelled by literary historians of Persian about the Qājār period is that there appeared but few quality works of poetry and none with a commanding expression of national awareness, a voice that might have been considered a response to real life, rather than an echo of court gossip.[33]

On the other hand, Bahār, perhaps the greatest poet of the late Qājār and early Pahlavi period, observes that Fatḥ-ʿAlī Shāh's reign (1797-1834) was a brilliant period for poetry. His view stands in marked contrast to those scholars who held that the poetry of this period was essentially useless.[34] Although Bahār's view is barely supported by evidence, it is clear that the poets of the Qājār period performed a great service to neoclassical literature by reviving the words and thematic styles of the master poets of the past, even though in some cases they were referred to as unoriginal imitators by some contemporary critics. Poets such as Ṣabā, Furūghī Basṭāmī, Ṣafī ʿAlī Shāh, Sabzivārī and many others continually manifest the influence of classical poets like Rūmī, Saʿdī and Ḥāfiẓ. Their attempts to emulate this remarkable literature and poetry and their appreciation of these great works led to a revival of neoclassical literature and poetry.

I do not entirely agree with the negative views held by many contemporary critics of these nineteenth-century poets. These commentators claimed that the poets were only able to imitate the classical poets. But one of the main roles of the neoclassical movement was to prevent the deterioration of the great works inherited from masters such as Firdawsī, Rūmī, Saʿdī and Hāfiz. In this sense, then, the movement proved highly successful and is thus deserving of our appreciation and gratitude. In what follows, I will examine the work of three critics and writers of the late Qājār and middle Pahlavi period, writers whose views on literary criticism are of great significance. While there were certainly other relevant writers and critics, an examination of all of them is beyond the scope of this study. The three examined here are Aḥmad Kasravī, Ṣādiq Hidāyat and Muḥammad Taqī Bahār. I will then continue to explore the poetic language of five poets of the late Qajar and early Pahlavi period: Bāhār, Nimā, Sipihrī, Shahriyār and Shāmlū. After presenting a brief biographical account of their lives, I will examine and compare their poetic language with that of Ḥāfiẓ, juxtaposing selected verses to demonstrate certain similarity and imitations of Ḥāfiẓ's language and thoughts.

Aḥmad Kasravī (d. 1325/1946)

Kasravī's writings on literary criticism are extremely important, not so much for their substance as for their lack of substance; that is to say, the impact made by his largely sensational and unbalanced extremist views, which for many years were (and among some still are) widely influential in Iran. In fact, it does appear odd that a scholar of Kasravī's character, who was led by a scientific and logical approach in his historical and critical works, permitted himself to be influenced by personal prejudice in literary scholarship.[35] Fortunately, we have accurate biographical details about Kasravī from his autobiography, in which he provides insight into the sociocultural and personal factors that helped shape his ideas.[36] He was born in September 1880 in the district of Hukmāvar (Tabriz). His father, Mīr Qāsim, gave him the name Mīr Aḥmad, which was the name of his own father (Kasravī's grandfather). Although his father had studied religion, he ultimately took up the rug trade. While a religious man, he did not approve of popular religious practices; nor did he wish to see his son become a preacher.[37] While a native speaker of Azerbaijani Turkish, young Kasravī studied the traditional curriculum of Persian, Arabic and the Qur'ān in elementary school and showed great ability in his studies.[38]

In general, Kasravī was a scholarly descendant of Ākhūndzāda, Mīrzā Āqā Khān Kirmānī, Malkam Khān, 'Abdul Raḥīm Ṭālibuf and Zayn al-'Ābidin Marāgha'ī. Like them, he thought it was his nationalistic obligation to fight illiteracy and misconceptions in Iranian culture, in order to establish a reasonable and structured ground for education. Kasravī pointed out that ignorance, whether literary, economic, or political, is a core source of social problems. Kasravī took up literary analysis as a mode of criticizing poetry and literature that did not advance social improvement.[39] He approached the works of classical poets and what he called 'wisdom' with a twentieth-century point of view. This prompted him to make rash and ill-considered attacks on Ḥāfiẓ. For instance, he failed to understand that the sensual and permissive nature of the work of Ḥāfiẓ was caused, for the most part, by his reaction to the religious orthodoxy of his time and his desire to subvert that hardline viewpoint.[40] Kasravī's opinion of the classical poets had much to do with the fact that the new poetry of the Constitutional period caused a union among the social reformers. These reformers believed that Persian literature had to be changed in order to make it more politically and socially appropriate and meaningful. As a result, there was a divergence of opinion about the means to achieve this end. The conservative group sought salvation in a return to a simpler pre-Mongolian style, which they tried to link up with, using Firdawsī, Nizāmī and Saʿdī as their examples. For the modernists, the answer was in a complete migration from all classical habits, whose rhetorical prescriptions and regulations they conceived to be so redundant as to prevent the poet from letting his thoughts expand and limitlessly soar. As we have seen, in the period after the First World War, the conflict erupted over the hithero untouchable and invincible hero of classical Persian literature, Saʿdī. Yet, as we shall see, the classification of reformists into two groups is simplistic, especially when the opinions of Kasravī are taken into account, since he held a favourable opinion of Firdawsī but rejected the verses of Saʿdī and Ḥāfiẓ as immoral.[41]

What united the reforming poets and writers was the rejection of poetry for the sake of poetry alone. This was the most significant feature of the sixteenth-century Iranian poets. Writers in Iran as diverse as Kasravī, Hidāyat, Aranī and Furūghī during the first half of the twentieth century all trusted that their writings were for the good of society. Poetry, however, was not the only form of literature that was influenced by Western literature, as the short story, or novella, became a trendy means for socially dedicated writers to get their message across.[42] In 1921, Jamālzāda published his short story, *Farsi Shekar Ast* (*Persian is Sugar*), which was quite innovative in its form, and which sustained the tradition of Persianism. The story criticizes the Arabic-Persian spoken by the mullas and the Franci-Persian of the Europeanized youths. The story is essential for popularizing fiction as a means to express a message; yet, in spite of the prospective benefits of this medium, Kasravī was to criticize fiction as little more than a 'lie'.[43] By the time Kasravī set his movement in motion to modernize Iran, chiefly through his writings on literature and mainly on poetry, the hostile contest about the preferred forms of Persian literature had been boiling for the better part of several generations. This argument assumed a national scale, as Kasravī claimed; literary associations accelerated all over the country at the same time that Browne sent his *Literary History of Persia* to Iran.

> All kinds of books related to poetry and composers were published, and domes were erected over the tombs of poets. It is difficult to substantiate whether this activity was integrated directly or indirectly by Browne, but it is clear that literary associations began to appear more frequently during the Constitutional period.[44]

At this time, Bahār was the supporter of modernism, and he respected and adored the old masters, such as Firdawsī, Sa'dī and Ḥāfiẓ. In fact, during this time, Kasravī, did not have many supporters as far as the condemnation of the classical poets was concerned. He claims that Muḥammad 'Alī Furūghī had once said that it is in the best interest of Iran to promote its great poets, including Ḥāfiẓ, Sa'dī, Khayyām and Firdawsī, in order to earn the respect of Europeans.[45]

Kasravī considers Ḥāfiẓ a *kharābātī*.[46] He ruthlessly attacks Ḥāfiẓ and accuses him of being an evil poet. Kasravī's opinion of the poet is derived from the belief that he was an individual with few ethical values, consumed by laziness and despair, and that he suffered from confused thoughts.[47] He criticizes the poet for praising tyrants such as Shāh Shujā', who blinded his own father, and Shāh Yaḥyā, who was known for his cowardly acts. Ḥāfiẓ, the criminal, he adds, wasted his life by spreading and composing foolish words with no meaning whatsoever. He states that if Ḥāfiẓ spent his life laying bricks he would have provided a greater service to mankind than writing so much rubbish.[48]However, in my opinion, Kasravī's ill views of the classical poets, in particular Ḥāfiẓ and Sa'dī, is without a doubt connected to his anti-fanaticism and religious beliefs, for they were two of the most mystical poets of Persia. In fact, both Ḥāfiẓ and Sa'dī shared this anti-fanaticism to some extent; critically, however, Kasravī failed, or perhaps was unwilling, to accept or even acknowledge this.

Ṣādiq Hidāyat (d. 1330/1951)

Ṣādiq Hidāyat was born in 1282/1903 and died in 1330/1951. During the first half of the twentieth century, much had transpired in Persian literature and Ṣādiq Hidāyat's participation in this evolution was considerable.[49]An assessment of Ṣādiq Hidāyat's legacy in literary criticism proves that, in addition to being a celebrated writer, he was a scholar in literary criticism and widely read in world literature.[50] Today, Hidāyat is considered one of the most important literary figures in modern Persian literature.[51] Hidāyat's popularity among readers and scholars has, similarly, been dominated by his psycho-fiction, which deals with universal problems; this is particularly notable in *Būf-i kūr* (*The Blind Owl*).

Hidāyat's prose is easy to read and understand, and is without literary embellishment. He employs common, well-liked, informal, natural expressions and proverbs where appropriate, and refrains from bookish and pedantic words of Arabic origin.[52] Occasionally, and indeed frequently in certain works, Hidāyat stammers in his grammar and speech. This is more common in his psycho-fiction than in other works, and most striking in *Būf-i kūr*. This gives the impression that he wrote in a rush, with overwhelming feeling. Metaphors and imagery, his literary devices of choice, are particularly apparent in *Būf-i kūr*.[53]

Hidāyat said that he was not particularly fond of rhythmic lyrics, such as Persian *ghazal*s, but that he believed Ḥāfiẓ's work was somewhat exceptional. He stated that there were some giants in Persian literature, such as Ḥāfiẓ, who was a master storyteller, and adds that there will never be another like him.[54] In his opinion, Ḥāfiẓ, Sa'dī and others are the mirrors of Persian literature and culture and the invaluable heritage of Iran.[55]

Muḥammad Taqī Bahār (d. 1330/1952)

Born in 1265/1886, Muḥammad Taqī Bahār ranks as the greatest modern and classical Persian poet of the last three hundred years. In addition to his talent for poetry, Bahār was a professional publisher, writer, critic and researcher. He was also the poet laureate of Iran who received a yearly stipend from Muẓaffar al-Dīn Shāh in the first decade of the twentieth century.[56] Some of his valuable published works are available, but unfortunately, many are out of print or have not been published at all.[57] Bahār's literary presentation was vast but, in his own mind and in the memory of his readers, he was first and foremost a poet. His *Dīvān* was published posthumously in two volumes by his brother, Muḥammad Malikzāda.[58] These two volumes represent the poet's work from his adolescence to the last few days of his life.

Bahār follows the Khurāsānī style in his panegyric writings and adheres to the 'Irāqī style in his lyrics.[59] We cannot say that all his works are masterpieces, but the majority of his poetry is clear in meaning and easy to understand.[60]

یاد باد آن عهد که ام بندی به پای اندر نبود　　　جز می اندر دست و غیر از عشقم اندر سر نبود[61]

May it be remembered, the time when my feet were not chained
Apart from wine in hand and love in mind, there was naught.

Bahār was primarily a panegyric poet. However, he also composed *ghazals*, exercising the traditional style of the elegant masters Saʿdī and Ḥāfiẓ. His style of poetry in panegyric writing matches the poets of fourth/tenth- and fifth/eleventh-century Persia, while his *ghazal*s follow the styles of the thirteenth- and fourtheenth-century master poets. Yet, he displays a certain originality of thought and expression that goes beyond pure imitation of the classical masters.[62] Bahār can rightfully be named as a poet who, while supporting and following the style of classical poetry, did much to advance new genres and widen the spectrum of Persian poetry, aiding the advent of modernist poetry.[63] More detailed biographical and poetic information about Bahār is given in the following section.

An Overview of Literary Development in Iran (1925-1978)

During the period of fifty-eight years between 1299/1920 and 1357/1978, forty-five different governments came to office.[64] This instability and the rise of so many prime ministers was caused by the uncertain foreign policies of the court and the changing views of the people. Riḍā Shāh at first focused on national improvements, bringing the state a degree of security and stability;[65] but this came at a price. Throughout his reign the police closely monitored the press.[66] Only journals and magazines supporting government policies were allowed circulation. The editors of some newspapers of the time experienced extreme hardship. Farrukhī Yazdī (d. 1318/1939), a political poet and writer, was among those who were imprisoned and later killed.[67] In the midst of the Constitutional Revolution in 1311/1905, and probably as a result of the sociopolitical turmoil, a transformation in the literature of Iran took place.

The Persian poetry and prose of four individuals who lived during the pre- and post-constitutional movement took a different course and became easier in context and style than works in the classical style. The first of these writers was Zayn al-ʿĀbidin Marāgha'ī, who introduced simplicity in prose, producing a travel book entitled *Sīyāḥat-nāma-yi Ibrāhīm Bayk*. The second was Ṭālibuf, who introduced simplicity and innovation in writing educational stories. Third was Dihkhudā, famous for his witticisms and his articles entitled '*Charand u parand*' (*Claptrap*); and finally, the fourth, was Jamālzāda, who introduced simple language for short stories and proverbs in his book entitled *Yakī būd yikī nabūd* (*Once Upon a Time*).[68] In fact, they competed over printing works with new concepts and meaning. Sometimes they were unsuccessful in producing the expressions they desired; consequently, they used Western vocabulary in their writings.[69] In 1288/1909 alone, ninety-nine new journals were published.[70] Moreover, these journals regularly published the works of poets such as 'Ārif, 'Ishqī and Yazdī, whose poems were manifestations of fluency and lucidity. These journals certainly had an immense effect on the common writing style.[71]

These scholars played an important role in the transformation of the Persian language in general. This change in language encouraged people to read more newspapers and books; this had always been an activity of the minority. As relations with the West increased, and the population became more acquainted with European countries, the school of romanticism began to flourish in Iran. Translations of western articles and short stories began to thrive. Western scripts gained popularity, and replaced the religiously based plays of the Qājār period. Ḥasan Muqadam (d. 1304/1925) was the founder of Iranian theater.[72] After Jamālzāda's short stories, the stories of Ṣādiq Hidāyat slowly found their way into the literary atmosphere of early Pahlavi Iran.

During this period, poets concentrated on patriotic poetry; among poets such as Bahār, 'Ārif Qazvīnī, Mīrzāda 'Ishqī (d. 1303/1924) and Adib Nayshābūrī this theme took precedence over any other subject.[73] However, some poets of this period still followed the style of the old masters such as Sa'dī and Ḥāfiẓ, and avoided politics. Parvin I'tisāmī was a famous poetess of the early Pahlavi period who mainly composed *qaṣīda*, *qaṭ'a* and *Mathnawī*, her masterpieces can be found in her couplets, and throughout her poetry one can sense a certain mysticism.[74]

Thus, after the Constitutional Revolution, poetry moved in two different directions: new poetry and classical poetry. The classical poetry included all those types of poetry that followed the styles of the old masters and was bound by the rules of prosody and metre. New poetry was different; it was not limited to prosody and metre, rather a verse was only bound by the profundity of its meaning, not the rhyme.[75] Gradually, new writers faced the traditionalists in a more structured way. The traditionalists, naturally, already had their own societies – for instance, Maktab-i Sa'dī (Sa'dī's School) and Anjuman-i Nizāmī (Nizāmī's Society) – and they published articles in journals such as *Naw Bahār* (*New Spring*) and *Āzādistān* (*The land of freedom*). The modernists formed similar official establishments, such as *Dānishgāh* (The place of knowledge), and informal groups such as *Rab'* (The four), headed by Ṣādiq Hidāyat.[76] All in all, the term *Persianism* (Pārsīgirā'ī) best describes the nature of the literary movement in this period. Its advocates had various important objectives to implement.

Immediately; namely, to condemn the use of Arabic terms and expressions; to attempt the refinement of the Persian language through poetry; to support a real language closer to common idiomatic language; to connect ancient Iran to the present and wipe out centuries of Islamic authority from the memories of the population.[77] In a personal interview with H. Katouzian, this issue was raised and his reply was as follows:

> This national sensitivity about *Persianism* began during the period of Riḍā Shāh's reign. It advanced to such an extent that some elites and scholars established a literary society called 'Farhangistān'; its role was to extract all Arabic words from the Persian language and replace them with similar words in Persian and then submit them to the Shāh, once approved, it would be officially recognized as a new vocabulary.[78]

Katouzian further asserts that this became somewhat ridiculous, when Taqizāda, who lived in Berlin at the time, wrote an article criticizing this method of language purification, claiming that it would do more harm than good; for Arabic had been so well blended with Persian that any attempt to reverse this would cause the collapse of the very structure of the Persian language. Riḍā Shāh was so enraged by his article that Taqizāda, out of fear for his life, did not return to Iran until Riḍā Shāh was deposed.[79]

Listed below are five poets (mentioned above) from the late Qājār period to the end of Pahlavi era. The life and work of each poet will be discussed, followed by an analysis of Ḥāfiẓ's influence upon them. These five poets are arguably some of the most important and popular figures in modern Persian poetry. Although the poets analyzed here represent only a fraction of those of the late Qājār and the whole Pahlavi period, they are some of the most important poets of early twentieth-century Persia:

1. Malik al-Shuʿarāʾ Bahār (d. 1330/1952)
2. Nimā Yūshij (d. 1338/1960)
3. Suhrāb Sipihrī (d. 1358/1980)
4. Shahriyār (d. 1366/1988)
5. Aḥmad Shāmlū (d. 1379/2000)

Malīk al-Shuʿarāʾ Bahār (d. 1330/1952)

Muḥammad Taqī Bahār was born in 1265/1886 in Mashhad, in northwest Iran. He is considered Iran's greatest twentieth-century poet. Furthermore, he was a great politician, scholar, journalist, historian and professor of literature. Although he was a contemporary poet, his poems were fairly traditional and strongly nationalistic in character. Some scholars believe that Bahār's style of writing, the beauty of his poetry, and his deeply patriotic sentiments earn him a place among the giants of Persian literature, such as Firdawsī, Saʿdī and Ḥāfiẓ.[80]

Bahār began his primary education when he was three, with his father, Muḥammad Kāzim Sabūrī, as his tutor. Muḥammad Kāzim Sabūrī was the poet laureate at the court of Muẓaffar al-Dīn Shāh Qājār; Sabūrī was given the honorific title the 'Malik al-Shuʿarāʾ' ('King of Poets'). In addition to his private schooling, Bahār attended a traditional school in Mashhad.[81] To enhance his knowledge of Persian and Arabic, he attended classes given by Adib-i Nayshābūrī.[82] It has been said that Bahār knew a good portion of the Qurʾān by heart from a very early age. According to Bahār himself, by the age of seven he had read the *Shāh-nāma* and fully grasped the meaning of Firdawsī's epic poem.[83]

At the age of eight Bahār composed his first poem and chose the name 'Bahār', meaning spring, as his pen name (*takhalluṣ*).[84] By the time he was fourteen Bahār was fluent in Arabic and he later mastered French. At eighteen, he lost his father and started to work as a Muslim preacher. It was during this time that he composed a long ode (*qaṣīda*) and sent it to Muẓaffar al-Dīn Shāh, who was so deeply impressed by it that he immediately appointed Bahār as court poet and, by royal decree, granted him the title of 'Malik al-Shuʿarāʾ'.[85]

At the start of the Constitutional Revolution of Iran in 1906, Bahār gave up his position as poet laureate and joined the revolutionary movement to establish a parliamentary system of democracy in Iran; he became an active member of the Mashhad branch of the Society for Prosperity (*Anjuman-i Saʿādat*) that campaigned for the establishment of a parliament (*majlis*) in Iran. He published the semi-covert newspaper, *Khurāsān*, in collaboration with Ḥusayn Ardibilī, and other periodicals such as: *Naw Bahār* (*New Spring*) and *Tāza Bahār* (*Fresh Spring*) in collaboration with his cousin, Ḥājj Shaykh Aḥmad Bahār.[86]Throughout his life, Bahār wrote poems in all the classical forms; he experimented a few times with canto forms of foreign style, but he utterly abandoned new forms of verse and returned, even at the end of his life, to the old convention. Yet his subjects, and frequently his speech, are distinctly contemporary.[87] Bahār's poetry employs the Khurāsānī and ʿIrāqī styles but replaces some of the older and more difficult words and themes with a more contemporary and simpler idiom.[88]

Bahār's scholarly works include *sabk shināsī* (3 vols., Tehran, 1321/1942), a thorough set of the history of Persian prose exemplified by many instances; *tārīkh-i mukhtaṣar-i aḥzāb-i sīyāsī* (Tehran, 1323/1944), a personal view of political developments of the time, important both as a primary historical source and for Bahār's biography; and *tārīkh-i tatavur-i shiʿr-i fārsī* (Mashhad, 1334/1955), a work on poetry originally intended to be similar to his *sabk shināsī*; only a few sections of *tārīkh-i tatavur-i shiʿr-i fārsī* were written before illness prevented him from working. His papers and miscellaneous works have been published by M. Gulbun in *Firdawsī-nāma-yi Bahār* (Tehran, 1345/1966), *tarjuma-yi chand matn-i Pahlavi* (Tehran, 1347/1968), and *Bahār va adab-i fārsī* (2 vols., Tehran, 1351/1972). Bahār also composed a number of songs (*taṣnīf*s), some of which are still quite popular. He published scholarly editions of *tārīkh-i sīstān* (Tehran, 1314/1935), *mujmal al-tawārīkh vaʾl-qisās* (Tehran, 1318/1939), and Balʿamī's *tārīkh-i balʿamī* (published after his death by M. Parvīn Gunābādī, Tehran, 1341/1962).[89]

Bahār's contribution to Persian poetry is vast and of great significance. His *Dīvān* consists of more than forty thousand couplets that include *rubāʿī*, *ghazal*, *qaṣīda*, *qaṭʿa*, and *Mathnawī*.[90] Bahār died in Tehran in 1330/1952.

Ḥāfiẓ and Bahār

On examining Bahār's *Dīvān*, it is clear that his poetry has a style of its own. In some aspects, namely meaning and rhyme, Ḥāfiẓ's influence can be detected, but only a small portion of his poetry was inspired directly by Ḥāfiẓ, as illustrated by the following examples:

Bahār — می خور ور خوری مدام مخور — جز شب، آن هم میان شام مخور[91]

Drink wine, but do not drink continuously,
Drink only at night, but not in between meals.

Ḥāfiẓ

روز در کسب هنر کوش که می خوردن روز   دل چون آینه در زنگ ظلام اندازد[92]

By day, strive in the acquisition of skill. For drinking wine by day
Casts the heart-like mirror into the blight of darkness.

Between the two poets, we find that Ḥāfiẓ influenced Bahār more in terms of profound sayings than in rhyme and metre.

Ḥāfiẓ

کمال سرّ محبت ببین نه نقص گناه   که هر که بی هنر افتد نظر به عیب کند[93]

Look at the perfection of the sincerity of love, not at the shortcomings of sin: It is whoever turns out lacking virtue that has an eye for faults.[94]

Bahār

عیب جوئی چو گشت عادت تو   بسته گردد در سعادت تو[95]

Once fault finding becomes your habit,
The doors to your prosperity shall close.

Ḥāfiẓ

به پیر میکده گفتم که چیست راه نجات   بخواست جام می و گفت عیب پوشیدن[96]

To the sage of the wine-house I spoke, saying 'Where is the path to salvation?'
He demanded the cup of wine, and said 'Concealing faults!'

Bahār

بده ساقی آن می که خواب آورد   شرابی که در مغز تاب آورد[97]

Sāqī, hand me the wine that brings sleepiness,
The wine that brings joy to the mind.

Ḥāfiẓ

بیا ساقی آن می که حال آورد   کرامت فزاید کمال آورد[98]
به من ده که بس بی دل افتاده ام   وزین هر دو بی حاصل افتاده ام

Sāqī come, give me the wine that brings raptures and perfection,
That increases blessings, for I have become heart-bereft, through lack of these.

In the following verse, he follows Ḥāfiẓ to a degree in meaning and ideas. There are also some similarities in rhyme and metre as in the following *taḍmīn* (insertion of another poet's hemistich into one's own poem):

Bahār بهار پردهٔ موبین حجاب عفت نیست هزار نکتهٔ باریکتر ز مو اینجاست[99]

'Bahār', the hair-like veil bears no honour!
Here are a thousand points finer than a hair.

Ḥāfiẓ هزار نکته باریکتر ز مو اینجاست نه هر که سر بتراشد قلندری داند[100]

Here are a thousand points finer than a hair:
Not everyone who shaves the head knows what it is to be a wandering dervish.[101]

Bahār's discussion of the principles of neoclassical poetry appears in a two-volume anthology of his works entitled *Bahār va adab-i fārsī*. In it, while speaking about the Indian style during the Ṣafavid period, Bahār emphasizes that many poets of the post-Ṣafavid period emulated the old masters of poetry, such as Rūmī, Sa'dī and Ḥāfiẓ.[102]

Bahār openly acknowledged Ḥāfiẓ as a master poet whose unique and pre-eminent style has had a profound impact on the general public of Iran as well as on scholars and specialists. Bahār refers to him as a genius, a miracle in the world of poetry and adds that Ḥāfiẓ was a mystic and a spiritual man.[103] Bahār believes that the love in a poet's heart is expressed in his compositions, which thus comprise the very essence of his spirit. His verse says,

ز قلب کسان قلب شاعر جداست دل شاعر آماج سهم خداست[104]

The poet's heart is different from all others;
The heart of the poet is the target of God's arrow.

Bahār was a political activist who could have enjoyed a comfortable life and high governmental position; instead, he chose a humble existence, in keeping with his moral beliefs.[105] According to Rastigār, Bahār spent most of his life defending his people against tyranny and hypocrisy; many examples of his love of freedom and condemnation of bigotry appear in his *Dīvān*.[106] This conduct brings to mind Ḥāfiẓ's philosophy, which Bahār had admired from the age of fifteen.

Nimā Yūshij (d. 1338/1960)

ʿAlī Nūrī, known from his early youth as Nimā Yūshij, was born in 1275/1897. He was a Persian poet who started the New Poetry (*Shiʿr-i naw*) movement, also known as the Nimāic poetry (*shiʿr-i Nimā'ī*) trend in Iran.[107] He is considered by supporters of modernist poetry to be the father of modern Persian poetry.[108]

Nimā Yūshij was the firstborn son of Ibrāhīm Nūrī of Yūsh.[109] He spent his youth helping his father on their farm. The images of this life, caring for cattle and walking the plains, telling stories of village and tribal life, touched him greatly. As a young poet, when he was able to articulate his ideas, he wrote of these images. Nimā recorded the events of his life, both great and small, in hundreds of letters, occasional memoirs, personal sketches, journals and daily notes. Most of these have recently come to light, making the biography of this significant poet easier to write.[110]

Nimā attended the St. Louis School in Tehran. Nizām Vafā (1889-1965),[111] a major poet of the time, took Nimā under his wing and nurtured his poetic talent.[112] Even though Nimā continued to write poetry in the tradition of Saʿdī and Ḥāfiẓ for quite some time, the way he expressed himself gradually and steadily altered, until it became more illustrative of the new style than classical poetry. In general, Nimā manipulated rhythm and rhyme and allowed the length of the line to be determined by the depth of the thought being expressed rather than by the conventional Persian metres that had, traditionally, dictated the length of a couplet (*bayt*). Nimā realized that while some readers were enthused by verses on the charms of lovers and the coquettish ways of the beloved, the majority preferred heroes with whom they could identify. His use of symbols, too, was different from the classical masters, in that he based the structural integrity of his creativity on the steady development of its symbols. In this sense, Nimā's poetry could be read as a dialogue between two or three symbolic references building up into a cohesive, semantic unit. In the past, only Ḥāfiẓ had attempted such creations in his mystical *ghazal*s. The basic device Nimā employed, however, was thematic, rather than symbolic unity.[113]

Muhmmad Ziā' Hashtrūdī and Abū'l Qāsim Jannatī ʿAtā'ī are among the first scholars to have studied Nimā's life and works.[114] The former included Nimā's works in an anthology entitled *Contemporary Writers and Poets*. The selections presented were 'Afsānih' (Myth), 'Ay Shab' (O Night), 'Mahbas' (Prison) and four short stories. Nimā's verses number 17,283.[115] Nimā died of pneumonia in Shimirān, in northern Tehran, and was buried in his native village of Yūsh, as he had willed.[116]

Ḥāfiẓ and Nimā

Nimā was generally dissatisfied with the way in which the public viewed his poetry. In a letter to Furūzānfar, Nimā complains about this situation and the lack of appreciation shown to him by the populace. He stresses that he is not as valued as he deserves because he does not fully follow the style of the classical poets.[117] He adds that one day he will be truly appreciated. He writes, 'My dear friend, the worst thing that can happen to a human being is that he is not comprehended by others; his thoughts and words are not understood and appreciated. This is like a living hell!'[118]

Nimā believed that everyday problems need not be broadcast in an exaggerated manner; rather, the poet should separate himself from these difficulties while illustrating them with an artistic view.[119]

According to Mihdī Akhavān Sālith, Nimā is a painter of meaning rather than a writer of it. In other words, he did not bind himself by the rules of poetry, but would end the verse wherever he perceived it necessary.[120] Sālith further believes that Ḥāfiẓ had a very important influence on Nimā's purity of speech and his complete honesty. Ḥāfiẓ says,

رنگ تزویر پیش ما نبود[121]

With us, the colour of deception exists not.

Furthermore, Īraj Jannatī 'Atā'ī, in his book, *Nimā Yūshij: Zindigānī va āthār-i aū* (*Nimā Yūshij: His Life and Works*), speaks of Nimā's revolutionary style of poetry and confirms that his mode of composition differs from that of all classical poets, including Ḥāfiẓ.[122]

'Atā'ī asserts that Nimā's mother taught her son the verses of Ḥāfiẓ which he memorized them as he grew up.[123] Moreover, we can see in some of his own verses that Nimā speaks to Ḥāfiẓ, asking him questions or challenging him in connection with his philosophy:

حافظ - این چه کید و دروغیست
کز زبان می و جام و ساقی است؟
نالی ار تا ابد، باورم نیست
که بر آن عشق بازی که باقی است
من بر آن عاشقم که رونده است![124]

Ḥāfiẓ, what deceit and lies are these,
Which you speak in the tongue of wine and cup and Sāqī?
If you wail for all eternity, I will not believe
That you are in love with that which is eternal,
I am in love with that which is passing.

Firoozeh Papan-Matin believes that Nimā's '*Afsānih*' (Myth), first published in 1922, is an exemplary composition, one that delineates the boundaries between the old and the new in Persian poetry.[125] Matin further asserts that in 'Afsana', the figure on the stage who presents the play of love lives in isolation, much like the paradigmatic lover in Ḥāfiẓ's verses.[126] Matin emphasizes that

> In Ḥāfiẓ's *ghazal*s, as in Afsāna, the poetic narrator perceives himself as a wanderer mystified on the path of love. This path is not definable; it may best be named as a nexus of anticipation, desire, wandering, and wayfaring. The path itself is not separate from the journey of the wayfarer or from his manner of travelling upon it: in an important sense, it is his way. The lover comes into contact with the tangibility of love as he passes upon the path.[127]

In Ḥāfiẓ's words:

از هر طرف که رفتم جز وحشتم نیافزود   زنهار از این بیابان وین راه بی نهایت[128]

From every direction I went, my terror only increased.
Beware of this desert and this never-ending road![129]

In Ḥāfiẓ's verses, as well as in '*Afsānih*,' the stricken lover, following his own persistent desire, discovers himself in a state of constant agony and ecstasy; an indescribable state, one like the torment of being in love.[130] Below are some exemplary verses by Nīmā that illustrate this condition:

سرگذشت منی ای فسانه!
که پریشانی و غمگساری؟
یا دل من به تشویش بسته
یا که دو دیدهٔ اشکباری؟
یا که شیطان رانده ز هر جای؟

قلب پر گیر و دار منی تو
که چنین ناشناسی و گمنام؟
یا سرشت منی که نگشتی
در پی رونق شهرت و نام؟
یا که بختی که از من گریزی؟
هر کس از جانب خود ترا راند
بی خبر که تویی جاودانه
تو که ای؟ ای از هرجای رانده!
با منت بوده راه دوستانه؟
قطرهٔ اشکی آیا تو، یا غم؟[131]

Are you my destiny, Afsāna!
You who are dishevelled and sorrowful.
Or are you my heart, bound with anxiety
Or are you two tear-stained eyes?
Or the devil chased out of every place?

Are you my preoccupied heart
You who are so unrecognised and anonymous?
Or are you my nature, that you didn't search
After splendour, fame and name?
Or are you fortune, you who escape me so?

Everybody has driven you away,
Not knowing that you are eternal.
Who are you? – Oh you, cast out of all places! –
for me you have been a companion:
Are you a tear-drop? Are you sorrow?[132]

It is easy to see how the following verses by Ḥāfiẓ express the same romantic ambience of erotic perplexity in very similar terms, without there being direct influence of rhyme or metre by Ḥāfiẓ on Nimā.

در زلف چون کمندش ای دل مپیچ کانجا　　　سرها بریده بینی بی جرم و بی جنایت[133]

Do not tangle with his lasso-like tresses, because there
You will see heads severed, guiltless and without crime.[134]

در این شب سیاهم گم گشت راه مقصود   از گوشه ای برون آی ای کوکب هدایت[135]

In this dark night, the way to my desire has been lost.
From a corner, O guiding star, shine out![136]

Nimā's poetry was profoundly influenced by Ḥāfiẓ in many ways, although Nimā himself tried very hard to separate his style from that of the classical masters, in particular Ḥāfiẓ. Yet still, subconsciously, his poetic language reflects some thematic similarities with Ḥāfiẓ, granted, perhaps not in rhyme and rhythm, but in many other aspects, as the examples above illustrate. Both Ḥāfiẓ and Nimā warn the heart against the trials and the excitement of the itinerary to the final destination. The lover's pursuit to fulfil his needs is a courageous course of self-realization. Just as for Nimā, the lover's sincere heart, the place of his desires, is enthralled far afield from salvation, so in Ḥāfiẓ's verse the heart is potentially subject to a vicious death.[137]

Suhrāb Sipihrī (d. 1358/1980)

Suhrāb Sipihrī was born in 1307/1929 in Kāshān, in the province of Iṣfahān. His father worked as a post office employee and enjoyed painting and playing the *tār*; Sipihrī learnt calligraphy and painting from him.[138] Sipihrī is considered one of the five most famous Persian members of the school of New Poetry (*Shiʿr-i naw*).[139] Others who wrote in this form were Nimā Yūshij, Aḥmad Shāmlū, Mihdī Akhavān Sālis, and Furūgh Farrukhzād. Suhrāb Sipihrī was also one of Iran's foremost modernist painters.[140]

Sipihrī's ideas about institutional religion in general and Islam in particular were quite enlightened and reflected the younger generation's way of thinking. He believed in faith, dignity and truth, but was not particularly religious in his poetry. His god was not Allah; Sipihrī's creator lies by the water, among the trees and all around him. He created a free and open environment in his poetry, giving people the right to question everything before believing. His most enthusiastic readers were and still are the younger generation, high school and college students. His poetry has become their language.

In Iran today many men and women look up to Sipihrī almost as a spiritual teacher and guide.[141] Sipihrī's poetry shows his concern for human values. He loved nature and referred to it frequently. Well-versed in

Buddhism, mysticism and western traditions, he gently mixed western concepts with eastern culture, thereby creating a type of poetry that cannot be easily compared to other poetry in the history of Persian literature.[142] His poetry has been translated into many languages, including French, English, Spanish, Italian, Swedish and Russian. In 1976, he published his final book, *Hasht kitāb* (*Eight Books*), which was a collection of almost all of his published poems in one volume, consisting of the following works:[143]

- '*Death of Colour*' (*Marg-i rang*) مرگ رنگ
- '*Lives of Dreams*' (*Zindagi-i khābhā*) زندگی خوابها
- '*Clash of the Sun*' (*Āvār-i āftāb*) آوار آفتاب
- '*East of Sorrow*' (*Sharq-i andūh*) شرق اندوه
- '*The Sound of Water's Footfall*' (*Ṣidā-yi pā-yi āb*) صدای پای آب
- '*Traveller*' (*Musāfir*) مسافر
- '*Measure of Green*' (*Ḥajm-i sabz*) حجم سبز
- '*We Naught, We Look*' (*Mā hīch, mā nigāh*)[144] ما هیچ، ما نگاه

Sipihrī made a significant contribution to Persian poetry; the number of lines in his collection reached approximately 8,850.[145] He died of cancer in Tehran in 1358/1980.

Ḥāfiẓ and Suhrāb Sipihrī

Sipihrī is generally considered more of a painter than a poet. However, his achievements in poetry are impressive, hence his influence on modern Persian poetry.[146] His paintings are reflections of his poetry and his poetry is the painting of his thought.[147] His work in both areas reflects his beliefs regarding Sufism and his pantheistic love of nature.[148] The *semi-précis* metaphors of his verses 'like the ochers and browns of his canvases – inspired by the desert around his native Kāshān – are always unexpectedly refreshing, and rarely artificial'.[149] His remarkable shifts in poetic themes are similar, in a poetic sense, to his love of chiaroscuro. Ultimately, the Cubist nature of his poetry recollects the world of his dramatic taste.[150]

Sipihrī's tendencies towards mysticism are apparent in his *Sharq-i andūh* (*East of Sorrow*), a compilation of twenty-five poems, many of which reveal the conspicuous influence of Rumi's *Dīvān-i Shams*, which is as transparent in ideology as it is in content, rhythm and inner rhyme.[151] The modest simplicity of verse in *Sharq-i andūh* forms an unusual blend of Sufism and eastern philosophy, permitting the first *coups d'oeil* at Sipihrī's vision of a superior spiritual being: an ubiquitous, yet momentary, creator whose mien can be felt in everything from nature to objects of daily life.[152]

The poems in *Sharq-i andūh* also divulge Sipihrī's extensive view on all faiths, their fundamental harmony, and the ineffectuality of their doctrines. These verses distinguish Sipihrī from his coevals, not only as a poet continuously searching for an unequalled personal voice, but also as an intellectual impelled by a vital force to conceive and convey a collective vision of life above and beyond the routine sociopolitical kinetics of everyday existence. During his youth, he studied the poetry of Ṣā'ib and Bidil, both of whom were undoubtedly influenced by Ḥāfiẓ and clearly influenced Sipihrī's work.[153]

In 1965, Sipihrī published *Ṣidā-yi pā-yi āb* (*The Sound of Water's Footfall*), a generally autobiographical work that presents not only another phase in his poetry, but also an original and, so far, unique voice in modern Persian poetry.[154] While the simple diction and common syntax of colloquial Persian give clear directions, the poem's *précis* imagery and baffling concepts make for road signs that are impossible to pursue. Yet, the frail balance between the plainness of the syntax and the complexity of the images summons the reader to enter into a meaning where none otherwise exists, 'ultimately to recognise that "the friend's house" (in the poem) is an otherworldly place beyond the familiar and ordinary parameters of day-to-day reality'.[155] While other characteristics add to the originality of Sipihrī's dialogue, his achievement in generating easily reachable abstractions in a straightforward and highly readable idiom rests at the centre of his accomplishment in striking a diction that has become so perfectly linked with him that the echo of its charm remains familiar to any reader of modern Persian poetry.[156] During his adolescence, Sipihrī was inspired by Nimā's poetry, considering it the most advanced style of poetry of his time.[157] The literature and poetry written during Sipihrī's lifetime reflect the depression and decline of the sociopolitical situation in the country, a recession clearly apparent in his own poetry.[158] In order to understand the situation society faced during this period, I quote from a letter Nimā wrote to his young friend, 'Jalāl Āl-i Aḥmad':

> It is obvious that we are going through a hot and dry desert. We do not know whether we are going through night or day. There is blood evaporating from the ground instead of dust. People are naked and hungry. Eyes are cold and wondering. They are told to pick up a weapon and shoot one another, but in reply, they say: 'we cannot' […].[159]

While Nimā's poetry reflects the problems faced by his fellow men, the key factor in Sipihrī's poetry is that, unlike most of the contemporary poets who invested their time and effort in composing poetry manifesting sociopolitical issues, it remains true to himself, for he carries the weight of his valuable heritage and is conscious of the profundity of the language of the classical poets, such as Rumī, 'Attār, Ḥāfiẓ and many others.[160] He informs us in some of his verses that he is inclined towards mysticism and that he seeks mystical wisdom:

من به مهمانی دنیا رفتم:
من به دشت اندوه،
من به باغ عرفان،
من به ایوان چراغانی دانش رفتم.[161]

I went to the banquet of the world:
to the field of sorrow,
to the garden of gnosticism,
I went to the bright foyers of wisdom.

Nūrbakhsh asserts that the following verses by Ḥāfiẓ provide evidence of this statement. He compares it to a poem by Sipihrī, to show that Sipihrī was under Ḥāfiẓ's influence, not in style, but rather in meaning and theme.[162]

حجاب چهره جان می شود غبار تنم   خوشا دمی که از این چهره پرده بر فکنم   Ḥāfiẓ
چنین قفس نه سزای چو من خوش الحانی است   روم به گلشن رضوان که مرغ آن چمنم[163]

The dust of my body is becoming the veil in front of the face of the soul.
O happy the moment when from that face I cast the veil aside!

A cage like this is unworthy of a sweet singer like me.
I will go to the rose bed of Paradise, because I am the bird of that Garen.[164]

In the following verses by Siphirī we see these same themes of spiritual alienation clearly reflected:

Sipihrī

دیر زمانی است روی شاخهٔ این بید
مرغی بنشسته کو به رنگ معماست
نیست هم آهنگ او صدایی، رنگی:
چون من در این دیار، تنها، تنهاست.[165]

On the stem of this willow, has been sitting awhile,
a bird with the colour of mystery,
One whose likeness doesn't exist in sound and colour,
in this land, he is all alone, just like me.

Further examples are given below:

Ḥāfiẓ

کمتر از ذره نه ای، پست مشو مهر بورز   تا به منزلگه خورشید رسی چرخ زنان[166]

You are not less than a mote. Do not be degraded. Practise love,
So that whirling now this side up, now that, to the private chamber of the sun you might arrive.[167]

Sipihrī

به روی شط وحشت برگی لرزانم
ریشه ات را بیاویز[168]

Like a shaky leaf, I am flowing on the river of awe,
Swing your roots.

Ḥāfiẓ

هرکه ترسد ز ملال انده عشقش نه حلال   سرِ ما و قدمش یا لب ما و دهنش[169]

For whoever is afraid of affliction, the grief of love is not sanctified;
It is a case of, our head and his foot, or our lip and his mouth.[170]

Sipihrī

می بویم، بو آمد. از هر سو، های آمد، هو آمد. من رفتم،
"او" آمد، "او" آمد.[171]

I smell, a fragrance came. From every direction, a sound came. I left,
'He' arrived, 'He' arrived.

Ḥāfiẓ

شهر خالیست ز عشاق بود کز طرفی   مردی از خویش برون آید و کاری بکند[172]

The city is empty of lovers. It might be that from some quarter
A man comes out of himself, and into action.[173]

Sipihrī

بدی تمام زمین را گرفت
هزار سال گذشت
صدای آبتنی کردن به گوش نیامد و
عکس پیکر دوشیزه ای در آب نیافتاد

The ugliness has covered the earth,
A thousand years have passed,
There was no sound of swimming to be heard
And there was no reflection of a virgin in the water.

While it is clear that the influence of Ḥāfiẓ on Siphirī cannot be understood in terms of the modern Iranian poet's use of traditional modes of poetic imitation such as *tattabu'*, *naẓira, istiqbāl*, or *taḍmīn* after the manner of the neoclassical poets (discussed in chapter III) who directly imitated their past masters (these devices were utterly alien to his modernist style), it is clear that Siphirī's verse is, as it were, 'haunted' by a Ḥāfiẓian ambience. This ambience, however, is quite elusive and only identifiable intuitively by the reader who is familiar with the symbolism and imagery of classical Persian poetry in general and Ḥāfiẓ in particular. The comparisons made above between the two poets remain, unfortunately, to a large degree subjective for this reason.

Shahriyār (d. 1366/1988)

Sayyid Muḥammad Ḥusayn Shahriyār was born in 1285/1907 in Tabriz. Shahriyār is considered one of the greatest lyricists/poets of twentieth-century Iran.[174] He started his primary education in 1912 and studied the Qur'ān and the *Dīvān* of Ḥāfiẓ.[175]

He later emphasized that one of the greatest fortunes in his life was his acquaintance with these works, adding that, since childhood, he had loved the musical verses of Ḥāfiẓ and had begun to memorize them.[176] It has been said that he composed his first poem at the age of four.[177] In 1914, he started studying Arabic and French with the aid of private tutors and four years later he composed his first *ghazal* in Persian. In 1921, he moved to Tehran and a year later met the great Persian music teacher, Abū'l-Ḥasan Ṣabā. In the same year, he enrolled in the polytechnic institute (*Dār al-Funūn*). In 1925, at his father's insistence, he entered medical school. He met Īraj Mīrzā, the most famous poet of the time, in 1925. He tells the story of their meeting as follows:

> In 1304/1925 at the age of twenty, Bahār took me to meet Īraj Mīrzā, the famous poet of the time. After I was introduced to Īraj by Bahār, I asked for permission to read a poem I had recently composed. After hearing the poem, Īraj Mīrzā said: 'You are not one of us, you are more on Ḥāfiẓ's level.'[178]

Two years later, in 1306/1927, he entered a poetry competition with the great poet and songwriter 'Ārif Qazvīnī and won. He refers to 'Ārif as a patriot and a sensitive man.[179] A collection of his poems, with a foreword by Bahār, Sa'īd Nafisī, and Pizhmān Bakhtīyārī, was published in 1932.[180] Three years later, in 1935, he met with the famous painter, Kamāl al-Mulk, and stayed at his house for ten days. In 1943, he met with Nimā Yūshij, and later became friends with the eminent poet, Hūshang Ibtihāj.[181] While the poetry of his youth was characterized mainly by romanticism, distinct traces of mysticism appeared in his verse towards the end of his life.[182] According to Kāvīyānpūr, who wrote a biography on Shahriyār, the poet (Shahriyār) was greatly influenced by Ḥāfiẓ throughout his life. Kāvīyānpūr further asserts that Ḥāfiẓ was his role model, teacher, and guide, and it was his lifelong desire to equal, or perhaps to follow him.[183] One of his masterpieces is *Ḥidar bābā-yi salām* completed in 1330/1951, in which he writes of the memories of his youth. To date this work has been translated into over seventy-five languages.

Shahriyār was a musician as well as a poet. He played the *sitār* very well which he was taught by the grand maestro Abū'l Ḥasan Ṣabā, who was one of the most outstanding musicians of his day. He always believed that a poet must also be familiar with music, he used to say: 'poetry without music is not poetry'.[184] According to the biography written by Zāhidī (this is a different biography than that mentioned above) Shahriyār fell in love during his youth for the first and the last time.[185] His style of poetry in *ghazal* writing follows that of Ḥāfiẓ, although in his *Dīvān* we can also see the influence of the new poetry style, which follows that of Nimā. In general, Shahriyār was more recognized as a *ghazal* writer than for his work in any other style of poetry.[186] Shahriyār's inspiration has always been Ḥāfiẓ and his poetic language. His utmost desire was to equal himself with Ḥāfiẓ, an aspiration which the following verse bears witness to:

بلی از این همه شاعر اگر ز من پرسید   کسی به خواجه و اوج کمال او نرسید[187]

Yes, if you ask me, among all these poets,
No one has been able to match Ḥāfiẓ's wisdom

Shahriyār believed that the so-called 'New Poetry' is not really new, but in fact was based on the groundwork of classical Persian poetry. This view is apparent in the following verse:

این نوع شعر که (آزاد) نام اوست جمع میان بحر طویل است و مستزاد[188]

This kind of poetry which is called (free verse),
Is made out of *tavīl* and *mustazād* metres.

Shahriyār was opposed to the Pahlavi dynasty and welcomed the Islamic revolution in 1979. Although patriotism and the love of country is visible throughout his poetry, his Islamic roots and beliefs drove him to compose a number of poems for officials of the Islamic Republic, Khomeini in particular, thus contributing to Khomeini's fame at the time. Today, however, these compositions stain his reputation, at least in the view of many now opposed to the figures he wrote of. Yet his ability and talent as a great poet should not be measured solely based on poems he composed at a specific time, in which he praised Khomeini and Rafsanjānī, the president of Iran at the time. Shahriyār died in 1988 in Tehran after an illness. His contribution to Persian poetry is deemed to be of major value. His entire collection of poetry consists of approximately 20,250 verses.[189]

Ḥāfiẓ and Shahriyār

Shahriyār's *ghazal*s generally follow those of Ḥāfiẓ, although in his *Dīvān* we can also see the influence of the 'New Poetry' style with verses occasionally composed in the vein of Nimā's school of poetics. The fact that Shahriyār always strove to emulate Ḥāfiẓ and to match the genius and poetic language of Ḥāfiẓ is reflected in the following verse:

Shahriyār به شهر عشق منم شهریار و چون حافظ منم که شهره شهرم به عشق ورزیدن[190]

In the city of love, like Ḥāfiẓ, I am the king,
It is I who am famous in town for love making

Ḥāfiẓ منم که شهره شهرم به عشق ورزیدن منم که دیده نیالوده ام به بد دیدن[191]

I'm the one who is the talk of the town for love-making.
It is I whose sight is not polluted by looking at evil.[192]

After studying Shahriyār's *Dīvān* and reviewing his notes and the forewords to his volumes of poetry, it is clear that this contemporary poet was greatly influenced by Ḥāfiẓ. A close study of Shahriyār's collection of poetry, and a juxtaposition of his *ghazal*s with those of Ḥāfiẓ reveals his admiration of Ḥāfiẓ. The similarities between the two poets are so numerous that a lengthy essay would be required to show all of them. Below, I have only given a few of Shahriyār's most popular verses, paralleling them with similar verses by Ḥāfiẓ:

Shahriyār

تا چشم دل به طلعت آن ماه منظر است طالع مگو که چشمه خورشید خاور است[193]

For as long as the eye of the heart is set on the countenance of that moon-face
Do not say that the fountain of the sun is located in the east!

Ḥāfiẓ باغ مرا چه حاجت سرو و صنوبر است شمشاد ساه پرور من از که کمتر است[194]

What need of cypress and pine has my garden? Less than whom
is my home-grown box tree?[195]

Shahriyār منم که شعر و تغزل پناهگاه من است چنانکه قول و غزل نیز در پناه من است[196]

It is I who find sanctuary in poetry and lyrics,
For it is I who provide sanctuary for them both

Ḥāfiẓ منم که گوشه میخانه خانقاه من است دعای پیر مغان ورد صبحگاه من است[197]

I am he whose dervish hospice is a corner of the wine-bothy
Prayer for the Magian elder is my dawn litany.[198]

Shahriyār به پیری مرا آنچه مانده لذت یاد دلم به دولت یاد است اگر کمی شاد است[199]

All I have left in old age are sweet memories
If I seem for a moment happy, it is owed to those memories

Ḥāfiẓ بیا که قصر امل سخت سست بنیاد است بیار باده که بنیاد عمر بر باد است[200]

Come, for the foundation of the mansion of hope is most unsound.
Bring wine: life's foundations are on wind.[201]

Shahriyār   ای چشم خمارین که کشد سرمه خوابت   وی جام بلورین که خورد بادهٔ نابت[202]

O drunken-eye, who will now decorate your sleepy eyes with collyrium,
O crystal-cup, who will now drink your pure wine?

Ḥāfiẓ   ای شاهد قدسی که کشد بند نقابت   وی مرغ بهشتی که دهد دانه و آبت[203]

O hallowed beauty, who might unfasten your veil?
Alas, bird of the celestial garden, who should your seed and water supply?[204]

Shahriyār
جبین بگشا که می بندیم از این غمخانه محملها   چه خرم سرزمینهایی که در پیش است و منزلها[205]

Smooth out the wrinkles on your brow for we are fastening down the camel leaders to depart from this house of sorrow
Pleasant the territories and destinations we shall explore!

Ḥāfiẓ   الا یا ایها الساقی ادر کاسا و ناولها   که عشق آسان نمود اول ولی افتاد مشکلها[206]

O Sāqī, pass the bowl round and offer it;
At first love seemed easy, snags have cropped up.[207]

Shahriyār   اگر آن دختر ترسا بیاراید کلیسا را   چراغان می کند قندیل راهب دیر ترسا را[208]

If that Christian girl decorates the church
The latticed lampshade of the monk shall illuminate the church.

Ḥāfiẓ   اگر آن ترک شیرازی بدست آرد دل ما را   به خال هندویش بخشم سمرقند و بخارا را[209]

If that Shīrāzī Turk captures our heart,
For his Hindu dark mole I would forgive Samarqand and Bukhara![210]

In the introduction to his *Dīvān*, Shahriyār emphasizes that great poetry in order to truly touch the soul and spirit must maintain a balance between meaning, rhyme, and subject matter. In this regard, he adds that the poetry of Ḥāfiẓ, written in 'sweet Persian', represents the zenith of Persian poetic tradition.[211] As if to prove this point, further on in the *Dīvān* of Shahriyār, we come across a poem called 'The School of Ḥāfiẓ' (*Maktab-i Ḥāfiẓ*), a title chosen by Shahriyār himself. The eleven-verse *ghazal* ends with this couplet, which stresses Shahriyār's literary attachment to Ḥāfiẓ and the strong influence this poet had on him:

سفر مپسند هرگز شهریار از مکتب حافظ　　سیر معنوی اینجا و کنج خانقاه اینجا[212]

Shahriyār, do not travel away from Ḥāfiẓ's school,
For the path to spirituality is here, the corner of the monastery is here.

It is also said that Shahriyār chose his pen name from the *Dīvān* of Ḥāfiẓ; while making a wish and opening the *Dīvān*, the following verse appeared, hence, his pen name 'Shahriyār':

غم غریبی و غربت چو بر نمی تابم　　به شهر خود روم و شهریار خود باشم[213]

When I cannot bear the misery of being alien and away from home,
Let me go to my own city and be my own prince.[214]

There are numerous *ghazal*s written by Shahriyār, in addition to those presented above, which were deeply influenced by Ḥāfiẓ, but it is not possible to cite them here for reasons of space. However, it seems indisputable, and his poem '*Maktab-i Ḥāfīz*' suffices to prove, as he himself admits, that all he has in the way sweetness of verse is due to the influence of Ḥāfiẓ.[215]

هر چه دارم همه از دولت حافظ دارم[216]

All I possess I owe to Ḥāfiẓ's rich largesse.

Aḥmad Shāmlū (d. 1379/2000)

Aḥmad Shāmlū was born in 1304/1925 in Tehran. Details of his adolescent life are scant. His poetry was initially very much influenced by the tradition of Nimā Yūshij.[217] Shāmlū's poetry is complex, yet his imagery, which greatly contributes to the quality of his poems, is simple. He begins with traditional imagery familiar to his Iranian audience through the works of Persian masters like Ḥāfiẓ and 'Umar Khayyām. For structure and impressions, he uses a kind of everyday imagery in which personified oxymoronic principles are illustrated with a false combination of the abstract.

The finished material, unprecedented in Persian poetry, has made some admirers of traditional poetry very unhappy.[218] He has written a number of plays and edited the works of major classical Persian poets, including Ḥāfiẓ. His six-volume work, *Kitāb-i kūcha* (*The Book of the Alley*) is a major contribution to the understanding of Iranian folklore beliefs and languages.[219] Shāmlū has translated extensively from German and French into Persian and his own works are translated into a number of languages. He died after an illness in 2000. The following table illustrates his works, poetry, prose and the approximate number of verses.[220]

Name of Poetry Collection		**Number of lines**	**Year of publication**
'Fresh Air'	هوای تازه	8/352	1363/1985
'Fragments'	قطعه نامه	6/264	1363/1985
'Dagger in Plate'	دشنه در دیس	18/792	1372/1994
'Moments and Always'	لحظه ها و همیشه ها	15/660	1372/1994
'Tales of the Dust'	مرثیه های خاک	7/308	1372/1994
'To Bloom in Fog'	شکفتن در مِه	8/352	1372/1994
'The Doors and the Big Wall of China'	درها و دیوار بزرگ چین	Short stories, few poems	1352/1974
'Phoenix in Rain'	ققنوس در باران	23/1012	1344/1966
'The Garden of Mirrors'	باغ آینه	45/1880	1338/1960
'Āidā in the Mirror'	آیدا در آینه	13/572	1343/1965

Shāmlū's contribution to Persian poetry is deemed to be of moderate value. His entire collection of poetry, according to my own calculations, consists of 6,132 lines.

Ḥāfiẓ and Aḥmad Shāmlū

Aḥmad Shāmlū published three editions of a controversial non-critical edition of the *Dīvān* of Ḥāfiẓ entitled *Ḥāfiẓ of Shīrāz, According to Aḥmad Shāmlū* (*Ḥāfiẓ-i Shīrāz, bi rivāyat-i Aḥmad Shāmlū*) between 1354/1975 and 1360/1981, followed by many reprints. A close study of his edition and a comparison between it and the editions of Qazvīnī/Ghanī and Khānlarī make clear that it totally lacks any scholarly foundation. In fact, his research is based more on his own taste than on any accurate or credible sources. Despite such imperfect editing, it has met with vast public popularity, especially among the younger generation.[221] It is believed that, to some extent, this may be due to Shāmlū's fame and his popular recorded declamation of Ḥāfiẓ's poetry.[222] In a broad assessment, Jalāl Matinī points out that 'In his introductions (which vary from edition to edition, and are missing in some) Shāmlū did not identify the manuscripts used and his long-standing pledge to list the verse variations in a posterior publication was never fulfilled.'[223]

Furthermore, Shāmlū's claims that he focused on establishing the 'logical' order of verses in each *ghazal* makes little sense if we bear in mind that in the older manuscripts the order of verses was highly consistent and in need of little, if any, improvement or alteration.[224] The texts of the *ghazals* vary from edition to edition; verses are excluded or interchanged together with entire poems, in some instances without logical reason.[225] Āshūrī, in a critical attack on Shāmlū in an article in the *Iranshenasi* journal, emphasizes that Shāmlū's views and interpretations of Ḥāfiẓ are without any scholarly foundation; they are based purely on his own taste and beliefs.

Āshūrī further asserts that Shāmlū's edition shows his lack of adequate knowledge of Ḥāfiẓ and that the author proves himself incompetent on the subject. Āshūrī adds that B. Khurramshāhī, in a critical and accurate article published thirty years ago, attacked Shāmlū over his interpretation of Ḥāfiẓ, rejecting his views and pointing out his lack of knowledge and competence.[226]

To conclude his review, Āshūrī adds that anyone attempting to undertake research on Ḥāfiẓ must have adequate knowledge of the poet before even beginning such a great task.[227] Khurramshāhī, in his *Dhihn va zabān-i Ḥāfiẓ*, (Ḥāfiẓ's language and Thoughts) criticizes Shāmlū's edition and questions his methods. Khurramshāhī quotes Shāmlū's own statement in the introduction of his edition: 'I have gathered all the manuscripts and the editions of the *Dīvān*, old and new, subsequently juxtaposing all the verses one by one, identifying the flaws'. In a sarcastic fashion, Khurramshāhī replies to Shāmlū, saying, 'I see, and that is easy I suppose'.

Khurramshāhī continues to criticize Shāmlū, adding, 'It is amazing and beyond me, how he has managed to put this edition together'. He expresses his opinion, saying, 'We have not seen such method since the appearance of Islam!' In general, Khurramshāhī states that Shāmlū's edition is a work based on purely subjective criteria invented by the poet himself (Shāmlū) which one cannot judge by normal academic or scholarly standards.[228] ʿAlī

Dastghiyb brings to the discussion yet another critical view, when he writes that Shāmlū acts as two different poets, one who speaks about the social, day-to-day life of ordinary people and a second, who speaks about love. Dastghiyb emphasizes that the second personality is more influenced by Ḥāfiẓ than by any other poet.[229]

Conclusion

Given the evidence provided throughout this section of the chapter, it is hoped that the extent of Ḥāfiẓ's influence over some of the key poets of the Pahlavi period has now been adequately demonstrated. The discussion of Ḥāfiẓ among contemporary poets and in the politics and literature of Pahlavi Persia is an extensive and complicated issue worthy of a monograph in itself. However, given the evidence provided throughout this section of the chapter, it is hoped that the extent of Ḥāfiẓ's influence over some of the key poets of the Pahlavi period has now been reasonably demonstrated. The poets selected in this chapter were carefully chosen to illustrate the differences in views of at least one or two of them – as has been demonstrated with Nimā and Shahriyār; while they were both contemporaries, one was more influenced by Ḥāfiẓ than the other. As was seen in the case of Shahriyār, Ḥāfiẓ has long been admired and emulated, but is admitted to be virtually impossible to equal.

This exercise shows the various degrees of influence that Ḥāfiẓ had on different poets. For example, Nimā grew up learning and memorizing Ḥāfiẓ's poetry and absorbing his style but, later in life, he developed his own style of poetry; though his work continued to reflect Ḥāfiẓ's philosophy. Shahriyār, too, was brought up with Ḥāfiẓ's poetry, and this influence continued; indeed, he found himself deeply inspired by Ḥāfiẓ and he followed his style, philosophy, beliefs and tendency to spirituality.

Other cases throughout this study also demonstrate the influence Ḥāfiẓ's teachings had on many scholars and poets of Persia – on their poetry, personalities, social behaviour or other aspects of life.

As Shahram Pazouki (I believe rightly) affirms, Ḥāfiẓ is a cultural treasure who has collated all the qualities of the spiritual masters and literary geniuses who flourished before him, improving and passing them on to the rest of humanity.[230]

> There is no poet in Persia who has not been influenced by Ḥāfiẓ. Even those who claim they are not, just don't realize it. Ḥāfiẓ is like a reservoir that has collected all the good qualities before him and passed them to all who came after him and those still yet to come. The spirit of Ḥāfiẓ flows in every Iranian who has the slightest interest in poetry and literature, not just the professional poets.[231]

The last word regarding the impact of Ḥāfiẓ on Iranian poets of the last century I leave to Bahā' al-Dīn Khurramshāhī:

> Reading the question of which particular poet was the more influenced by Ḥāfiẓ, I can only say that anyone with the slightest familiarity with Persian poetry is under Ḥāfiẓ's influence. No one has been able escape this. This is a reality, a factual statement. Now, if some choose not to believe it, that is unfortunate.[232]

CHAPTER V

From Medieval to Modern Ḥāfiẓology: Five Hundred Years of Editions and Compilations of the *Dīvān*, from 1500 to 2000

This chapter examines some of the most important commentaries of Ḥāfiẓ's work produced by scholars and investigates the history of compilations of critical and non-critical editions of his *Dīvān*, while highlighting some of the most important critical studies of the poet. Commentaries on the poetry of Ḥāfiẓ have improved over time, particularly in terms of literary analysis; however, his symbolic lexicon and deeper mystical allusions continue to elude scholars and we still lack a single commentary that addresses both the literal and mystical aspects of Ḥāfiẓ's verses. Another central problem for commentators relates to verses that appear to be extremely libertine, if not altogether irreligious; these have been addressed by authors such as Riḍā Nūr Niʿmatullāhī and Sayyid Yaḥyā Yathrabī, both of whom have interpreted Ḥāfiẓ from a mystical point of view. Bahāʾ al-Dīn Khurramshāhī's commentary, by contrast, focuses on a select number of the most arcane and problematic *ghazal*s in the *Dīvān* and explains the accurate pronunciation of difficult words.

In terms of the compilations of the *Dīvān* made by editors, the two most reliable editions available today (which both serve as a basis for many other studies) are those of Qazvīnī/ Ghanī and Khānlarī. Other authors have tackled what they feel are the most significant issues in *Ḥāfiẓ-shināsī* in need of clarification; as a researcher I am indebted to them all for their contributions.

In section one of this chapter, I will outline a selection of compilations of the *Dīvān* chosen from the vast array of studies undertaken on the *Dīvān* of Ḥāfiẓ during the nineteenth and twentieth centuries and I will discuss some of the important critical studies produced in the twentieth century. The information presented here illustrates the plethora and complexity of Ḥāfiẓology research. We must accept, however, that the lack of an accurate and authentic version of the *Dīvān* is a major problem facing Ḥāfiẓology today in Iran and throughout the world.

Section two examines, in closer detail, eleven commentaries on Ḥāfiẓ written in Persia during the period from 1939 to 2010. The composition of commentaries written on Ḥāfiẓ is not new; the practice goes back approximately four hundred years; the purpose of this section is to assess in detail the most significant works produced in Persia over the past seventy odd years.

As other very important and much earlier commentaries on the *Dīvān* of Ḥāfiẓ have been produced outside Persia, in section three I will assess two of the most significant of these, those of Sūdī and Lāhūrī, before drawing some final conclusions.

An Outline of the Study of Ḥāfiẓ in the Nineteenth and Twentieth Centuries

This section outlines a selection of the most significant studies on the *Dīvān* of Ḥāfiẓ published in the nineteenth and twentieth centuries and some of the important critical studies of Ḥāfiẓ produced in the twentieth century. Bibliographies produced by Niknām in 1988 and by Rādfar in 1989 reference over three hundred and 225 printed editions, respectively.[1] Since the publication of these two bibliographies, further editions have materialized.[2] However, only those of specific significance will be addressed here.

The first lithograph volume of Ḥāfiẓ was published in Calcutta in 1791 by Richard Johnson.[3] This edition had been collated by Abū Ṭālib Khān Landanī and was based on twelve different manuscripts; 1,200 copies were published.[4]

Further editions followed: one, edited by Muḥammad ʿAlī Pāshā (d. 1849),[5] was printed in 1243/1827 and another, with the traditional foreword by Gulandām, was edited by Badr-ʿAlī ʿAzimābādī.[6]

In 1854, Hermann Brockhaus published an edition of Ḥāfiẓ's *Dīvān* based on the version used by Sūdī (d. 1006/1589) for his commentary in Turkish.[7] Jarrett's reproduction of the Brockhaus edition was based on that Turkish analysis. In 1838, the initial lithograph of this version (Jarrett's reproduction of the Brockhaus edition) of the *Dīvān* was printed in Persia. Subsequently, the number of editions printed in Iran gradually increased, although the figure was, for a long time, surpassed by the number printed elsewhere, such as Calcutta, Bombay (now Mumbai) and Istanbul.[8]

In 1881, a noteworthy edition of the *Dīvān*, edited by H.S. Jarrett was printed in India and used by the military and civil service for their examinations. H. Wilberforce Clarke made comprehensive references to this book in his interpretation.[9] My careful inspection of Jarrett's edition has revealed 573 recorded *ghazal*s together with some *Mathnawīhā*, *qaṭaʿāt* and *rubāʿīyāt*.

A credible edition based on a manuscript dated 827/1423 was published by ʿAbdul Raḥīm Khalkhālī in 1306/1927.[10] He produced three subsequent editions based on manuscripts dated 898/1492-1493, 901/1495-1496 and 984/1576-1577.[11] As editor, he later became cognizant of his many errors.[12] 'When I first heard Mr. Qazvīnī's views on my edition of the *Dīvān*, I felt so proud that I almost disregarded the flaws in the manuscript. However, after a while, I realized the errors and faults in my edition.'[13] He then quotes this verse from Ḥāfiẓ:

از آن گناه که نفعی رسد به غیر چه باک

Fear not the sin that benefits others.

Khalkhālī asserts that he compiled his edition of the *Dīvān* because he had in his possession a rare and valuable manuscript of the *Dīvān* of Ḥāfiẓ. He refers to this valuable copy as very old and thus closer to the time of the poet; this encouraged Khalkhālī to compile an edition of the *Dīvān* and later pass the same manuscript to Qazvīnī.[14] Khalkhālī informs us that in his edition of the *Dīvān* he juxtaposed the verses of many other poets contemporary to Ḥāfiẓ, in order to be reasonably certain that the verses he had in his possession did not belong to other poets and that they were authentic and from Ḥāfiẓ.[15] This method is referred to by Khurramshāhī and Jāvid as the most reliable.[16] Furthermore, Khānlarī asserts that the most reliable and effective method for compiling the *Dīvān* is to rely on the evidence as close to the time of the poet as possible; he adds that, to date, only a few have used this method, and refers to Khalkhālī as one of the very few who have implemented it.[17] This fact is also mentioned by Qazvīnī in the introduction to his edition of the *Dīvān*.[18] Moreover, Khurramshāhī expresses his view about Khalkhālī's edition and states:

> Khalkhālī was not aware of the detailed problems embedded throughout the *Dīvān* and for this reason alone his edition bore many flaws, which were later corrected by Qazvīnī/Ghanī and Minuvī. Later Khalkhālī became aware of such flaws and because of his personality (he was a person

> who was 'open to criticism') he subsequently published a very profound book entitled: *Ḥāfiẓ-nāma*; in it he explained the errors in his edition in detail.[19]

Khurramshāhī claims that Khalkhālī's edition contained over four hundred errors, one of which I will give here as an example:

سحر بلبل حکایت با صبا کرد   که عشق روی گل با ما چها کرد[20]

> At dawn the nightingale related to the breeze,
> 'What things love of the face of the rose has done to us!'[21]

صبا[23] بلبل حکایت با صبا کرد   که عشق روی گل با ما چها کرد[22]

> At the beginning the nightingale related to the breeze,
> 'What things love of the face of the rose has done to us!'[24]

سحر بلبل حکایت با صبا کرد   که عشق روی گل با ما چها کرد[25]

> At dawn the nightingale related to the breeze,
> 'What things love of the face of the rose has done to us!'[26]

Khalkhālī's manuscript has served as the foundation for many printed editions of Ḥāfiẓ's *Dīvān*, not least for that of Qazvīnī/Ghanī. In the preface of this collaborative version, Muḥammad Qazvīnī/Ghanī, the pioneers in publishing a critical edition of the *Dīvān* in Persia, identified numerous uncorrected mistakes in Khalkhālī's first edition. It should be noted, however, that the essentials for their edition were gleaned from Khalkhālī's prior publication.

A well-known early publication was produced by Mir Sayyid Muḥammad, a scholar whose pen name was 'Qudsī' (d. 1361/1944).[27] Qudsī's edition, which took eight years to complete, was the result of a comprehensive study of fifty manuscripts and published books.[28] A. Hikmat, the editor of another edition of the *Dīvān*, maintains that Qudsī was a fervent admirer of Ḥāfiẓ and that he had loved his poetry since childhood. Qudsī's edition was published in two lithographed volumes in 1314/1896 and 1322/1904 in Bombay.[29]

According to H. Dhulfaqārī and A. 'A. Muḥammadī, the editors of the latest edition (1381/2002) of the *Dīvān* of Ḥāfiẓ, originally edited by Mir

Sayyid Muḥammad Qudsī and entitled *Dīvān-i Ḥāfiẓ-i Qudsī* (1314/1896), Qudsī's edition was one of the most credible editions of the *Dīvān* prior to that of Qazvīnī/Ghanī.[30] Dhulfaqārī and Muḥammadī add that Qudsī's edition is comprised of six hundred *ghazal*s. In addition to this, they further believe that the most reliable editions to date are those of Qazvīnī/Ghanī, Khānlarī, Naysārī and Sāya.[31] By juxtaposing this edition with those of Qazvīnī/Ghanī, Khānlarī, Naysārī and Sāya I have observed many discrepancies for which none of the mentioned editors provides any explanation. For example, Qudsī records one hundred extra *ghazal*s, for which we have no reasonable explanations about their origins, or why the editor believes, contrary to other scholars, that they belong to Ḥāfiẓ.[32] Qudsī's edition, as stated earlier, is also flawed, yet was considered one of the best, until the appearance of the editions of Qazvīnī/Ghanī, after which it gradually lost popularity. In my opinion, Qudsī provides a valuable edition of the *Dīvān* whose accuracy I believe is reasonably credible, excluding the extra one hundred *ghazal*s.

In 1315/1937 Ḥusayn Pizhmān Bakhtīyārī published an edition of the *Dīvān*.[33] In it, he condemns the methods employed by Qazvīnī/Ghanī in compiling their edition.[34] While Bakhtīyārī emphasizes that his own copy is not without flaws, he stresses that Qazvīnī/Ghanī fail to identify the true meaning and beauty of Ḥāfiẓ's verses and they tended to judge a verse's authenticity or lack thereof purely on the basis of its historical context – this is a result of Qazvīnī's and Ghanī's academic backgrounds and expertise in history.[35] Bakhtīyārī further asserts that the popularity of the edition of Qazvīnī/Ghanī is due mainly to the fame of one of the authors (Qazvīnī) rather than the intrinsic value of the work. He adds that such an important task should have been given to poets and scholars such as Humā'ī or Furūzānfar.[36] In agreement with Bakhtīyārī, Dr. Meisami believes that

> Every edition has its pluses and minuses. Working on Ḥāfiẓ, I tend to use Pizhman's edition; I think he had a better feeling for the poetry. But I also compare with Qazvīnī-Ghanī and Khānlarī. Later (post-Revolution) editions, if there are any new ones (i.e., not re-editions of earlier ones), I'm not familiar with.[37]

Pizhmān Bakhtīyārī's *Dīvān-i Khawja Shams al-Dīn Muḥammad Ḥāfiẓ Shīrāzī* was a popular edition of the *Dīvān* and was widely accepted by the general public. Bakhtīyārī's edition comprises fifty-five pages of introduction and foreword, with a total of 489 *ghazal*s, falling six short of Qazvīnī's and Ghanī's edition. Scholars such as Bakhtīyārī, have relied on their own personal biases and tastes while editing the *Dīvān*. Thus, in Khurramshāhī's view, scholars such as Bakhtīyārī, Īnjavī, Yiktā'ī and Shāmlū have not adhered to the standard rules and regulations necessary for compiling an accurate edition.[38] Without naming a particular scholar in his critical note, Khurramshāhī further adds that some scholars do not consider it essential to rely on the manuscripts close to the time of the poet.[39] In this respect, Qazvīnī believes that editors and scholars must not rely solely on their own taste in compiling editions of the *Dīvān*, rather their task is to concentrate on accuracy.[40]

According to Khurramshāhī, who wrote his own commentary on the *Dīvān* in *Ḥāfiẓ-nāma* (*The Book of Ḥāfiẓ*), although Qazvīnī/Ghanī's edition is considered one of the best published, it is far from perfect. Their publication is based on the manuscript used by Khalkhālī dated 827/1424 in his 1927 edition of the *Dīvān* together with seventeen manuscripts. In further detailed reviews, Khurramshāhī adds that the editors do not systematically annotate their deviations from Khalkhālī's manuscript, nor do they identify the sources for the additional verses provided.[41] However, Khurramshāhī goes on to say that the most reliable edition of the *Dīvān* still remains that written by Qazvīnī/Ghanī, because of the simple fact that they have not based their research on just one old edition and have employed a comparative method to reach a conclusion.[42]

According to Khānlarī, Qazvīnī/Ghanī relied heavily on the edition of Khalkhālī and some other manuscripts close to the time of the poet. Khānlarī believes that Qazvīnī/Ghanī's edition is one of the most reliable editions to date, with the exception of some minor errors, which Khānlarī claims he has corrected in his edition.[43] Khurramshāhī also seems to agree with Khānlarī in believing that Qazvīnī/Ghanī's edition is one of the most reliable editions produced to date for the very reasons mentioned before – that they have gone as far back to the time of the poet as possible.[44] This is a view shared by Dr. Meisami as well.[45] Khurramshāhī further asserts that this marks a revolution in editions of the *Dīvān*.[46]

In agreement with Khurramshāhī, Īnjavī states that Qazvīnī's edition is one of the most credible editions to date. Mīnuvī's edition of the *Dīvān* published in 1346/1968 is also based on that of Qazvīnī/Ghanī.[47] Following Qazvīnī's death, M. Mīnuvī professed that Qazvīnī/Ghanī's edition of the *Dīvān* is one of the most reliable copies available today and a solid base for many published editions.[48] Hiravī agrees that Qazvīnī/Ghanī's edition is still considered the most accurate, even after over forty years.[49]

Hiravī, in connection with Qazvīnī/Ghanī's edition, says: 'I am deeply fond of this copy, because I have enjoyed its accurate contents many times and have not come across any other more credible editions.'[50] I must agree that Qazvīnī/Ghanī's edition is, to date, the most reliable edition available for students and researchers of Ḥāfiẓology. In his work, entitled *Dawlat-i pīr-i mughān* (*The Wisdom of the Sage of Magi*), Kirmānī juxtaposes some verses from Qazvīnī/Ghanī's edition with those of Khānlarī to demonstrate dissimilarities between the two editions, favouring Khānlarī's version over that of Qazvīnī/Ghanī. I believe, having studied the views of many scholars about this issue, that it would be accurate to confirm that Qazvīnī/Ghanī's edition remains the most credible today; thus, my view remains the same as that of Khurramshāhī. Clearly, Qazvīnī/Ghanī's work is of major significance in the field of Ḥāfiẓology.

Injavī Shīrāzī first published his edition of the *Dīvān*, entitled *Dīvān-i Khawja Ḥāfiẓ-i Shīrāzī*, in 1346/1967. In the introduction he informs us that to date there is no completely reliable edition of the *Dīvān* on which researchers can totally rely.[51] In his view, this is because Ḥāfiẓ did not compile his verses in his lifetime and therefore, the burden of this task has fallen to scholars and admirers. He further asserts that every scholar, according to his own comprehension and taste, has inserted verses in the *Dīvān* and this has become a major problem over the centuries. For researchers, the question remains, which verses are authentic and which ones are dubious?[52] Injavī asserts that in many cases those who attempted to produce an accurate version of the *Dīvān* have failed, mistaking some words, either because the original handwriting is unclear, or for other unknown obstacles. Below he provides an example.[53]

اسم اعظم بکند کار خود ای دل خوش باش　　　که ز تلبیس و حیل دیو مسلمان نشود[54]

[Invocation of] the Supreme Name of God shall [in due course] work its own effect – rest content, O heart/Because by means of fraud and deceit, the demon shall never become 'Muslim' (*musalmān*).

اسم اعظم بکند کار خود ای دل خوش باش　　　که ز تلبیس و حیل دیو سلیمان نشود

[Invocation of] the Supreme Name of God shall [in due course] work its own effect – rest content, O heart/Because by means of fraud and deceit, the demon shall never become 'Solomon' (*Suliyman*).

Injavī believes that the correct verse should read as Suliyman, not Muslim, as underlined above. However, according to Khurramshāhī, Injavī's edition is one of those editions that rely more on personal taste than on objective scholarship.[55]

Khānlarī's two-volume *Dīvān-i Ḥāfiẓ Khawja Shams al-Dīn Muḥammad* (1362/1983) is widely believed by many scholars to be a great improvement on that of Qazvīnī/Ghanī. As Khānlarī himself claims, his edition is free from the errors found in Qazvīnī/Ghanī's edition. Khānlarī informs us that his primary sources were the edition by Mīnuvī, along with a manuscript he had access to at the British Museum, dated 813-814/1431-1432. This manuscript is therefore very close to the time of the poet and various other manuscripts, which are mixtures of poems of Ḥāfiẓ and some of his contemporaries, poets such as Sāvajī.[56] Khānlarī's edition is very similar to Qazvīnī/Ghanī's, though he (Khānlarī) states that the various errors in their edition have been corrected in his edition. Clearly, most recent editions of the *Dīvān* are based, in one way or another, on either Qazvīnī's/Ghanī's or Khānlarī's edition.

Khānlarī was considered a poet as well as a scholar, thus he is more skilful in modifying verses in an agreeable and stylish manner.[57]

Naysārī records that his own edition, the *Dīvān daftar-i dīgarsānīhā dar ghazalhā-yi Ḥāfiẓ* (*The Book of Variation in the Lyrics of Ḥāfiẓ*), was based on, and compared to, that of Qazvīnī/Ghanī, as well as thirty-two other editions, and for this reason he claims that his version was an improvement on theirs.[58] In 1372/1993, Hūshang Ibtihāj, otherwise known as Sāya, produced an edition of the *Dīvān*, entitled *Ḥāfiẓ bi saʿ-yi Sāya*. Ibtihāj's edition comprises only 484 *ghazals*. According to the author, his edition was based on the editions previously produced by Qudsī, Khalkhālī, Qazvīnī/Ghanī, Farzād, and by examining various manuscripts currently held in Tajikistan, Istanbul, the British Museum, India and America.

The evidence of the existence of these manuscripts is given at the end of his edition of the *Dīvān*, where Sāya provides reproductions of their title pages and colophons.[59]

Sāya informs us that he has produced this edition with major help from Kadkanī; he emphasizes that because Kadkanī was a poet, the task of identifying and replacing errors with correct words was considerably eased.[60] In my interview with Khurramshāhī, he stated that Sāya's edition is one of the most credible ones to date and that many scholars prefer it to other editions currently available.[61] Dr. Pazouki also agreed with Khurramshāhī's statement.[62] In my opinion, Sāya's edition, because of the talent of the author and his profession as a poet, is of immense help to the student of Ḥāfiẓ's poetry in need of a reliable edition of the *Dīvān*, and the fact that Sāya has benefited from other contemporary poets and scholars such as Kadkanī makes his edition quite credible and reliable for the researcher of the *Dīvān*.

Important Critical Studies of Ḥāfiẓ

Ḥāfiẓ and the study of Ḥāfiẓ (*Ḥāfiẓ-shināsī*) are important elements of Iranian culture. Perhaps the primary reason for this significance is that Ḥāfiẓ's poetry and his language are blended with honesty and sincerity, presented in witty poetic forms, and reflects the problems manifested in the day-to-day life of the Iranian nation. Moreover, in today's sociopolitical milieu of Iran, people come to realize that what this supreme classical poet uttered seven centuries ago has proven to be truer than ever.

In 1319/1941 Muḥammad Muʿīn, whose grand stature as a literary scholar in Pahlavi Persia is well known to all contemporary Iranian scholars, published his two-volume *Ḥāfiẓ-i shirīn sukhan* (*Sweet-spoken Ḥāfiẓ*). The volumes address many aspects of Ḥāfiẓ's life that are of interest to the student, including the following biographical details: his birthplace, pen name, family name and ancestry, education, marital status, and other matters of literary, historical, and anecdotal importance.[63]

The first volume ends with an analysis and close study of the meaning of some of Ḥāfiẓ's verses, with illustrative poetry as supportive evidence. Muʿīn's method of analysis relies heavily on the words of the poet, although some historical facts are taken into account as primary sources of reference.

The second volume begins with an analysis of Ḥāfiẓ's poetry, an examination of his style and some technical aspects of the lyrics.[64] Key words, metaphors, ambiguities and imagery are assessed and a study of major events at the end of the poet's life is offered. The book continues with discussions about Ḥāfiẓ's tomb and his *Dīvān* and an analysis of the influence of Ḥāfiẓ on the people and literature of Iran. This examination provides insights on a number of critical views, articles and essays about Ḥāfiẓ, the views of international scholars and, finally, a general analysis of his poetry.[65]

With regard to Muʿīn's *Ḥāfiẓ-i shirīn sukhan*, I must emphasize the importance of this book in the realm of research. According to Mahdukht Muʿīn (Muʿīn's daughter), her father utilized the editions of Khalkhālī, Bakhtīyārī, and Qazvīnī/Ghanī to produce this book and thus it is considered highly accurate by contemporary scholars.[66] According to Muʿīn, in order to write about the life of a poet, one must base one's research on three primary sources: narrations directly attributed to the poet, statements about him given by his contemporaries and any additional details given by those who have come after the poet. These three elements form the basis for the analysis conducted in Muʿīn's book, thus making it a very valuable tool for the purpose of research. I have partly relied on this book for this research and believe that most of its details are largely accurate.[67]

Javād Majdzāda Sahbā published *Sukhanī chand dar bāb-i aḥvāl va ashʿār-i Ḥāfiẓ* (*A Brief Discussion about the Life and Poetry of Ḥāfiẓ*) in 1321/1943.[68] Later, Sahbā speaks about the Muẓaffarīd dynasty, presenting illustrative verses as supportive evidence for his various statements and connecting some verses to the beliefs and philosophy of Ḥāfiẓ. For example, the following verse from the *Dīvān* is offered as evidence that Ḥāfiẓ was a teacher who conferred lessons about humanity and moral behaviour:

نگویمت که همه ساله می پرستی کن　　　سه ماه می خور و نه ماه پارسا میباش[69]

> I do not tell you: Worship wine throughout the year,
> For three months drink wine, but for nine be abstinent.[70]

The book consists of 103 pages with no index or table of contents.

In 1321/1943, Saʿīd Nafisī published *Dar pīrāmūn-i ashʿār va aḥvāl-i Ḥāfiẓ* (*An Overview of Ḥāfiẓ's Poetry, Life and Times*). His book contains 279 pages comparing 100 *ghazal*s by Ḥāfiẓ with those in Khalkhālī's edition of the *Dīvān*. In the foreword of this book, Nafisī expresses his admiration for Ḥāfiẓ with a profound passion, unsurpassed – as far as I have witnessed – by any other devotee of Ḥāfiẓ. The book includes a foreword by ʿAbbās Iqbāl. In the introduction, Sahbā claims that the verses chosen for his book rely on an undated and unnamed manuscript in his possession, and are, therefore, more authentic than other available manuscripts.[71]

Not long after Nafisī's book was published in 1943, a major two-volume study by Qāsim Ghanī (d. 1331/1953), *Baḥth dar āthār va afkār va aḥvāl-i Ḥāfiẓ* (*A Discussion About the Works, Thought and Life of Ḥāfiẓ*), was produced in 1322/1944. It begins with a foreword by Qazvīnī, detailing the history of his friendship with Ghanī. Qazvīnī expands his discussion, acknowledging the great poets of Persia and categorizing them into three different classes. Class one consists of poets like Rūmī, Saʿdī, Ḥāfiẓ and so on. Class two is made up of 'second-class poets,' such as Khājū and Salmān Sāvajī, and the third class consists of poets from the Ṣafavid period. The book begins by considering the name and pen name of Ḥāfiẓ, moving on to his early years, education and relationship with kings and rulers.

Ghanī emphasizes that researchers must not waste valuable time conducting research on the third or even the second class of poets, but rather they should concentrate on the superior poets.[72] To conclude his criticism, Ghanī quotes the following verse by Rūmī:

من بندهٔ خوبانم هر چند بدم گویند   با زشت نیامیزم هرچند کند نیکی

I am the servant of the fair ones; however much they criticize me!
With the ill and ugly I do not associate; however much good they do!

I believe that the above quote is somewhat different in meaning than Ghanī suggests and actually indicates that all works of scholarly value should be explored without prejudice. Ghanī's introduction establishes the aims and importance of such research. He stresses that in order to understand Ḥāfiẓ, we must first familiarize ourselves with the period in which he lived, those he associated with, and the political and historic situation of his time. Ghanī believes that to understand Ḥāfiẓ, one must take daring steps in exploring these matters.[73] In addition, he believes that artists are products of (or influenced by) their environment, and Ḥāfiẓ was no exception to this reality.

Ghanī's book consists of extensive research into Ḥāfiẓ's era and includes an analysis of the impact of different sovereigns on the city of Shīrāz. Ghanī begins with the Chūpānīd era and ends with the last part of the Muẓaffarīd dynasty. The most significant method of Ghanī's analysis of Ḥāfiẓ is his reliance on the words of the poet – these he uses more than any other source, while juxtaposing such verses with the available historical facts.

In 1338/1960, over a decade after the publication by Ghanī, a work by Muḥammad ʿAlī Bāmdād, *Ḥāfiẓ-shīnāsī yā ilhāmāt-i Khawja* (*Ḥāfiẓology or Khawja's Inspirations*), was published. As Bāmdād asserts in his foreword, the book concentrates mostly on the meaning of Ḥāfiẓ's verses. He focuses on defining frequently used metaphors and key phrases in the *Dīvān*. Illustrative verses are followed by detailed explanations of the intended meaning. There are also references to the life and education of Ḥāfiẓ during his youth and throughout his old age.[74] Further on, we come across references to kings and the rulers of the time, in particular to Shāh Shujāʿ and his family.[75] Bāmdād goes on to investigate Ḥāfiẓ's personality, with the aim of presenting an accurate statement of his philosophy. The book is 174 pages, with a partial glossary and line index.

In 1344/1966, a few years after Bāmdād's publication, Maḥmūd Hidāyat produced *Muntakhabātī az Dīvān-i Ḥāfiẓ-i Shīrāzī* (*Selections from the Dīvān of Ḥāfiẓ of Shīrāz*).[76] This book focuses mainly on the different periods of Ḥāfiẓ's life and is illustrated with appropriate *ghazal*s from the *Dīvān*. It consists of 329 pages, with a line index and corrections of some words in previous publications of the *Dīvān*. Muḥammad ʿAlī Muʿayyirī published *Ḥāfiẓ rā ham az Ḥāfiẓ bishnāsīm* (*Let's Learn Ḥāfiẓ from Ḥāfiẓ Himself*) in 1354/1974.[77] Interestingly, the book begins with a picture of the tomb of Ḥāfiẓ and a *ghazal* composed by Muʿayyirī, praising Ḥāfiẓ. The *ghazal* starts with the verse:

بوی جان میوزد از تربت حافظ به جهان　　　زندهٔ عشق در این خاک گرفته است مکان[78]

The tomb of Ḥāfiẓ exudes the scent of spirit to the world,
He, who is alive with love, rests here in this ground.

In the foreword of this book, Muʿayyirī courageously attacks those who slander Ḥāfiẓ and express opinions without solid evidence. He emphasizes that there are two very important rules that must be taken into account before any research on Ḥāfiẓ is conducted: fairness and concentration.[79] Illustrative verses are presented to support his belief, for example:

شعر حافظ همه بیت الغزل معرفتست　　　آفرین بر نفس دلکش و لطف سخنش[80]

Each of Ḥāfiẓ's verses is a masterpiece of wisdom,
Bravo to his fascinating words and the charm of his utterance!

Another important and interesting point in this book, frequently emphasized by the author, is Ḥāfiẓ's references to wine-drinking. Muʿayyirī claims that these should be interpreted purely in a literal sense and that no other assumption can be derived from his poems, apart from a few exceptional verses. He further asserts that Ḥāfiẓ did have a tendency towards wine and that he very openly admitted such behaviour. One of the most appealing points about Ḥāfiẓ's verses is 'his honesty', which is what makes people love his poetry; he makes no attempt to hide his behaviour, but rather openly admits it and emphasizes that drinking wine is no sin, but that deception and deceit are![81] Muʿayyirī presents the following verse as an example to support his claim:

من و انکار شراب؟ این چه حکایت باشد!　　غالبا اینقدرم عقل و کفایت باشد[82]

Me, deny wine? What tale is this?
I do, apparently, have just enough reason and character never to do that.

The rest of the book is written in the same manner, with references to Ḥāfiẓ's religiosity, beliefs, education and Ḥāfiẓ as a mystic, with relevant illustrative verses to support the author's claims. This book consists of 122 pages and, in the field of Ḥāfiẓology, it is considered moderately significant.

Commentaries and Studies on Ḥāfiẓ

Published in Persia from 1939 to 2010

Having outlined a selection of important critical editions and studies of the *Dīvān* of Ḥāfiẓ in the nineteenth and twentieth centuries, in this section I will concentrate on commentaries on the *Dīvān* of Ḥāfiẓ published in Persia between 1939 and 2010. Sūdī's work is not included here, although it is considered one of the most important commentaries. However, given its importance, I will address it towards the end of this chapter in a separate section devoted to 'Commentaries and Studies on the *Dīvān* of Ḥāfiẓ Published Outside Persia.' Here, my main focus will be on conducting a detailed examination and assessment of the works of the following scholars:

Muḥammad Dārābī	*Laṭifa-yi ghaybī* (*Subtleties of the World of the Invisible*)
Riḍā Nūr Niʿmatullāhī	*Nubūgh-i Ḥāfiẓ-i Shīrāz va nūr-i ashʿārash* (*The Genius of Ḥāfiẓ of Shīrāz and the Light of his Poetry*)
M. Murtaḍavī	*Maktab-i Ḥāfiẓ* (*The School of Ḥāfiẓ*)
Bahā'al-Dīn Khurramshāhī	*Ḥāfiẓ-nāma* (*The Book of Ḥāfiẓ*)
Saʿīd Niāz Kirmānī	*Dawlat-i pīr-i mughān* (*The Magian Master's Kingdom*)
Sayyid Yaḥyā Yathrabī	*Āb-i ṭarabnāk* (*Delightful Waters*)
Raḥīm Dhū'l-Nūr	*Dar justujū-yi Ḥāfiẓ* (*In Search of Ḥāfiẓ*)
Muḥammad Riḍā Khāliqī	*Shākh-i nabāt-i Ḥāfiẓ* (*A Stalk of Sugarcane from Ḥāfiẓ's Verse*)
M.S. Kadkanī	*In kimīyā-yi hastī* (*This Elixir of Existence*)

Ḥusayn Hiravī	*Sharḥ-i Dīvān-i Ḥāfiẓ* (*Commentaries on the Dīvān of Ḥāfiẓ*)
Muḥammad Isti'lāmī	*Dars-i Ḥāfiẓ* (*Ḥāfiẓian Studies*)

Muḥammad Dārābī

The commentary by Muḥammad b. Muḥammad al-Dārābī, *Laṭifa-yi ghaybī* (*Subtleties of the World of the Invisible*), was originally published in 1317/1939. The book is 154 pages, beginning with a ten-page introduction extolling Ḥāfiẓ's greatness and the charm of his utterances.

Unlike the commentary by Sūdī (discussed below at the end of this chapter), Dārābī's commentary is a patchwork study of enigmatic and difficult verses in the *Dīvān* and is by no means comprehensive. Although his approach is primarily mystical, some of Ḥāfiẓ's poems are defined in almost the same literal manner as in Sūdī's work. There are also references to the poems of Rūmī, Sa'dī, Shabistarī, Maghribī and 'Attār.[83]

The book is divided into several thematic sections. The first offers explanations of Ḥāfiẓ's more difficult poems; the second details relevant points in relation to Sufism; and finally, Dārābī presents a comparison of Ḥāfiẓ's verses with verses from the Qur'ān. This commentary includes some useful explanations of difficult words and phrases; however, the style in which the research is conducted is not of a scholarly standard, thus causing problems for the student and researcher. Consequently, although it is one of the older commentaries, it cannot be relied on as a sole source of reference. Furthermore, only a handful of *ghazal*s are included, without proper justification or explanation of their selection. It should be noted, however, that Dārābī's commentary does offer some mystical views and interpretations that are not present in anybody else's work, and the mystical depth of his exegesis is often exceedingly revealing and helpful to the modern students.[84] It should be underlined that Dārābī's incomplete commentary does contain one of the most important mystical analyses of Ḥāfiẓ. Although brief and random in its reference to *ghazal*s as a whole, Dārābī breaks a poem into fragments and analyzes those elements with a spiritual meaning verse by verse, in order to uncover deeper mystical aspects of Ḥāfiẓ's poetry. While he does explain the chosen verses, the full meaning of the *ghazal* is often lost, given that Ḥāfiẓ sometimes introduces up to seven different subjects in any one poem; if only the mystical verses are studied, we do not do justice to the entire poem. Although Dārābī's approach may have been acceptable a few decades ago, it certainly is not now.[85] In order to define Ḥāfiẓ's poetry, Dārābī relies heavily on verses from the Qur'ān, and utilizes Qudsī's edition of the *Dīvān*. Definitions of mystical verses are given, as well as the meanings of difficult verses, and Dārābī tries to resolve some problems of ambiguity in his commentary; however, a number of his definitions and conclusions are without academic foundation; there are no credible references or sources on which the reader can rely.[86] His work is considered only moderately significant in the field of Ḥāfiẓology.

Riḍā Nūr Niʿmatullāhī

In a personal interview conducted in 2010 in Tehran with Dr. Shahram Pazouki, a well-known scholar of Islamic mystical philosophy and Sufism, I was shown a copy of the commentary by Riḍā Nūr Niʿmatullāhī, *Nubūgh-i Ḥāfiẓ-i Shīrāz va nūr-i ashʿārash* (*The Genius of Ḥāfiẓ of Shīrāz and the Light of his Poetry*), which is no longer in print and almost impossible to find. It is a mystical commentary on the *Dīvān*, undertaken by a mystic whose intended audience were dervishes and mystics. Since Sufism is an important element in Ḥāfiẓ's poetry, this commentary is quite important, as Dr. Pazouki observes:

> Becoming a companion in the world of Ḥāfiẓ is not a task everyone can manage. It requires far more than knowledge and research alone – one must be a genius to be able to think in parallel with Ḥāfiẓ and comprehend his language in detail. Many have tried and failed.[87]

Since the author was familiar with Sufi mysticism and considered a gnostic, his work belongs in the same genre of commentaries as Dārābī and Lāhūrī. No publication date is recorded in this book; however, by examining the introduction and explanations given by the author, it can be estimated at around 1328/1950. Unlike more contemporary commentaries, this book draws on randomly selected *ghazal*s from the *Dīvān*, the roots of which are considered mystical by the author. The book consists of 917 pages, with a foreword by the author explaining the difficulties involved in compiling a commentary on Ḥāfiẓ, along with information on the methods employed. Niʿmatullāhī claims that his commentary is based on the editions of Qazvīnī/Ghanī and Khalkhālī; he also mentions the credibility of the versions produced by Qudsī, Khānlarī and Naysārī. Niʿmatullāhī's interpretation of Ḥāfiẓ's poetry is based purely on his knowledge of Sufi mysticism, and this makes his work different from many others published to date.

Poems and verses from Rūmī, ʿAttār, Saʿdī and Khājū are presented as evidence of mystical connotations in the wording and meaning of Ḥāfiẓ's verses, and analyzed for their influence on Ḥāfiẓ. In addition, the details of Ḥāfiẓ's biography and the period in which he lived are included and Ḥāfiẓ's relationship with kings and rulers is studied in some detail. Further on, some interesting passages consider Ḥāfiẓ's advice to all mankind. Supported by his verses, these words of wisdom are as follows:

- Listen to the spiritual masters – this is the key to prosperity and the avoidance of harm and misfortune.
- Live by your own hard work, obtain knowledge and be thankful.
- Do not believe that your misfortune is the worst kind, for what lies ahead might be worse – if you are not thankful.
- I am thankful to God that my arms lack the strength to cause harm to others.
- Do not drink during the day, for this is the time to learn and work.
- Constantly search to improve and find wisdom in these efforts.
- Be kind to your friends and patient with your enemies.
- Learn from love, for it is the ultimate healer.
- Live in such a manner that when you die you will not be considered dead.

The evidence for verses supporting the above claims is given below, in the same order as found in the original text.

- نصیحتی کنمت یاد گیر و در عمل آر — که این حدیث ز پیر طریقتم یاد است
- چو باد از خرمن دونان ربودن خوشه تا چند — زهمت توشه ای بردار و خود تخمی بکار آخر
- روزی اگر غمی رسدت تنگدل مباش — رو شکر کن مباد که از بد بدتر شود
- من از بازوی خود دارم بسی شکر — که زور مردم آزاری ندارم
- روز در کسب هنرکوش که می خوردن روز — دل چون آینه در زنگ ظلام اندازد
- شکر آنرا که دگر باز رسیدی به بهار — بیخ نیکی بنشان و ره تحقیق بجوی
- آسایش دو گیتی تفسیر این دو حرف است — با دوستان مروت با دشمنان. مدارا
- عشقت رسد بفریاد گر خود بسان حافظ — قرآن زبر بخوانی با چارده روایت
- چنان زندگی کن اندر جهان — که چون مرده باشی نگویند مرد

Similar examples of wise verse-adages appear throughout the *Dīvān* and this is one of the few commentaries to identify them one by one, discussing them for easy comprehension while presenting a mystical definition.[88]

The commentary of Niʿmatullāhī is an exceptional book for two reasons: first, the author was a mystic and familiar with mystical poetry; and, second, he was a poet himself. (At the end of his book he includes a profound mystical *ghazal* that he composed.)[89]

Niʿmatullāhī's method of examining the *ghazal*s of Ḥāfiẓ is not scholarly in the modern sense of the word, rather it is mystical. If one is to come to an accurate understanding of Ḥāfiẓ's poetry, it is necessary to have an insight into this dimension as well. Although I do not believe that all of Ḥāfiẓ's poetry bears mystical interpretation, in order to identify those verses which do, such an approach and background is necessary. The main shortcoming of this book is that it is not a full commentary; only a fraction of the poems are analyzed, for reasons not clearly explained. The author also examines verses of *ghazal*s that would seem to be randomly chosen, those that he considers mystical; thus the structure of each poem is broken into fragments. With regard to mystical concepts, the significance and importance of this commentary is major.

M. Murtaḍavī

Murtaḍavī's book, *Maktab-i Ḥāfiẓ* (*The School of Ḥāfiẓ*), makes no attempt to unlock the mystery of Ḥāfiẓ's poetry; however, it does focus on some difficult words and symbols that have been the cause of ambiguity. Murtaḍavī believes that in order to understand Ḥāfiẓ's language, one must unpack and decipher the key phrases in his verses and investigate words such as *rind*, *qalandar*, *wine*, *pīr* and so on. He emphasizes that the key to understanding such words lies with the poet's philosophy.[90]

This study, which is 478 pages long, consists of various articles previously published elsewhere. The first section of the book presents some information about Sufism (*taṣawwuf*). This chapter mentions figures such as Abū Saʿīd Abū'l Khayr, ʿIrāqī, Rūmī and Saʿdī, and examines their philosophies, comparing their thought to that of Ḥāfiẓ.[91] After studying this section carefully, it is clear that the author's purpose is to distinguish Ḥāfiẓ from the Sufis, to prove that the poet had a tendency towards gnosticism rather than asceticism.[92] The author tries to acquaint the reader with what he conceives to be 'Ḥāfiẓ's school of thought', thus trying to make it easy to understand why the poet criticizes the formalist ascetics and the fake Sufis. He hypothesizes that Ḥāfiẓ created a new school of philosophy, which he calls: *Maktab-i rindī* (The inspired libertine's school) – *rindī* being one of the most troublesome terms in the poetry of Ḥāfiẓ. The second chapter discusses piety through obedience and love. Brief histories of the beliefs and philosophies of mystics such as Rābiʿa al-Adawīyyih, Ḥasan al-Basrī, Ibrāhīm Adham, Ibn Khafif, Yūsuf b. Ḥusayn Manṣūr al-Hāllāj and many others are recounted in order to connect them to Ḥāfiẓ and his love of God.[93]

Overall, this book concentrates more on the mystical aspects of Ḥāfiẓ's poetry than on any other aspect of Ḥāfiẓ. Randomly selected illustrative *ghazal*s are followed by explanations and definitions of difficult words, with some references to the poetry of Rūmī and ʿAttār; in this way, Murtaḍavī implies that Ḥāfiẓ also adhered to the thought of such mystical poets who followed a philosophy of divine love.

The fundamental aim of Murtaḍavī's book is to prove that Ḥāfiẓ is not an ascetic, but a mystic filled with the love of God – a mystic whose mission is to combat hypocrisy and anything that deceives people by distracting them from righteousness and absolute honesty. By presenting arguments from various philosophies, thinkers and theologians and providing an insight into the history and roots of Sufism, Murtaḍavī makes a solid argument to support his hypotheses, and although only a fraction of Ḥāfiẓ's poems are discussed in this book, the analysis of those included are most often cogently presented, and, to a large extent, convincingly argued.

Bahāʾ al-Dīn Khurramshāhī

The commentary by Bahāʾ al-Dīn Khurramshāhī, *Ḥāfiẓ-nāma* (*The Book of Ḥāfiẓ*), consists of 654 pages concentrating on the exposition and explanation of certain *ghazal*s that contain phrases and words in the *Dīvān* of Ḥāfiẓ. In his twenty-four page foreword, Khurramshāhī explains that other commentaries and works on Ḥāfiẓ are great in quantity, but not in quality.[94]

Khurramshāhī commends the greatness and status of Ḥāfiẓ among other Persian poets, and describes his philosophy. He goes on to discuss difficult phrases such as *rind* and *rindī*, before moving on to demonstrate Ḥāfiẓ's position in the realm of mysticism and spirituality.[95] He explains Ḥāfiẓ's status in Iranian society and examines the witticism of his language, the music of his poetry and the melody of his verses. Khurramshāhī investigates the influence some of the great poets had on Ḥāfiẓ and his contemporaries, juxtaposing their verses with those of Ḥāfiẓ as illustrative evidence. He discusses poets such as Sanāʾī (d. 538/1137), Anvarī, Khāqānī, Fāryābī (d. 598/1197),

Nizāmī, ʿAttār (d. c. 618/1217), Kamāl al-Dīn Ismāʿīl Iṣfahānī (d. 635/1234), ʿIrāqī, Saʿdī, Nizārī Quhistānī (d. 720/1319), Amīr Khusru (d. 725/1324), Awhadī Marāgha'ī (d. 738/1337), Khājū Kirmānī, ʿUbayd Zākānī, Nāṣir Bukhārā'ī, Salmān Sāvajī and Kamāl Khujandī.[96]

Not every *ghazal* of the *Dīvān* is analyzed, only those which are problematic and abstruse. The first *ghazal* is followed by nine pages of interpretation.[97] Other *ghazals* follow in the same manner, with the number of each *ghazal* given at the top of the page, as recorded by Qazvīnī.

Khurramshāhī explains words that might, in some way, bear mystical meanings and, because the meaning of 'love' could be mystical, earthly, or literal, he classifies the *ghazals* of Ḥāfiẓ into these different categories. In this sense, he perceived the *ghazals* as being written in three different languages.[98]

According to Movahedi, Khurramshāhī's commentary is a valuable one, not least because, at the time of writing, there were many useful sources to which he could refer. Thirty to forty scholars are named in this book, each of whom specialized in Ḥāfiẓology. Movahedi, referring to his own work as a professor of literature at the university, observed: 'I have used Khurramshāhī's books in all my classes as a reference and I believe them to be the most balanced and realistic commentaries published today.'[99]

Saʿīd Niāz Kirmānī

In his study, *Dawlat-i pīr-i mughān* (*The Magian Master's Kingdom*), Kirmānī introduces Ḥāfiẓ as a superior mystical poet-genius. In this 362-page book, Kirmānī writes mostly about Ḥāfiẓ's views in connection with the mystical and religious issues of the time, presenting verses from other known mystical poets such as Rūmī, ʿAttār, ʿIrāqī and others as supportive evidence. He begins with an exploration of the poet's philosophy and sociopolitical issues of the era, mentioning Shāh Shujāʿ and the Muẓaffarīd dynasty. Much like Murtaḍavī's book, Kirmānī focuses on Ḥāfiẓ's philosophy and attempts to define the mystical aspects of his poetry, though he includes somewhat less detailed studies on the different ideologies of various mystics. Kirmānī does not include many illustrative *ghazals* as a whole, but instead offers some verses with a commentary and different angles of interpretation. Certain verses, however, are interpreted in three aspects: social, political and mystical. There are also explanations of key words, phrases and certain imaginary figures in Ḥāfiẓ's poetry, such as the old Magī and the inspired libertine (*rind*).[100] After a careful study of this commentary, I cannot see any reliable evidence to back up the interpretations of the author, which seem to be pure speculation on his part and thus easily challenged.[101] Indeed, in some instances he presents a poem followed by an interpretation, claiming: 'This is what Ḥāfiẓ intended to say,' without any credible evidence. Kirmānī tries to portray Ḥāfiẓ as a great mystical poet rather than a superior literary genius. In a few rare instances, he demonstrates that some verses can also be related to sociopolitical issues.

Sayyid Yaḥyā Yathrabī

The work *Taḥlil-i muḍūʿī-yi Dīvān-i Ḥāfiẓ* (*A Thematic Analysis of the Dīvān of Ḥāfiẓ*) by Sayyid Yaḥyā Yathrabī is a 488-page study of the mystical issues of Ḥāfiẓ's poetry. The book is not, in itself, a commentary, but as the title explains, is a thematic analysis. It begins with an introduction to the world of mysticism and the rules and regulations by which mystics should abide. A detailed explanation is offered of the divine beloved, the phenomenon of love, the definition of union and separation in mystical language, and so on.[102] Explanations of human love and mystical love follow, as well as a description of the way to purify one's soul by choosing solitude, sleeplessness and hunger, defining each stage as a condition of walking on the path to enlightenment.[103] In addition, he examines Ḥāfiẓ's style of poetry and the perfect poetic style in general, naming various rules necessary for the composition of flawless verses.

Yathrabī emphasizes that the fundamental problem facing commentators of Ḥāfiẓ's poetry is that some do not perceive his verses as mystical, instead they regard them literally. Although this commentary recognizes the poet as a mystic, only random verses are selected to support the author's stance. Further on, explanations about creation and the mystic's philosophy are given, with illustrative verses by Ḥāfiẓ offered as supportive evidence.[104] In addition, there is a chapter about love and the endless difficulties it presents; this relates to a particular *ghazal* in the *Dīvān*:

روز اول که سر زلف تو دیدم گفتم　　　که پریشانی این سلسله را آخر نیست[105]

The very first day I saw your tresses, I said:
'There will be no end to this dishevelled bond!'

This commentary is more a study of mysticism than an interpretation of Ḥāfiẓ's verses. By familiarizing the reader with mystical knowledge, words and phrases, the author attempts to unveil the ambiguities of Ḥāfiẓ's poetry. Yathrabī approaches the problem presented by Ḥāfiẓ's language through the lens of mysticism; however, very little evidence is given to support his interpretations of verses and, although some explanations might seem reasonably acceptable, one is left with more questions than answers.

Raḥīm Dhū'l-Nūr

In the fourth publication of his two-volume book, *Dar justujū-yi Ḥāfiẓ* (*In Search of Ḥāfiẓ*), published in 1381/2003, Raḥīm Dhū'l-Nūr explains his methods of investigation and states that his commentary on the *ghazals* is based on the edition of Qazvīnī/Ghanī. In this book he offers a commentary on each and every line in the *ghazals* in the Qazvīnī/Ghanī edition, explaining that he used the same calligraphy and style of writing as in Qazvīnī/Ghanī's version and that the numbers allotted to the *ghazals* are also the same for easy reference. All the *ghazals* in Dhū'l-Nūr's commentary have been juxtaposed with those in Khānlarī's version, and the differences in readings are inserted as footnotes.[106] Dhū'l-Nūr explains that all the previously missing phrases and overlooked words have been reprinted and added to his book. The number on the top right-hand side of each *ghazal* is the same as the number in Qazvīnī/Ghanī's edition, while the numbers on the top left of each *ghazal* are those found in Khānlarī's edition.

Dhū'l-Nūr claims that his method of commentary is closer to that of Muʿīn and Humā'ī than any other scholars (he adds that the classes at the University of Tehran he found most interesting were those given by Muʿīn and Humā'ī; indeed, he spent most of his time attending their lectures).[107] Furthermore, in producing his commentary, he claims that his standard of methodology matches that of Muʿīn and Nafisī. Dhū'l-Nūr contends that, since 1946, the situation of Ḥāfiẓology has improved considerably and that now a scholar or teacher of the subject can at least find a few *ghazals* in alphabetical order and be confident that he can accurately comment on the chosen poems, knowing that the text has some academic foundation.[108] Dhū'l-Nūr admits that his commentary is far from perfect and that, prior to his version, the most reliable commentary available was that of Sūdī. He further adds that a researcher in Ḥāfiẓology must expand his research and not rely solely on this book. For this reason alone, he adds, 'I have therefore named this book *Dar justujū-yi Ḥāfiẓ* (*In Search of Ḥāfiẓ*), for I claim nothing more than that, it most certainly does not mean that a researcher is necessarily a discoverer; he is, I insist, only a researcher, nothing more.'[109] In addition, he states that all the explanations given in the two-volume book are based on interpretations by other credible scholars whose names are given in footnotes. According to the author, this commentary on Ḥāfiẓ is only a compilation and juxtaposition of the works of the reliable scholarly sources previously published.

After studying both volumes closely, I believe that it is a fairly reliable source for the study of Ḥāfiẓ for beginners and enthusiasts who wish to know more about his verses; it does explain the meaning of some difficult words and phrases. As the author so honestly and openly admits, his edition is by no means the only source of reference and wider research must be conducted to develop a more accurate enlightenment of this endless subject.

Like Khurramshāhī, Dhū'l-Nūr does not claim to have made a mystical commentary on Ḥāfiẓ, although there are some mystical interpretations of various words and phrases in his commentary. Because his edition is based on the scholarly works of Muʿīn, the life and times of Ḥāfiẓ and the poems of Ḥāfiẓ (based on the editions of Qazvīnī/Ghanī and Khānlarī), his interpretations thus appear to be quite genuine and fair-minded, inspiring confidence in the reader.

Muḥammad Riḍā Khāliqī

Shākh-i nabāt-i Ḥāfiẓ (*A Stalk of Sugarcane from Ḥāfiẓ's Verse*), written by Muḥammad Riḍā Khāliqī, is a commentary on every *ghazal* of the *Dīvān*. It consists of one large volume of 1,145 pages and contains the accurate pronunciation of difficult words, a guide to the correct reading of verses and a glossary of mystical words and phrases.

In the preface, Khāliqī offers, somewhat randomly, specific verses from the *Dīvān* as evidence of statements presented on mystical issues. He does not support this selection by any logical evidence; rather it would seem to be based purely on his personal preferences. Throughout the book, although he identifies *ghazal*s and the metres and prosody for each poem verse by verse, and he interprets some mystical words and phrases, but does not provide references or sources for further research. Some of the sources to which Khāliqī refers, such as Dawlatshāh Samarqandī and others, are not reliable and are essentially the same as that of earlier commentaries. The level of scholarship and research in this book is, in my opinion, inadequate for the serious researcher in the field of Ḥāfiẓology.

For instance, in connection with Ḥāfiẓ's date of birth and death, he refers to E.G. Browne and other early scholars. Therefore, this work is not truly a commentary, but rather a compilation and comparison of works of other scholars and thus not particularly innovative.[110]

In summary, while Khāliqī's commentary demonstrates his general knowledge of Ḥāfiẓ's life and philosophy, it is based purely on the works of scholars such as Hidāyat, Zarrinkūb and Khānlarī. There are also references to western scholars and historians, such as Browne. The interpretations of mystical words and phrases are pure speculation on the part of the author, and although some may be correct, no solid reference is given for his definitions. This is not an academic work of high quality, and although it does contain much useful material, in my opinion it is not a credible source of reference for a researcher on Ḥāfiẓ's poetry.

Shafīʿī-Kadkanī

In Kimīyā-yi hastī (*This Elixir of Existence*), a study by Kadkanī, is a collection of his previously published articles on Ḥāfiẓ, not a comprehensive study in itself. According to Durūdīyān, the editor of the book, all Kadkanī's previous works on Ḥāfiẓ were collected and compiled in this single-volume book of 464 pages.[111] Durūdīyān adds that he referred to the editions of Qazvīnī/Ghanī, Khānlarī, Ibtihāj and Injavī Shīrāzī, emphasizing that these sources were also referred to by Kadkanī in all of his works on Ḥāfiẓ.

The book begins with a *ghazal* in praise of Ḥāfiẓ, clearly demonstrating the admiration the author has for him:

هر کس درون شعر تو جویای خویش و تو   آینه دار خاطر هر مرد و هر زنی[112]

Everyone, within your verse goes in search of themselves and you
Are the holder of every man and woman's mirror of the mind.

After studying this work and examining Kadkanī's interpretations, it is clear that the majority of its content relates to the style of Ḥāfiẓ's poetry rather than interpretations of his verses; it concentrates on purely literary, phonetic and syntactical aspects of the poetry of Ḥāfiẓ more than it does any of the deeper mystical and philosophical characteristics of his verse.[113]

Kadkanī asserts that Ḥāfiẓ, in his opinion, is a political poet, and he names two other poets, Firdawsī and Nāṣir Khusru, who he considers to be in the same category and of a similarly high calibre.[114] In this context, he presents and analyzes the political significance of some social observations and witticisms found in Ḥāfiẓ's poetry.

Often, only fragmentary verses, those the authors consider difficult to understand, are presented instead of an entire *ghazal*. An example of one such complex phrase is given below:

در نهانخانهٔ عشرت صنمی خوش دارم　　کز سر زلف و رخش نعل در آتش دارم[115]

In the secret place of pleasure, I have a sweet idol,
Because of whose tresses and cheek, I have a horseshoe in the fire.

In this verse, the word 'horseshoe' creates a difficulty in understanding the verse since it personifies a love charm and, without knowing this interpretation, the phrase is meaningless. According to Kadkanī, in medieval times, there was a superstition that by throwing a horseshoe in the fire and making a wish to charm one's beloved, one's love could be enticed to return.[116]

Although this book is a collection of Kadkanī's articles and is, therefore, somewhat different from the studies previously mentioned, it can be considered a valuable tool for the researcher of Ḥāfiẓ's poetry. Kadkanī examines selections of key definitions and interpretations using verses from other poets to provide supporting evidence and also analyzes some aspects of Ḥāfiẓ's poetry that are not dealt with in other commentaries. However, in my opinion, since it is merely a collection of academic studies and essays on Ḥāfiẓ and not a complete interpretation of his poetry, Kadkanī's book, while useful, is of limited value for the researcher.

H. Hiravī

Hiravī's three-volume commentary, *Sharḥ-i Dīvān-i Ḥāfiẓ* (*A Commentary of the Dīvān of Ḥāfiẓ*), comes with a slim volume containing a general index, an index to verses, and a bibliography. The thirty-page preface focuses briefly on the life and times of Ḥāfiẓ and refers the reader to a more comprehensive discussion by Ghanī, *Baḥth dar āthār va aḥvāl-i Ḥāfiẓ*. It also discusses Ḥāfiẓ's status among the Iranian people.[117] Hiravī believes that Ḥāfiẓ is not just any poet; he is a poet whose words and wisdom attract all classes and religions. He states that Ḥāfiẓ's language is cherished by every household in Iran and people of every profession enjoy his wisdom and the sweetness of his utterances.

The first volume consists of an introduction with information about the poet, his life, the charm of his poetry and the magnificence of his words. It includes the first *ghazal* of the *Dīvān*, the opening verse of which has long been the subject of doubt and criticism, as it resembles the work of Yazīd. Hiravī confirms that he is in possession of the full printed collections of Yazīd's poetry and that no such verse is to be found there.[118]

According to Hiravī, the absence of a complete commentary on Ḥāfiẓ represents a serious gap in Persian literature, a gap that is more significant because of the way that Ḥāfiẓ's work encompasses the realms of literature, culture and the socioreligious traditions of Persia. He adds that the most complete commentary available is that of Sūdī. However, this work contains a number of inaccuracies with respect to the Persian language, and is certainly an inadequate source of reference for Iranians interested in Ḥāfiẓ today.

In the preface, Hiravī discusses the edition by Qazvīnī/Ghanī, emphasizing that Qazvīnī/Ghanī used Sūdī's commentary written in Turkish (it had not yet been translated into Persian). Sūdī's commentary was first translated into Persian in 1342/1964.[119] Many commentaries have been produced since that of Sūdī, and many have considerable flaws. Every edition on the *Dīvān* produced to date contains errors, including that of Qazvīnī/Ghanī; therefore, any commentary based on such editions is bound to include flaws. This particular commentary is no exception.

Hiravī discusses the technical points of Ḥāfiẓ's poetry, taking key words (such as *zulf*, *ṭurra*, *khāl*, *kamand*, *kamān-i abrū* and so on) that may be ambiguous and tries to resolve them.[120] In addition, he presents them in a simpler, more straightforward language so that they can be more widely comprehended. He claims that if the reader refers to his commentary often, he will gain a better understanding of Ḥāfiẓ's poetry. Hiravī breaks the *ghazals* down by verses, and explains each verse in detail, sometimes over quite a few pages. The poems, however, are not recorded as a whole in his commentary – a major fault that B. Khurramshāhī emphasized in his communication with me. The author also examines the language of Ḥāfiẓ, contending that the witticisms in his utterances play an important role in the sweetness of his poetry.[121]

Finally, Hiravī explains his technique for handling the problem of interpreting mystical issues and emphasizes that only in very clear and unquestionable instances has he defined specific mystical words. He is the first to admit that his commentary on Ḥāfiẓ is far from being a book of mystical interpretation.[122]

In sum, Hiravī's commentary concentrates on the literal, rather than the mystical meaning of Ḥāfiẓ's poetry. While the commentary seems accurate, it is, in my opinion, of more use to Ḥāfiẓ's admirers than to serious researchers of Ḥāfiẓology. It can be used as a point of reference at some stage by students, but it is not of a standard that can be used as a complete guide to comprehending Ḥāfiẓ's language.

Muḥammad Istiʿlāmī

This two-volume commentary, *Dars-i Ḥāfiẓ* (*Ḥāfiẓian Studies*), consists of a thorough analysis of every line in all 497 *ghazal*s of the Ghanī/Qazvīnī edition of the *Dīvān*. The foreword by Istiʿlāmī attracted my attention because in it, he asks the reader, very openly and honestly, a series of questions. The translated text follows:

1. You, who read this book, what is it you want of me and this book? What are your expectations?
2. Do you want to read the *Dīvān* smoothly and easily, while understanding every verse?
3. Do you want me to juxtapose the other scholarly works and analyze them so you can agree and disagree with whichever you like?
4. Do you want to just read a poem and enjoy it?
5. Do you want me to use difficult words and show off my knowledge?
6. Do you want to hear something sensational about Ḥāfiẓ?
7. Do you want…?

> Let me make it clear right now. I have no problem acting as a teacher for the second question. However, if there is anything else you, the 'reader', are after, let us just say goodbye and part company this very minute.[123]

The author's questions make the intention of this commentary very straightforward. The first thirty-eight pages of the introduction present discussions about Ḥāfiẓ's philosophy, with various relevant illustrative verses given as evidence of his statements.

The second part consists of a number of explanations on the language of Ḥāfiẓ's verses. The third part discusses the logical comprehension of Ḥāfiẓ's poetry and, finally, in the fourth part, Isti'lāmī speaks about miscellaneous issues and his method for compiling the *ghazal*s.

Isti'lāmī asserts that his commentary is based on the editions of Qazvīnī/Ghanī,[124] and adds that the numbers allotted to each *ghazal* are consistent with those in their edition. This commentary, I believe, is among the more reliable studies published to date. It is noteworthy that Isti'lāmī's explanations of the *ghazal*s have one structure: for each poem he provides a short paragraph of commentary summing up the gist of the *ghazal*, followed by an analysis of its key themes and terms. He divides the *ghazal*s into various types or combinations of types: gnostic (*'ārifāna*), romantic-erotic (*'āshiqāna*), etc. The commentary examines nearly every line of every *ghazal* and his explanations are very easy for the reader to understand. Isti'lāmī's commentary is composed mainly from a literary viewpoint although he also presents some mystical definitions.

Commentaries and Studies on the *Dīvān* of Ḥāfiẓ Published outside Persia

According to 'A. Nūshāhī, during a one-hundred-year period beginning in the ninth/sixteenth century, commentaries on Ḥāfiẓ reached a peak in the Punjab and Turkey.[125] He adds that during this time nine commentaries on Ḥāfiẓ, short and long, were produced in these two areas of the Muslim world.

Author's Name	**Composition Date**
Surūrī	c. 959/1558
Sham'ī (Turkey)	c. 1000/1591
Sūdī (Turkey)	c. 1006/1589
Mawlānā 'Abdullāh Khūishī Qasūrī	1106/1697
Khātmī Lāhūrī	1077/1668
Shāh Bahūl Kūl Barakī	1119/1710
Badr al-Dīn Akbarābādī	1254/1845
Yusif 'Alī Shāh Chashtī Nizāmī (Punjab)	1307/1897

Below, I examine the two best known and, I believe, most important commentaries, those by Sūdī and Lāhūrī.[126]

Sūdī

One of the most important, although not the most scholarly, commentaries on the *Dīvān* of Ḥāfiẓ is that of Sūdī (d. 1006/1589). The foreword of this four-volume book was written by Saʿīd Nafisī; in it, he gives a brief account of Sūdī's origins. According to Nafisī, Sūdī was originally from Bosnia, but spent most of his life in Turkey.[127] He adds that his commentary on Ḥāfiẓ was published almost three hundred years ago and that he wrote other commentaries on the works of Rūmī and Saʿdī.

This commentary begins with the first *ghazal* in the *Dīvān*, explaining the first verse and stating that it originally belonged to Yazīd b. Muʿāwīya:

انا المسموم ما عندی بترياق ولاراق　　ادرکاسا و ناولها الا يا ايها الساقی[128]

O Sāqī, pass the bowl around,
For I am poisoned and in need of an antidote!

Sūdī presents evidence to support his claim and further states that the poet also used the second verse, changing its original arrangement, as the first verse of a *ghazal* in his own *Dīvān*. He presents a couple of verses by Ahlī Shīrāzī as illustrative evidence for this statement:

خواجه حافظ را شبی دیدم به خواب　　گفتم ای در فضل و دانش بی حساب
از چه بستی بر خود این شعر یزید　　با وجود اینهمه فضل و کمال[129]

I saw Khwaja Ḥāfiẓ in my dream one night.
I said to him: 'You, who have endless knowledge and wisdom,

Why did you use this verse from Yazīd
With all that wisdom you possess?'

A poem from Kātibī Nishābūrī is presented as further evidence:

عجب در حیرتم از خواجه حافظ　　بنوعی کش خرد زان عاجز آید
چه حکمت دید درشعر یزید او　　که در دیوان نخست از وی سر آید[130]

I am awed by Khawja Ḥāfiẓ,
In a way that reason cannot comprehend.

What wisdom did he perceive in Yazīd's verse,
To make him make his own *Dīvān* begin with a verse by him?

There are interpretations of 569 *ghazals* in the four volumes produced by Sūdī. Each *ghazal* is broken into couplets (*bayt*) with a minimum of two to six, and sometimes even eight lines of explanation given. Sūdī named this interpretation 'the couplet's sense' (*maḥsūl-i bayt*).

In some instances Sūdī explains various key words employed by Ḥāfiẓ, such as, to take the case of the first *ghazal*, love (*'ishq*), ease (*āsān*) and difficulty (*mushkil*), etc. In addition, verses by other poets are presented to the reader as illustrative evidence of a particular word's meaning or the meaning of a theme. On the top left-hand side of each *ghazal*, the metres of the particular poem are recorded.

Sūdī's commentary, although one of the oldest and most venerable available, today is viewed as somewhat antiquated and thus considered unreliable by many scholars of Ḥāfiẓology. In my opinion, it is not necessary to break down the *ghazals* and produce so many pages (2,890 in total) in order to explain the verses of Ḥāfiẓ. As Khurramshāhī stated, this kind of work can do more harm than good, as the message to the reader is that Ḥāfiẓ's poems are incomprehensible. In agreement with Khurramshāhī, I believe that each *ghazal* has a character of its own, and in order to understand the words of Ḥāfiẓ fully, one must analyze the *ghazals* as a total unit rather than decipher and interpret the poem as if it were composed of independent verses.

According to Khurramshāhī, Sūdī's commentary is detailed but has many flaws, in particular, it has a number of grammatical errors. In fact, given that many better scholarly commentaries have been produced over the past sixty years, in many respects Sūdī's work is now quite dated. Sūdī's saving grace may be in the exhaustive quantity of detail he provides, an amount of detail seldom found in other commentaries.[131]

Abū'l-Ḥasan 'Abd al-Rahmān Khātmī Lāhūrī

One of the most credible and complete commentaries on Ḥāfiẓ is the four-volume book entitled, *Sharḥ-i 'irfānī-i ghazalhā-yi Ḥāfiẓ* (*A Mystical Commentary on Ḥāfiẓ's Dīvān*) by Abū'l-Ḥasan 'Abd al-Raḥmān Khātmī Lāhūrī.[132]

It was originally written in India in the seventeenth century and an introduction was added by its editors, Bahā' al-Dīn Khurramshāhī, Kūrush

Manṣūrī and Ḥusayn Muṭīʿī-Amīn.[133] By examining the whole of this four-volume commentary and comparing it with those similar in scope, such as the works of Sūdī and Istiʿlāmī, one can perceive vast differences between them. Just like Sūdī and Istiʿlāmī, Lāhūrī breaks down the structure of each *ghazal* and presents a detailed explanation for each verse, also giving the whole of the *ghazal* at the beginning of the commentary on each poem (with variant readings of verses in Khānlarī's edition recorded in notes added by the editors). As in the two commentaries, this book also contains verses from other poets as evidence of statements, while explaining the verses in great detail. Lāhūrī's commentary is entirely Sufi and mystical in its approach.

In some instances, Lāhūrī goes into great detail, defining a verse over four pages. The commentary on the first *ghazal* in the *Dīvān* occupies fifteen pages in total.[134] However, after comparing the *ghazal*s in this commentary with the editions by Qazvīnī/Ghanī and Khānlarī, I encountered a number of discrepancies in the length of the *ghazal*s, because Qazvīnī/Ghanī and Khānlarī unaccountably excluded some verses with no apparent reason or justification. For example, the following *ghazal*, named as the twentieth *ghazal* (*ghazal-i bistum*), begins with this verse:

بی مهر رخت چشم مرا نور نماندست وز عمر مرا جز شب دیجور نماندست[135]

Without the sun of your face, the light has left my eye,
And of my life, except a dark night, there is nothing left.

The following verses were excluded from the original *ghazal* recorded by Qazvīnī/Ghanī and Khānlarī, and although the authors state in the footnote that there was an exclusion, they do not offer any reason.

هنگام وداع تو زبس گریه که کردم   دور از رخ تو چشم مرا نور نماندست
صبر است مرا چارهٔ هجران تو لیکن   چون صبر توان کرد که مقدور نماندست

I cried so much at the time of your departure,
Away from your countenance, the light of my eye is gone.

The cure for my separation is patience, but
How can I be patient, when I am not able?

In my opinion this commentary is one of the best I have so far examined – despite its exclusively mystical approach. As Ḥāfiẓ says:

فکر معقول بفرما گل بی خار کجاست؟

Think about it rationally: Tell me, where is a flower free of thorns?

In the course of interviewing Khurramshāhī, I asked for his opinion about this particular commentary. He stated:

I can only say that Professor Manūchihr Murtaḍavī, the prominent Ḥāfiẓ researcher at the Tabriz University, approved this book and greatly encouraged me [to use it], emphasizing that it is a very valuable scholarly work and therefore should be appreciated. Anyway, if you ask me: Which one is the best? I must say that I do not know! This is an impossible question to answer.[136]

Conclusion

According to Khurramshāhī, Ḥāfiẓ's literary works are the result of the 500 years of poetry that came before him. In turn, Ḥāfiẓ affected the poets who have followed him, and no doubt will continue to influence those who have yet to come. Ḥāfiẓ did not compose lyrics like other poets; instead, he blended his poetry with his culture and wrote with reason and intelligence.[137] Khurramshāhī adds that the readers of Ḥāfiẓ's poetry are divided into two different categories: serious researchers and ordinary readers.[138]

In recent years, commentaries such as those by Khurramshāhī, Hiravī, Istiʿlāmī, Khāliqī and others have greatly enhanced the field of Ḥāfiẓology. Sūdī's commentary, in comparison with the most recent ones published in Iran, differs greatly in terms of meaning and the resolution of key issues and difficulties in understanding Ḥāfiẓ's language. Ḥāfiẓ's poetry is, on the surface, easily understood; however, most verses in the *Dīvān* have deeper meanings that can be gleaned from more detailed examinations of ambiguous terms and phrases. All contemporary scholars address these deeper issues by offering their own interpretations, which have various degrees of originality, depth and scope of scholarly insight. In the vast majority of cases, their interpretations are more or less the same, with very few distinctions in meaning and idiom.

Although some authors have gone into great detail in their interpretation of verses, and others have limited their interpretation to only a few paragraphs, the overall conclusions are quite consistent. A noteworthy aspect of recent commentaries is the scholarly manner in which research has generally been conducted; one rarely comes across any recently published commentary with a low standard of interpretation. On the contrary, I have found solid explanations of the verses supported by reasonable evidence and adequate research.

While commentary on the poetry of Ḥāfiẓ has vastly improved with regard to literary concepts, the mystical and symbolic context of his language remains a hotly debated topic among scholars. In my opinion, to date there has not been an adequate commentary on the *Dīvān* that interprets both literal and mystical meanings, the symbolic dimension of the language of Ḥāfiẓ and the enigmas voiced by both. This is a problem that can only be addressed by a scholar versed in both dimensions. Such a scholar has yet to appear and such a commentary has yet to be written.

I believe the future of Ḥāfiẓology is bright; scholars and researchers are motivated to conduct ever broader research on the subject. The works of contemporary scholars continue to shed light on the language and thought of Ḥāfiẓ. We are indebted to scholars such as Khurramshāhī, Hiravī, Anjavī, Kadkanī, Murtaḍavī and many others who tirelessly continue their research to unlock the mystery of the poetic language of Ḥāfiẓ.

Yet even with the vast improvements in the research of Ḥāfiẓology, as one can see from the present book, the study of Ḥāfiẓ's poetry remains a problematic and lengthy undertaking. Any commentary on Ḥāfiẓ must rely on his verses and, therefore, to produce a dependable academic commentary on Ḥāfiẓ, scholars must have on hand a completely reliable and accurately edited text of the *Dīvān*, which to date does not exist. While some more scholarly and accurate editions have been produced over the last sixty years, none of these have provided the student with a reliable text which is even relatively flawless.

CHAPTER VI

Conclusion

Our foregoing survey of the reception of the poetry of Ḥāfiẓ in Iran during the nineteenth and twentieth centuries raises many issues. Despite the wide chronological sweep of the historical and literary ground covered in the research, several questions remain to be resolved. These can be roughly narrowed down to the following seven outstanding issues.

First, one may ask, what progress, if any, has been made towards producing a good critical edition of Ḥāfiẓ's poetry over the last two hundred years?

Secondly, which are the best editions of the *Dīvān* compiled and printed during the latter part of the last century, and what key approaches and what consensus exists among scholars about the principles that should govern the compilation of a critical edition of Ḥāfiẓ's *Dīvān*?

Third, in light of the material reviewed in this study, what future directions should Ḥāfiẓology take?

Fourth, what advantages does understanding Ḥāfiẓ have for Persians, and precisely what relationship do Persian readers have with their own tradition of Ḥāfiẓology?

Fifth and sixth are the issue of the reception history of Ḥāfiẓ during the Qājār and Pahlavi period (the subject of chapters III and IV). This raises two key questions: What was Ḥāfiẓ's impact on the seven poets of Qājār Persia and the five poets of Pahlavi Persia discussed above?

Seventh and last, exactly what original contributions does this book make to the study of the poetic legacy of Ḥāfiẓ?

Each of these questions will be carefully considered and answered to the best of my ability below.

What progress, if any, has been made towards producing a good critical edition of Ḥāfiẓ's poetry over the last two hundred years?

Scholars have long been aware of the value and need for accurate research works on the poetry of Ḥāfiẓ. Because Ḥāfiẓ did not personally compile and collate his *Dīvān* during his lifetime, later researchers and admirers have been tasked with the compilation of his poetry. The editions that have reached us today contain numerous discrepancies, and thus there is a need for serious research into the language and variant readings of his lyrics. The editions outlined in the foregoing chapter are useful to the researcher of Ḥāfiẓ's poetry. Although many credible editions are available, they are not without flaws and considerable errors and although tremendous effort has been made to overcome such problems, this task is far from complete. Much further research is necessary. No poet in Iran has been discussed, debated or written about as much as Ḥāfiẓ. Current research continues to change our understanding of Ḥāfiẓ, even in comparison with what we knew fifty years ago. But while the quantity of research on Ḥāfiẓ is great, the quality does not always meet current academic standards. According to Khurramshāhī, there is much work that needs to be done in an academic and scholarly fashion.[1]

How should a scholar approach the task of publishing a correct edition of the *Dīvān*? How should he choose between so many editions and how should he know which poems are authentic and which ones are not? Should he base his work on copies that contain more verses, or less, or on whichever versions please him more? According to Muḥammad Qazvīnī, the only certain way a scholar can approach such a task is to go as far back to the time of the author as possible. He would then have to study the manuscripts that survived from the period of the poet and his contemporaries.

Qazvīnī emphasizes that anyone with an interest in the *Dīvān* of Ḥāfiẓ who is keen to research his poetry must eventually refer to other manuscripts. The scholar's research should preferably include a comparison of the most ancient and relatively recent handwritten manuscripts in order to determine their authenticity; the researcher would doubtless realize that no two copies of the *Dīvān* are identical and that such discrepancies are apparent in the quantity, quality and meaning of the verses.

Scholars are still far from reaching their common goal of compiling an authoritative collection of Ḥāfiẓ's poetry. Though this problem may never be solved, we may establish a good, accurate and reliable edition of Ḥāfiẓ's *Dīvān* which bears fewer errors than other editions available to date.[2]

Muḥammad Qazvīnī contends that the manuscripts published after the fifteenth century are more reliable than more recent manuscripts;[3] however, when they are studied closely, one can see that the number of *ghazal*s in the earliest manuscripts does not exceed 500, and in some cases, they do not even reach that figure. For instance, the edition of ʻAbdul Raḥīm Khalkhālī, which is based on notes and handwritten evidence made no later than thirty-five years after the death of Ḥāfiẓ, comprises only 496 *ghazal*s, one of which is repeated (*ghazal* 365); this leaves a total of 495.[4] In the manuscripts written during the fourteenth and fifteenth centuries, the number of *ghazal*s often exceeds 500. As one moves further away in time from Ḥāfiẓ's era, the number of *ghazal*s grows even higher. By the end of the fifteenth century, some editions contain over 600 *ghazal*s, thus over the course of two centuries roughly 100 *ghazal*s were added (we cannot know if they were added to the *Dīvān* arbitrarily or with intent). This increase, however, seems to have stopped around the end of the fifteenth-century or beginning of the sixteenth-century.

In a two-hour personal interview that I conducted with Iran's leading Ḥāfiẓologist, Bahā' al-Dīn Khurramshāhī, I enquired about his opinion concerning the progress that has been made in establishing a critical edition of the *Dīvān*. He commented that 'the earliest reference here is that of Qudsī; although we cannot be sure of the methods he used in his edition. Nevertheless, it can be referred to as a fairly reliable edition'.[5]

All in all, much progress has been made towards producing a good critical edition of the *Dīvān* during the last two hundred years; yet while the achievements are noteworthy, much research remains to be done. Ultimately, a completely reliable commentary on the *Dīvān* cannot be written, nor a totally accurate understanding of the language of Ḥāfiẓ obtained, while there are yet inaccuracies in the text of his poems, and this problem has no solution because Ḥāfiẓ did not compile his own work. What we have in our possession today, although partly accurate, includes verses that remain dubious; in many instances some words have been changed and replaced with different words, even in a single verse, transmitting a totally different meaning. These changes bring into question the lifestyle and the character of the poet. One such example, given below, clearly illustrates the discrepancies among the most prominent scholars such as Qazvīnī/Ghanī and Khānlarī. Cases such as these raise many unanswered questions:

Dīvān-i Ḥāfiẓ, ed. Khānlarī, *ghazal* 223:

حافظ خلوت نشین دوش به میخانه شد   از سر پیمان برفت با سر پیمانه شد[6]

Ḥāfiẓ the recluse last night went to the wine-shop:
From thought of the pledge he went to contemplating the cup.[7]

Dīvān-i Ḥāfiẓ, ed. Qazvīnī/Ghanī, *ghazal* 170:

زاهد خلوت نشین دوش به میخانه شد   از سر پیمان برفت با سر پیمانه شد[8]

Ascetic the recluse last night went to the wine-shop:
From thought of the pledge he went to contemplating the cup.[9]

Which are the best editions of the *Dīvān* compiled and printed during the latter part of the last century?

The following scholars have produced, in my opinion, the principal and most important editions of Ḥāfiẓ during the past hundred years:

1. ʿAbdul Raḥīm Khalkhālī, ed., *Dīvān-i Khawja Ḥāfiẓ Shīrāzī*, 1306/1927
2. Mir Sayyid Muḥammad Qudsī, ed., *Dīvān-i Ḥāfiẓ-i Qudsī*, 1314/1935
3. Ḥusayn Pizhmān Bakhtīyārī, ed., *Dīvān-i Khawja Shams al-Dīn Muḥammad Ḥāfiẓ Shīrāzī*, 1315/1937
4. Muḥammad Qazvīnī and Qāsim Ghanī, ed., *Dīvān-i Ḥāfiẓ*, 1320/1942
5. Khānlarī, ed., *Dīvān-i Ḥāfiẓ Khawja Shams al-Dīn Muḥammad*, 1362/1983
6. Salīm Naysārī, ed., *Daftar-i dīgarsānīhā dar ghazalhā-yi Ḥāfiẓ*, 1371/1992
7. Injavī Shīrāzī, ed., *Dīvān-i Khawja Ḥāfiẓ Shīrāzī*, 1371/1992
8. Hūshang Ibtihāj (Sāya), ed., *Ḥāfiẓ bi saʿyi Sāya*, 1372/1993

According to Shahram Pazouki,

> One of the most outstanding scholarly works undertaken on the edition of the *Dīvān* is that of Qazvīnī/Ghanī. However, with regard to the accuracy of the scholarship, I would assert that the work of Khānlarī is superior. It is regrettable that this work [of editing Ḥāfiẓ's *Dīvān*] has not been undertaken by a scholar and mystic; this is a fundamental problem in the area of Ḥāfiẓology and in mystical literature in general.

> In other words, we do not have an edition by a scholar who was also a mystic, who could edit and undertake an accurate correction of the *Dīvān*. They have all been academic scholars and men of letters, but none have been mystics. This is the fundamental weakness facing our literature today.[10]

Dr. Pazouki makes a very important point, that we do not have a critical edition of the *Dīvān* by a mystic scholar. This issue has always been a problem in the field of Ḥāfiẓology and, in my opinion, will only be resolved when such an edition is produced by a scholar with a background in Islamic mysticism.

Regarding the edition of Īnjavī Shīrāzī, I concur with Khurramshāhī's opinion that 'although his research has no solid base, it is a fairly good edition.'[11] Likewise, in respect to Naysārī's edition, I agree with his opinion that Naysārī's criticisms of the Qazvīnī and Ghanī edition are largely spurious and 'although some of his critical views are not without foundation, many of them cannot be justified.'[12]

In my opinion, Khalkhālī's edition has considerable merit because he used manuscripts close to the time of the poet and heavily relied on sources written just thirty-five years after Ḥāfiẓ's death. Likewise, Qudsī's edition is very important for the student of Ḥāfiẓ's *Dīvān* because Qudsī employed the same method as Khalkhālī and further expanded his research by including numerous additional manuscripts. As noted in chapter v, the edition by Pizhmān Bakhtīyārī is one of the best available today because Bakhtīyārī, unlike Qudsī and Khalkhālī, was himself a poet as well as a scholar. Thus, he was a highly-qualified editor, able to analyze the verses in each *ghazal* and correct any discrepancies that might be invisible to the untrained eye.

With regard to more recent progress on publishing a better edition of the *Dīvān*, Khurramshāhī, when I interviewed him, sagely commented:

> Now we speak of the past twenty years. After much hardship and effort, Ibtihāj produced a very good edition, on which I wrote a critical review expressing my appreciation and approval. However, to answer your original question, regarding which is the best edition so far, I must say that there is no such thing yet, although I can name some that are best so far [...] Naysārī, Sāya, Qazvīnī and Ghanī and Khānlarī [...]. Each of these researchers and scholars have worked almost fifty-odd years to achieve what has been produced [...].[13]

According to the earlier statements presented in chapter v, the most accurate edition of the *Dīvān*, in my opinion, are respectively those of Qazvīnī/Ghanī and Khānlarī. A further edition worthy of mention is that of Sāya; most contemporary scholars approve this edition for the simple reason that Sāya is a scholar and a poet himself and thus better qualified to evaluate and juxtapose verses, identify any flaws and discrepancies. Although his edition is based on that of Khalkhālī and Qazvīnī/Ghanī, I consider it an improvement on their versions. As Pazouki stated earlier, the one problem in producing a better edition of the *Dīvān* is the lack of a scholar versed in Islamic mysticism or Sufism.

The other problem is that, with the exception of Qazvīnī/Ghanī's, most editions have been produced by only one scholar. I believe that the only certain way to produce a better edition of the *Dīvān* is to involve more than one or two scholars. A few scholars who are experts in Ḥāfiẓology with different points of view about Ḥāfiẓ's poetry would be able to produce a superior edition. For example, Khurramshāhī believes that the edition produced by Sāya is fairly good, for the reasons already mentioned, and Pazouki believes in that of Qazvīnī/Ghanī, while Meisamī believes in that of Bakhtīyārī and also Qazvīnī/Ghanī. If scholars share their views and come to agreement about various points that continue to pose problems in the *ghazal*s of Ḥāfiẓ and work to solve such obstacles, then an excellent edition of the *Dīvān* could certainly be produced. In this respect, there is a general consensus among scholars that the key factor to collating a correct edition lies in reference to the oldest manuscripts, those nearest in time to the poet, and that these should be relied on more than any other evidence. Likewise, another important point of agreement among scholars today is that the number of *ghazal*s should not exceed 500; in general there is a consensus that Ḥāfiẓ did not compose more than 500 *ghazal*s. The final problem scholars face is the mystical aspect of the verses of Ḥāfiẓ, which, as mentioned before, has still not been resolved.

What future directions should Ḥāfiẓology take, in light of the material reviewed in this study?

There seems to be no end to the subject of Ḥāfiẓology. According to Āshūrī, this is due to the talent and greatness of Ḥāfiẓ, who immersed himself in the language and the culture of the nation to such an extent that they became inseparable.[14] Ḥāfiẓ intoxicated millions with his utterances, and it can certainly be said that his admirers, who are quite sensitive, value his words as a sacred text. Muḥammad Muʿīn, in an article in the *Kilk* journal, expands on this passion: 'Ever since I was a child and learnt to read and write I became intoxicated with Ḥāfiẓ's language.' He adds: 'I did not fully understand the meaning of his words at the time; however, I enjoyed the sweetness of his words very much.' In a poem that Muʿīn composed in praise of Ḥāfiẓ he admires this superior poet and the importance of his influence on the language and culture of Iran.[15]

According to Khurramshāhī, while the corrections and commentaries on the *Dīvān* of Ḥāfiẓ have vastly improved, he adds,

> When I first started to work on my book, all I had to work on was the commentary of Sūdī and that of Dārābī, and whenever I encountered a problem I had no idea where to start in solving it. My task was very difficult, bearing in mind that Sūdī's commentary has many flaws, especially with regard to Persian grammar. The future of Ḥāfiẓology, in my opinion, lies in such works as the one Jāvid has accomplished, [producing] single and multiple volumes. However, I sincerely do not see a need for multi-volume works. I do not believe in such works because, in order to complete them, one must write commentaries in prose on every single verse; this makes no sense. If we make such an attempt, do you know what it means? It means Ḥāfiẓ makes no sense, for if he did, there would be no need for such worthless effort. This would mean that Ḥāfiẓ's *ghazal*s do not make sense as a whole with their full structure intact and that, therefore, there is a need to break them down and explain them one by one.[16]

Here Khurramshāhī refers to his book entitled *Ḥāfiẓ-nāma*, first published in 1366/1987 in Tehran. The book makes various references to key difficult words in the *ghazal*s of Ḥāfiẓ, explaining the difficult phrases and verses in his *Dīvān*. He also mentions the work produced by Hāshim Jāvid, a book that also addresses key difficult words in the *ghazal*s of Ḥāfiẓ, while ignoring the rest of the *ghazal*. It is entitled *Ḥāfiẓ-i Jāvid (Eternal Ḥāfiẓ)* and is much like that of *Ḥāfiẓ-nāma* by Khurramshāhī.[17] After studying this book it is clear that the editor has used many previously published editions to juxtapose and compare different variations – editions such as that of Khalkhālī, Khānlarī, Nāʾīnī, Viṣāl, Naysārī, Ayuḍī, Bihrūz and Sāya.

Khurramshāhī then continued:

> There is a book recently published by Dr. K. Ḥasanlī: *Rāhnamā-yi mūḍū-ʿī-yi Ḥāfiẓ Pazhūhī* (*A Thematic Guide to Ḥāfiẓology*) which is a very important book; it contains 130,000 subjects that the scholars of Ḥāfiẓology have worked on during the past century. I see the future of Ḥāfiẓology in such new criticism. It is said that authors must be considered dead. It is the text we have to concentrate on; we must admire the writing not the writer. It must also be said that all scholars claim that they speak from the tongue of Ḥāfiẓ, but this is not at all the case. Like Mr. Āshūrī, it is their own tongues they speak from, not Ḥāfiẓ's. Another point concerns the massive gap in the world of Ḥāfiẓology – the biography of Ḥāfiẓ. I am very well aware of the fact that we do not have accurate data on his biography, however, we can still extract some factual points about the poet, even by studying Gulandām's introduction. For example, I have written an article based on Gulandām's records, stating which books Ḥāfiẓ used to read. Of course, at some point we have to make guesses about some parts of such a biography, but this guesswork can be based on factual clues and starting points. Moreover, we also need a good dictionary of his key words, words mostly used in his poetry, not in the general literature of Persia.[18]

Contrary to Khurramshāhī's view, as far as the biography of Ḥāfiẓ is concerned, I believe the two-volume biography of Ḥāfiẓ by Muʿīn *Ḥāfiẓ-i shirīn sukhan* (The Sweet Spoken Ḥāfiẓ) is a fairly accurate book of the life and times of Ḥāfiẓ. The other is one produced by Ghanī, entitled *Tārīkh-i ʿaṣr-i Ḥāfiẓ* (The History of Ḥāfiẓ's Time), which is also valuable in introducing Ḥāfiẓ to his admirers and researchers, and finally, there is one written by Zarrinkūb, entitled *Az kūcha-yi rindān* (From the Alley of the Libertines). These scholarly works, although not perfect, are very valuable to the field of Ḥāfiẓology and in my opinion, very useful to researchers.

It should also be noted that, although many edited *Dīvān*s of Ḥāfiẓ have been published to date, and many opinions have been expressed, there is still an enormous gap in the academic study of Ḥāfiẓ. In comparison with western literature and research undertaken on western poets such as Shakespeare, Dante, Homer and so on, the study of Ḥāfiẓ is still in its infancy! In this regard, I would draw attention to the following learned comments from Dr. Meisami, who I questioned about the issue. She answered me as follows:

> I think it will probably go on as much as it has done in the past, with debates as to whether Ḥāfiẓ was, or was not, a 'mystical poet'. (In my opinion, he was not, although mystical themes and images infuse his poetry, as they do most of the poetry of the period. This is a stylistic issue, but has seldom been addressed as such.) There will always be the search for 'new' or 'earlier' manuscripts; they don't add much to our knowledge of Ḥāfiẓ's poetry, although they may shed light on the transmission and reception of that poetry – again, an issue which has received little discussion. There has been little study of how the poems work to convey their meaning; this is a field just waiting for a breakthrough. (I've tried, but my efforts seem to have fallen on deaf ears.) I suppose there will always be a 'cult of Ḥāfiẓ' (just as there is a 'cult of Rumi', or a 'cult of Khayyam'). Ḥāfiẓ needs to be studied in (a) the context of the poetic production of his time (including religious, social and political circumstances surrounding that poetry), and (b) in relation to the literary tradition on which he so creatively draws.[19]

In light of the above information and the views of various prominent scholars based on the editions of the *Dīvān* discussed here – and considering that each edition is the result of decades of hard work and research – in addition to the fact that each of these editions has something completely different and new to offer the researcher, I believe that the future of Ḥāfiẓology is much brighter than it was a hundred years ago. However, I also strongly believe that this task should be encouraged by governments; financial and moral support for those scholars who work tirelessly to produce better and more accurate versions of the *Dīvān* should be provided without hesitation. In agreement with Dr. Meisami, I believe there has been little research undertaken on how the poems convey their meaning in the field of Ḥāfiẓology. As I have shown in this research, the legacy of Ḥāfiẓ is to be found in the poets, both past and present, both Persian and non-Persian (western or from other oriental civilizations) who revered and imitated him. So the future of Ḥāfiẓology is a living and dynamic movement of ideas that is inseparable from the future of Persian poetry and poetics. There is probably a whole field of Ḥāfiẓ studies waiting to be inaugurated by novelists writing historical novels on his life and times.

There may also be a field of Ḥāfiẓ studies related to the art of music (operas based on his *ghazal*s, etc.) and dramatists who will write plays about him. The field of Ḥāfiẓ commentaries is a sub-field of Ḥāfiẓology which remains unexplored, particularly given that commentaries on the

Dīvān, especially those written in India and the Ottoman empire, remain in unpublished manuscript form. The mystical dimension (*ʿirfān*, *taṣawwuf* and so forth) of Ḥāfiẓ's imagery and symbolism has not been adequately expounded (*cf.* Pazouki's remarks) and understood, so this remains a future field of study.

What advantages does understanding Ḥāfiẓ have for Persians and what relationship do Persian readers have with their own tradition of Ḥāfiẓology?

The most important subject in Ḥāfiẓ's language is the language of love; it is love that he invites us to seek and cherish, for it is the only tool one needs for self-purification. During the seventh/fourteenth century, Ḥāfiẓ warned us about religious fanaticism and the danger of extremism, and today the people of Iran appreciate Ḥāfiẓ's views on this aspect perhaps more than anything else, for they realize the ecumenical truth embedded in Ḥāfiẓ's poetry. In this book, I have shown how Ḥāfiẓ's language is blended with the Persian language and the Persian people in an unbreakable bond. Ḥāfiẓ is part of the Iranian tradition and is considered a national treasure. He is the representative of the Iranian heritage and the keeper of the Persian language. By understanding his verses and, better still, his school of thought, we can move towards understanding not only what is quintessentially 'Iranian' but what is quintessentially poetic about the Persian language. In Khurramshāhī's words: 'Anyone with the slightest familiarity with Persian poetry is under Ḥāfiẓ's influence. No one has been able to escape this fact, and I daresay, reality.'[20]

In addition to Khurramshāhī's observation, I would add that Ḥāfiẓ's influence on Persian poetry is not only limited to the poetry, but also includes the very fibre of the Persian language as well. 'Ḥāfiẓ's *Dīvān* holds the same status for the Persian-speaking people as does the Holy Qurʾān among Muslims.'[21] Ferdowsi asserts that the *Dīvān*, like the holy Qurʾān, is impervious to the depredation of time; it is a book, moreover, whose equivalent can never be produced.[22] This union of the Qurʾān and the *Dīvān* is a result of the mystical communion between the poet and the nation, for which Hazhir offers the following explanation:

> It must be said that Ḥāfiẓ is an abstract existence and a pure spirit which is either created by blending all the souls of all the vivacious

> (*zinda dil*) Iranians, or is divided before birth and after death by nature, with the parts implanted in the hearts of various individuals, making them masters of awareness and purification (*maʿrifat va kamāl*). In the terminology of the mystics who see unity in plurality, we can say that Ḥāfiẓ is no one but the Iranian nation that is unified in one entity, and the Iranian nation is the same Ḥāfiẓ who is manifested as a plurality.[23]

With regard to the relationship that Persian readers have with their tradition, I would note that when Persians read the poetry of Ḥāfiẓ, they connect it not only to their traditional culture and literature, but with the current sociopolitical situation of Iran. In other words, Ḥāfiẓ's wise verse-adages still remain (as they have for the past six centuries) very much part and parcel of every man and woman's inner life, his poems capable of representing both the timeless ethical values and expressing the temporal political views of ordinary Iranians.

The reception history of Ḥāfiẓ during the Qājār and Pahlavi period

Fifth and sixth, I would like to examine the impact of Ḥāfiẓ on the poets of nineteenth- and twentieth-century Persia in general and his impact on the seven poets of Zand and Qājār Persia (discussed in chapter III) and the five poets of Pahlavi Persia (discussed in chapter IV) in particular. The transformation of Persian poetry that took place between 1797 and 1979 coincided with the start of the neoclassical school. Almost all the poets of this period, such as Mijmar, Ṣabā Kāshānī, Yaghmā Jandaqī, Basṭāmī and others revived the Khurāsānī and ʿIrāqī styles. Here only two examples of this sort of verse may be cited

نیک چون می نگرم، هست خیال تو زمن　　　شادمانم که همه شب بتو گرم سخنم[24]

When I focus, I see your image within me,
Happy I am that every night I speak with you!

زیبا شود به کارگه عشق کار من　　　هرگه نظر به صورت زیبا کنم ترا[25]

Every time I look at your beautiful face,
I shall have a beautiful portrait in the workshop of love!

The major influence on neoclassical poetry was the power of religion, specifically, Sufi mysticism, which was usually the main subject matter in the poetry of the neoclassical period. Poets such as Nishāṭ, Ṣafī ʿAlī Shāh and Sabzivārī continued to compose mystical verses, many inspired by Ḥāfiẓ. A few examples highly typical of this tendency may be cited here:

به کس نیاز ندارم به خویش نیز مگر   یکی خدا و یکی سایهٔ خدای من است[26]

I need no one, nor do I need myself,
God alone and God's shadow suffice.

تصوف نیست آن کز وی نشانی   توان دادن بتعریف و بیانی[27]

Sufism is not something from which indication can be given
By way of explanation or exposition

آب حیوان که خضر زندهٔ جاوید از اوست   هست یک قطره ای از چشمهٔ جان پرور عشق[28]

The water of life from which 'Khizr' found immortality,
Is only a drop in comparison to the reviving fountain of love!

As was demonstrated in chapter III, poets such as Sabzivārī were inspired by Ḥāfiẓ and continued to benefit from his wisdom and style of poetry throughout their lives. None of the poets mentioned in this book would take exception to Sabzivārī's *ghazal*:

هزاران آفرین بر جان حافظ   همه غرقیم در احسان حافظ
ز هفتم آسمان غیب آمد   لسان الغیب اندر شان حافظ
پیمبر نیست لیکن نسخ کرده   اساطیر همه، دیوان حافظ
چه دیوان کز سپهرش رجم دیوان!   نموده کوکب رخشان حافظ
هر آن دعوی کند سحر حلال است   دلیل ساطع البرهان حافظ
ایا غواص دریای حقیقت   چه گوهر هاست در عمان حافظ
نه تنها آن و حسنش در نظر هست   طریقت با حقیقت آن حافظ
بیا اسرار تا ما بر فشانیم   دل و جان در ره دربان حافظ
ببند اسرار لب را چون ندارد   سخن پایانی، اندر شان حافظ[29]

A thousand praises upon the spirit of Ḥāfiẓ,
We are all drowned in the beneficence of Ḥāfiẓ!

He has come from the seventh heaven of mysteries,
The name 'tongue of the mysteries' truly suits Ḥāfiẓ.

He is not a prophet, yet the previous myths and fables
Have been abrogated by the *Dīvān* of Ḥāfiẓ...

What a *Dīvān*! For from his heaven the demons,
Have been driven away by the radiant star of Ḥāfiẓ.
Whatever claim he makes is lawful as the white magic [of poetry]
The tangible proof of which is [the verse of] Ḥāfiẓ...

O you who are a diver in the sea of truth,
How many jewels rest in the ocean of Ḥāfiẓ!

Not only do we still regard his mystery-of-beauty and loveliness,
The Sufi path and the divine reality are the mystery-of-beauty of Ḥāfiẓ.

Come 'Asrār' let us sacrifice
Heart and soul at the path of the door-keeper of Ḥāfiẓ,

Seal your lips and remain silent, O 'Asrār',
For there is no end to the praising of Ḥāfiẓ.

While the proportion of imitation of Ḥāfiẓ varies from poet to poet, it is evident that all the poets studied in chapter III emulated our poet from Shīrāz to some degree. Below I will summarize some of the conclusions concerning the poetry of Ādhar, Yaghmā, Viṣāl, Qā'ānī and Basṭāmī from chapter III.

Ādhar closely imitates Ḥāfiẓ in one-sixth of his *Dīvān*. In his *ghazal*s, we encounter similar wording, style and rhyme. In addition, he emulated Ḥāfiẓ when writing of his strife with the hypocritical puritan ascetics. Mijmar, like many other poets of his period, generally followed Ḥāfiẓ in style, although less so in *ghazal* writing. There is some evidence of his imitation of Ḥāfiẓ in rhyme and meaning, and in themes in his *Dīvān* that are frequently similar.

In examining Viṣāl's *Dīvān*, we see that almost a quarter of his poems are similar to those of Ḥāfiẓ. Another contemporary poet, Qā'ānī Shīrāzī, was greatly influenced by Ḥāfiẓ when writing his lyric poetry. In some of Qā'ānī's verses, we can see imitations of rhyme and meaning. In examining his *Dīvān*, one-fifth of his poems are clearly similar to those of Ḥāfiẓ. Another mystical poet of this era, Furūghī Basṭāmī, followed Ḥāfiẓ in the sphere of meaning and rhyme. With regard to mysticism, he imitated Ḥāfiẓ by using similar mystical statements and themes. Clearly, over a quarter of his verses are similar to those written by Ḥāfiẓ. He also reflects the works of Ḥāfiẓ in his love poems and criticism of hypocrisy.

Yaghmā Jandaqī, who died fourteen years after Viṣāl Shīrāzī, was influenced by Ḥāfiẓ both in meaning and rhyme and this can be plainly observed in his collection of poems. In his hostility towards clerics, he uses Ḥāfiẓ's style to deliver his message and nearly a quarter of his *ghazal*s are similar to those of Ḥāfiẓ. His mystical language is also similar.

Throughout the history of Persian literature, classical poetry reflecting the ideas of the old masters was virtually always deemed superior to any other form of poetry. As illustrated in chapter III and IV, as well as the Appendix to this book, the seven selected poets of the Qājār period (who largely belonged to the neoclassical school) and the five poets of the Pahlavi period (two of whom – Bahār and Shahriyār – were highly influenced by the neoclassical school) and the other poets mentioned in the Appendix followed in the steps of the classical masters, some more consistently than others. From this, we can conclude that the influence of the classical masters still prevails on the poets and poetry of Persia, so much so that it can be said to be the predominant influence. The impact Ḥāfiẓ had on the seven selected poets discussed in chapter III was astonishing. Clearly, these poets were hugely influenced by the mastery of his lyrics and utterance.

The modern poets of the new style (Nīmā, Sipihrī, Shāmlū...) from the latter half of twentieth-century Persia were also affected by Ḥāfiẓ, in spite of the fact that their form of poetry was so different. However, whether in idea, essence, style, commentary or worldview, in one way or another they all followed the classical masters. Even Nimā Yūshij, who was considered the father of New Poetry, followed Ḥāfiẓ, first in his *ghazal*s and, although he changed course, later towards the end of his life.

Ḥāfiẓ's anticlericalism continued to be an issue throughout the nineteenth and twentieth centuries and remains a topic of discussion to the present day. Many poets of the Qājār period imitated Ḥāfiẓ's language in the sphere of anticlericalism, as was demonstrated in chapter III. Ḥāfiẓ's many reflections on deceit and hypocrisy were appreciated by readers, particularly in nineteenth-century Persia, when many poets, inspired by Ḥāfiẓ, emulated his language and criticism of the ascetic and religious preachers. Poets such as Basṭāmī, Nishāṭ, Mijmar and, towards the late nineteenth-century, the likes of Īraj Mīrzā, ʿĀrif, Bahār and Sabzivārī also used the same language when writing about religion and anti-asceticism. I have given comparisons and verse similes on this issue in chapter III.

In the nineteenth century, Persian literature experienced a spectacular transformation and entered a new era. The prelude of this change was illustrated by an incident in the mid nineteenth century at the court of Nāsir al-Dīn Shāh. The Prime Minister, Amīr Kabīr, disciplined the poet Habībullāh Qāʾānī for 'lying' in a panegyric *qaṣīda* written in Amīr Kabīr's honour. Amīr Kabīr saw poetry in general, and the type of poetry that had developed during the Qājār period, as detrimental to 'progress' and 'modernization' in Iranian society, which he believed was in urgent need of change. Such concerns were also expressed by others, such as Fatḥ-ʿAlī Ākhūndzāda, Mīrzā Āqā Khān Kirmānī and Mīrzā Malkam Khān. Malkam Khan also expressed a need for a change in Persian poetry in literary terms as well, always linking it to social concerns.

The new Persian literary movement cannot be understood without an awareness of the intellectual movements in Iranian philosophical circles. The social and political climate of Persia in the late nineteenth and early twentieth centuries that led to the Persian Constitutional Revolution (*inqilāb-i mashrūṭa*) in 1906-1911, and the idea that changes in poetry were essential spread. Many argued that Persian poetry should reflect the realities of a country in transition. This idea was propagated by prominent scholars such as ʿAlī-Akbar Dihkhudā and Abū'l Qāsim ʿĀrif Qazvīnī, who challenged the traditional system of Persian poetry by introducing new content with new lexico-semantics and rhetorical structure. Dihkhudā, for instance, used a lesser-known traditional form to elegize the execution of a revolutionary journalist. ʿĀrif employed the *ghazal* to write his anthem: *Payām-i āzādī* (*Message of Freedom*).

Some researchers argue that sociopolitical ramifications of artistic changes led to the idea of poets 'as social leaders trying the limits and possibilities of social change'. An important question in modern Persian literature concerns the terms modernization and westernization – and whether these had similar meanings when describing the evolution of Iranian society. It can be argued that almost all advocates of modernism in Persian literature, from Ākhūndzāda, Kirmānī, and Malkam Khān to Dihkhudā, ʿĀrif, Bahār and Rafʿat, were inspired by the developments and changes that had occurred in western, particularly European, literature. Such inspiration did not lead to the blind imitation of western models, but rather to the adaptation of aspects of western literature.

The most important issue portrayed in the birth of 'New Poetry' was the advancement towards westernization in Iran. The evolution of new literary techniques was based on modern literary tendencies in the West after 1910; it was from the beginning of this period that contemporary Persian poets became interested in foreign literature, notably French. The translation of works from European languages into Persian and their effects on the poets of the time greatly influenced a new shift from the neoclassical movement. Furthermore, the influence of communism and anti-religious attitudes among the later New Poetry poets, such as Nimā Yūshij and Aḥmad Shāmlū, also contributed to the progression and direction of neoclassical literature towards the West, thereby expanding the potential for the New Poetry.

'Abdul Ḥusayn Zarrinkūb, a scholar in Persian literature and literary criticism and a historian, studied the works of Aḥmad Kasravī, Ṣādiq Hidāyat and many others as the wave of Iranian comparative literature and literary criticism reached a symbolic crest. This comparative literature, he notes, was influenced by Ḥāfiẓ, and reflected his style and philosophy, even in the new poetry. In some cases the poets did not realize this until many years later. There has been an extensive discussion of Ḥāfiẓ among contemporary poets with regard to the politics and literature of Pahlavi Persia. In this research, I have carefully chosen poets of the period to illustrate their differences of opinion and to demonstrate the wide gap between the views of at least one or two poets, for example, Nimā and Shahriyār. While they were contemporaries, one was more influenced by Ḥāfiẓ than the other. For example, Nimā grew up with knowledge of Ḥāfiẓ's poetry and style but, later in life, introduced a new style of poetry, though his own work continued to reflect Ḥāfiẓ's ideology and philosophy in life. The same situation was true of Shahriyār's youth. He, too, was brought up studying Ḥāfiẓ's poetry and later in life found his style, ideology, beliefs and spiritual tendency to be similar to those of Ḥāfiẓ. Likewise, Ḥāfiẓ exerted his influence on the political writings of twentieth-century poets such as Bahār, Shāmlū and Nādirpūr.

They were all patriots who despised hypocrisy, deceit, tyranny and injustice, and came to reflect Ḥāfiẓ in their behaviour, words and poetry, in both prose and poetic writings.

During the Pahlavi period, and in particular between 1940 and 1978, the subject of Ḥāfiẓology thrived due to the political and economic stability of the government. Financial aid was granted to scholars for research and there was no censure on the subject. On issues of classical Persian poetry, scholars were able to discuss and debate freely, without fear of reproach. Intellectual thought was generously shared and the government seldom interfered with the teaching of literature and poetry. Great scholars, such as Khānlarī, Muʿīn, Furūzānfar, Zarrinkūb, Hiravī and many others thrived during the period. Unfortunately, circumstances in modern day Iran are markedly different. For a millennium, Persian governments and central power were controlled by monarchs and kings; now, for the first time in the history of Persia this system has been replaced by an Islamic republic.

The policies of the current Islamic republic have had a negative impact on the study of Ḥāfiẓology because the philosophy and language of Ḥāfiẓ is anti-religious, against extremism, fundamentalists and hypocrisy. Unfortunately, many outstanding contemporary Iranian scholars who are actively studying Ḥāfiẓology have only a limited freedom of expression and the areas in which they are able to expand their research are somewhat circumscribed. Therefore, the full potential of their research remains unrealized. Until recently, the poetry of Ḥāfiẓ and ʿUmar Khayyām was forbidden in Iran and it was only because of the immense popularity of these superior poets that this prohibition was overcome.

Research in Ḥāfiẓology requires broadmindedness, not fanaticism and prejudice. There are many facets to the language of Ḥāfiẓ, the most important being the language of criticism – specifically against religious fanaticism and hypocrisy; hence, the opposition of the current government of Iran to this aspect of his verse. In my opinion, Ḥāfiẓ must be studied and interpreted with an open mind, free from prejudice. Only then can we see true progress in Ḥāfiẓology. Through the history of Persian poetry and literature, Ḥāfiẓ stands firm against dishonesty and deceit. Where there is a lack of sincerity, Ḥāfiẓ appears to defend the victims with his sharp, witty and profound language.

زاهد ار رندی حافظ نکند فهم چه شد   دیو بگریزد از آن قوم که قرآن خوانند[30]

If the ascetic does not comprehend Ḥāfiẓ as being a *rind*, what matter?
A demon flees those tribes who recite the Qur'ān!

In brief, this book also demonstrates the influence of the teachings of Ḥāfiẓ on many poets and men of letters in Persia – on their poetry, personality, social behaviour and indeed on other aspects of their lives. Ḥāfiẓ was not just a poet; he was and still is a great spiritual teacher, showing mankind the way to humanity and a comprehension of love. Movahedi, in this context, ironically observes:

> In the past, our society placed Ḥāfiẓ in the heavens, referring to him as a divine poet. Only recently has he been placed back on earth through the examination of those angles of his poetry aside from the mystical aspects. Today, Iranian society does not need a divine Ḥāfiẓ – they only want him as a divine poet during the Night of Yaldā. The rest of the time we need an earthly Ḥāfiẓ so we can understand and communicate.[31]

A final point concerning the reception of Ḥāfiẓ in the Persian speaking world in general and Iran in particular is the universal acknowledgement of his inimitability as a poet on the part of all critics, scholars and poets. The talent of Ḥāfiẓ cannot be matched, although many have faithfully followed and emulated him. During the past seven hundred years, not one Persian poet has succeeded in attaining the same level of skill, and although some have come close, Ḥāfiẓ remains unequalled. I leave the final observation on the poetic language of Ḥāfiẓ to one of the most prominent scholars and contemporary poets of Persia, Mr. Hushang Ibtihāj, with whom I conducted a telephone interview. Ibtehaj produced and edited one of the most credible editions of the *Divan* of Ḥāfiẓ in print today.

> I don't believe that Ḥāfiẓ had any influence on the poetic language of the Zand and Qājār periods, for the simple reason that they [the poets of those periods] were not in the same literacy level as Ḥāfiẓ. As for imitation, I would say they may have employed some words and phrases that Ḥāfiẓ too had used in his poetry, but that is not something new and goes back much further than Ḥāfiẓ's time… However, I believe some poets had made such attempts to put themselves under the influence of Ḥāfiẓ, but still, that in itself would also require work and abilities of a genus. Unfortunately, Persian literature has never witnessed any supreme figure like Ḥāfiẓ, whose work can be greatly relied on. Even Jāmī, who was considered a great mystical poet after Ḥāfiẓ, was no match for this supreme figure of poetry. We cannot, however, deny the fact that during the period since the death of Ḥāfiẓ and the emergence of Pahlavi era, Persian poetry sharply declined, and if there has been a slight improvement since, it is owed to the Pahlavi dynasty. I should also add that the entire art and subtleties of Persian literature and poetry are

> embedded in Ḥāfiẓ's utterance; this is why that for almost seven hundred years, no one has been able to compete with his poetry or even come close.[32]

What original contributions does this book make?

There is a great deal of scholarly research available on the subject and the studies of Ḥāfiẓology, as already discussed in chapters III, IV and V of this book. However, I have not encountered any research that comprehensively analyzes the reception of Ḥāfiẓ at any particular time in the history of Persia. In my interviews with them, Khurramshāhī and Pazouki both expressed that they also have not found anyone who has to date addressed this subject.[33]

Part of my original intention in undertaking this research was to illustrate the importance of Ḥāfiẓ in Persian literature, culture, sociopolitical life and the very fibre of the Iranian nation. Many of the poets who followed Ḥāfiẓ and who are cited above in this book, considered him as a beacon for the conscience and psyche of Persians, if not for all mankind in general, capable of guiding them through dark paths to enlightenment. This seems to be the message of one of his verses as well:

بعد از این نور به آفاق دهم از دل خویش   که به خورشید رسیدیم و غبار آخر شد[34]

> My heart will light up the skies from this day onwards, because we have reached the Sun and the dust is now settled.

The original material, ideas and discoveries presented in this book hopefully provide adequate proof that both the superior classical and the significant modern poets of Persia have all, in one way or another, participated in and been influenced by the social teachings and mystico-romantic philosophy of Ḥāfiẓ. As we have seen above, Ḥāfiẓ's language continues to influence the language and thought of many scholars and poets of Persia, just as it had changed the lives and ways of thinking of their forebears. By comparing Ḥāfiẓ's verses with those of other poets, the fact has been amply demonstrated that, since his death, Ḥāfiẓ's poetry has always enjoyed a warm reception in Persia, and the influence of his verse has remained strong over the past seven hundred years. Hopefully, as well, this book has opened up a new window on the future of Ḥāfiẓology and has cast light on the high place of Ḥāfiẓ among his countrymen, as well as among Western and Eastern scholars.

APPENDIX

The Influence of Ḥāfiẓ on Eight Persian Poets of the Zand and Qājār Period

In chapter III, I discussed and demonstrated the influence of Ḥāfiẓ on seven of the most important poets of Qājār Persia. Ḥāfiẓ's influence on Persian poets and poetry of the nineteenth century, however, was far more extensive than I was able (for reasons of space) to show there. Therefore, in this appendix, in order to widen the scope of my analysis, I examine the influence of Ḥāfiẓ on the following eight (mostly minor) poets of the Qājār period: Ḥazīn Lāhījī (d. 1180/1763), Mijmar-i Zavāri'ī (d. 1225/1810-1811), Nishāṭ Iṣfahānī (d. 1244/1827), Surūsh Iṣfahānī (d. 1285/1868), Furṣat Shīrāzī (d. 1290/1873), Humā-yi Shīrāzī (d. 1290/1873) and Īraj Mīrzā (d. 1344/1926). I have provided short biographies of each poet, followed by some notable examples of parallels between their verse and that of Ḥāfiẓ. At the end I offer a brief conclusion containing general observations about the significance of Ḥāfiẓ's impact on these eight poets.

Ḥazīn Lāhījī (d. 1180/1763)

Muḥammad 'Alī ibn Abī Ṭālib Ḥazīn Lāhījī (1103-1180/1692-1763), born in Iṣfahān, was a Persian poet and scholar who emigrated to India in 1145/1734.[1] Ḥazīn was born into a family of scholars and landholders in Gilān (a town in the northern province of Iran); his descent traces back to Shaykh Zāhid Gilānī, who was also a learned individual and a scholar of the time. His father moved to Iṣfahān as a student during the reign of Shāh Sulayman I; thus, Muḥammad grew up at the Ṣafavid court as an intelligent learned person and a talented poet.[2] He learnt to read and write at the age of six and at the age of eight it is said that he learnt the Qur'ān and in a very short time became fluent in the subject of logic and theology.[3] He began to study various subjects such as medicine, mathematics and philosophy; he also developed an interest in other religions and studied the Bible, Torah and Zoroastranism.[4]

He travelled far and wide in Iran and to India and Arabia. In 1135/1722, when the Afghan army defeated the Ṣafavid forces and occupied Iṣfahān, Ḥazīn attempted, without success, to convince Shāh Sulṭān Ḥusayn and his own family and friends to leave the ruined capital before it was too late; eventually, he had to sell all his possessions (with the exception of his books – he gave away two thousand and left the rest behind). He fled only days before the Afghans under Maḥmūd entered the city of Iṣfahān.[5] He made several journeys by sea in and beyond the Persian Gulf, and also to Yemen. He stayed at Najaf for three years, and then travelled through Gilān to Mashhad. Returning via Tehran to Iṣfahān, he found the former capital desolated. After further adventures and voyages in the Gulf, he was so appalled by the continuing subjugation of the population under the rule of the future Nādir Shāh that he left Iran permanently.[6]

Of his later life and travels in India, his memoirs (compiled in 1154/1742) give us relatively few details; although Indians knew of his fame, he thought ill of India and its people and wrote satires of them.[7]

He was for some time sponsored by the Mughal court of Muḥammad Shāh in Delhi. He later moved to Benares, where he died and is buried.[8] Ḥazīn (this *pen name* means 'anguished') claims to have compiled four *Dīvāns* of verse, of which only the fourth survives; all forms of poetry are represented, including several *Mathnawīs*, though his *ghazals* were exceptional. His panegyrics *qaṣā'īd* are addressed mainly to the Imams. His poetic diction is generally less elaborate than that of contemporary poets of the sabk-i Hindi school, such as Sā'ib, whose work he dismissed. Ḥazīn's prose style is remarkably simple and direct.[9]

His style of poetry is known as the Indian style and the theme of his poems lean towards concepts somewhat mystical and romantic. The level of profundity in the meaning of his verses is maintained and blended with simplicity.[10]

In 1135/1724, Ḥazīn left Iṣfahān for Khurram Ābād.[11] There he suffered from a severe depression that continued for almost a year. He fully recuperated and decided to publish a book comprising his most valued works. In 1136/1725, he accomplished this task and entitled the book, *Muddat al-'umr* (*Life's Duration*). Today, this book is in the British Library.[12] In 1154/1743, he wrote an autobiography entitled *Tadhkirat al-Mu'āṣirīn* (*Memoirs of my Contemporaries*), which is important for its account of contemporary events.

Engraved on his stone is the following couplet:

حزین از پای ره پیما بسی سرگشتگی دیدم   سر شوریده بر بالین آسایش رسید اینجا[13]

Ḥazīn: From travelling on these feet, so much confusion I saw,
Here, the troubled head has reached its bed of tranquillity.

According to Ḥazīn, his collections total some thirty thousand couplets in four books.

سی هزار است در چهار کتاب   نظم کلک بدایع آثاری[14]

The original compositions writ by my marvellous pen,
amount to thirty-thousand verses in four books.

Ḥazīn and Ḥāfiẓ

In examining Ḥazīn's *Dīvān*, it is clear that a large number of his verses are similar to those of Ḥāfiẓ. The following comparisons illustrate some of the parallels and similarities between Ḥazīn's and Ḥāfiẓ's poetry.

Ḥazīn

در مجلس ما خون دل است این که به جام است   هر قطره که از دل نتراویده حرام است[15]

In our assembly, the blood of the heart is in the cup,
Any drop not spilt from the heart is unlawful!

Ḥāfiẓ   در مذهب ما باده حلال است ولیکن   بی روی تو ای سرو گل اندام حرام است[16]

In our order, the wine is lawful; but, O Cypress Roselike Stature,
Without your face it is forbidden!

Ḥazīn   با جلوهٔ او در چه حسابست وجودم؟   چون صبح دمد شمع سحرگاه تمام است[17]

With such a manifestation of the beloved, what good is my existence?
Because with brilliance, the dawn extinguishes the morning candle.

Ḥāfiẓ　　گو شمع میارید در این جمع که امشب　　در مجلس ما ماه رخ دوست تمام است[18]

Say: Into this assembly bring not the candle, for in our circle tonight,
The friend's face is as radiant as the full moon.

Ḥazīn　　نامم به بدی در همه آفاق علم باد　　رسوا شدهٔ عشق تو را ننگ ز نام است[19]

May my name be known as bad to the whole world,
For the one exposed to your love is ashamed of his name!

Ḥāfiẓ　　از ننگ چه گویی که مرا نام ز ننگ است　　وز نام چه پرسی که مرا ننگ ز نام است[20]

Of shame, why do you speak? My name is shame.
Of name, why do you ask? I am ashamed of my name.

Ḥazīn　　از سر کوی تو نبود ره بیرون شدنم　　بس که بر روی هم اینجا، دل و جان افتادست[21]

There is no way for me to leave off haunting your alley's Entrance way,
So many hearts and souls lie strewn about and piled up there.

Ḥāfiẓ　　تا سر زلف تو در دست نسیم افتادست　　دل سودا زده از غصّه دو نیم افتادست[22]

Since the ends of your tresses fell into the hands of the breeze,
My heart, distraught with grief, broke into two pieces.

Ḥazīn　　در و دیوار جهان گوش بر آواز دلند　　مگشا پردهٔ این راز که غما/زی هست[23]

The walls and doors of the world hearken to the heart's melody,
Do not unveil this mystery, for there is an informer about!

Ḥāfiẓ　　من با کمر تو در میان کردم دست　　پنداشتمش که در میان چی[24]/زی هست[25]

My hand, I put within your girdle,
Within which, I thought to find something.

Ḥazīn　　از دلق می آلود مپرسید حزین را　　کایّام گل و جوش مُل و عهد شباب است[26]

Do not ask Ḥazīn about the wine-stained gown,
Because it is the time of the rose, the brewing of wine and of youth.

Ḥāfiẓ

حافظ منشین بی می و معشوق زمانی　　کایّام گل و یاسمن و عید صیام است[27]

Ḥāfiẓ, sit not a moment without the beloved,
Because it is the time of the rose, jasmine and festival of Sayām.[28]

Ḥazīn

یارب این غنچه دهن مست ز میخانهٔ کیست؟　　عهد و پیمان لبش با لب پیمانهٔ کیست؟[29]

O Lord! That rosebud mouth, by whose tavern is it intoxicated?
The fidelity and loyalty of Her lip rests with the lip of whose cup?

Ḥāfiẓ

بادهٔ لعل لبش کاز لب من دور مباد　　راح روح که و پیمان ده پیمانهٔ کیست؟[30]

The ruby-wine of Her lip, be not far from mine!
Whose cup does it replenish, to whose soul does it bring joy?

Ḥazīn

عشق اگر یار شود سود و زیان اینهمه نیست　　سر جانانه سلامت، غم جان اینهمه نیست[31]

In the presence of love, profit and loss is naught,
The health of the beloved comes first; the sorrow of the soul is naught.

Ḥāfiẓ

از دل و جان شرف صحبت جانان غرضست　　غرض اینست وگرنه دل و جان اینهمه نیست[32]

The desire of the heart and soul is the honour of the beloved,
This is the purpose; else the heart and soul are naught!

Ḥāfiẓ

نام حافظ رقم نیک پذیرفت ولی　　پیش رندان رقم سود و زیان اینهمه نیست[33]

The name of Ḥāfiẓ has been well-inscribed in the books, but
In the opinion of *rind*s, the measure of profit and loss is naught.

Mijmar-i Zavāraʿī (d. 1225/1810-1811)

Sayyid Ḥusayn Ṭabātabāʾī Ardistānī, whose pen name was 'Mijmar', was the son of Sayyid ʿAlī, and was born during the late twelfth/early nineteenth century in Zavāra near Iṣfahān. Mijmar's father, Sayyid ʿAlī, had two sons. The elder was Sayyid Muḥammad Bahrī and the other Mijmar. The brothers

(Mijmar and Muḥammad) never married and died without any family.[34] Mijmar's origins were from the Mīr ʿAlī Bābā tribes, whose heritage goes back to the Ṣafavid dynasty. His place of birth (Zavāra) was home to many of the elite, and a number of poets. He studied in Iṣfahān, but as he preferred not be indebted to anyone, he earned his livelihood solely by exhibiting and selling his literary work. In 1209/1792 at the age of nineteen, Mijmar proved a notable talent, as can be seen in an inverse description of Āghā Muḥammad Khān Qājār's personality. In this characterization, he presents the diction of an individual with experience and cultural wisdom.[35] Mijmar followed in the footsteps of Muʿizzī, Anvarī, in the *qaṣīda*, and Saʿdī in the *ghazal*. He imitated Saʿdī's *Gulistān* (Rose Garden) in a basic way.[36] After finishing his studies, Mijmar travelled through many Iranian cities and then visited India. On his return, he met with the distinguished poet of the time, Nishāṭ, and furthered his education under his supervision.[37] It is believed that Mijmar and Nishāṭ developed a firm friendship that continued to the last days of their lives. When Mijmar came to Iṣfahān, he was already a well-known poet and had no difficulty in mixing with the literary elite and poets known for their good poetic style. On the invitation of Nishāṭ, Mijmar left Iṣfahān in 1219/1802 and travelled to Tehran.

He was introduced to Ḥasan ʿAlī Mīrzā, the son of Fatḥ-ʿAlī Shāh and a man of literature, who paid special attention to Mijmar, treating him with kindness and care.[38]

Mijmar can safely be placed among the poets of the neoclassical school for following the styles of Khāqānī, Muʿizzī and Anvarī, and in *ghazal* writing, Saʿdī and Ḥāfiẓ. His *Dīvān* consists of five thousand verses, most of which were composed in Tehran. As a panegyrist, Mijmar bettered all his contemporaries. He took the poet Rafīq Iṣfahānī[39] as his particular model, along with the Iṣfahān group of poets as a whole, to which Nishāṭ had given an immense boost during his period.[40]

Mijmar died at the age of thirty-four, in 1225/1810-1811.[41] There are varying accounts as to the cause of his premature death; some believe he was poisoned by his rivals or some of the Shah's courtiers. In fact, Mijmar died from an unknown illness. His resting place is now in Qum.[42]Mijmar's work was first published in 1312/1894, in Tehran.[43] His *Dīvān* consists of five thousand verses, most of which were composed in Tehran. As a panegyrist, Mijmar bettered all his contemporaries. Mijmar followed in the footsteps of Muʿizzī, Anvarī, in the *qaṣīda*, and Saʿdī in the *ghazal*, imitating Saʿdī's *Gulistān* in his prose. Consequently, he can safely be placed among the poets of the neoclassical school. He took the poet Rafīq Iṣfahānī as his particular model, along with the Iṣfahān group of poets as a whole, to which Nishāṭ had given an immense boost during his period. He made a major literary contribution to nineteenth-century Persian poetry.[44]

Mijmar and Ḥāfiẓ

Although Mijmar was a neoclassical poet who adhered to the style of Khāqānī and Muʿizzī in his odes and followed Saʿdī, Hātif and Rafiq Iṣfahānī in his lyrics, there are also some traces of Ḥāfiẓ's style in his poetry. In particular, he imitates Ḥāfiẓ in rhyme, meaning and occasionally imitates him through certain phrases (*naẓira*) and also by inserting Ḥāfiẓ's verse in his own work (*taḍmīn*). This is evident throughout his *Dīvān*.

The following couplets are illustrations of the similarity of Mijmar's poetry to that of Ḥāfiẓ,

Mijmar   مپرس از مجمر و زاهد که دیدم   گریبانش به دست جاهلی بود[45]

Ask not of Mijmar or the ascetic, for I have seen
That his collar was grasped by a fool.

Ḥāfiẓ   مگو دیگر که حافظ نکته دانست   که ما دیدیم و محکم جاهلی بود[46]

Do not repeat that Ḥāfiẓ was subtle,
For we have seen that he was a chronic fool.

Mijmar   چه توان کرد که میل همه بر جانب تست   ور نه زین بیش شکایت همه جا نتوان کرد[47]

What can I do? Everyone desires you,
One cannot complain incessantly!

Ḥāfiẓ   غیرتم کشت که محبوب جهانی لیکن   روز و شب عربده با خلق خدا نتوان کرد[48]

Passion and jealousy killed me. You are the beloved of the world,
But I cannot be in conflict with the creatures of God day and night.

Mijmar   همین بود ار بعشقم حاصلی بود   که مشکل تر شدم گر مشکلی بود[49]

If anything was gained by this love,
It was greater problems!

Ḥāfiẓ مسلمانان مرا وقتی دلی بود که با وی گفتی گر مشکلی بود[50]

O Muslims! Once I possessed my heart,
And spoke to it if a difficulty arose.

Mijmar مرا در دست دل تا منزلی بود که از هر گوشه دستی بر دلی بود[51]

In my hand, the heart journeyed to a certain destination;
Travelling, I saw from every corner comes a hand on a heart.

Ḥāfiẓ دلی همدرد و یاری مصلحت بین که استظهار هر اهل دلی بود[52]

A heart, fellow-sufferer, friend and counsellor,
This was the supporter of every man of heart.

After spending many hours studying Mijmar's *Dīvān*, it is clear that a good amount of his *ghazal*s closely parallel those of Ḥāfiẓ, either in rhyme, meaning, metaphor, or phonemic arrangement. In poetic terms he also practises literary plagiarism (*siraqat-i shiʿrī*) of Ḥāfiẓ in his poetry.

Nishāṭ Iṣfahānī (d. 1244/1827)

Mīrzā ʿAbdul Wahhāb Mūsavī, pen name 'Nishāṭ'[53] was born in 1175/1761 in Iṣfahān.[54] He was descended from a wealthy family. Out of sheer generosity, he spent all his inherited wealth within a very short time. This brilliant and cultured poet, whose life was ruined, found a way to alleviate his poverty and make a decent living by writing panegyric verses that won him popularity at court. Further consequences of his talent were his appointment as mayor, and later, governor of Iṣfahān, which also improved his financial state. He paid special attention to the local literary scene. Still later, in Tehran, he was assigned important duties such as being a diplomat to the court of Napoleon in Paris, the mollification of the Ghuriyān in East Khurāsān in 1233/1818; and the crushing of an uprising of certain Afghan tribes in 1237/1821. He performed these tasks to the best of his ability and proved himself worthy of his cognomen, 'The Trusted Man of the Empire' (*Muʿtamid al-Dawla*).[55] In the literary circle of the Shāh, he was one of the leading poets. He wrote prose in Persian, Arabic and Turkish. His *qaṣā'id* find their inspiration in the school of Ṣabā,[56] but are somewhat simpler in form. By decree of Nāṣir al-Dīn Shāh, Nishāṭ's verse and prose were collected and published in a lithographed edition titled *Ganjīna* (*Treasure*).[57] Nishāṭ learnt to speak Turkish and Arabic and studied philosophy, calligraphy, theology, mathematics, logic and mysticism.[58]

As a mystic he was inspired by Sa'dī and Ḥāfiẓ in his lyrics and Anvarī in his elegy writing.[59] His *Dīvān* consists of around five thousand couplets. Among the poets of his day, it may be said that he was a master of the *ghazal* genre, and indeed the best poet of his generation. He made a major contribution to neoclassical Persian poetry, as well as being a celebrated calligraphist. He died in 1244/1827.[60]

Nishāṭ and Ḥāfiẓ

Nishāṭ greatly admired Ḥāfiẓ and closely imitated his style in all aspects of his *ghazal* writing. According to Bahār,[61] Nishāṭ's talent in poetry lay in *ghazal* writing. He was truly one of the best poets of the period because of his devotion to Ḥāfiẓ and the way in which he follows his style in detail.[62] The comparisons below illustrate the parallels between Nishāṭ's poetry and that of Ḥāfiẓ.

Nishāṭ

راه بیرون شدن از هردو جهانم هوس است   خیمه بیرون زدن از کون و مکانم هوس است[63]

It is my desire to die to both worlds;
It is my desire to dwell outside time and space.

Ḥāfiẓ

حال دل با تو گفتنم هوس است   خبر دل شنفتنم هوس است[64]

It is my desire to speak with you about the state of the heart
It is my desire to hear news of the heart.[65]

Nishāṭ

با ما قدحی خواجه سپردن نتواند   اورا حذر از ننگ و مرا ننگ ز نام است[66]

The honourable ascetic would not drink with us out of fear of his good name,
But I am ashamed of all honour and good names.

Ḥāfiẓ از ننگ چه گوئی که مرا نام ز ننگ است   وز نام چه پرسی که مرا ننگ ز نام است[67]

Of shame, why do you speak? My name comes from shame.
Of name, why do you ask? I am ashamed of my name.

Nishāṭ دو چشم مست تو فرهنگ هشیارانند   دو بند زلف تو زنجیر رستگارانند[68]

The two drunken eyes of yours are guides to the sober,
The two locks of your hair are chains to those who enjoy salvation.

Ḥāfiẓ خلاص حافظ از آن زلف تابدار مباد   که بستگان کمند تو رستگارانند[69]

May Ḥāfiẓ not be free of those entangling tresses,
Because those bound by you are in salvation.

Nishāṭ چو پشت بر ره مقصود می روند چه باک   که من پیاده و این همرهان سوارانند[70]

Since they are travelling away from their destination,
Why should I fear that I am on foot while my fellow travellers are on horseback?

Ḥāfiẓ تو دستگیر شو ای خضر پی خجسته که من   پیاده می روم و همرهان سوارانند[71]

O Khizr[72] of auspicious origin, be my guide, for I
Travel on foot and my fellow travellers are on horseback.

Nishāṭ شب است و بخت من و یاد زلف او آنجا   سپیده سر نزند کاین سیاهکارانند[73]

Here is the night, my fate, and the memory of the beloved's tresses,
May there not be the gleam of dawn, for they are miscreants.

Ḥāfiẓ بیا بمیکده و چهره ارغوانی کن   مرو به صومعه کانجا سیاهکارانند[74]

Come to the tavern and put some colour in your cheek,
Do not go to the cloister, where sinners abide.

Nishāṭ پرده افتاد و دگر حاجت مشاطه نماند   شیشه بر سنگ شد و تیشه به بنیاد آمد[75]

The veil fell, thus no need for the adorner;
The glass hit the rock, so thus there's no need for the axe.

Ḥāfiẓ باده صافی شد و مرغان چمن مست شدند موسم عاشقی و کار به بنیاد آمد[76]

The wine was strained clear and the birds of the meadow drunk;
It is the lovers' season and all affairs have become well grounded.

Nishāṭ بی تو میل گل و گلشن نکنم هوس سوری سوسن نکنم[77]

Without you, I yearn for no rose or rose garden;
I yearn for no joyous feasting or lily.

Ḥāfiẓ بی تو ای سرو روان با گل و گلشن چه کنم زلف سنبل چه کشم عارض سوسن چکنم[78]

Without you, O Walking Cypress, what would I do with a flower and a rose garden?
Why touch a hyacinth tress? With the cheek of the lily, what would I do?

Nishāṭ نشاید ار چو تویی در کنار من باشی همین بس است که گویند یار من باشی[79]

It may not be for someone like you to be at my side,
But as long as they say you are my dear companion, that will be enough.

Ḥāfiẓ هزار جهد بکردم که یار من باشی مراد بخش دل بیقرار من باشی[80]

I have attempted a thousand times to make you my dear companion;
For you to grant my restless heart's desire.

Nishāṭ تو کز میان دل من قدم برون ننهی نمیشود که دمی در کنار من باشی[81]

You, who do not step out of the midst of my heart,
Could you not stay at my side for a moment?

Ḥāfiẓ من این مراد ببینم به خود که نیم شبی بجای اشک روان در کنار من باشی[82]

For myself, I pondered this desire, that one midnight,
Instead of running tears, you would be at my side.

In examining Nishāṭ's *Dīvān*, as the above few examples demonstrate, it is clear that a substantial portion of his verses are similar to those of Ḥāfiẓ and that Ḥāfiẓ had a profound impact on the style, metrics, expressions, imagery and content of Nishāṭ's verse.

Surūsh Iṣfahānī (d. 1285/1868)

Mīrzā Muḥammad ʿAlī, the son of Qanbar ʿAlī Sadihī Iṣfahānī, was born in 1228/1813.[83] Interested in poetry since his childhood, he finished his studies in Iṣfahān and started composing panegyric verse, but had little success. He left Iṣfahān in his late twenties, first for Qum and later Kāshān. There he stayed only three years; he left Kāshān for Tabriz, where he met with two of the Qājār princes and benefited from their hospitality. He eventually became a courtier and made the acquaintance of the crown prince, Nāṣir al-Dīn Mīrzā, who came to the throne after the death of his father Muḥammad Shāh. Surūsh accompanied the Shāh to Tehran and resided at the court where Nāṣir al-Dīn Shāh gave him the title of 'Khān' ('Sir').[84] In addition, he was also given the title 'Shams al-Shuʿarā'' ('Sun of the Poets').[85]

His poetry shows the influence of Anvarī, Sanā'ī and Muʿizzī, he is thus considered to follow the style of the neoclassical school. Some of the events of his lifetime can be found in his poetry; for instance, the establishment of the electric telegraph is mentioned in his verses. He praised Fatḥ-ʿAlī Shāh a great deal; one of his most impressive works is his interpretation of famous stories from the *One Thousand and One Nights*. Surūsh also follows Saʿdī and Ḥāfiẓ in his poetry and sometimes mixes their verses with his own.[86]

Surūsh's works consist of *qaṣā'id* and *Mathnawīhā*. Among his most well-known works are *Shams al-munāqīb* (Goodness of the Sun) *Ruḍatt al-anvār* (School's Light) and *Ziynatt al-madāyiḥ* (Decorated Praise).[87] His entire collection contains approximately thirty thousand verses, as he mentions in one of his elegies:

در این سی سال مدحت گستری از سی هزار افزون   بمدح شاه و مدح اولیا نظم دری دارد[88]

After these thirty years of panegyric writing,
over thirty thousand verses
Can be found in praise of the king and the saints in Persian verse.

His contribution is of moderate significance in Persian poetry. Mīrzā Muḥammad ʿAlī Surūsh Iṣfahānī died in 1285/1868 in Tehran. His poetry shows little evidence of innovation and is characterized by a considerable amount of empty flattery. Indeed, Surūsh's poetry has been criticized for the bombastic excesses he went to in self-praise; he unjustifiably and continually makes exaggerated claims that no other poet matches his talent.

نداند هیچ ثنا گر چنین ثنا ترتیب   نگفته هیچ سخنور سخن بدین ترتیل[89]

No elegy writer knows such elegiac techniques;

کس در سخن امروز سزاوار ثنا نیست   ور هست بجز حضرت شمس الشعرا نیست[90]

Today no one deserves commendation in poetry,
Save His Grace, the Sun of Poets.

دو شعر شیرین در یک قصیده گر گویند   ز شعر منشان رفته است چاشنی بکلام[91]

If they write two sweet verses in an elegy,
My words must have inspired them.

No speaker has ever uttered such phonemic words.

دل گفت غلام پادشاه خواهی شد   از مدح و ثنا کامروا خواهی شد[92]

The heart said: You shall become the Shāh's servant,
You will become prosperous by praising him.

Surūsh and Ḥāfiẓ

The following comparisons illustrate the relationship between Surūsh's style of poetry and that of Ḥāfiẓ. The comparisons are slightly superficial and do not reflect the poet's preoccupation with Ḥāfiẓ, but these correlations, however slight, are worthy of mention.

Surūsh   فرخنده خسروا ملکا فضل پرورا   بنگر بدین قصیدهٔ دوشیزهٔ ثمین[93]

O Glorious King, O Prince, thou the promoter of wisdom,
Perceive such precious, virgin elegy!

Ḥāfiẓ   خسروا دادگرا شیردلا بحرکفا   ای جلال تو به انواع هنر ارزانی[94]

O Prince! O Just One! O Lion-Hearted One! O Generous One!
O thou whose glory with varied forms of art, is adorned!

Surūsh پریانند که پوشیده لباس بشرند[95] شرط انصاف نباشد که قمر خوانمشان

It is not just to refer to them as the moon,
These nymphs in human clothing.

Ḥāfiẓ رنج ما را که توان برد به یک گوشهٔ چشم شرط انصاف نباشد که مداوا نکنی[96]

Since with a glance from the corner of your eye you can relieve our dolor,
It is unbecoming of justice for you to withhold the remedy.

Another method of imitation that Surūsh employs is the use of metaphors and the inclusion of the tales of the holy cup of Jamshīd (*Jām-i Jam*) and the story of the prophet Solomon in a manner similar to that of Ḥāfiẓ:

Surūsh چون به بر شاه ستاده باشد گویی آصف بن برخیا ستاده بر جم[97]

As he stands next to the Shāh,
You might say that Āṣif, the son of Barkhīyā, stood next to the 'Jam'.

Ḥāfiẓ زبان مور به آصف دراز گشت و رواست که خواجه خاتم جم یاوه کرد و بازنجست[98]

If an ant's tongue has gone to excess in reproaching the vizier, it's okay for the owner of Jamshid's ring let it be lost and did not seek its recovery.

Humā-yi Shīrāzī (d. 1290/1873)

Muḥammad Riḍā Qulī Khān,[99] known as Humā-yi Shīrāzī, was born in 1212/1795 in Shīrāz and died in 1290/1873 in Iṣfahān.[100] Humā was a mystic and a dervish who was utterly disinterested in worldly possessions and unconcerned with social status, power and titles. It has been narrated that Muḥammad Shāh Qājār granted him land and properties as gifts, but he refused to accept them.[101] When the Shāh insisted that he accept something from him, he sent the Shāh this verse in reply:

خواستن در درویشی کفر است درویش را با خواست و خواسته چه کار؟[102]

To a dervish, desires are acts of infidelity,
What business has a dervish with claims and demands?

As an alternative, the Shāh persisted in sending him cash, but by the sunset of the very same day, Humā had donated all the money to the destitute and needy, to the extent that he left himself nothing to buy food that night. Humā's master (teacher) was Viṣāl Shīrāzī and after his death Humā was given the title of 'Malik al-Shuʿarā'' ('King of the Poets'). However, his Sufi temperament did not allow him to accept the title or render his services to the Nāṣir al-Dīn Shāh. Flouting the custom of the court, he left the service of the king without permission and, some months later, sent a letter of apology, excusing himself on behalf of obligations concerning personal and family matters.

In addition to poetry, Humā was also a calligrapher. His three sons, Mīrzā Muḥammad Ḥusayn, with the pen name of "Anqā'; Mīrzā Muḥammad, with the pen name of 'Sahā'; and Mīrzā Abū'l Qāsim, with the pen name of 'Ṭarab', were also poets and calligraphers.[103] His eldest son, ʿAnqā, began compiling his father's work throughout his lifetime and this continued after Humā's death.

His *Dīvān*, which consists of *qaṣīda*, *ghazal*, *musammaṭ*, *rubāʿī*, *tarkib-band*, *qaṭʿa* and *Mathnawī* was named *Shikkaristān* (*Sugar Land*).[104] It consists of approximately 5,560 verses, and is the combination of all his works. His style of *ghazal* writing follows that of Ḥāfiẓ and his panegyric writing utilizes the Khurāsānī style.

Humā and Ḥāfiẓ

The phrases used in Humā's poems reveal his mystical beliefs and view of the world, resulting in some similarities with Ḥāfiẓ's poetry. The following comparisons demonstrate this.

چه غم گر کاروان چین نیارد نافهٔ مشکین   تو بگشا طرهٔ پر چین و مشکین ساز محفلها[105] Humā

There would be no anxiety if no perfume was delivered by
The caravan from China, you free your wavy tresses and fill assemblieses with perfume.

همه کارم ز خود کامی به بد نامی کشید آری   نهان کی ماند آن رازی کز آن سازند محفلها[106] Ḥāfiẓ

By following my own fancy, all my affairs led to disrepute,
How do secrets remain secrets if spoken in every assembly?

Humā   حیات جاودان خواهی هما در بادهٔ باقی   الا یا ایها الساقی ادر کسأ و ناولها[107]

Humā, you seek eternal life in the eternal wine,
O Sāqī, pass around and offer the bowl.

Ḥāfiẓ   الا یا ایها الساقی ادر کسأ و ناولها   که عشق آسان نمو اول ولی افتاد مشکلها[108]

O Sāqī, pass around and offer the bowl,
For love at first appeared easy, but difficulties occurred.

Humā   با همه آلودگی ها پاک از آلایشیم   گرچه رند و مست و بدنام و نظربازیم ما[109]

Despite all the sins, we are free of impurities,
Although we're rogues, drunkards and men of ill-repute who gaze on lovely faces.

Ḥāfiẓ   عاشق و رند و نظربازم و می گویم فاش   تا بدانی که به چندین هنر آراسته ام[110]

I am a lover, libertine and play the sport of gazing on beautiful faces. I state it plainly
So you may understand that I am decked out with so many fine arts.

Humā
بزمی که تو ساقی شوی آن بزم بهشت است   عیشی که نه با تو بود آن عیش حرام است[111]

The assembly in which you are the Sāqī is paradise,
The joyous moments without you are thus forbidden.

Ḥāfiẓ   در مذهب ما باده حلال است ولیکن   بی روی تو ای سرو گل اندام حرام است[112]

In our order, the wine is lawful, but O Cypress Rose of Stature,
Without your face it would be unlawful.

It is clear that Humā was influenced by Ḥāfiẓ not only in respect to meter and rhyme, but in his metaphors, imagery and mystical expressions. From my examination and analysis of Humā's poetry, it is evident that more than a third of his *ghazal*s were written as virtual parallels to those of Ḥāfiẓ.

Furṣat Shīrāzī (d. 1339/1922)

Sayyid Mīrzā Muḥammad Nāṣīr al-Ḥusaynī-yi Shīrāzī, otherwise, known as Furṣat al-Dawla, whose pen name was 'Furṣat', was born in 1271/1854 in Shīrāz. In addition to being a well-known and accomplished poet, he was familiar with mathematics, astrology, logic and mysticism; he was also fluent in English.

Furṣat taught Arabic and literature in Shīrāz then accepted several government posts. During his retirement he chose solitude, spending most of his time in isolation reading and doing research. He never married and had plenty of time to travel. Furṣat was also a professional artist whose paintings of many of the places he visited are quite valuable. As a dervish and a humble individual he spent a great deal of time helping the needy.

A few years before Furṣat's death, he sought complete solitude. He used to say: 'I am now preparing for the final journey'. He ordered his gravestone and had some of own verses engraved on it. Furṣat wanted to be laid to rest next to Ḥāfiẓ's tomb. He visited the shrine of Ḥāfiẓ and sought an answer as to whether Ḥāfiẓ would object to his being laid to eternal rest nearby. He referred to Ḥāfiẓ's *Dīvān*, searching for insight, and found the following verse:

رواق منظر چشم من آشیانهٔ تست   کرم نما و فرود آ، که خانه خانهٔ تست[113]

Your doorstep is the gateway to the vision of my eye,
Show affection and enter this house as your home.[114]

After reading this profound verse, Furṣat became so emotional that he began to cry, and the next day he reserved a grave for himself next to Ḥāfiẓ's mausoleum.[115]

Furṣat and Ḥāfiẓ

In studying Furṣat's poetry and in analyzing his lyrics, it is clear that he was influenced by Ḥāfiẓ's *ghazal*s. Almost a quarter of his *ghazal*s parallel those of Ḥāfiẓ. The idioms used in his poems illustrate his mystical doctrines and view of the world, which reflect those found in Ḥāfiẓ's poetry. The following comparisons demonstrate some of these similarities and parallels between the poetry of Furṣat and Ḥāfiẓ:

Furṣat هر زمان گویمش ای یار دلم بیمار است لب لعل تو دوای دل بیمار من است[116]

To the beloved, I constantly say: 'I have an ill heart,
Your ruby lip is thus the remedy.'

Ḥāfiẓ شربت قند و گلاب از لب یارم فرمود نرگس او که طبیب دل بیمار من است[117]

Her narcissus prescribed sweet nectar and rose water from
My beloved's lips, for it is the healer of my ill heart.

Furṣat تیغ ابرو کشد و طره خود را ببرد گر ببیند زوی آشفتگی کار من است[118]

If she sees that my business is naught but being dishevelled by her,
She shall draw the sword of her eyebrow to cut her curly lock.

Ḥāfiẓ لعل سیراب بخون تشنه لب یار من است وز پی دیدن او دادن جان کار من است[119]

The luscious ruby, thirsty for blood, is the lip of my adored one,
And in longing to have a glimpse of her, my work is sacrifice of self and life.

Furṣat دلبرا با دل دیوانه چه تدبیر کنم مگرش آرم و در زلف تو زنجیر کنم[120]

O Beloved, how prudent can I be with this crazy heart?
Perhaps, I may drag and entangle it in the midst of your tresses.

Ḥāfiẓ دل دیوانه از آن شد که نصیحت شنود مگرش هم ز سر زلف تو زنجیر کنم[121]

The lunatic heart is beyond listening to advice,
Unless I were to fashion a chain for it from your tresses' strands.

Furṣat قصه های شب هجران تو را روز وصال کو زبانی که یکایک همه تقریر کنم[122]

Where is a tongue that, on the day of union, may recite one by one, in detail, the tales of the night of separation.

Ḥāfiẓ با سر زلف تو مجموع پریشانی خود کو مجالی که سراسر همه تقریر کنم[123]

With your tresses distracting me entirely,
Where is my skill to narrate each detail?

Furṣat محو چون صورت تصویر شوم سر تا پای روی زیبای تو در دیده چو تصویر کنم[124]

From foot to face, I shall become like an image erased,
The moment I picture before my eyes your beautiful face!

Ḥāfiẓ آنزمان کارزوی دیدن جانم باشد در نظر نقش رخ خوب تو تصویر کنم[125]

When my desire is to see my soul,
I picture the image of your fair cheek.

Īraj Mīrzā (d. 1344/1926)

Īraj Mīrzā was born in 1290/1874 in Tabriz.[126] His ancestors were of royal blood from the house of Fatḥ-ʿAlī Shāh Qājār, the second Shāh of the Qājār dynasty (r. 1797-1834). Ghulām Ḥusayn Mīrzā, Īraj's father, was a poet laureate of Muẓaffar al-Dīn Mīrzā, the brother of Nāṣir al-Dīn Shāh, the crown prince of Iran at the time. By the time he was fifteen, Īraj was fluent in French, Turkish and Arabic; he was also familiar with the art of calligraphy. His handwriting was very artistic and he was considered one of the notable calligraphers of Iran. At sixteen, Īraj got married and at nineteen, he lost both his father and wife. Later, like his father, he became the poet laureate of Muẓaffar al-Dīn Mīrzā. In 1313/1896, at twenty-two, when Muẓaffar al-Dīn Mīrzā succeeded to the throne and became Muẓaffar al-Dīn Shāh, Īraj was given the title 'Sadr al-Shuʿarā'' ('Head of the Poets'). He was then given a second title, 'Jalāl al-Mamālik'[127] ('Majesty of the Countries').[128] In 1322/1905 he moved to Tehran where he soon became involved in the Constitutional Revolution.

Īraj's simple poetic language is also famous for its witticism and satire.[129] His style is rich in the art of simile (*hunar-i tashbīh*). His striking sarcasm, caustic and venomous words point at dishonest clergy and religious hypocrisy, businessmen, merchants and statesmen. In addition to his colloquial poems, Īraj also composed elegies to praise Muẓaffar al-Dīn Shāh, but his praise never descended into flattery. Īraj composed very good *Mathnawī* and *qaṭaʿāt* on the raising and education of children, maternal affection, love and romance.

Īraj was influenced by the political circumstances of his age, in particular the Persian Constitutional Revolution (1906-1911); his environment and these events are manifested in the particular style of poetry that he created, a blend of modern and imported concepts. He criticizes the social conditions of the country and employed striking originality in his use of metaphor when addressing diverse social problems. He was an enlightened, innovative poet who tended towards European thought. Despite his famous technical skills, he sometimes used similar cases of rhyme, a practice that is considered by some poetry critics as an intentional rejection of strict traditional and poetic rules. However, it is believed that he did not intend to reject those rules. Some scholars maintain that because of the time in which he lived, his depth of literary knowledge and his familiarity with French and other foreign languages, he could also have been a master of free verse had he devoted himself to it.[130] He is known for his ribald and profane poetry. The following is a verse that characterizes this well.

زمن مترس که کنم تورا خطاب خانم   از او بترس که همشیره ات خطاب کند

> Fear me not for addressing you as 'lady';
> Fear he who addresses you as 'sister'.[131]

Among the many poems that Īraj composed, his most well-known include 'Satan', 'Mother', 'A Letter to a Poet 'Ārīf Qazwīnī', 'Woman's Picture', 'Story of the Veil' or 'Hijāb' and the 'Story of Zuhra and Manūchihr', which is based on Shakespeare's Venus and Adonis.[132]In 1335/1917 he held a number of ministerial positions in the Qājār government. He died from a heart attack at the age of fifty-two in Tehran, 1344/1925.[133] Īraj is considered one of the most famous contemporary poets of Iran and the first Iranian master of colloquial poetry, making use of everyday language in his verses.[134] Although Īraj was one of the founders of the creative movement (*Naw āvarī*) in Persian poetry, he never abandoned the rules of classical Persian poetry.[135]

Īraj Mīrzā and Ḥāfiẓ

After a detailed investigation and reading of Īraj's entire *Dīvān*, I calculated that a minor part of his poetry follows the style of Ḥāfiẓ in terms of rhyme, mystical phrases, metaphors and meter. Īraj's imitation of Ḥāfiẓ's language and style appears, as is shown in the parallels between the two poets presented below, in his use of the devices of 'poetic following' (*tattabu*ʿ) and 'poetic emulation' (*naẓira*) as well as a number of similar rhetorical devices, used in a way similar to that of Ḥāfiẓ.

The following comparisons illustrate the similarity of the poetry written by Īraj and Ḥāfiẓ. While these analogies are somewhat superficial and do not fully demonstrate the poet's obsession with Ḥāfiẓ, they are worthy of mention nonetheless.

Īraj خواهم که دهم جان بتو، میل دلم این است ترسم که پسندت نشود، مشکلم این است[136]

The desire of my heart is to give you my life,
My problem is I fear it might not meet your approval.

Ḥāfiẓ خم زلف تو دام کفر و دین است ز کارستان او یک شمه این است[137]

The curl of your lock is the trap of both unbelief and faith,
This is but the slightest part of His wonderous works.

Īraj زندگی عشق – عجب زندگیست زنده که عاشق نبود – زنده نیست[138]

A life with love – what a life that will be!
One who is alive and not in love – is not alive!

Ḥāfiẓ از صدای سخن عشق ندیدم خوشتر یادگاری که در این گنبد دوار بماند[139]

I have heard nothing more delightful than the sound of love's song
Left as a memento beneath this dome of the whirling heavens.

Īraj کار دشوار بود لیک مرا می باید حیلتی از پی آسانی دشوار کنم[140]

My affairs are complex, so I must
Search out duplicities to ease them.

Ḥāfiẓ   هزار حیله برانگیخت حافظ از سر فکر   درآن هوس که شود آن نگار رام و نشد[141]

Out of craftiness, Ḥāfiẓ has put up a thousand duplicities
In the desire for that idol to be tamed, but She was not!

Īraj   سبحه و سجاده و مهری، مرتب کرده شیخ   تا چه پیش آید خدایا ؟ دام تزویر است ومن[142]

A rosary prayer, a prayer mat and a praying stone have been set by the Shaykh, O God, what may now lie ahead? Here is the bait of deceit and here am I.

Ḥāfiẓ   واعظان کاین جلوه بر محراب و منبر می کنند   چون به خلوت می روند آن کار دیگر می کنند[143]

Ministers, who make all this display in the prayer-niche and on stage,
In private, they turn to practise in totally other ways!

Īraj   سوزیم در آتش فراقت   گرییم ز درد اشتیاقت[144]

We burn in the flames of your separation;
We weep in the sorrow of your love.

Ḥāfiẓ   صبا گر چاره داری وقت وقت است   که درد اشتیاقم قصد جان کرد[145]

Ṣabā, if you know of a cure, now is the time,
For the bane of desire has threatened my life!

Īraj   چون با ادب و تمیز باشی   پیش همه کس عزیز باشی[146]

If you are polite and clean,
You will be dear to everyone.

Ḥāfiẓ   حافظا علم و ادب ورز که در مجلس شاه   هرکه را نیست ادب لایق صحبت نبود[147]

Ḥāfiẓ: Practise knowledge and manners. For, in the king's assembly
He who has not manners, is not worthy of conversation.

This appendix is designed to provide solid and relevant evidence of the reception of Ḥāfiẓ in nineteenth- and twentieth-century Persia. I have presented clear evidence as far back as eighteenth-century Persia, demonstrating examples of the works of poets such as Ḥazīn Lāhījī in order to firmly establish the influence of Ḥāfiẓ on the poets of Persia even much earlier than the nineteenth and twentieth centuries.

This appendix aims to direct the attention of the reader to examples that, because of the limitation of space, have been excluded from the main text of this study. The poets and the comparative verses presented with those of Ḥāfiẓ bring to light the reception of this fourteenth-century master poet on an enormous range of Persian poets and writers. While I have already established that Ḥāfiẓ's influence has inspired scholars, intellectuals, writers and even the ordinary people of Iran, my main focus throughout this research has been the poets, in particular those of nineteenth- and twentieth-century Persia. Ḥāfiẓ's influence on the eight poets mentioned above displays the strong and unbreakable bond of this superior poet on Persian literature, culture and in particular nineteenth- and twentieth-century Persian poets. By adding the appendix to this study, I hope to clarify the central focus of this research and thereby bring this research to a logical and conclusive end.

Notes

Acknowledgements

1 P. Avery, *The Collected Lyrics of Hafiz of Shiraz* (Cambridge: Archetype, 2007), p. 423; *ghazal* 344.

Preface

1 See *Hafiz and the Religion of Love in Classical Persian Poetry*, ed. Leonard Lewisohn (London: I.B. Tauris 2010).

2 *Dīwān-i Khwāja Shams al-Dīn Muḥammad Ḥāfiẓ*, ed. Parvīz Nātil Khānlarī (Tehran: Intishārāt-i Khawārazmī 1359 A.Hsh./1980), *ghazal* 310: 1. All translations, unless otherwise stated, are mine.

3 *Dīvān*, ed. Khānlarī, ghazal 329: 3.

4 Dīvān, ed. Khānlarī, ghazal 211: 7.

5 For a fuller discussion, see Leonard Lewisohn, "Sufi Erotic Theology from the Revelation of the Qur'an to the Fusus al-hikam," forthcoming in Lloyd Ridgeon (ed.), The Cambridge Companion to Sufism (Cambridge: CUP 2014).

6 *Dīvān*, ed. Khānlarī, *ghazal* 305: 2.

7 *Dīvān*, ed. Khānlarī, *ghazal* 385: 1. From *The Angels Knocking on the Tavern Door: 30 Poems of Hafez*, trans. Robert Bly and Leonard Lewisohn, (New York: HarperCollins 2008), p. 21.

8 See Leonard Lewisohn, "The Religion of Love and the Puritans of Islam: Sufi Sources of Ḥāfiẓ's Anti-clericalism," in Lewisohn (ed.), *Hafiz and the Religion of Love*, pp. 159-196.

9 *Dīvān*, ed. Khānlarī, ghazal 126: 10.

10 "Ḥāfiẓ's entire *Dīvān* is one long manifesto of opposition to religious hypocrisy." – Bahā al-Dīn Khurramshāhī, "Mayl-i Ḥāfiẓ bih gunāh," in

his *Dhihn u zabān-i Ḥāfiẓ*, (Tehran: Intishārāt-i Nāhīd 1379 A.Hsh./2000), p. 77.

11 *Dīvān*, ed. Khānlarī, ghazal 278: 6.

12 *Measure for Measure*, III.ii.253-261.

13 *Samson Agonistes*, 514.

14 For a good exposition of this doctrine of Ḥāfiẓ, see Taqī Pūrnāmdāriyān, *Gumshuda-yi lab-i daryā: Tā'ammulī dar ma'nā va ṣūrat-i sh'ir-i Ḥāfiẓ*, (Tehran: Intishārāt-i Sukhan 1382 A.Hsh./2003), pp. 18-19. See also my discussion of this issue: "The Religion of Love and the Puritans of Islam," in Lewisohn (ed.), *Hafiz and the Religion of Love*, pp. 164-166.

15 *Dīvān*, ed. Khānlarī, ghazal 76: 6. Exactly the same moral message, "eternal salvation is found in causing as little distress as possible" (ghazal 67: 10) is repeated in a number of other verses in his *Dīvān*.

16 *Dīvān*, ed. Khānlarī, ghazal 154: 3. On the term *rindī*, which I translated here as 'Romance', see my "Prolegomenon to the Study of Ḥāfiẓ, 2 – The Mystical Milieu: Ḥāfiẓ's Erotic Spirituality," in Lewisohn (ed.), *Hafiz and the Religion of Love*, pp. 31-73. See also Rafiq Ajani, "The Development of the Mystical Theology and Ethics of *Rindi* in Persian Poetry from the Eleventh to Fifteenth Centuries" (Ph.D. dissertation, Exeter University, forthcoming 2014).

17 *Dīvān*, ed. Khānlarī, ghazal 220: 1.

18 *Dīvān*, ed. Khānlarī, ghazal 385: 9.

19 *Dīwān-i Khwāja Ḥāfiẓ-i Shīrāzī*, ed. S. 'Abū'l-Qāsim Anjawī-Shīrāzī (Tehran: Sāzmān-i Intikhābāt-i Jāwidān 1358 A.Hsh./1979), p. 205.

20 *Dīvān*, ed. Khānlarī, ghazal 179: 4. One Sufi commentator on this verse explains that the poet means that one cannot recognize the truth of religion until one first perceives the Reality (*ḥaqīqat*) of faith and attain inward certainty. As a consequence of that certainty, "one looks with compassion and mercy on the followers of all other faiths and creeds. One does not deny them however benighted and misguided they may be. This is one of the ideas especially recognized by the Sufis… As long as the Reality (*ḥaqīqat*) of religious faith is not unveiled to one, the aspirant will rely on his powers of deduction and personal striving (*qiyās va ijtihād*), and these only generate religious differences (*ikhtilāf*)." Abū'l-Ḥasan 'Abd al-Raḥmān Khatmī Lāhūrī, *Sharḥ-i 'irfānī-yi ghazalhā-yi-i Ḥāfiẓ*, ed. Bahā' al-Dīn Khurramshāhī, Kūrush Manṣūrī, and Ḥusayn Muṭī'ī-Amīn (Tehran: Nashr-i Qaṭra 1374 A.Hsh./1995), III, pp. 1183-1184.

21 *Dīvān*, ed. Khānlarī, ghazal 78: 2-3.

22 *Dīvān*, ed. Khanlari, *ghazal* 190: 5.

23 *Dīvān*, ed. Khānlarī, *ghazal* 279: 3.
24 *Dīvān*, ed. Khānlarī, *ghazal* 190: 5.
25 *Dīvān*, ed. Khānlarī, *ghazal* 306: 3.
26 *Dīwān-i Ḥāfiẓ*, ed. Khānlarī, *ghazal* 275: 9.
27 See Leonard Lewisohn, "The Ḥāfiẓocentricism of Persianate Civilization and the Qur'ān," in Lewisohn (ed.), *Hafiz and the Religion of Love*, pp. 16-18.
28 See Ata Karim Burke, "The Contribution of Hafiz of Shiraz to Secular Aspects of Humanism," *Indo-Iranica*, XLV (1992), pp. 132-142.
29 See Ali Ferdowsi, 'The "Emblem of the Manifestation of the Iranian Spirit": Hafiz and the Rise of the National Cult of Persian Poetry', *Iranian Studies*, Vol. 41, No. 5 (2008), pp. 665-691.
30 One of Iran's greatest living novelists, recently composed an interesting work of historical fiction based on legends in medieval Persian chronicles about Ḥāfiẓ, portraying him as a free-thinking, rabidly anticlerical iconoclast. See Īraj Pizhiskhzād, *Ḥāfiẓ nāshinīda-pand: bargī chand az daftar-e khāṭirāt-e Muḥammad Gulandām* (Tehran; Nashr-e Qaṭra 1383 A.Hsh./2004).
31 See Shāpūr Pasāvand's unconvincing interpretation of Ḥāfiẓ's mystical thought as of Mithraic inspiration: "Ḥāfiẓ, 'ishq va mashrab-e ū," in Kāvūs Ḥasanlī, *Sādih-i bisyār-naqsh: Dāstān-nivīsān va shā'irān-i imrūz, Ḥāfiẓ rā chigūna mībīnand?* (Tehran: Intishārāt-i 'ilmī u farhangī 1384 A.Hsh./ 2005), pp. 43-59.
32 'Alī-Riḍā Dhakāvatī Qarāguzlū, "Ḥāfiẓ dar miyān-i haftād u dū millat," *Taḥqīqāt-i Islāmī*, Year 3, Nos. 1&2 (1367 A.Hsh./1988), pp. 61-74.
33 *Tadhkira-ye Riyāḍ al-'ārifīn*, ed. Nuṣratu'llāh Furūhar (Tehran: Amīr Kabīr 1388 A.Hsh./2009), p. 616. *Ḥakīmī ast ṣāḥib-māyih va 'ārifī buland-pāyih… Ash'ār-i ḥikmat-i 'āthārash chinān dar dil-i har ṭā'ifa nishasta kih ākthar-i faraq mukhtalafa ū rā ham maslak- khwīsh dānista-and.*
34 See Ferdowsi, 'The "Emblem of the Manifestation of the Iranian Spirit," pp. 665-691.
35 Khurrāmshāhī, "Ḥāfiẓ dar farhang-i mā u farhang-i mā dar Ḥāfiẓ," in idem., *Ḥāfiẓ Ḥāfiẓa-yi mā'st* (Tehran: Intishārāt-i nashr-i Qaṭra 1385 A.Hsh./2006; 3rd printing), p. 128 – drawing heavily on the depth psychology of C.G. Jung. His statement is echoed by the view of 'Abbās Zaryābkhū'ī's view that "Ḥāfiẓ is a compendium of our [Persian] culture and the symbol and archetype of the Persian spirit." – *Ā'yina-yi jām* (Tehran: Intishārāt-i 'Ilmī 1368 A.Hsh./ 1989), p. 24.
36 Khurrāmshāhī, "Ḥāfiẓ dar farhang-i mā," p. 132.
37 Khānlarī, ed. *Dīwān-i … Ḥāfiẓ*, ghazal 218: 3; Browne, *Literary History*, III, p. 283.

38 Khānlarī, ed. *Dīwān-i … Ḥāfiẓ*, ghazal 431: 9; Browne, *Literary History*, III, p. 283.

39 Cited by Muḥammad Muʿīn, *Ḥāfiẓ-i shīrīn-sukhan*, (Tehran: Intishārāt-i Muʿīn 1370 A.Hsh./1991), II, p. 684.

40 *Dīvān-i Kamāl al-Dīn Masʿūd Khujandī*, ed. ʿAzīz Dawlatābādī (Tehran 1958), introduction, p. vii.

41 *Kulliyāt-e Busḥaq Aṭʿamah-i Shīrāzī*, ed. Manṣūr Rastigār-Fasāʾī (Tehran: Mīrāth-e Maktūb 1382 A.Hsh./2003).

42 Iḥsān Yārshātir, *Shiʿr-i fārsī dar ʿahd-i Shāh Rukh: yā āghāz- inḥiṭāṭ-i shiʿr-i fārsī* (Tehran: University of Tehran Press 1334 A.Hsh./1954), p. 81.

43 Faraḥ Niyāzkār, "Dāʿī Shīrāzī," *Dānishnāma-ye zabān va adab-e fārsī*, ed. Ismāʿīl Saʿādat, (Tehran: Farhangistān-i zabān va adab-i fārsī 1391 A.Hsh./ 2012), vol. III, p. 129; Ṣafā, *Tārīkh-i Adabiyyāt dar Īrān*, (Tehran: Intishārāt-i Majīd 1373 A.Hsh./1994; 10th edition), IV, p. 336.

44 Yārshātir, *Shiʿr-i fārsī*, pp. 80-81.

45 Yārshātir, *Shiʿr-i fārsī*, p. 80.

46 Dhabīḥu'llāh Ṣafā, *Tārīkh-i Adabiyāt-i Īrān*, (Tehran: Intishārāt-i Firdaws 1373 A.Hsh./1994, 13th edition), IV, p. 329.

47 *Dīvān-e Ādharī Isfarāyenī*, ed. Muḥsin Kiyānī and Sayyid ʿAbbās Rastakhīz (Tehran: Mūzih va markaz-e asnād-e Majlis-e Shūrā-ye Islāmī 1389 A.Hsh./2010), introduction, pp. lxxvi–lxxvii. Likewise, Several pages of Adharī's prose treatise *Jawāhir al-asrār (Jewels of the Mysteries) (Jawāhir al-asrār)* are devoted to explanation of abstruse imagery in selected verses of many of the great classical Persian poets, including Ḥāfiẓ. See his *Jewels of the Mysteries (Jawāhir al-asrār)*: British Library manuscript No. 1269, in the Hermann Ethé, *Catalogue of Persian Manuscripts in the India Office Library* (London: India Office Library 1980), pp. 1128-1129 (no. 2036).

48 *Dīvān-e Ghazālī Mashhadī (Āthār al-shabāb)*, ed. Ḥusayn Qarbānpūr Ārānī (Tehran: Intishārāt-e ʿIlmī va Farhangī 1387 A.Hsh./2009), introduction, p. xxvii.

49 Aḥmad Gulchīn-Maʿānī, *Maktab-e vuqūʿ dar shiʿr-e fārsī* (Tehran: Intishārāt-e Bunyād-e Farhang-e Īrān 1348 A.Hsh./1969), p. 390.

50 Gulchīn-Maʿānī, *Maktab-e vuqūʿ*, p. 297.

51 Kayvān Samīʿī, "Taḍmīn dar ghazaliyāt-i Ḥāfiẓ," in his selected essays entitled: *Taḥqīqāt-i adabī: sukhanānī pīrāmūn-i shiʿr va shāʿirī* (Tehran: 1982), pp. 378-379.

52 Cf. J. Schimdt. "Ḥāfiẓ and Other Persian Authors in Ottoman Bibliomancy: the Extraordinary Case of Kefevī Hüseyn Efendi's *Rāznāme* (Late Sixteenth Century)," *Persica*, 21 (2006-2007): 63-74.

53 *Dīwān-i Ḥāfiẓ*, ed. Khānlarī, *ghazal* 201: 3.

Introduction

1 Ḥāfiẓ, *Dīvān-i Khawja Shams al-Dīn Muḥammad Ḥāfiẓ Shīrāzī*, ed. Muḥammad Qazvīnī and Qāsim Ghanī (Tehran: Intishārāt-i Zavvār 1320/1941), *ghazal* 206, v. 10.

2 P. Avery, *The Collected Lyrics of Hafiz of Shiraz*, p. 265; *ghazal* 202.

3 Mu'īn, *Ḥāfiẓ-i shirīn-sukhan* (Tehran: Ṣidā-yi Mu'āṣir, 1375/1966), Vol. 1, p. 690.

4 'Alī Ferdowsi, 'The 'Emblem of the Manifestation of the Iranian Spirit': Hafiz and the Rise of the National Cult of Persian Poetry', *Iranian Studies*, Vol. 41, No. 5 (2008), p. 667.

5 Ḥāfiẓ, *Dīvān-i Khawja Shams al-Dīn Muḥammad Ḥāfiẓ Shīrāzī*, ed. Muḥammad Qazvīnī and Qāsim Ghanī (Tehran: Intishārāt-i Zavvār 1320/1941), *ghazal* 86, v. 8.

6 M. Thābitī, 'Khawja-yi Faqīr', *Majala-yi muḥīṭ*, No. 5 (Autumn 1321), p. 35.

7 a *ghazal* (Persian lyric) is a poetic form entailing of rhyming verses and a refrain, with each line distributing the same meter. A *ghazal* may be assumed as a poetic manifestation of both the pain of loss or separation and the magnificence of love, despite its pain. The form is ancient, originating in sixth-century Arabic poetry. It is derived from the Arabian panegyric *qaṣida* (panegyric). The fundamental requirements of the *ghazal* are alike in stringency to those of the sonnet. In style and content it is a type that has demonstrated capable of a bizarre variety of expression around its central themes of love and separation. It is one of the primary poetic forms which the Indo-Perso-Arabic civilization offered to the eastern Islamic world.

8 Verse-adages by other poets such as Sā'ib are similarly famous and, had space permitted, might have been cited here.

9 Dihkhudā, *Amthāl va hikam* (Tehran: Sipihr, 1352/1974), Vol. 1, p. 99. *Cf.* Ḥāfiẓ, *Dīvān-i Ḥāfiẓ Shīrāzī*, ed. M. Qazvīnī and Q. Ghanī, *ghazal* 299, v. 1.

10 Dihkhudā, *Amthāl va hikam*, Vol. 1, p. 104. *Cf.* Ḥāfiẓ, *Dīvān-i Ḥāfiẓ Shīrāzī*, ed. M. Qazvīnī and Q. Ghanī, *ghazal* 80, v. 2.

11 Ḥāfiẓ, *Dīvān-i Ḥāfiẓ Shīrāzī*, ed. M. Qazvīnī and Q. Ghanī, *ghazal* 471, v. 7.

12 Dihkhudā, *Amthāl va hikam*, Vol. 1, p. 98.

13 Ibid., Vol. 1, p. 105.

14 Ibid.

15 Ibid., Vol. 1, p. 110.

16 Ibid., Vol. 2, p. 807.

17 Ibid., Vol. 1, p. 96.

18 Ḥāfiẓ, *Dīvān-i Ḥāfiẓ Shīrāzī*, ed. M. Qazvīnī and Q. Ghanī, *ghazal* 387, v. 7.

19 Dihkhudā, *Amthāl va hikam*, Vol. 2, p. 802. *Cf.* Ḥāfiẓ, *Dīvān-i Ḥāfiẓ Shīrāzī*, ed. M. Qazvīnī and Q. Ghanī, *ghazal* 493, v. 2.
20 Ḥāfiẓ, *Dīvān-i Ḥāfiẓ Shīrāzī*, ed. M. Qazvīnī and Q. Ghanī, *ghazal* 123, v. 7.
21 Dihkhudā, *Amthāl va hikam*, Vol. 1, p. 146.
22 Ibid.
23 Ibid.
24 Ḥāfiẓ, *Dīvān-i Ḥāfiẓ Shīrāzī*, ed. M. Qazvīnī and Q. Ghanī, *ghazal* 126, v. 5.
25 Ibid., *ghazal* 484, v. 10.
26 Ibid., *ghazal* 481, v. 4.
27 ʿA. Dashtī, *Kākh-i ibdāʿ: Andishahā-yi gūnāgūn-i Ḥāfiẓ* (Tehran: Shirkat-i Qalam, 1385/2007), p. 50.
28 Ḥāfiẓ, *Dīvān-i Ḥāfiẓ Shīrāzī*, ed. M. Qazvīnī and Q. Ghanī, *ghazal* 440, v. 7.
29 Avery, *Collected Lyrics*, p. 520; *ghazal* 431.

Chapter I – The Life and Times of Ḥāfiẓ

1 M. Nīknām, *Muqaddama-i kitāb shināsī-i Ḥāfiẓ* (Shīrāz: Markaz-i Ḥāfiẓ-Shināsī, 1381/2003), p. 6. *Cf.* K. Ḥasanlī, *Chishma-i khurshid: Bāz khānī-i zindagī, andisha va sukhan-i Ḥāfiẓ-i Shīrāzī* (Shīrāz: Navīd, 1385/2007), p. 19.
2 H. Dabāshī, 'Taʿbirī bar taʿbirāt-i Ḥāfiẓ', *Iran Nameh*, Vol. 6, No. 4 (Summer 1988), p. 574.
3 L. Lewisohn, 'Zindagī va dawrān-i Kamāl-i Khujandī', *Iran Nameh*, Vol. 10, No. 4 (Autumn 1992), pp. 689-706.
4 E.T. Gray (trans.), *Ḥāfiẓ the Green Sea of Heaven: Fifty Ghazals from the Dīwān of Ḥāfiẓ* (Ashland, OR: White Cloud Press, 2002), pp. 11-17. *Cf.* Taqī al-Dīn M. Awhadī, *Tadhkira-yi ʿarafāt al-ʿāshiqin va ʿarasāt al-ʿārifin* (Tehran: Asāṭir, 1388/2010), Vol. 2, p. 1069.
5 ʿA.A. Dihkhudā, *Lughat-nāma*, ed. M. Muʿīn and M. Jaʿfar Shahidi (Tehran: Muʿassissi-yi Lughat-nāma Dihkhudā and Tehran University Press, 1373/1994), Vol. 5, p. 7490, s.v. 'Ḥāfiẓ Shīrāzī'. Dihkhudā asserts his date of birth to be 720/1320. *Cf.* M.M. ʿA. Mudarris, *Rihānat al-adab fi tarjuma al-maʿrūfīn bil kunīyat al-laqab* (Tabrīz: Shafaq, [n.d.]), Vol. 2, pp. 12-14; Arberry, *Classical Persian Literature* (London: George Allen and Unwin Ltd, 1958), p. 330; B. Khurramshāhī, 'Ḥāfiẓ's Life and Times', *EIr*, Vol. 11, p. 468. Scholars cite a variety of birth and death dates, however, the most accurate are believed to be 715-792/1315-1392.

6 J. Rypka, *History of Iranian Literature*, ed. K. Jahn (Dordrecht-Holland: D. Reidel Publishing Company, 1968), p. 271.

7 ʿA. Zarrinkūb, *Az kūcha-yi rindān* (Tehran: Kitābhā-i Jibī, 1349/1971), pp. 35-37. *Cf.* R.Q. Hidāyat, *Majmaʿ al-fuṣaḥā*, ed. M. Muṣaffā (Tehran: Amīr Kabīr, 1382/2003), Vol. 2, p. 37.

8 Zarrinkūb, *Az kūcha-yi rindān*, p. 37.

9 Ḥāfiẓ, *Dīvān-i Ḥāfiẓ Shīrāzī*, ed. M. Qazvīnī and Q. Ghanī, *ghazal* 154, v. 5.

10 Avery, *Collected Lyrics*, p. 205; *ghazal* 150.

11 Ḥ. Imdād, *Shīrāz dar guzashta va ḥāl* (Shīrāz: Itiḥādīyi-yi Maṭbūʿātī-i -i Fārs, 1341/1963), pp. 28-31.

12 H. Roemer, 'The Jalayirids, Muẓaffarids and Sarbadārs', in P. Jackson and L. Lockhart (eds.), *The Cambridge History of Iran*, Vol. 6: *The Timurid and Ṣafavid Periods* (Cambridge: Cambridge University Press 1986), p. 13. *Cf.* M. Zarkūb, *Muʿīn al-Dīn Abū'l ʿAbbās Aḥmad ibn Abī al-Khayr Shīrāzī, Shīrāz-nāma*, ed. Ismāʿīl Vāʿiz Javādī (Tehran: Bunyād-i Farhang-i Iran, 767/1350), p. 123; R.Q. Hidāyat, *Tadhkira-yi rīyāḍ al-ʿārifīn* (Tehran: Mahdīyyi, 1316/1937), Vol. 2, p. 131.

13 G. Bell, *The Garden of Heaven*: *Poems of Hafiz* (Mineola, NY: Dover Publication, 2003), pp. 1-7.

14 J. Limbert, *Shiraz in the Age of Hafez*: *The Glory of a Medieval Persian City* (Seattle: University of Washington Press, 2004), pp. 32-33. *Cf.* Arberry, Shiraz: *Persian City of Saints and Poets* (Norman: University of Oklahoma Press, 1960), p. 141.

15 Ḥāfiẓ, *Dīvān-i Ḥāfiẓ Shīrāzī*, ed. M. Qazvīnī and Q. Ghanī, *ghazal* 207, v. 8.

16 Limbert, *Shiraz in the Age of Hafez*, p. 33.

17 E.G. Browne, *A Literary History of Persia* (Cambridge: Goodword Books, 2002), Vol. 3, p. 163.

18 Zarkūb, *Shīrāz-nāma*, pp. 199-200. *Cf.* Annemarie Schimmel, 'Ḥāfiẓ and his Contemporaries', in P. Jackson and L. Lockhart (eds.), *The Cambridge History of Iran*, Vol. 6: *The Timurid and Ṣafavid Periods* (Cambridge: Cambridge University Press 1986), pp. 929-932.

19 Ḥāfiẓ, *Dīvān-i Ḥāfiẓ Shīrāzī*, ed. M. Qazvīnī and Q. Ghanī, *ghazal* 327, v. 10.

20 Limbert, *Shiraz in the Age of Hafez*, p. 148.

21 Ghanī, *Baḥth dar āthār va afkār va aḥvāl-i Ḥāfiẓ: Tārīkh-i ʿ aṣr-i Ḥāfiẓ yā tārīkh-i Fārs va muzāfāt va ayālāt-i mujāvirī dar qarn-i hashtum* (Tehran: Zavvār, 1344/1966), pp. 124-125.

22 Qāḍī Majd al-Dīn (662/1261-756/1355) was from a well-known Shīrāzī family of religious jurists who had been in charge of religious affairs for 150 years. Ghanī, *Baḥth dar āthār va afkār va aḥvāl-i Ḥāfiẓ*, p. 125.

23 Ibid., p. 124.

24 Zarkūb, *Shīrāz-nāma*, p. 187.

1. An adviser and minister of the king: Ḥājjī Qavām al-Dīn Tamghachī (d. 754/1353).
2. The supreme judge (Qāḍī al-Quḍāt) of Fārs: Qāḍī Majd al-Dīn Ismāʿīl Fālī (669/1268-755/1355).
3. A judge and theologian: Qāḍī ʿAzud al-Dīn Ījī (d. 755/1355).
4. A Sufi master: Shaykh Amīn al-Dīn Balyānī Kāzirunī (d. 744/1344).

25 The Qalʿi-i sifid was the only fortress that survived the Mongol attack, due to its strong structure and impenetrable geographical location. ʿA.M. Āyatī, *Tārīkh-i vaṣṣāf* (Tehran: Intishārāt-i Bunyād-i Farhang-i Iran 1346/1968), pp. 96-99.

26 Limbert, *Shiraz in the Age of Hafez*, p. 38.

27 M.A. Razavī-Nizhād, *Chihār ṣad shāʿir-i barguzidi-i pārsī gūī: Hikmat-i ʿilmi-i zindagī-yi insānhā* (Tehran: Intishārāt-i Tehran, 1369/1990), p. 205. *Cf.* Dalal, *Ethics in Persian Poetry* (Calcutta: Abhinav Publication, 1995), pp. 229-242, and Arberry, *Classical Persian Literature*, p. 330.

28 Dalal, *Ethics in Persian Poetry*, pp. 330-333.

29 Gray (trans.), *Ḥāfiẓ the Green Sea of Heaven*, p. 2.

30 Schimmel, 'Ḥāfiẓ and his Contemporaries', p. 936.

31 Ḥāfiẓ, *Dīvān-i Ḥāfiẓ Shīrāzī*, ed. M. Qazvīnī and Q. Ghanī, *ghazal* 128, v. 6.

32 Ibid., *ghazal* 365, v. 2.

33 Ibid., *ghazal* 490, v. 6.

34 Ibid., *ghazal* 327, v. 4. *Cf.* Ḥāfiẓ, *Dīvān-i Khawja Shams al-Dīn Muḥammad: Mulhaqāt-i ghazalīyāt, qaṣāʾid, mathnavīyyāt, qaṭaʿāt va rubāʿīyāt*, ed. P.N. Khānlarī (Tehran: Khārazmī, 1362/1984), Vol. 1, *ghazal* 481, v. 4.

35 M. Muʿīn, *Ḥāfiẓ-i shirin sukhan*, ed. Mahdukht Muʿīn (Tehran: Sidāyi Muʿāṣir, 1389/2011), Vol. 1, p. 140.

36 Ḥāfiẓ, *Dīvān-i Ḥāfiẓ Shīrāzī*, ed. M. Qazvīnī and Q. Ghanī, *ghazal* 216, v. 1, 2. *Cf.* Ḥāfiẓ, *Dīvān-i Ḥāfiẓ*, ed. Khānlarī, Vol. 1, *ghazal* 210, v. 1, 2, and Muʿīn, *Ḥāfiẓ-i shirīn sukhan*, Vol. 1, p. 139 – this verse is an indication of the loss of Ḥāfiẓ's wife and he composed this verse in mourning for her.

37 Muʿīn, *Ḥāfiẓ-i shirīn sukhan*, Vol. 1, p. 141.

38 Ḥāfiẓ, *Dīvān-i Ḥāfiẓ Shīrāzī*, ed. M. Qazvīnī and Q. Ghanī, *ghazal* 54, v. 7; see also: Ḥāfiẓ, *Dīvān-i Ḥāfiẓ*, ed. Khānlarī, Vol. 1, *ghazal* 55, v. 7. I am following certain commentators here who state that Ḥāfiẓ wrote this verse in mourning for his son: *Cf.* Muʿīn, *Ḥāfiẓ-i shirīn sukhan*, Vol. 1, p. 141, and R. Dhūʾl-Nūr (ed.), *Dar justujū-yi Ḥāfiẓ* (Tehran: Zavvār, 1362/1984), Vol. 1, p. 130.

39 Zarrinkūb, *Az kūcha-yi rindān*, p. 41.
40 Ibn Battūta, *Safar-nāma*, trans. M. ʿA. Muvvahid (Tehran: Bungāh-i Tarjūma va Nashr-i Kitāb 1337/1959), p. 199.
41 Browne, *Literary History*, Vol. 3, pp. 163-164. *Cf.* Muʿīn, *Ḥāfiẓ-i shirīn sukhan*, Vol. 1, p. 192.
42 Browne, *Literary History*, Vol. 3, p. 163.
43 Ibid.
44 H. Roemer, 'The Jalayirids', p. 13.
45 N. Inqitāʿ, *Ḥāfiẓ va Kish-i Mihr: Shaydā-yi shūrida-yi Shīrāz, dar kārgāh-i Kishī Kuhan* (Tehran: Shirkat-i Kitāb, 1387/2008), p. 17.
46 Schimmel, 'Ḥāfiẓ and his Contemporaries', pp. 932-935.
47 Ḥāfiẓ, *Dīvān-i Ḥāfiẓ Shīrāzī*, ed. M. Qazvīnī and Q. Ghanī, *ghazal* 202, v. 6.
48 Limbert, *Shiraz in the Age of Hafez*, p. 37.
49 Literally sheriffs and policemen; a person who constantly reminds sinners of their sins, in this case drinking wine. These individuals were assigned to watch and, if necessary, arrest citizens who violated Islamic laws by consuming or purchasing alcoholic beverages, which were forbidden during certain periods of the Islamic history of Iran. Dihkhudā, *Lughat-nāma*, Vol. 12, p. 17978, s.v. '*muḥtasib*'. *Cf.* Abū'l Faḍl-i Bayhaqī-yi Dabīr, ed. J.M. Ṣādiqī, *Tārīkh-i Beyhaqī* (Tehran: Nashr-i Markaz, 1377/1999), p. 441; C-H De Fouchécour, describes *muḥtasib*, '[…] as a strict *Censor morum* and officer of the Vice-squad in Shīrāz.' C-H De Fouchécour, 'Ḥāfiẓ and the Sufi', *Ḥāfiẓ and the Religion of Love*, (ed.), L. Lewisohn (London and New York: I.B.Tauris, 2010), p. 144.
50 Ghanī, *Baḥth dar āthār va afkār va aḥvāl-i Ḥāfiẓ*, p. 174.
51 Roemer, 'The Jalayirids', p. 13. *Cf.* Arberry, *Shiraz*, pp. 141-147.
52 Ḥāfiẓ, *Dīvān-i Ḥāfiẓ Shīrāzī*, ed. M. Qazvīnī and Q. Ghanī, *ghazal* 165, v. 4.
53 Ibid., *ghazal* 178, v. 4.
54 Muʿīn, *Ḥāfiẓ-i shirīn sukhan*, Vol. 1, p. 197.
55 Ḥāfiẓ, *Dīvān-i Ḥāfiẓ Shīrāzī*, ed. M. Qazvīnī and Q. Ghanī, *ghazal* 200, v. 2.
56 Ghanī, *Baḥth dar āthār va afkār va aḥvāl-i Ḥāfiẓ*, p. 173.
57 Ḥāfiẓ, *Dīvān-i Ḥāfiẓ Shīrāzī*, ed. M. Qazvīnī and Q. Ghanī, *ghazal* 206, v. 2.
58 Ibid., *ghazal* 204, v. 7.
59 Fasten on his belt: this refers to the Shāh, getting ready to ride to engage in battle.
60 Ghanī, *Baḥth dar āthār va afkār va aḥvāl-i Ḥāfiẓ*, p. 174.
61 Shiblī Nuʿmānī, *Shiʿr al-ʿajam*, ed. Fakhr Dāʾī Gilānī (Tehran: Ibn Sinā, 1339/1961), pp. 10-14.
62 Browne, *Literary History*, p. 277. *Cf.* Limbert, *Shiraz in the Age of Hafez*, p. 39.

63 M. Kutbī, *Tārīkh-i āl-i Muẓaffar*, ed. A.H. Navā'ī (Tehran: Ibn Sinā, 1334/1956), pp. 56-59. *Cf.* Hidāyat, *Majma' al-fuṣaḥā*, Vol. 1, p. 142.

64 Ḥāfiẓ, *Dīvān-i Ḥāfiẓ Shīrāzī*, ed. M. Qazvīnī and Q. Ghanī, p. 376, v. 9.

65 Limbert, *Shiraz in the Age of Hafez*, p. 39.

66 Ḥāfiẓ, *Dīvān-i Ḥāfiẓ Shīrāzī*, ed. M. Qazvīnī and Q. Ghanī, p. 366.

67 Shāh Shujā' (b. 733) was Mubāriz's second son. Sharaf al-Din Muẓaffar II (b. 725) was his eldest, but he had died on 754, his father was still alive, blinded, and languishing in a fortress in the Garmsir of Shīrāz. He was alive for about four years after Shāh Shujā' ascended to the throne following the coup of 759/760 in the month of Ramazān against his father.

68 Zarrinkūb, *Az kūcha-yi rindān*, p. 110. On Abarqūh, see C.E. Bosworth, 'Abarqūh,' in *EIr*, Vol. 1, pp. 64-65.

69 Zarrinkūb, *Az kūcha-yi rindān*, pp. 110-112.

70 Ḥāfiẓ, *Dīvān-i Ḥāfiẓ Shīrāzī*, ed. M. Qazvīnī and Q. Ghanī, *ghazal* 156, v. 5.

71 Zarrinkūb, *Az kūcha-yi rindān*, p. 110. Bosworth asserts that 'The Islamic geographers of the tenth/fourteenth century describe Abarqūh as lying in the Shīrāz-Iṣfahān-Estakr road. [...] Geographers describe Abarqūh as prosperous and populous in 'Abbāsid and Buyid times; it was fortified, with a citadel, and had a fine Friday mosque (the precursor of the present Friday mosque, which dates from post-Mongol times). [...] The streets and houses were jumbled together in a close network, and the houses were of a vaulted construction in sun-dried brick, as at Yazd. Although the surrounding region was treeless and arid, and gardens and orchards were lacking, ample provisions were brought in from outside. The town produced cotton cloth for export.' 'Abarqūh,' *EIr*, Vol. 1, pp. 64-65.

72 Zarrinkūb, *Az kūcha-yi rindān*, pp. 110-120.

73 Ibid., p. 111.

74 Kutbī, *Tārīkh-i āl-i Muẓaffar*, ed. A.H. Navā'ī, p. 104.

75 Zarrinkūb, *Az kūcha-yi rindān*, p. 110.

76 Ibid., pp. 120-121.

77 Ibid., pp. 118-119.

78 Ibid., p. 119.

79 Ghanī, *Baḥth dar āthār va afkār va aḥvāl-i Ḥāfiẓ*, p. 276.

80 According to Islamic law, a man cannot be ruler if he is blind; for this reason, aspirants to the throne sometimes blinded their rivals.

81 Bosworth, *New Islamic Dynasties*, pp. 264-265.

82 Schimmel, 'Ḥāfiẓ and his Contemporaries', p. 935.

83 Roemer, 'The Jalayirids', pp. 15-16.

84 Zarkūb, *Shīrāz-nāma*, p. 112.
85 Muʿīn, *Ḥāfiẓ-i shirīn sukhan*, Vol. 1, p. 228.
86 Ḥāfiẓ, *Dīvān-i Ḥāfiẓ Shīrāzī*, ed. M. Qazvīnī and Q. Ghanī, *ghazal* 242, v. 1.
87 Ibid., *ghazal* 153, v. 10.
88 Dihkhudā, *Lughat-nāma*, Vol. 9, p. 12425, s.v. 'Shāh Manṣūr'.
89 Ḥāfiẓ, *Dīvān-i Ḥāfiẓ Shīrāzī*, ed. M. Qazvīnī and Q. Ghanī, *ghazal* 402, v. 1. *Cf.* Dihkhudā, *Lughat-nāma*, Vol. 9, p. 12425, s.v. 'Shāh Manṣūr'.
90 B. Khurramshāhī, 'Ḥāfiẓ's Life and Times', *Elr*, Vol. 11, p. 468. Ḥāfiẓ's death date is recorded as 791/1388 in Hidāyat, *Majmaʿ al-fuṣaḥā*, Vol. 2, p. 37.
91 Ḥāfiẓ, *Dīvān-i Ḥāfiẓ Shīrāzī*, ed. M. Qazvīnī and Q. Ghanī, *ghazal* 205, v. 3.
92 F. Mīrzā'ī, *Mafhūm-i rindī dar shiʿr-i Ḥāfiẓ* (Tehran: Kavīr, 1373/1995), pp. 55-64. For a further study of the meaning of *rind* in Ḥāfiẓ's poetic language, see Mīrzā'ī, *Mafhūm-i rindī dar shiʿr-i Ḥāfiẓ*; Franklin Lewis, 'Hafez and *Rendi*', *EIr*, Vol. 11, pp. 483-491; R. Bly and L. Lewisohn (trans.), *The Angels Knocking on the Tavern Door: Thirty Poems of Hafez* (New York: Harper Collins, 2008), pp. 74-75; L. Lewisohn, 'Prolegomenon', *Ḥāfiẓ and the Religion of Love* (London and New York: I.B.Tauris, 2010), pp. 31-53, and M. Ḥ. Tabrīzī, *Burhān-i Qātiʿ*, ed. M. Muʿīn (Tehran: Ibn Sinā, 1342/1964), Vol. 2, p. 963, s.v. '*Rind*'.
93 Browne, *Literary History*, Vol. 3, pp. 182-186.
94 B.F. Manz, *The Rise and Rule of Tamerlane* (Cambridge: Cambridge University Press, 1989), p. 28. *Cf.* Beatrice Forbes Manz, 'Temür and the Problem of a Conqueror's Legacy', *Journal of the Royal Asiatic Society*, Vol. 8, No. 1 (April 1998), p. 25.
95 Rypka, *History of Iranian Literature*, p. 279.
96 Browne, *Literary History*, Vol. 3, p. 182.
97 The Dajjāl is a figure associated with the apocalypse, Muslims believe that he (or some say more than one) will come towards the end of time as a religious imposter to deceive believers.
98 Rypka, *History of Iranian Literature*, p. 279.
99 Ḥāfiẓ, *Dīvān-i Ḥāfiẓ Shīrāzī*, ed. M. Qazvīnī and Q. Ghanī, *ghazal* 242, v. 6.
100 Avery, *Collected Lyrics*, p. 303; *ghazal* 238.
101 M. Axworthy, *Iran: Empire of the Mind, A History from Zoroaster to the Present Day* (London: Penguin Books, 2007), p. 119.
102 Rypka, *History of Iranian Literature*, p. 279.
103 E.G. Browne, *A History of Persian Literature Under Tatar Dominion (A.D. 1265-1502)* (Cambridge: University Press, 1920), p. 181. *Cf.* Rypka, *History of Iranian Literature*, p. 279.

104 'The bloody struggles preceding the final Mozaffarid collapse had been the blinding of Zein al-Abedīn in 1391, the death of Abū Yazid b. Amīr Mohammad in 1390, the death in battle of Shāh Mansur in 1393, and the slaughter of 50,000 Esfahanis by Amīr Timur's forces in 1387.' Limbert, *Shiraz in the Age of Hafez*, p. 42.

105 Zarrinkūb, *Az kūcha-yi rindān*, p. 247. *Cf.* Ḥāfiẓ, *Dīvān-i Ḥāfiẓ*, ed. Khānlarī, *ghazal* 431, v. 3.

106 'Ubayd Zākānī, *Kullīyāt-i 'Ubayd Zākānī*, ed. 'A.I. Āshtīyānī (Tehran: Iqbāl, 1334/1956), p. 4.

107 Khwājū Kirmānī, *Dīvān of Khwājū Kirmānī*, ed. M. Burhānī (Tehran: Zavvār, 1370/1992), p. 8.

108 Frye, *Anatomy*, 90: 'We have actual allegory when a poet explicitly indicates the relationship of his images to examples and precepts, and so tries to indicate how a commentary on him should proceed.'

109 A. Fletcher, Allegory, *the theory of a symbolic mode* (Princeton and Oxford: Princeton University Press, 2012), pp. 221-222.

110 Ibid.

111 Ibid.

112 Milton's two poems, *L'Allegro* and *il Penseroso*, interweaves to create dramatic tension between the personified characters (*L'Allegro* or the "Joyful man" and *il Penseroso* or the "Contemplative man"). See Michael O'Connell, John Powell, "Music and Sense in Handel's Setting of Milton's *L'Allegro* and *Il Penseroso*" (Autumn 1978). Eighteenth-Century Studies, *12*' (1): pp. 16-46.

113 Salmān Sāvajī, *Dīvān-i Salmān Sāvajī*, ed. M. Mushfiq (Tehran: Ṣafī 'Alī Shāh, 1336/1958), p. 9.

114 Khawja 'Imād al-Dīn 'Alī Faqih-i Kirmānī, *Dīvān-i qaṣā'id va ghazalīyāt-i Khawja 'Imād al-Dīn 'Alī Faqih-i Kirmānī*, ed. R. Humāyūn-Farrukh (Tehran: Ibn Sinā, 1348/1970), p. 20.

115 Kamāl Khujandī, *Dīvān-i Kamāl Khujandī*, ed. 'A. Dawlatābādī (Tehran: Sazimān-i Chāp va Intishārāt-i Islāmī, 1375/1997), p. 25.

116 Jahān Malik Khātūn, *Dīvān-i kāmil-i Jahān Malik Khātūn, qarn-i hashtum-i hijrī qamarī*, ed. P. Kāshānīrād (Tehran: Zavvār, 1374/1996), p. 9.

117 Shāh Ni'matullāh Valī, *Kullīyāt-i ash'ār-i Shāh Ni'matullāh Valī*, ed. J. Nūrbakhsh (Tehran: Intishārāt-i Yaldā Qalam, 1385/2007), p. 12.

118 Nāṣir Bukhārā'ī, *Dīvān-i Nāṣir Bukhārā'ī, az sukhanvarān-i qarn-i hashtum-i hijrī*, ed. M. Dirakhshān (Tehran: Nūryānī, 1353/1957), pp. 1-5.

119 Ḥāfiẓ, *Dīvān-i Ḥāfiẓ Shīrāzī*, ed. M. Qazvīnī and Q. Ghanī, *ghazal* 41, v. 7.

120 Nu'mānī, *Shi'r al-'ajam*, p. 14.

121 Jahān Malik Khātūn, *Dīvān*, pp. 1-7.

122 My analysis here is indebted to certain observations by Losensky. P. Losensky, *Welcoming Fighānī, Imitation and Poetic Individuality in the Ṣafavid-Mughal Ghazal* (Costa Mesa, CA: Mazda Publication, 1998), p. 71.

123 'Sincerity is a function of style, involving a relation between the artist and the public; it has to do with the presentation of a self appropriate to the kind of verse being written, to the genre, not with the personality of the poet. [...] In ancient literature it is the personality expressed in the poem, not the personality of the historical poet, that signifies.' Robert C. Elliot, *The Literary Persona* (Chicago: University of Chicago Press, 1982), pp. 43-45.

124 J.T.P. de Bruijn, 'Hafez's Poetic Art', *Elr* 11, pp. 400-474.

125 Ibid.

126 This ability allowed the poets to create a unique style known as the 'Ḥāfizian style' (*sabk-i Ḥāfiẓ*), M.S. Kadkanī, *Advār-i shiʿr-i fārsī* (Tehran: Sukhan, 1380/2002), pp. 154-157. Lewis partly confirms Kadkanī's statement, observing: 'Complementing this themetic sensuality in the *ghazal*s of Ḥāfiẓ is an often tactile sonority created by a thick texture and complex patterning of sounds. We know Ḥāfiẓ to have been competitively conscious of the work and wording of other poets, which he often quotes, adapts and improves upon.' M.S. Kadkanī, 'Ḥāfiẓ and Music', *EIr*, Vol. 11, p. 493.

127 M.J. Maḥjūb, *Sabk-i Khurāsānī dar shiʿr-i fārsī* (Tehran: Firdawsī, [n.d]), pp. 40-41.

128 During Shāhrukh's age, the poetry market was buoyant; both literature and art were sponsored and cultivated. However, after Shāhrukh's death, this attention to the arts faded away and was never recovered. This decline was a result of the problems the state faced, particularly the poor economic and sociopolitical situation. There was neither social, nor economic security, and high rates of unemployment and crime existed. Losensky, *Welcoming Fighānī*, p. 50.

129 E. Yarshater, *Shiʿr-i fārsī dar ʿahd-i Shāhrukh* (Tehran: Chāpkhāna-yi Dānishgāh, 1334/1956), pp. 79-81.

130 Ibid., p. 80.

131 Ibid., p. 81.

132 Ibid.

133 Shamīsā, *Sabk shināsī-i shiʿr*, pp. 256-257. *Cf.* Losensky, *Encyclopedia of Iranica*, 'Jāmī: Life and Works', www.iranica.com/articles/jami-i (accessed 18 April 2011).

134 Shamīsā, *Sabk shināsī-i shiʿr*, p. 259.

135 Ibid., pp. 260-261. The above table is partly adopted from Shamīsā, *Sabk shināsī-i shi'r*, p. 242.
136 S. Shamīsā, *Naqd-i adabī* (Tehran: Firdawsī, 1383/2005), p. 98.
137 M.T. Bahār, *Malik al-Shu'arā': Sabk shināsī* (Tehran: Amīr Kabīr, 1373/1994), Vol. 2, p. 4.
138 M. Gulbun, *Bahār va adab-i fārsī* (Tehran: Kitābhā-yi Jibī, 1351/1972), Vol. 4, pp. 3-6.
139 Bahār, *Sabk shināsī*, Vol. 2, p. 2.
140 Ḥāfiẓ, *Dīvān-i Ḥāfiẓ Shīrāzī*, ed. M. Qazvīnī and Q. Ghanī, *ghazal* 292, v. 3.
141 Avery, *Collected Lyrics*, p. 358; *ghazal* 287.
142 E. Yarshater, 'Ḥāfiẓ's Life and Times', *EIr*, Vol. 11, p. 465.
143 B. Khurramshāhī, 'Ḥāfiẓ's Life and Times', *EIr*, Vol. 11, p. 468.
144 Culler notes that in the medieval tradition, 'rhetoric was considered the art of eloquence and poetry (since it seeks to teach, to delight, and to move) [and] was a superior instance of this art'. J. Culler, *Literary Theory* (Oxford: Oxford University Press, 1997), p. 69.
145 Losensky, *Welcoming Fighānī*, p. 210.
146 W.J. Bate, *The Burden of the Past and the English Poet* (New York: W.W. Norton, 1970), pp. 89-90.

Chapter II – Ḥāfiẓ in Historical Perspective, from the Late Tīmūrīds to the Qājārs

1 Bābā Fighānī, *Dīvān-i 'ash'ār-i Bābā Fighānī*, ed. A.S. Khunsārī (Tehran: Iqbāl, 1362/1984), p. 8. *Cf.* DH. Ṣafā, *Tārīkh-i adabīyāt dar Iran* (Tehran: Firdawsī, 1370/1992), Vol. 4, p. 434, and 'I. Shakībāpūr, *'Iṭilā'āt-i 'umumī* (Tehran: Ishrāqī, 1384/2006), p. 78.
2 Browne, *A Literary History of Persian*, vol, 3, p. 507. *Cf.* R.Q. Hidāyat, *Rīyāḍ al-'ārifīn* (Tehran: Amīr Kabīr, 1388/2009), p. 104.
3 W. Hanaway, 'Comments on Literature before the Ṣafavid Period, "Studies on Iṣfahān"', *Iranian Studies*, Vol. 7 (Winter-Spring 1974), p. 134.
4 Jāmī, *Dīvān-i Kāmil-i Jāmī*, ed. H. Razī (Tehran: Pirūz, 1341/1963), pp. 22-23.
5 Ibid. *Cf.* Arberry, *Classical Persian Literature*, p. 426.
6 Arberry, *Classical Persian Literature*, p. 426.
7 R.Q. Hidāyat, *Rīyāḍ al-'ārifīn* (Tehran: Āftāb, 1316/1938), p. 80.
8 Jāmī, *Dīvān-i Kāmil-i Jāmī*, *ghazal* 290, v. 1.

9 Ḥāfiẓ, *Dīvān-i Ḥāfiẓ Shīrāzī*, ed. M. Qazvīnī and Q. Ghanī, *ghazal* 42, v. 1.
10 N.M. Haravī, *Jāmī* (Tehran: Ṭarh-i Naw, 1377/1999), p. 200.
11 Ibid., p. 203.
12 Jāmī, *Dīvān-i Kāmil-i Jāmī*, p. 147.
13 Ḥāfiẓ, *Dīvān-i Ḥāfiẓ Shīrāzī*, ed. M. Qazvīnī and Q. Ghanī, *ghazal* 1, v. 1.
14 Avery, *Collected Lyrics*, p. 18; *ghazal* 1. The above translation follows peter Avery's, with some modifications.
15 Ḥāfiẓ, *Dīvān-i Ḥāfiẓ Shīrāzī*, ed. M. Qazvīnī and Q. Ghanī, *ghazal* 244, v. 1.
16 Jāmī, *Dīvān-i Kāmil-i Jāmī*, p. 422.
17 Haravī, *Jāmī*, p. 205.
18 Muʿīn, *Ḥāfiẓ-i shirin sukhan*, ed. Mahdukht Muʿīn, Vol. 2, p. 712.
19 Rypka, *History of Iranian Literature*, p. 288. *Cf.* R.Q. Hidāyat, *Majmaʿ al-fuṣaḥā*, ed. M. Musaffā (Tehran: Amīr Kabīr, 1388/2009), Vol. 1, p. 328.
20 Rypka, *History of Iranian Literature*, p. 288.
21 M. Ṣ. Hāshimī, *Shiʿr va shāʿirī dar ʿaṣr-i Ṣafavī* (Tehran: Naqsh-i Jahān, 1323/1945), p. 10.
22 Losensky, *Welcoming Fighānī*, pp. 36-39.
23 Z. Ṣafa, 'Baba Faghani', *EIr*, Vol. 3, p. 291. *Cf.* S. Mīrzā Ṣafavī, *Tazkiri-i Sāmī*, ed. Rukn al-Dīn Humāyūn Farrukh (Tehran: ʿIlmī, 1967), pp. 184-185.
24 Bābā Fighānī, *Dīvān-i ʿashʿār-i Bābā Fighānī*, ed. Khunsārī, introduction, p. 19.
25 Losensky, *Welcoming Fighānī*, p. 5.
26 E.G. Browne, *A Literary History of Persia* (Cambridge: Cambridge University Press, 1920-1924), Vol. 4, pp. 229-230. *Cf.* Arberry, *Classical Persian Literature.*
27 Ehsan Yarshater, 'Persian Poetry in the Timurid and Ṣafavid Period', in P. Jackson and L. Lockhart (eds.), *The Cambridge History of Iran*, Vol. 6: *The Timurid and Ṣafavid Periods* (Cambridge: Cambridge University Press, 1986), p. 992.
28 R. Akbar, *Sharḥ-i aḥvāl va sabk-i ashʿār-i Bābā Fighānī* (Hyderabad: Shālīmār, 1974), pp. 133-134.
29 Ṣafā, *Tārīkh-i adabīyāt dar Iran* (Tehran: Firdawsī, 1364/1985), Vol. 4, p. 414.
30 Shiblī Nuʿmānī, *Shiʿr al-ʿajam*, trans. M.T. Fakhr-i Dāʿī Gilānī (Tehran: Ibn Sinā, 1335/1956), Vol. 3, p. 22.
31 Bābā Fighānī, *Dīvān-i ʿashʿār-i Bābā Fighānī*, p. 19.
32 Ibid., *ghazal* 62, v. 7.
33 Ḥāfiẓ, *Dīvān-i Ḥāfiẓ Shīrāzī*, ed. M. Qazvīnī and Q. Ghanī, *ghazal* 49, v. 2.
34 I.H. Kausar, *Fighānī's Life and Work* (Pakistan: Pakistan Historical Society, 1963), p. 94.

35 Losensky, *Welcoming Fighānī*, p. 86.
36 Ibid.
37 E.J.W. Gibb, *A History of Ottoman Poetry* (London: Luzac, 1900-1909), Vol. 5, pp. 10-22.
38 Nuʿmānī, *Shiʿr al-ʿajam*, Vol. 3, pp. 66-111.
39 Ṣafā, *Tārīkh-i adabīyāt dar Iran*, Vol. 5/2, pp. 799-814.
40 A. Tamimdari, *ʿIrfān va adab dar ʿaṣr-i Ṣafavī* (Tehran: Ḥikmat, 1993), Vol. 1, pp. 255-269, 417-435.
41 Ḥamida Ḥujjatī, "ʿUrfī-i Shīrāzī", in Ḥasan Anūshā (ed.), Dānish-nāma-i Adab-i fārsī (Tehran, 2001), pp. 1760-1764.
42 ʿUrfī Shīrāzī, *Kullīyāt-i ʿUrfī Shīrāzī*, ed. Gh. Javāhirī (Tehran: Muḥammad ʿAlī ʿIlmī, [n.d]), pp. 50-51.
43 Ibid., p. 304.
44 Ḥāfiẓ, *Dīvān-i Ḥāfiẓ Shīrāzī*, ed. M. Qazvīnī and Q. Ghanī, *ghazal* 46, v. 3.
45 ʿUrfī Shīrāzī, *Kullīyāt-i ʿUrfī Shīrāzī*, ed. Muḥammad Valī al-Ḥaqq Anṣārī (Tehran: Intishārāt-i Dānishgāh-i Tehran, 1378/1999), Vol. 1, *ghazal* 676, v. 1.
46 Ḥāfiẓ, *Dīvān-i Ḥāfiẓ Shīrāzī*, ed. M. Qazvīnī and Q. Ghanī, *ghazal* 336, v. 1.
47 Avery, *Collected Lyrics*, p. 407; *ghazal* 328.
48 ʿUrfī Shīrāzī, *Kullīyāt-i ʿUrfī Shīrāzī*, ed. Anṣārī, Vol. 1, *ghazal* 641, v. 1.
49 Ḥāfiẓ, *Dīvān-i Ḥāfiẓ Shīrāzī*, ed. M. Qazvīnī and Q. Ghanī, *ghazal* 298, v. 1.
50 Avery, *Collected Lyrics*, p. 364; *ghazal* 292.
51 Ṣā'ib Tabrīzī, *Dīvān-i Ṣā'ib Tabrīzī*, ed. S. Shamīsā (Tehran: Mustuwfī, 1373/1995), p. 1.
52 Rypka, *History of Iranian Literature*, p. 301.
53 Ṣā'ib Tabrīzī, *Dīvān-i Ṣā'ib*, ed. A. Firūzkūhī (Tehran: Anjuman-i Āthār-i Millī, 1345/1966), pp. 1-10. *Cf.* Ṣā'ib Tabrīzī, *Dīvān-i Ṣā'ib*, M. ʿA. Ṣā'ib Tabrīzī, ed. M. Qahrimān (Tehran: Shirkat-i Intishārāt-i ʿIlmī va Farhangī, 1363/1985), pp. 1-5.
54 Ṣā'ib Tabrīzī, *Dīvān-i Ṣā'ib Tabrīzī*, ed. Shamīsā, p. 1.
55 Ibid., p. 15.
56 Ibid.
57 Ibid., p. 22.
58 Ḥ. S. Nāṣirī, *Ātashkada-yi Ādhar* (Tehran: Amīr Kabīr, 1336/1958), Vol. 1, p. 126. *Cf.* Ṣā'ib Tabrīzī, *Dīvān-i Ṣā'ib*, ed. S. Betler and C.I. Djamili (Tehran: Akhtar, 1381/2002), pp. 3-7; Hidāyat, *Majmaʿ al-fuṣaḥā*, ed. M. Musaffā, Vol. 2, p. 75.
59 Hāshimī, *Shiʿr va shāʿirī*, p. 8.

60 Ṣā'ib Tabrīzī, *Dīvān-i Ṣā'ib Tabrīzī*, ed. Shamīsā, p. 17.
61 Ṣā'ib Tabrīzī, *Dīvān-i Ṣā'ib Tabrīzī*, ed. J. Manṣūr (Tehran: Nigāh, 1383/2004), Vol. 1, *ghazal* 682. v. 1.
62 Ḥāfiẓ, *Dīvān-i Ḥāfiẓ Shīrāzī*, ed. M. Qazvīnī and Q. Ghanī, *ghazal* 49, v. 4.
63 Avery, *Collected Lyrics*, p. 86; *ghazal* 50.
64 Ṣā'ib Tabrīzī, *Dīvān-i Ṣā'ib Tabrīzī*, ed. Manṣūr, Vol. 1, *ghazal* 1006, v. 1.
65 Ḥāfiẓ, *Dīvān-i Ḥāfiẓ Shīrāzī*, ed. M. Qazvīnī and Q. Ghanī, *ghazal* 19, v. 1.
66 Avery, *Collected Lyrics*, p. 57; *ghazal* 27.
67 Rypka, *History of Iranian Literature*, p. 281. *Cf.* M. Alam and Sanjay Subrahamanyan, *Indo-Persian Travels in the Age of Discoveries 1400-1800* (Cambridge: Cambridge University Press, 2007), pp. 180-185.
68 L. Lockhart, 'The Timurid and Ṣafavid Period' in P. Jackson and L. Lockhart (eds.), *The Cambridge History of Iran*, Vol. 6: *The Timurid and Ṣafavid Periods* (Cambridge: Cambridge University Press, 1986), p. 189.
69 Ibid. *Cf.* Y. Āzhand, *Tajadud-i adabī dar dawra-yi mashrūṭa* (Tehran: Mu'assasa-yi Taḥqiqāt va 'Ulūm-i Insānī, 1384/2006), p. 1.
70 Ṣafā, *Tārīkh-i adabīyāt dar Iran*, Vol. 4, p. 434.
71 R. Savory, *Iran under the Ṣafavids* (Cambridge: Cambridge University Press, 1980), p. 203. *Cf.* Rypka, *History of Iranian Literature*, p. 301.
72 Roemer, 'The Jalayirids', p. 189.
73 Ibid.
74 Ibid., p. 947.
75 Ibid., p. 948.
76 W. Floor, *A Fiscal History of Iran in the Ṣafavid and Qajar Periods 1500-1925* (New York: Bibliotheca Persica Press, 1999), pp. 243-258.
77 Bahār, *Sabk shināsī*, Vol. 3, pp. 316-317.
78 Sykes, *History of Persia*, p. 279. *Cf.* Bahar, *Sabk shināsī*, Vol. 3, pp. 316-319.
79 Gh. Varherām, *Tārikh-i sīyāsī va ijtimā'-yi Iran dar 'aṣr-i Zand* (Tehran: Mu'īn, 1366/1988), pp. 167-168.
80 Cyrus, *Iran and the Rise of the Riḍā Shāh*, pp. 1-14.
81 Yarshater, *Iran Faces the Seventies*, pp. 287-289.
82 The four above-mentioned poets will be discussed in later chapters.
83 J. Rypka, *History of Iranian Literature*, pp. 320-337.
84 E.G. Browne, *A Literary History of Persia: Modern Times*, Vol. 4, p. 30. Fatḥ-'Alī Khān Ṣabā Kāshānī with the pen name Ṣabā (d. 1238/1822) was the poet laureate to Fatḥ-'Alī Shāh.
85 H. Subḥānī, *Tārīkh-i adabīyāt-i Iran* (Tehran: Zavvār, 1386/2007), pp. 480-485.

86 A.L. Beelaert, 'Ḵāqāni Šervān', *EIr*, Vol. 15, pp. 521-529. *Cf.* Ṣafā, *Tārīkh-i adabīyāt dar Iran*, Vol. 2, pp. 776-794.

87 Ḥ. 'A. Mallāh, *Manūchihrī Dāmghānī va mūsīqī* (Tehran: Intishārāt-i Hunar va Farhang, 1363/1984), p. 5.

88 Dihkhudā, *Lughat-nāma*, Vol. 11, p. 16410, s.v. "Unṣurī'.

89 Bahār, *Sabk shināsī*, Vol. 3, p. 339. *Cf.* Dihkhudā, *Lughat-nāma*, Vol. 11, p. 17050, s.v. 'Farrukhī'; and Ṣafā, *Tārīkh-i adabīyāt dar Iran*, Vol. 1, pp. 531-546.

90 Katouzian, *State and Society in Iran*, pp. 62-65.

91 'Ārif-i Qazvīnī, *Dīvān-i Mīrzā Abū'l Qāsim 'Ārif-i Qazvīnī*, ed. Sayf-i Āzād, p. 361.

92 Bahār, *Sabk shināsī*, Vol. 3, pp. 368-369. *Cf.* A.K. Hakkak, *Recasting Persian Poetry: Scenarios of Poetic Modernity in Iran* (Salt Lake City: University of Utah Press, 1995), p. 41.

93 M. Malakī, 'Mashrūṭīyat va Riḍā Khān' *Iran shināsī*, Vol. 28, No. 1 (Spring 2006), p. 67.

94 Bahār, *Sabk shināsī*, Vol. 3, p. 362. *Cf.* M.T. Ṭarqī, 'Mīrzā Āqā Khān Kirmānī, Nāmahā-i Tab'īd', *Iran Nameh*, Vol. 9, No. 3 (Summer 1991), p. 479, and Ī. Parsinejad, 'Mīrzā Āqā Khān Kirmānī, Muntaqid-i adabī', *Iran Nameh*, Vol. 8, No. 4 (Autumn 1990), pp. 541-546. Also for an analysis of Mīrzā Āqā Khān Kirmānī's view on Persian poetry, see Hakkak, *Recasting Persian Poetry*, p. 42.

95 Hakkak, *Recasting Persian Poetry*, p. 41.

96 Bahār, *Sabk shināsī*, Vol. 3, p. 362.

97 Mongol Bayat, 'Āqā Khan Kermānī', *Elr*, Vol. 2, pp. 175-177. *Cf.* Bahār, *Sabk shināsī*, Vol. 3, p. 362.

98 Parsinejad, *A History of Literary Criticism in Iran (1866-1951)* (Bethesda, MD: Ibex Publishers, 1382/2003), p. 30. *Cf.* F. Adamīyyat, *Andishahā-yi Mīrzā Āqā Khān Kirmānī* (Tehran: Ṭahūrī, 1364/1986), pp. 3-10.

99 'A.H. Zarrinkūb, *Naqd-i adabī* (Tehran: Amīr Kabīr, 1354/1976), pp. 637-638.

100 M.M. Bahādur, *Haftād u du millat: Mīrzā Āqā Khān Kirmānī* (Berlin: Iranshahr, 1343/1965), pp. 3-8.

101 Ferdowsi, 'The "Emblem"', pp. 677-691.

102 Ibid., p. 677.

103 Hakkak, *Recasting Persian Poetry*, p. 42. *Cf.* Nazm al-Islām Kirmānī, *Tā rikh-i bidārī-i Iranian*, ed. 'Alī-Akbar Sa'īd Sirjānī (Tehran: Bunyād-i Farhang-i Iran, 1345/1967), p. 175.

104 Ibid., p. 70.

105 Bahār, *Sabk shināsī*, Vol. 3, pp. 357-359.

106 Y. Āryānpūr, *Az Ṣabā tā Nimā* (Tehran: Zavvār, 1372/1994), Vol. 2, pp. 262-264. *Cf.* R.M. Burrell and R.L. Jarman (eds.), *Iran Political Diaries 1881-1965* (Oxford: Archive Editions Ltd. 1997), Vol. 12, p. 443.

107 M.Q. Hidāyat, *Khāṭirāt: nivishta'i az tārīkh-i shish pādishāh va gūsha'i az duwra-i zindagī-i man* (Tehran: Rangīn, 1329/1951), Vol. 1, p. 1.

108 This is a paraphrase of God's reply to Moses in Rūmī's story about Moses and the shepherd in the *Masnawī*, which underlines his mystical romanticism. For the verse in question, see Muwlānā Jalāl al-Dīn Muḥammad Balkhī: *Mathnawī*, ed. M. Isti'lāmī (Tehran: Mahārat, 1379/2001), II, v. 1785.

109 P.E. Losensky, 'Hedayat, Riḍāqolī Khān', *EIr*, Vol. 12, p. 120.

110 Hakkak, *Recasting Persian Poetry*, p. 33.

111 Malakī, 'Mashrūṭīyat va Riḍā Khān', p. 66.

112 H. Algar, 'Ākhūndzāda,' *EIr*, Vol. 1, p. 736. J. Rypka, *History of Iranian Literature*, p. 340.

113 Ibid.

114 Ibid., p. 64.

115 Hakkak, *Recasting Persian Poetry*, p. 40.

116 Ibid., p. 35. *Cf.* F. 'A. Ākhūndzāda, *Maqālāt-i fārsī* (Tehran: Āvā, 1350/1972), p. 56.

117 Parsinejad, *History of Literary Criticism in Iran*, p. 64.

118 Bahār, *Sabk shināsī*, Vol. 3, p. 363.

119 L. Ridgeon, *Religion and Politics in Modern Iran* (London: I.B.Tauris, 2005), p. 14.

120 F. Ādamīyat, *Fikr-i āzādī va Muqadama-yi nihzat-i Mashrūṭīyat* (Tehran: Intishārāt-i Sukhan, 1340/1962), p. 104. *Cf.* Āryānpūr, *Az Ṣabā tā Nimā*, Vol. 2, pp. 314-322.

121 J. Afary, *Iranian Constitutional Revolution*, p. 26.

122 Keddie and Richard, *Modern Iran*, pp. 431-432. *Cf.* Bahār, *Sabk shināsī*, Vol. 3, pp. 363-368.

123 Bahār, *Sabk shināsī*, Vol. 3, p. 363.

124 Ibid., Vol. 3, pp. 363-368.

125 Keddie and Richard, *Modern Iran*, pp. 431-432.

126 H. Algar (trans.), *Mirza Malkam Khan: A Study in the History of Iranian Modernism* (Berkeley: University of California Press, 1977), pp. 4-10.

127 Parsinejad, *A History of Literary Criticism in Iran (1866-1951)*, p. 110.

128 Algar (trans.), *Mīrzā Malkam Khān*, pp. 3-7.

129 Ibid., pp. 4-10.

130 Āryānpūr, *Az Ṣabā tā Nimā*, Vol. 1, pp. 321-322.

131 *Yāddāshthā-yi Qazvīnī*, ed. Iraj Afshar, vol. 7, 1332 Sh./1953, pp. 132-136. *Cf.* Parsinejad, *A History of Literary Criticism in Iran*, p. 98.

132 Ḥ. Asīl, *Zindagī va andisha-yi Mīrzā Malkam Khān* (Tehran: Nashr-i Nay, 1376/1998), p. 83. *Cf.* Parsinejad, *A History of Literary Criticism in Iran*, p. 111.

133 A. Milani, *Eminent Persians: The Men and Women Who Made Modern Iran 1941-1979* (Syracuse, NY: Syracuse University Press, 2008), Vol. 1, p. 152.

134 M. Mīnuvī, Naqd-i ḥāl (Tehran: [n. p], 1351/1972), pp. 534-550.

135 H. Itiḥād, *Pazhūhishgaran-i Mu'āṣir-i Iran* (Tehran: Farhang-i Mu'āṣir, 1382/2004), Vol. 1, pp. 54-55.

136 Fakhreddin Azimi and Iraj Afshar, *Encyclopedia Iranica*, 'Forūgī, Mohammad-Alī Ḏokā'-Al-Molk,' *EIr*, Vol. 10, pp. 108-111.

137 Ibid., Vol. 10, p. 111. *Cf.* Ī. Afshār (ed.), *Nathr-i fārsī-i mu'āṣir: muntakhabātī az bihtarīn āthār-i muvarrikhīn va muḥaqqiqīn-i nāmī-i Irān az ṣadr-i Mashrūṭīyat tā mu'āṣir* (Tehran: Kānūn-i Ma'rifat, 1330/1951), pp. 67-68.

138 Itiḥād, *Pazhūhishgaran-i Mu'āṣir-i Iran*, p. 61.

139 M. 'Alī Dhakā' al-Mulk Furūghī, *Maqālāt-i Furūghī* (Tehran: Ṭūs, 1354/1976), Vol. 1, pp. 224-226.

140 Furūghī, *Maqālāt-i Furūghī*, Vol. 1, p. 226.

141 Ibid., Vol. 1, pp. 203-208.

142 Ḥāfiẓ, *Dīvān-i Ḥāfiẓ Shīrāzī*, ed. M. Qazvīnī and Q. Ghanī, *ghazal* 271, v. 3.

143 Milani, *Eminent Persians*, Vol. 1, p. 156.

144 Furūghī, *Maqālāt-i Furūghī*, Vol. 1, pp. 252-255.

145 Ibid., Vol. 1, pp. 232-243. *Cf.* Milani, *Eminent Persians*, Vol. 1, pp. 156-157.

146 Furūghī, *Maqālāt-i Furūghī*, Vol. 1, pp. 238-241.

147 F. Ādamīyat, *Andishahā-yi Ṭālibuf Tabrīzī* (Tehran: Damāvand, [n.d]), p. 1.

148 M. Qazvīnī, 'Ṭālibuf Tabrīzī,' *Majala-yi Yādigār*, Nos. 4/5 (1327/1949), p. 86. *Cf.* Āryānpūr, *Az Ṣabā tā Nimā*, Vol. 1, p. 287.

149 Parsinejad, 'Ṭālebof-e Tabrīzī' *Iran shināsī*, Vol. 7, No. 3 (Autumn 1990), p. 40.

150 Ibid.

151 Malakī, 'Mashrūṭīyat va Riḍā Khān,' p. 66.

152 Ādamīyat, *Andishahā-yi Ṭālibuf Tabrīzī*, p. 5.

153 Ibid., p. 3.

154 Bahār, *Sabk shināsī*, Vol. 3, p. 361. *Cf.* Āryānpūr, *Az Ṣabā tā Nimā*, Vol. 1, pp. 294-295.

155 Ī. Afshār, *'Abdul Rahīm Ṭālibuf Tabrīzī: Āzādī va sīyāsat* (Tehran: Sahar, 1357/1979), pp. 18-22.

156 Kasravī, *Tārikh-i mashrūṭa-i Iran*, pp. 43-46.

157 ʿA.R. Ṭālibuf, *Masālik al-muḥsinīn* (Tehran: Shabgīr, 1356/1978), p. 2.

158 Ḥāfiẓ, *Dīvān-i Ḥāfiẓ Shīrāzī*, ed. M. Qazvīnī and Q. Ghanī, *ghazal* 323, v. 5.

159 Avery, *Collected Lyrics*, p. 395; *ghazal* 318.

160 ʿA.R.N. Tabrīzī, *Masālik al-muḥsinīn* (Tehran: Shirkat-i Sahāmi-i Kitābhā-i Jibī, 1323/1906), pp. 4-8.

161 F. Ādamīyat, *Andishahā-i Mīrzā Āqā Khān Kirmānī* (Tehran: Amīr Kabīr, 1357/1978), p. 267.

162 Dihkhudā, *Lughat-nāma: Muqadama* (Tehran: Tehran University Press, 1336/1958). *Cf.* Bahār, *Sabk shināsī*, Vol. 3, p. 361.

163 Bahār, *Sabk shināsī*, Vol. 3, p. 361. *Cf.* Ī. Parsinejad, 'Zayn al-ʿĀbidin Marāqi'ī, muntaqid-i adabī' *Iran Nameh*, Vol. 9, No. 3 (Summer 1991), p. 427.

164 Browne, *Literary History of Persia*, Vol. 4, p. 467. *Cf.* Parsinejad, 'Zayn al-ʿĀbidin Marāqi'ī, muntaqid-i adabī', p. 428; E.G. Browne, *The Press and Poetry of Modern Persia* (Cambridge: Cambridge University Press, 1941), p. 25.

165 Parsinejad, *History of Literary Criticism in Iran*, p. 147.

166 Kasravī, *Tārikh-i mashrūṭa-yi Iran*, p. 46.

167 Marāgha'ī, *Sīyāḥat-nāma-i Ibrāhīm Bayk, yā, balā-yi aū*, ed. B. Mu'minī (Tehran: Nashr-i Andīsha, 1353/1975), Vol. 3, pp. 27-30. Also cited by Parsinejad, *History of Literary Criticism in Iran*, p. 148.

168 Marāgha'ī, *Sīyāḥat-nāma-yi Ibrāhīm Bayk*, p. 208.

169 Āryānpūr, *Az Ṣabā tā Nimā*, Vol. 1, pp. 304-307.

170 Parsinejad, *History of Literary Criticism in Iran*, p. 147.

171 Marāgha'ī, *Sīyāḥat-nāma-yi Ibrāhīm Bayk*, Vol. 1, p. 241. *Cf.* Āryānpūr, *Az Ṣabā tā Nimā*, Vol. 1, p. 309; Parsinejad, 'Ziyn al-ʿĀbidin Marāqi'ī, muntaqid-i adabī', p. 433.

172 Marāgha'ī, *Sīyāḥat-nāma-yi Ibrāhīm Bayk*, pp. 88-89.

173 Ibid., p. 82.

174 Ḥāfiẓ, *Dīvān-i Ḥāfīz Shīrāzī*, ed. M. Qazvīnī and Q. Ghanī, *ghazal* 449, v. 5.

175 A mythical bird that symbolizes luck and glory, it was mentioned in the *Shāh-nāma* of Firdawsī.

176 ʿA. Rāzī, *Tārikh-i Iran* (Tehran: Sipihr, 1316/1938), p. 518.

177 Ḥāfiẓ, *Dīvān-i Ḥāfīz Shīrāzī*, ed. M. Qazvīnī and Q. Ghanī, *ghazal* 324, v. 5.

178 Ibid., *ghazal* 418, v. 4.

179 Ibid., *ghazal* 169, v. 1, 4.

180 Avery, *Collected Lyrics*, p. 221; *ghazal* 164.

181 Parsinejad, *History of Literary Criticism in Iran*, p. 30.

182 Ibid., p. 64.

183 Hakkak, *Recasting Persian Poetry*, p. 57.

Chapter III – The Influence of Ḥāfiẓ on the Poets of Zand and Qājār Persia

1 M.J. Maḥjūb, *Sabk-i Khurāsānī dar shiʿr-i fārsī: bar rasī-i mukhtassāt-i shiʿr-i fārsī, az āghāz-i zuhūr tā pāyān-i qarn-i panjum-i hijri* (Tehran: Firdawsī, 1363/1985), pp. 48-49. *Cf.* DH. Ṣafā, *Tārikh-i adabīyāt-i Iran* (Tehran: Firdawsī, 1378/2000), Vol. 4, pp. 236-237.
2 Tajrubikār, *Sabk-i shiʿr dar ʿaṣr-i Qājārīya*, pp. 35-61.
3 Tajrubikār, *Sabk-i shiʿr dar ʿaṣr-i Qājārīya*, pp. 35-61.
4 Hakkak, *Recasting Persian Poetry*, p. 54.
5 Rypka, *History of Iranian Literature*, p. 362.
6 Ibid., pp. 320-337.
7 Subḥānī, *Tārīkh-i adabīyāt-i Iran*, pp. 480-485.
8 Rypka, *History of Iranian Literature*, p. 355. *Cf.* A.K. Karimi-Hakkak, 'Naqd-i adabī', *Iran Nameh*, Vol. 9, No. 1 (Winter 1994), pp. 3-5.
9 Rypka, *History of Iranian Literature*, p. 355. *Cf.* Kasravī, *Tārikh-i mashrūṭa-yi Iran*, p. 18.
10 Hakkak, *Recasting Persian Poetry*, p. 101.
11 Ibid.
12 Kasravī, *Tārikh-i mashrūṭa-yi Iran*, p. 45.
13 Rypka, *History of Iranian Literature*, p. 380.
14 ʿA. Ḥ. Zarrinkūb, *Advār-i shiʿr-i fārsī: Az Mashrūṭīyat tā suqūt-i saltanat* (Tehran: Intishārāt-i Ṭūs, 1359/1980), pp. 34-48. *Cf.* Hakkak, *Recasting Persian Poetry*, p. 103.
15 Huma'i, *Funūn-i balāghat*, p. 395.
16 Leonard Lewisohn, 'The Life and Poetry of Mashreqi Tabrizi', *The Journal of the Society for Iranian Studies*, Vol. XXII, Nos. 2-3 (1998), p. 115. Mohammad Qazvini summarizes the relationship of four of these devices as follows: 'The principle and basis of *taḍmīn, eqtebās, ersāl-e methāl*, and *talmīh* is the poet's adoption of something from someone else without consciously intending to 'use' it or to 'plagiarize' it (*serqat*), yet also without this happening after the manner of an 'inspired coincidence between two poems' (*tavvarod*). In reality, if the item adopted by the poet be someone else's verse or poem, this art is called *taḍmīn*; if it be something from the Koran or Prophetic tradition it is called *eqtebās*; if it be proverb it is called *ersāl-e methāl*; and if it be an illusion indirectly pointing to one of these things, or to famous historical tale, then it is termed *talmih*.' – Leonard Lewisohn, 'The Life and Poetry of Mashreqi Tabrizi', Vol. XXII, Nos. 2-3 (1998), pp. 115-116.

17 Losensky, *Welcoming Fighānī*, p. 215.
18 Leonard Lewisohn, 'The Life and Poetry of Mashreqi Tabrizi', Vol. XXII, Nos. 2-3 (1998), p. 115.
19 Ādhar Bigdilī, *Ātashkada*, ed. Sādāt (Tehran: Amīr Kabīr, 1339/1961), Vol. 3, pp. 15-17. *Cf.* Ṣafā, *Ganj-i sukhan* (Tehran: Ibn Sinā, 1339/1961), Vol. 3, p. 143.
20 Hidāyat, *Majmaʿ al-fuṣaḥā*, Vol. 1, p. 159. *qaṣāʾid*: (elegies), *ghazalīyāt*: (lyrics), *qaṭiʿāt*: (fragments) and a *Mathnawī*: *mathnawī* is the name of a poem transcribed in rhyming couplets, or more specifically, "a poem based on independent, internally rhyming lines". Most *mathnawī* s follow a meter of eleven, or seldom ten syllables, but have no limit in their length.
21 Browne, *A Literary History of Persia: Modern Times*, Vol. 4, pp. 282-284.
22 J. Humāʾī, *Funūn-i balāghat va ṣanāʿāt-i adabī* (Tehran: Intishārāt-i Ṭūs, 1363/1985), Vol. 2, p. 395.
23 Bigdilī, *Dīvān-i Lutf-ʿAlī Bayk Ādhar Bigdilī*, ed. N. Sādāt, p. 5.
24 Ḥāfiẓ, *Dīvān-i Ḥāfiz Shīrāzī*, ed. M. Qazvīnī and Q. Ghanī, *ghazal* 71, v. 10.
25 The word *kharābāt* means, literally, ruins; in mystical poetry it is used to mean an estate in which taverns and cheerful places for rogue and footloose libertines are located.
26 Bigdilī, *Dīvān-i Lutf-ʿAlī Bayk Ādhar Bigdilī*, ed. Sādāt, *ghazal* 140, v. 1.
27 Ḥāfiẓ, *Dīvān-i Ḥāfiz Shīrāzī*, ed. M. Qazvīnī and Q. Ghanī, *ghazal* 374, v. 5.
28 Bigdilī, *Dīvān-i Lutf-ʿAlī Bayk Ādhar Bigdilī*, ed. N. Sādāt, *ghazal* 140, v. 7.
29 Ḥāfiẓ, *Dīvān-i Ḥāfiz Shīrāzī*, ed. M. Qazvīnī and Q. Ghanī, *ghazal* 374, v. 8.
30 Bigdilī, *Dīvān-i Lutf-ʿAlī Bayk Ādhar Bigdilī*, ed. Sādāt, *ghazal* 110, v. 3.
31 Ḥāfiẓ, *Dīvān-i Ḥāfiz Shīrāzī*, ed. M. Qazvīnī and Q. Ghanī, *ghazal* 276, v. 3.
32 Bigdilī, *Dīvān-i Lutf-ʿAlī Bayk Ādhar Bigdilī*, ed. Sādāt, *ghazal* 110, v. 7.
33 Ḥāfiẓ, *Dīvān-i Ḥāfiz Shīrāzī*, ed. M. Qazvīnī and Q. Ghanī, *ghazal* 276, v. 2.
34 See the article prepared by Grūh-i Farhangī-yi huza-yi adabīyāt va kitāb in an article at the following website: www.farsnews.net/newstext.php?nn =8707260390 (accessed 16 July 2009).
35 Viṣāl Shīrāzī, *Kullīyyāt-i Viṣāl Shīrāzī, Ganjīna-i adab va ʿirfān-i Iranī*, ed. A. Muḥammad (Tehran: Fakhr Āzād, 1339/1960), p. 726.
36 Hidāyat, *Tadhkira-yi rīyāḍ al-ʿārifīn*, p. 598.
37 Viṣāl Shīrāzī, *Dīvān-i Viṣāl Shīrāzī*, ed. M. Ṭavūsī (Shīrāz: Navīd Shīrāz, 1378/2000), Vol. 1, p. 19.
38 Ibid., Vol. 2, p. 342, v. 10.
39 Ḥāfiẓ, *Dīvān-i Ḥāfiz Shīrāzī*, ed. M. Qazvīnī and Q. Ghanī, *ghazal* 64, v. 3.
40 Avery, *Collected Lyrics*, p. 102; *ghazal* 65. 'Abū Lahab (Literally, 'Father of the Flame') was the Prophet Muḥammad's half uncle. He became the

Prophet's implacable foe in opposition to the preaching of Islam. Sura cxi of the Koran names him and says that he will roast in Hell, his wife carrying the fuel.'

41 Viṣāl Shīrāzī, *Dīvān-i Viṣāl Shīrāzī*, Vol. 2, *ghazal* 650, v. 9.
42 Ḥāfiẓ, *Dīvān-i Ḥāfiz Shīrāzī*, ed. M. Qazvīnī and Q. Ghanī, *ghazal* 278, v. 1.
43 Viṣāl Shīrāzī, *Dīvān-i Viṣāl Shīrāzī*, Vol. 2, *ghazal* 254, v. 1.
44 Ḥāfiẓ, *Dīvān-i Ḥāfiz Shīrāzī*, ed. M. Qazvīnī and Q. Ghanī, *ghazal* 73, v. 1.
45 Viṣāl Shīrāzī, *Dīvān-i Viṣāl Shīrāzī*, Vol. 2, *ghazal* 287, v. 1.
46 Ḥāfiẓ, *Dīvān-i Ḥāfiz Shīrāzī*, ed. M. Qazvīnī and Q. Ghanī, *ghazal* 85, v. 1.
47 Subḥānī, *Tārīkh-i adabīyāt-i Iran*, pp. 493-497. *Cf.* Āryānpūr, *Az Ṣabā tā Nimā*, Vol. 1, p. 93.
48 Browne, *A Literary History of Persia*, Vol. 4, p. 326.
49 Subḥānī, *Tārīkh-i adabīyāt-i Iran*, p. 497. *Cf.* Dihkhudā, *Lughat-nāma*, Vol. 9, p. 12464, s.v. 'Shiblī'.
50 Qā'ānī Shīrāzī, *Dīvān-i Ḥakīm Qā'ānī Shīrāzī*, ed. M.J. Maḥjūb (Tehran: Amīr Kabīr, 1336/1957), p. 897.
51 Ḥāfiẓ, *Dīvān-i Ḥāfiz Shīrāzī*, ed. M. Qazvīnī and Q. Ghanī, *ghazal* 77, v. 2.
52 Losensky, *Welcoming Fighānī*, p. 106.
53 Qā'ānī Shīrāzī, *Dīvān-i Ḥakīm Qā'ānī Shīrāzī*, p. 897.
54 Ḥāfiẓ, *Dīvān-i Ḥāfiz Shīrāzī*, ed. M. Qazvīnī and Q. Ghanī, *ghazal* 77, v. 8.
55 Qā'ānī Shīrāzī, *Dīvān-i Ḥakīm Qā'ānī Shīrāzī*, p. 903.
56 Ḥāfiẓ, *Dīvān-i Ḥāfiz Shīrāzī*, ed. M. Qazvīnī and Q. Ghanī, *ghazal* 220, v. 7.
57 This translation follows that of Peter Avery, with some modifications.
58 Qā'ānī Shīrāzī, *Dīvān-i Ḥakīm Qā'ānī Shīrāzī*, p. 904.
59 Ḥāfiẓ, *Dīvān-i Ḥāfiz Shīrāzī*, ed. M. Qazvīnī and Q. Ghanī, *ghazal* 220, v. 6.
60 Qā'ānī Shīrāzī, *Dīvān-i Ḥakīm Qā'ānī Shīrāzī*, p. 904.
61 Ḥāfiẓ, *Dīvān-i Ḥāfiz Shīrāzī*, ed. M. Qazvīnī and Q. Ghanī, *ghazal* 220, v. 4.
62 This translation follows that of Peter Avery, with some modifications.
63 Qā'ānī Shīrāzī, *Dīvān-i Ḥakīm Qā'ānī Shīrāzī*, p. 904.
64 Ḥāfiẓ, *Dīvān-i Ḥāfiz Shīrāzī*, ed. M. Qazvīnī and Q. Ghanī, *ghazal* 220, v. 3.
65 Qā'ānī Shīrāzī, *Dīvān-i Ḥakīm Qā'ānī Shīrāzī*, p. 913.
66 Ḥāfiẓ, *Dīvān-i Ḥāfiz Shīrāzī*, ed. M. Qazvīnī and Q. Ghanī, *ghazal* 136, v. 1.
67 Qā'ānī Shīrāzī, *Dīvān-i Ḥakīm Qā'ānī Shīrāzī*, p. 914.
68 This translation follows that of Peter Avery, with some modifications.
69 Ḥāfiẓ, *Dīvān-i Ḥāfiz Shīrāzī*, ed. M. Qazvīnī and Q. Ghanī, *ghazal* 327, v. 9.
70 This translation follows that of Peter Avery, with some modifications.
71 Qā'ānī Shīrāzī, *Dīvān-i Ḥakīm Qā'ānī Shīrāzī*, p. 914.
72 Ḥāfiẓ, *Dīvān-i Ḥāfiz Shīrāzī*, ed. M. Qazvīnī and Q. Ghanī, *ghazal* 342, v. 3.
73 Qā'ānī Shīrāzī, *Dīvān-i Ḥakīm Qā'ānī Shīrāzī*, p. 915.

74 Ḥāfiẓ, *Dīvān-i Ḥāfiz Shīrāzī*, ed. M. Qazvīnī and Q. Ghanī, *ghazal* 233, v. 2.
75 The first line of this translation follows that of Peter Avery.
76 Qā'ānī Shīrāzī, *Dīvān-i Ḥakīm Qā'ānī Shīrāzī*, p. 971.
77 Ḥāfiẓ, *Dīvān-i Ḥāfiz Shīrāzī*, ed. M. Qazvīnī and Q. Ghanī, *ghazal* 218, v. 9.
78 Dihkhudā, *Lughat-nāma*, Vol. 12, p. 18443, s.v. 'Miskīn'.
79 Furūghī Basṭāmī, *Dīvān-i Furūghī Basṭāmī*, ed. Ḥ. R. Qilichkhānī (Tehran: Rūznih, 1376/1998).
80 Ibid., pp. 11-20.
81 Ibid., *ghazal* 195, v. 9.
82 Ḥāfiẓ, *Dīvān-i Ḥāfiz Shīrāzī*, ed. M. Qazvīnī and Q. Ghanī, *ghazal* 336, v. 4.
83 The first line of this translation follows that of Avery, with some modifications.
84 Furūghī Basṭāmī, *Ghazalīyāt-i Furūghī Basṭāmī*, ed. M. Mushfiq (Tehran: Ṣafī 'Alī Shāh, 1336/1958), p. 131.
85 Ḥāfiẓ, *Dīvān-i Ḥāfiz Shīrāzī*, ed. M. Qazvīnī and Q. Ghanī, *ghazal* 152, v. 4.
86 Yaghmā Jandaqī, *Dīvān-i ash'ār-i Yaghmā Jandaqī*, ed. S. 'A.A. Dāvūd (Tehran: Intishārāt-i Ṭūs, 1369/1990), p. 5.
87 Yaghmā Jandaqī, *Dīvān-i ash'ār-i Yaghmā Jandaqī*, Vol. 1, p. 99, v. 11.
88 Ḥāfiẓ, *Dīvān-i Ḥāfiz Shīrāzī*, ed. M. Qazvīnī and Q. Ghanī, *ghazal* 352, v. 3.
89 Yaghmā Jandaqī, *Majmu'a-yi āthār-i Yaghmā Jandaqī*, ed. S. 'A.A. Dāvūd (Tehran: Intishārāt-i Ṭūs, 1357/1979), Vol. 1, *ghazal* 8, v. 1.
90 Ḥāfiẓ, *Dīvān-i Ḥāfiz Shīrāzī*, ed. M. Qazvīnī and Q. Ghanī, *ghazal* 10, v. 1.
91 This translation follows that of Avery, with some modifications.
92 Yaghmā Jandaqī, *Majmu'a-yi āthār-i Yaghmā Jandaqī*, Vol. 1, *ghazal* 8, v. 9.
93 Ḥāfiẓ, *Dīvān-i Ḥāfiz Shīrāzī*, ed. M. Qazvīnī and Q. Ghanī, *ghazal* 10, v. 2.
94 This translation follows that of Avery, with some modifications.
95 Yaghmā Jandaqī, *Majmu'a-yi āthār-i Yaghmā Jandaqī*, Vol. 1, *ghazal* 50, v. 1.
96 Ḥāfiẓ, *Dīvān-i Ḥāfiz Shīrāzī*, ed. M. Qazvīnī and Q. Ghanī, *ghazal* 36, v. 1.
97 Yaghmā Jandaqī, *Majmu'a-yi āthār-i Yaghmā Jandaqī*, Vol. 1, *ghazal* 74, v. 5.
98 Ḥāfiẓ, *Dīvān-i Ḥāfiz Shīrāzī*, ed. M. Qazvīnī and Q. Ghanī, *ghazal* 195, v. 1.
99 Yaghmā Jandaqī, *Majmu'a-yi āthār-i Yaghmā Jandaqī*, Vol. 1, *ghazal* 74, v. 6.
100 Zahhāk is the name of a mythical tyrant king who frequently appears in Firdawsī's epic of kings (*Shāh-nāma*).
101 Ḥāfiẓ, *Dīvān-i Ḥāfiz Shīrāzī*, ed. M. Qazvīnī and Q. Ghanī, *ghazal* 195, v. 8.
102 Yaghmā Jandaqī, *Majmu'a-yi āthār-i Yaghmā Jandaqī*, Vol. 1, *ghazal* 76, v. 5.

103 Ḥāfiẓ, *Dīvān-i Ḥāfiz Shīrāzī*, ed. M. Qazvīnī and Q. Ghanī, *ghazal* 136, v. 1.
104 Yaghmā Jandaqī, *Majmu'a-yi āthār-i Yaghmā Jandaqī*, Vol. 1, *ghazal* 76, v. 6.
105 Ḥāfiẓ, *Dīvān-i Ḥāfiz Shīrāzī*, ed. M. Qazvīnī and Q. Ghanī, *ghazal* 136, v. 10.
106 Yaghmā Jandaqī, *Majmu'a-yi āthār-i Yaghmā Jandaqī*, Vol. 1, *ghazal* 84, v. 1.
107 To tear one's clothes in the street is a metaphor representing a state of love and insanity.
108 Ḥāfiẓ, *Dīvān-i Ḥāfiz Shīrāzī*, ed. M. Qazvīnī and Q. Ghanī, *ghazal* 182, v. 1.
109 This translation follows that of Avery, with some modifications.
110 Yaghmā Jandaqī, *Majmu'a-yi āthār-i Yaghmā Jandaqī*, Vol. 1, *ghazal* 90, v. 2.
111 Ḥāfiẓ, *Dīvān-i Ḥāfiz Shīrāzī*, ed. M. Qazvīnī and Q. Ghanī, *ghazal* 219, v. 4.
112 Dihkhudā, *Lughat-nāma*, Vol. 6, p. 8046, s.v. 'Ḥikmat'. *Cf.* R.Q. Hidāyat, *Majma' al-fuṣaḥā*, ed. Musaffā (Tehran: Amīr Kabīr, 1388/2009), Vol. 1, p. 339.
113 Rypka, *History of Iranian Literature*, pp. 343-344.
114 J. Nurbakhsh, *Farhang-i Nūrbakhsh, Iṣṭilāḥāt-i taṣawwuf*, Vol, 3, pp. 291-302, s.v. 'Sālik'. This is usually said to a devoted individual whose only aims are to seek the truth through faith and to unite with the Beloved, God. A *sālik* is a person engaged in an Islamic spiritual path or Sufism. The word is derived from the Arabic word *sulūk*, which means to walk a spiritual path to God. To become a *sālik*, one must follow both the outer path and the inner path, the *ṭariqa* and the *ḥaqīqa* of Islam virtuously. Dihkhudā, *Lughat-nāma*, Vol. 8, p. 11759, s.v. 'Sālik'.
115 Mu'īn, *Ḥāfiẓ-i shirīn-sukhan*, Vol. 1, p. 743.
116 Ibid., Vol. 1, p. 737.
117 Ḥāfiẓ, *Dīvān-i Ḥāfiz Shīrāzī*, ed. M. Qazvīnī and Q. Ghanī, *ghazal* 73, v. 1.
118 Sabzivārī, *Dīvān-i Asrār*, ed. Amīn, *ghazal* 24, v. 7.
119 Ḥāfiẓ, *Dīvān-i Ḥāfiz Shīrāzī*, ed. M. Qazvīnī and Q. Ghanī, *ghazal* 1, v. 6.
120 Sabzivārī, *Dīvān-i Asrār*, ed. Amīn, *ghazal* 45, v. 3.
121 Ḥāfiẓ, *Dīvān-i Ḥāfiz Shīrāzī*, ed. M. Qazvīnī and Q. Ghanī, *ghazal* 49, v. 2.
122 Ṣafī 'Alī Shāh, *Dīvān-i Ṣafī 'Alī Shāh*, ed. A.K. Baraq (Tehran: Amīr Kabīr, 1336/1957), p. 1.
123 Leonard Lewisohn, 'An Introduction to the History of Modern Persian Sufism', *The Bulletin of the School of Oriental and African Studies*, Vol. 61 (1998), part 1, p. 454.
124 Ibid., p. 3.
125 Ibid., p. 70.
126 Ḥāfiẓ, *Dīvān-i Ḥāfiz Shīrāzī*, ed. M. Qazvīnī and Q. Ghanī, *ghazal* 21, v. 5.
127 Baraq, *Justujū dar aḥvāl va āthār-i Ṣafī 'Alī Shāh*, p. 72.

128 Ḥāfiẓ, *Dīvān-i Ḥāfīz Shīrāzī*, ed. M. Qazvīnī and Q. Ghanī, *ghazal*178, v. 4. For further comparative examples of Ḥāfiẓ and other poets of the Qājār period, refer to the appendix.

129 J. Kh. Mutlaq, 'Ḥāfiẓ va himāsi-yi milli-yi Iran', *Iran Nameh*, Vol. 6, No. 4 (Summer 1988), pp. 565-572.

130 Ḥāfiẓ, *Dīvān-i Ḥāfīz Shīrāzī*, ed. M. Qazvīnī and Q. Ghanī, *ghazal* 105, v. 4.

131 Avery, *Collected Lyrics*, p. 144; *ghazal* 101.

132 Ḥāfiẓ, *Dīvān-i Ḥāfīz Shīrāzī*, ed. M. Qazvīnī and Q. Ghanī, *ghazal* 345, v. 5.

133 Avery, *Collected Lyrics*, p. 416; *ghazal* 337.

134 Ḥāfiẓ, *Dīvān-i Ḥāfīz Shīrāzī*, ed. M. Qazvīnī and Q. Ghanī, *ghazal* 470, v. 5.

135 'Chigil is situated to the southwest of Lake Issyk'kul'. Avery, *Collected Lyrics*, p. 88.

136 Avery, *Collected Lyrics*, p. 556; *ghazal* 501.

137 Ḥāfiẓ, *Dīvān-i Ḥāfīz Shīrāzī*, ed. M. Qazvīnī and Q. Ghanī, *ghazal* 324, v. 5.

138 This translation follows that of Avery, with some modifications.

139 M. 'Alī Islāmī Nudūshan, *Chihār sukhangu-yi vijdān-i Iran, Firdawsī, Muwlavī, Sa'dī va Ḥāfiẓ* (Tehran: Nashr-i Qatra, 1381/2002), p. 183. *Cf.* Ferdowsi, 'The "Emblem"', p. 670.

140 Ferdowsi, 'The "Emblem"', p. 670.

141 Ḥāfiẓ, *Dīvān-i Ḥāfīz Shīrāzī*, ed. M. Qazvīnī and Q. Ghanī, *ghazal* 9, v. 13.

142 Avery, *Collected Lyrics*, p. 31; *ghazal* 9.

143 J. Humā'ī, *Funūn-i balāghat va ṣanā'āt-i adabī* (Tehran: Intishārāt-i Ṭūs, 1363/1985), Vol. 2, p. 395.

144 L. Lewisohn, 'Ḥāfiẓ and Islamic Philosophy,' in *Journal of Persianate Studies* (forthcoming 2013) – private manuscript lent to me by the author.

145 Ibid.

146 Ibid.

Chapter IV – Ḥāfiẓ and the Poets of Pahlavi Iran

1 W.M. Shuster, *The Strangling of Persia: A Personal Narrative* (Washington, D.C.: Mage Publishers, 1987), p. 311.

2 Ibid. Interestingly, but not surprisingly, I came across the verse by Ḥāfiẓ, with which Shuster starts his book (p. 1). It is appropriate to note it, as it is clear evidence that Ḥāfiẓ influences nations other than the Iranians. The verse reads:

ما بدین در نه پی حشمت و جاه آمده ایم　　　از بد حادثه اینجا به پناه آمده ایم

Not in pursuit of pomp and pageant, to this door we have come:
For shelter from ill fortune, here we have come.

3 Keddie and Richard, *Modern Iran*, p. 88.

4 ʿA. Ḥ. Banisard, *Muqiʿīyat-i Iran va naqsh-i Muṣaddiq* ([n.p], 1356/1978), p. 2. *Cf.* Ḥ. Makki, *Muddaris qahrimān-i āzādī* (Tehran: Bungāh-i Tarjuma va Nashr-i Kitāb, 1358/1980), p. 49.

5 Keddie and Richard, *Modern Iran*, p. 88.

6 A. Milani, *Eminent Persians*, Vol. 1, p. 236. *Cf.* J. Buzurgmihr, *Risidigi-yi farjāmī dar Dīvān-i kishvar* (Tehran: Shirkat-i Sahāmī-i Intishār, 1367/1989), pp. 5-9.

7 Keddie and Richard, *Modern Iran*, p. 88.

8 Milani, *Eminent Persians*, Vol. 1, p. 321.

9 Keddie and Richard, *Modern Iran*, p. 88.

10 Ibid., p. 88. *Cf.* J. Groot, *Religion, Culture and Politics in Iran from the Qājārs to Khomeini* (London: I.B.Tauris, 2007), pp. 167-168.

11 C. Ghanī, *Iran and the Rise of Reza Shah* (London: I.B.Tauris, 1998), pp. 43-44.

12 Malakī, 'Mashrūṭīyat va Riḍā Khān', p. 72.

13 B. Mu'minī, *Dīn va Dawlat dar ʿaṣr-i Mashrūṭīyat* (Sweden: Bārān, 1993), p. 336.

14 Ibid.

15 Ḥāfiẓ, *Dīvān-i Ḥāfiz Shīrāzī*, ed. M. Qazvīnī and Q. Ghanī, *ghazal* 351, v. 3.

16 Avery, *Collected Lyrics*, p. 422; *ghazal* 343.

17 Malakī, 'Mashrūṭīyat va Riḍā Khān', p. 72.

18 Abrahamian, *Iran Between Two Revolutions*, p. 61.

19 E. Yarshater, *Iran Faces the Seventies* (New York: Praeger, 1971), p. 289.

20 Ibid.

21 H. Gulshirī, *Jidāl-i naqsh bā naqqāsh dar āthār-i Simin-i Dānishvar* (Tehran: Intishārāt-i Nilūfar, 1376/1998), p. 10.

22 ʿA. Dastghayb, *Naqd-i āthār-i Ṣādiq Chūbak* (Tehran: Kānūn-i Taḥqīqāt-i Iqtiṣādī va Ijtimāʿī-i Pāzand, 1353/1974), p. 5. *Cf.* M. Ḥasan, *Naqd va taḥlīl va guzīda-yi dāstānhā-yi Ṣādiq Chūbak* (Tehran: Nashr-i Rūzgār, 1381/2002). 'Born on 5th August 1916; and died in Berkeley, Calif., 3rd July 1998, one of most acclaimed Persian short story writers and novelists of the twentieth century'. M.R. Ghanoonparvar, 'Chubak, Sadeq', Encyclopedia Iranica Online, www.iranicaonline.org/articles/chubak-sadeq.

23 Yarshater, *Iran Faces the Seventies*, p. 289. These poets will be properly introduced later in this chapter.

24 K. Talattof, *The Politics of Writing in Iran* (Syracuse, NY: Syracuse University Press, 2000), p. 22.

25 Ibid., p. 23.

26 Ibid., pp. 23-24.

27 Parsinejad, *A History of Literary Criticism in Iran*, p. 27.

28 Ibid., p. 27.

29 Ibid., p. 30.

30 Muʿīn, *Farhang-i Muʿīn* (Tehran: Amīr Kabīr, 1373/1994), Vol. 6, p. 2262, s.v. 'Hidāyat'.

31 Rypka, *History of Iranian Literature*, p. 340.

32 Ibid., p. 326.

33 Ibid., p. 324.

34 Bahār, *Bahār va adab-i fārsī* (Tehran: Kitabhā-yi Jibī, 1351/1932), Vol. 1, p. 49.

35 Parsinejad, *A History of Literary Criticism in Iran*, p. 175. *Cf.* Ī. Parsinejad, 'Aḥmad Kasravī va naqd-i adabī', *Iran Nameh*, Vol. 11, No. 3 (Summer 1993), pp. 481-483.

36 A. Kasravī, *Zindigānī-yi man: Dah sāl dar ʿadlīyih, va chirā az ʿadlīya bīrūn āmadam* (Tehran: Pāzand, 1377/1960), p. 21.

37 Ibid., p. 9.

38 Ibid., p. 38.

39 Parsinejad, *A History of Literary Criticism in Iran*, pp. 176-178.

40 Ibid., pp. 178-179.

41 L. Ridgeon, *Sufi Castigator: Aḥmad Kasravi and the Iranian Mystical Tradition* (New York: Routledge, 2006), p. 138.

42 Ibid.

43 Ibid.

44 Ibid., p. 139.

45 Ibid., p. 139.

46 L. Ridgeon, *Sufi Castigator*, pp. 147-148. *Cf.* A. Kasravī, *Ḥāfiẓ chi migūyad* (Tehran: Intishārāt-i Mihr, 1335/1956). Kasravī admits that this is a term he has coined. He expands on the meaning of *kharābātī* in some depth in his work '*Ḥāfiẓ chi migūyad?*' and makes somewhat daring claims concerning the appearance of the *kharābātī*s in Iran. For Kasravī, *kharābātī*s were characters who considered the world purposeless and vain. It was impossible to understand the world's objective and for that reason, the *kharābātī*s even criticized its maker.

47 'A. Dastghayb, *Naqd-i āthār-i Aḥmad Kasravī* (Tehran: Pāzand, 1357/1979), p. 175.
48 Ridgeon, *Sufi Castigator*, pp. 181-183. *Cf.* A. Kasravī, *Dar pīrāmūn-i falsafa* (Tehran: Pāydār, 1344/1966), p. 13.
49 H. Katouzian, 'Hedayat,' *EIr*, Vol. 12, p. 121.
50 Parsinejad, *A History of Literary Criticism in Iran*, p. 201.
51 Khawsrū Ardāqī, 'Ṣādīq-i Ḥidāyat nivisanda-yi buzurg-i Mu'āṣir-i Iran darguzasht,' *Rūz-nāma-yi parcham-i ṣulḥ*, Year 1, No. 2490 (Tehran: 1330/1950), p. 11.
52 D.S. Kumisarov, *Ṣādiq Hidāyat muhaqiq va mutarjim*, trans. A. Āzmūda (Tehran: Markaz-i Nashr-i Sipihr, [n.d.]), p. 9.
53 Katouzian, 'Hedayat', *EIr*, Vol. 12, p. 124.
54 M.F. Farzāna, *Āshinā'ī bā Ṣādiq Hidāyat*: *Ānchi Ṣādiq Ḥidāyat bi man guft* (Tehran: Nashr-i Markaz, 1372/1994), pp. 209-210.
55 R. Mustafavī, *Baḥth-i kūtāhī dar murad-i Ṣādiq Hidāyat va āthārash* (Tehran: Amīr Kabīr, 1350/1972), p. 1.
56 Ṣafā, *Ganj-i sukhan*, Vol. 3, p. 327.
57 Gulbun, *Bahār va adab-i fārsī*, Vol. 1, p. 1.
58 M.G. Morony, 'Bahār,' *EIr*, Vol. 3, p. 477.
59 Subḥānī, *Tārīkh-i adabīyāt-i Iran*, p. 602.
60 Bahār, *Dīvān-i ash'ār*, Vol. 1, p. 38.
61 Ibid., Vol. 1, *ghazal* 203, v. 1.
62 Ibid., Vol. 1, p. 479.
63 Ibid.
64 Subḥānī, *Tārīkh-i adabīyāt-i Iran*, p. 633.
65 Abrahamian, *Iran Between Two Revolutions*, p. 149. *Cf.* Keddie and Richard, *Modern Iran*, pp. 88-89; S. Mackey, *The Iranians: Persia, Islam and the Soul of a Nation* (New York: Penguin, 1998), pp. 158-159, and Talattof, *Politics of Writing in Iran*, p. 20.
66 Subḥānī, *Tārīkh-i adabīyāt-i Iran*, p. 633.
67 Dihkhudā, *Lughat-nāma*, Vol. 10, p. 15039, s.v. 'Farrukhī'.
68 Subḥānī, *Tārīkh-i adabīyāt-i Iran*, p. 634. *Cf.* Āryānpūr, *Az Ṣabā tā Nimā*, Vol. 2, pp. 278-279.
69 Talattof, *Politics of Writing in Iran*, p. 20.
70 M. Sipanlu (ed.), *Bāz āfarinī-yi vāqi'īyat: Bist u haft qiṣṣa az bist u haft nivisanda-yi Mu'āṣir-i Iran* (Tehran: Nigāh, 1366/1988), introduction.
71 Ibid.
72 Āryānpūr, *Az Ṣabā tā Nimā*, Vol. 2, pp. 302-304.
73 Ibid., Vol. 2, p. 20.

74 Parvin Iʿtisāmī, *Dīvān-i ashʿār-i Parvin Iʿtisāmī*, ed. A. Iʿtisāmī and V. Durūdīyān (Tehran: Nashr-i Nay, 1382/2003), pp. 13-18.
75 Subḥānī, *Tārīkh-i adabīyāt-i Iran*, p. 634.
76 Talattof, *Politics of Writing in Iran*, p. 21.
77 Ibid., p. 25.
78 Personal communication from Dr. Homayoon Katouzian, Oxford, 20 July 2009.
79 Ibid.
80 C. Bahār (ed.), *Muḥammad Taqī-yi Bahār* (Tehran: Ṭūs, 1380/2001), Vol. 2, pp. 5-20. *Cf.* Āryānpūr, *Az Ṣabā tā Nimā*, Vol. 2, pp. 332-340.
81 Maktab Khāna.
82 Adib-i Nayshābūrī was a traditional poet and a literary scholar who promoted the style of the poets of Khurāsān in the early Islamic era, in the tradition of the so-called *bāzgasht-i adabī* (neoclassical school). Bahār (ed.), *Muḥammad Taqī-yi Bahār*, Vol. 2, pp. 5-20.
83 M.B. Loraine, 'Bahār, Malek al Šoʿarā', i. Life and Work', *Elr*, Vol. 3, pp. 476-479.
84 It has been said that Bahār chose this pen name after the death of Bahār Shirvānī, a poet and close friend of his father. Shirvānī was a famous poet during the reign of Nāṣir al-Dīn Shāh Qājār.
85 Bahār (ed.), *Muḥammad Taqī-yi Bahār*, Vol. 2, pp. 23-41. *Cf.* Loraine, 'Bahār,' *Elr*, Vol. 3, 476-479.
86 Āryānpūr, *Az Ṣabā tā Nimā*, Vol. 2, pp. 332-340.
87 Loraine, 'Bahār', *Elr*, Vol. 3, pp. 477-478.
88 Subḥānī, *Tārīkh-i adabīyāt-i Iran*, pp. 602-607.
89 Loraine, 'Bahār', *Elr*, Vol. 3, pp. 477-478. *tārīkh-i sīstān* (The History of Sīstān), (Tehran, 1314/1935), *mujmal al-tawārīkh va'l-qisās*: (All Dates and Retribution), (Tehran, 1318/1939), and Balʿamī's *tārīkh-i balʿamī*: (The Record of History by Balʿamī).
90 S. ʿA. Khalkhālī, *Tazkiri-yi shuʿarā-yi muʿāsīr-i Iran* (Tehran: Ṭahūrī, 1331/1953), p. 28.
91 Bahār (ed.), *Muḥammad Taqī-yi Bahār*, Vol. 2, p. 158.
92 Ḥāfiẓ, *Dīvān-i Ḥāfiẓ Shīrāzī*, ed. M. Qazvīnī and Q. Ghanī, *ghazal* 150, v. 5.
93 Ibid., *ghazal* 188, v. 2.
94 Avery, *Collected Lyrics*, p. 243; *ghazal* 183.
95 Bahār (ed.), *Muḥammad Taqī-yi Bahār*, Vol. 2, p. 129.
96 Ḥāfiẓ, *Dīvān-i Ḥāfiẓ Shīrāzī*, ed. M. Qazvīnī and Q. Ghanī, *ghazal* 393, v. 3.
97 G.F. Rastigār, *Muntakhab-i shiʿr-i Bahār va barrisi-i kūtāhī az ashʿār-i aū* (Tehran: Bāstān, 1351/1973), p. 38.

98 Ḥāfiẓ, *Dīvān-i Ḥāfiẓ Shīrāzī*, ed. M. Qazvīnī and Q. Ghanī, *Sāqī-nāma*, p. 356.

99 Rastigār, *Muntakhab-i shi'r-i Bahār*, p. 52.

100 Ḥāfiẓ, *Dīvān-i Ḥāfiẓ Shīrāzī*, ed. M. Qazvīnī and Q. Ghanī, *ghazal* 177, v. 7.

101 Avery, *Collected Lyrics*, p. 232; *ghazal* 174.

102 Gulbun, *Bahār va adab-i fārsī*, pp. 54-55.

103 Ibid., p. 158.

104 Rastigār, *Muntakhab-i shi'r-i Bahār*, p. 26.

105 Ibid., p. 13. *Cf.* Āryānpūr, *Az Ṣabā tā Nimā*, Vol. 2, p. 328.

106 Rastigār, *Muntakhab-i shi'r-i Bahār*, p. 14.

107 The impact of Nimā's poetry was felt in Iran after World War Two, and a decade or two later in Afghanistan and Tajikistan. His influence there grew, indirectly at first, mostly through the works of the Iranians who followed his path; poets such as Mihdi Akhavān Sālis, Sīyāvash Kasrā'ī, Furūgh Farrukhzād and Nādir Nādirpur.

108 C. Ṭāhbāz, *Kamāndār-i buzurg-i kuhistān: zindigi va sh'ir-i Nimā Yūshij* (Tehran: Sālis, 1380/2002), p. 19. *Cf.* Khalkhālī, *Tazkiri-yi shu'arā-y i mu'āsīr-i Iran*, pp. 413-420.

109 This is a village in Nūr county, which is situated in Māzandarān province of Iran. Dihkhudā, *Lughat-nāma*, Vol. 14, p. 21130, s.v. 'Yūsh'.

110 A.K. Hakkak, 'Poetic Signs, Critical Frames', *Critique: Journal for Critical Studies of the Middle East*, 4 (1994): 35-50.

111 Khalkhālī, *Tazkiri-yi shu'arā-yi mu'āsīr-i Iran*, pp. 395-411. Nizām Vafā was born in the village of Aran, near Kāshān. He was the son of the village preacher and prayer leader. His mother wrote poetry under the pen name 'Ḥayā' (Modesty). In his youth, Vafā went to Tehran and joined the constitutional movement. In 1923, he published a journal by the name of *Vafā*, a name he later adopted as his own pen name and surname.

112 Nizām Vafā, *Dīvān-i Nizām Vafā*, ed. A. Karīmi (Tehran: Tālār-i Kitāb, 1362/1984), p. 2.

113 A. K-Hakkak, 'Nima Yushij: A Life', in A. Karimi-Hakkak and K. Talattof (eds.), *Essays on Nima Yushij: Animating Modernism in Persian Poetry* (Leiden and Boston: Brill, 2004), pp. 28-34.

114 Āryānpūr, *Az Ṣabā tā Nimā*, Vol. 2, p. 467.

115 Nimā Yūshij, *Majmū'a-yi kāmil-i ash'ār-i Nimā Yūshij*, ed. S. Ṭāhbāzī (Tehran: Nigāh, 1371/1993). This book has only been used to count Nimā's verses.

116 Ibid., p. 1.

117 S. Ṭāhbāz (ed.) *Nāmahā-yi Nimā Yūshij* (Tehran: Nashr-i Ābī, 1363/1972), pp. 72-75.

118 Ibid., p. 72.
119 Ibid., p. 251.
120 Ibid., p. 250.
121 Ḥāfiẓ, *Dīvān-i Ḥāfiẓ Shīrāzī*, ed. M. Qazvīnī and Q. Ghanī, *ghazal* 381, v. 9.
122 ʿA.J. ʿAtāʾī (ed.), *Nīmā Yūshij: Zindagī va āthār-i aū* (Tehran: Ṣafī ʿAlī Shāh, 1346/1955), pp. 15-16.
123 Ibid., p. 19.
124 Ibid., p. 51.
125 F.P. Matin, 'Love: Nima's Dialogue with Hafez', in Hakkak and Talattof (eds.), *Essays on Nima Yushij*, p. 173.
126 Ibid., p. 177.
127 Ibid., p. 181.
128 Ḥāfiẓ, *Dīvān-i Ḥāfiẓ Shīrāzī*, ed. M. Qazvīnī and Q. Ghanī, *ghazal* 94, v. 7.
129 Avery, *Collected Lyrics*, p. 134; *ghazal* 93.
130 Matin, 'Love', p. 182.
131 Nimā Yūshij, *Majmūʿa-yi kāmil-i ashʿār-i Nimā Yūshij*, p. 44. Also cited by Matin, 'Love', p. 180.
132 Matin, 'Love', pp. 179-180.
133 Ḥāfiẓ, *Dīvān-i Ḥāfiẓ Shīrāzī*, ed. M. Qazvīnī and Q. Ghanī, *ghazal* 94, v. 4.
134 Avery, *Collected Lyrics*, p. 134; *ghazal* 93.
135 Ḥāfiẓ, *Dīvān-i Ḥāfiẓ Shīrāzī*, ed. M. Qazvīnī and Q. Ghanī, *ghazal* 94, v. 6.
136 Avery, *Collected Lyrics*, p. 134; *ghazal* 93.
137 Matin, 'Love', p. 182.
138 Lute – A string musical instrument which is claimed to be originated from the names of the Iranian *sitār* and the guitar as well as less prevalent instruments such as the *dutār*. However it was definitely developed in Persia, the precise region in which it was first made and played cannot be confirmed.
139 This refers to the modernist school of poetry founded by Nimā, in which verse was, more often than not, written with scant regard for metre and rhyme.
140 Subḥānī, *Tārīkh-i adabīyāt-i Iran*, pp. 642-644.
141 Ibid.
142 K. ʿĀbidī, *Az muṣāḥibat-i āftāb: Taʾamulāt va justujūhāʾī dar shiʿr-i Suhrāb Sipihrī* (Tehran: Rivāyat, 1996), pp. 18-99.
143 S. Sipihrī, *Hasht kitāb* (Tehran: Tahūrī, 1383/2004).
144 Ibid.
145 Ibid., pp. 1-5.
146 Subḥānī, *Tārīkh-i adabīyāt-i Iran*, pp. 642-644.

147 Ibid., p. 643.
148 Hakkak, *Anthology of Modern Persian Poetry*, p. 95.
149 Ibid.
150 Ibid.
151 D. Āshūrī, K. Imāmī, Ḥ. M. Hamadānī (eds.), *Payāmī dar rāh: naẓarī bi shiʿr va naqāshī-i Suhrāb Sipihrī* (Tehran: Ṭahūrī, 1358/1980), pp. 84-86.
152 S. Bihbahānī, *Yik rūz bā hasht kitāb* (Tehran: [n.p.], 1376/1998), pp. 327-371.
153 Ṣ. Ḥusaynī, *gulhā-yi niāyish: shiʿr va naqd-i suhrāb sipihrī* (Tehran: Nilūfar, 1996), pp. 131-164. *Cf.* Ḥ. Ḥusaynī, *Bidil, Sipihrī va sabk-i Hindī* (Tehran: Surūsh, 1368/1989).
154 S. Shamīsā, *Nigāhī bi Sipihrī* (Tehran: Murvārid, 1371/1993), pp. 185-191.
155 H. Sarshar, 'Sepehri, Sohrab', Encyclopedia Iranica online, www.iranica-online.org/articles/sepehri-sohrab.
156 Ibid. *Cf.* Yarshater, *Iran Faces the Seventies*, p. 300.
157 M. Ḥuqūqī, *Shiʿr-i zamān-i mā*: *Suhrāb Sipihrī* (Tehran: Nigāh, 1371/1993), p. 7.
158 M. Nūrbakhsh, *Bi surāgh-i man agar miāʾīd: Sirr-i andisha-yi Suhrāb Sipihrī dar āʾina-yi ashʿārash* (Tehran: Murvārid, 1376/1998), p. 29.
159 Ṭāhbāz (ed.), *Nāmahā-yi Nimā Yūshij*, p. 179.
160 Sipihrī did not discuss sociopolitical issues directly. He is conscious of the heritage of classical poets – but that is not the way he wrote.
161 Sipihrī, *Hasht kitāb*, p. 276.
162 Nūrbakhsh, *Bi surāgh-i man agar miāʾīd*, p. 31.
163 Ḥāfiẓ, *Dīvān-i Ḥāfiẓ Shīrāzī*, ed. M. Qazvīnī and Q. Ghanī, *ghazal* 342, v. 1, 2.
164 Avery, *Collected Lyrics*, p. 413; *ghazal* 334.
165 Sipihrī, *Hasht kitāb*, p. 20.
166 Ḥāfiẓ, *Dīvān-i Ḥāfiẓ Shīrāzī*, ed. M. Qazvīnī and Q. Ghanī, *ghazal* 387, v. 4.
167 Avery, *Collected Lyrics*, p. 463; *ghazal* 380.
168 Sipihrī, *Hasht kitāb*, p. 135.
169 Ḥāfiẓ, *Dīvān-i Ḥāfiẓ Shīrāzī*, ed. M. Qazvīnī and Q. Ghanī, *ghazal* 281, v. 8.
170 Avery, *Collected Lyrics*, p. 344; *ghazal* 275.
171 Sipihrī, *Hasht kitāb*, p. 226.
172 Ḥāfiẓ, *Dīvān-i Ḥāfiẓ Shīrāzī*, ed. M. Qazvīnī and Q. Ghanī, *ghazal* 189, v. 6.
173 Avery, *Collected Lyrics*, p. 244; *ghazal* 184.
174 Kāvīyānpūr, *Zindigi-yi adabī*, p. 192.
175 A. Mihrin, *Tārīkh-i zabān va adabīyāt-i Iran az zamān-i Qājār tā ʿaṣr-i Pahlavi* (Tehran: Mānī, 1353/1934), p. 198.

176 J. ʿAlī Zāda (ed.), *Bi hamīn sādigi va zibāʾī: Yād-nāma-yi ustād Sayyid Muḥammad Ḥusayn Shahriyār 1285-1376* (Tehran: Nashr-i Markaz, 1374/1995), p. 546.
177 A. Kāvīyānpūr, *Zindagi-yi adabī va ijtimāʿī-yi ustād Shahriyār* (Tehran: Iqbāl, 1381/2001), p. 6.
178 Ibid., p. 28.
179 Ibid., p. 31.
180 Āryānpūr, *Az Ṣabā tā Nimā*, Vol. 2, p. 18.
181 ʿAlī Zāda (ed.), *Bi hamīn sādigi va zibāʾī*, pp. 1-10.
182 Ibid.
183 Ibid.
184 Ibid.
185 Shahriyār, *Dīvān-i Shahriyār*, biography by Zāhidī, 2 vols. (Tehran: Nigāristān-i Kitāb, 1388/2009), Vol. 1, p. 12.
186 Ibid., Vol. 1, p. 30.
187 Ibid., Vol. 1, p. 60.
188 Ibid.
189 Shahriyār, *Kullīyāt-i Dīvān-i Shahriyār*, ed. M. Ḥ. Shahriyār, 3 vols. (Tabrīz: Maṭbūʿāt-i Saʿdī, 1345/1967).
190 Shahriyār, *Dīvān-i Shahriyār*, Vol. 1, p. 343.
191 Ḥāfiẓ, *Dīvān-i Ḥāfiẓ Shīrāzī*, ed. M. Qazvīnī and Q. Ghanī, *ghazal* 393, v. 1.
192 Avery, *Collected Lyrics*, p. 470; *ghazal* 385.
193 Shahriyār, *Dīvān-i Shahriyār*, Vol. 1, p. 105.
194 Ḥāfiẓ, *Dīvān-i Ḥāfiẓ Shīrāzī*, ed. M. Qazvīnī and Q. Ghanī, *ghazal* 39, v. 1.
195 Avery, *Collected Lyrics*, p. 72; *ghazal* 40.
196 Shahriyār, *Dīvān-i Shahriyār*, Vol. 1, p. 110.
197 Ḥāfiẓ, *Dīvān-i Ḥāfiẓ Shīrāzī*, ed. M. Qazvīnī and Q. Ghanī, *ghazal* 53, v. 1.
198 Avery, *Collected Lyrics*, p. 91; *ghazal* 54.
199 Shahriyār, *Dīvān-i Shahriyār*, Vol. 1, p. 103.
200 Ḥāfiẓ, *Dīvān-i Ḥāfiẓ Shīrāzī*, ed. M. Qazvīnī and Q. Ghanī, *ghazal* 37, v. 1.
201 Avery, *Collected Lyrics*, p. 68; *ghazal* 37.
202 Shahriyār, *Dīvān-i Shahriyār*, Vol. 1, p. 100.
203 Ḥāfiẓ, *Dīvān-i Ḥāfiẓ Shīrāzī*, ed. M. Qazvīnī and Q. Ghanī, *ghazal* 15, v. 1.
204 Avery, *Collected Lyrics*, p. 42; *ghazal* 16.
205 Shahriyār, *Dīvān-i Shahriyār*, Vol. 1, p. 92.
206 Ḥāfiẓ, *Dīvān-i Ḥāfiẓ Shīrāzī*, ed. M. Qazvīnī and Q. Ghanī, *ghazal* 1, v. 1.
207 This translation follows that of Peter Avery, with some modifications.
208 Shahriyār, *Dīvān-i Shahriyār*, Vol. 1, p. 75.
209 Ḥāfiẓ, *Dīvān-i Ḥāfiẓ Shīrāzī*, ed. M. Qazvīnī and Q. Ghanī, *ghazal* 3, v. 1.

210 Avery, *Collected Lyrics*, p. 21; *ghazal* 3.

211 Shahriyār, *Kullīyāt-i Dīvān-i Shahriyār*, ed. M. Ḥ. Shahriyār, Vol. 1, p. 10.

212 Ibid., Vol. 1, p. 96.

213 Ḥāfiẓ, *Dīvān-i Ḥāfiẓ Shīrāzī*, ed. M. Qazvīnī and Q. Ghanī, *ghazal* 337, v. 2.

214 Avery, *Collected Lyrics*, p. 409; *ghazal* 330.

215 Gulbun, *Bahār va adab-i fārsī*, p. 209.

216 Shahriyār, *Kullīyāt-i Dīvān-i Shahriyār*, ed. M. Ḥ. Shahriyār, p. 5.

217 ʻA. Dastghayb, *Naqd-i āthār-i Aḥmad Shāmlū* (Tehran: Chāpār, Shāhanshāhī 2537), p. 1.

218 Hakkak, *Anthology of Modern Persian Poetry*, p. 53.

219 N. Taqīpūr, *Ta'amulī dar shiʻr-i Aḥmad Shāmlū* (Tehran: Ābān, Shāhanshāhī 2537), pp. 3-5.

220 Shāmlū, *Havā-yi tāza* (Tehran: Nigāh, 1363/1985).
Shāmlū, *Dashna dar dīs* (Tehran: Murvārīd, 1372/1994).
Shāmlū, *Lahzihā va hamīshihā* (Tehran: Nigāh, 1372/1994).
Shāmlū, *Marsīyihā-yi khāk va shikuftan dar mih* (Tehran: Nigāh, 1372/1994).
Shāmlū, *Darhā va dīvār-i buzurg-i chīn* (Tehran: Nimūna, 1352/1974).
Shāmlū, *Qaqnūs dar bārān* (Tehran: Nīl, 1344/1966).
Shāmlū, *Bāgh-i āyina* (Tehran: Murvārīd, 1338/1960).
Shāmlū, *Āidā dar āyina* (Tehran: Nīl, 1343/1965).

221 Ḥāfiẓ, *Dīvān-i Ḥāfiẓ: Qarāʻt guzīnī intiqādī*, ed. B. Khurramshāhī (Tehran: Farzān, 1378/2000), p. 7.

222 Ibid., p. 8.

223 Ḥāfiẓ, *Dīvān-i Ḥāfiẓ mīras-i girānqadr-i farhangi-i mā*, ed. J. Matinī (Tehran: Iran-nāma Majala-yi Tahqīqāt-i Iran Shināsī, 1376/1998), pp. 606-607.

224 Ibid., pp. 609-611; pp. 627-638.

225 Ibid., pp. 627-638.

226 D. Āshūrī, 'Ḥāfiẓ bi rivāyat-i ʻAbbās Kīārustamī', *Iran shināsī*, No. 4 (Winter 1386/2008), pp. 757-758.

227 Ibid., p. 761.
In an article in *Kilk*, a monthly cultural journal, Shāmlū engages in a debate with Khānlarī after interpreting a verse of Ḥāfiẓ's poetry. He rejects Khānlarī's view on the verse:

عبوس زهد به وجه خمار بنشیند   مرید فرقهٔ دردی کشان خوش خویم

Let the gloomy, ill-tempered asceticism match the appearance of the hangover,
I am the disciple of the order of pleasant drunkards.

There have been many debates in connection with this verse, suggesting that the influence of Ḥāfiẓ on scholars and men of letters is a topic ripe for exploration. The debate continues in a ten-page article by Khānlarī, Shāmlū, Khurramshāhī, Islāmī, 'Alavī, Khatīb Rahbar and Shu'ār. 'A. Ravāqī, 'Shab-i tārīk va bīm-i mūj va...', *Māh-nāma-yi Kilk*, No. 21 (Autumn 1370/1992), pp. 70-81.

228 B. Khurramshāhī, *Dhihn va zabān-i Ḥāfiẓ* (Tehran: Nāhid, 1384/2005), pp. 381-388. Shahram Pazouki, Tehran, 2010, believes Shāmlū's edition has no credibility or scholarly value; 'it is just a view by someone who likes Ḥāfiẓ, not an academic work'.

229 'A. Dastghiyb, *Naqd-i āthār-i Aḥmad Shāmlū* (Tehran: Āfarīn, 1373/1995), p. 115.

230 Personal communication from Dr. Shahram Pazouki, Tehran, 20 May 2010.

231 Personal communication from Dr. Shahram Pazouki, Tehran, 20 May 2010.

232 Personal communication from Bahā' al-Dīn Khurramshāhī, Tehran, 18 May 2010.

Chapter V – From Medieval to Modern Ḥāfiẓology: Five Hundred Years of Editions and Compilations of the *Dīvān*, from 1500 to 2000

1 M. Nīknām, *Kitāb shīnāsī-i Ḥāfiẓ* (Shīrāz: Markaz-i Ḥāfiẓ Shināsī, 1381/2003), Vol. 2, pp. 1-30. Cited in B. Khurramshāhī, 'Ḥāfiẓ. Printed Editions,' *EIr*, Vol. 11, p. 477. *Cf.* 'A.Q. Rādfar, *Majmu'a-yi zabān va adabīyāt-i fārsī: Ḥāfiẓ pazhuhān va Ḥāfiẓ pazhuhī* (Tehran: Gustara, 1367/1989), Vol. 3, pp. 247-263. Cited in Meisami, 'Manuscripts of Hafez', *EIr*, Vol. 11, p. 477.

2 Meisami, 'Manuscripts of Hafez', *EIr*, Vol. 11, p. 477.

3 Khurramshāhī, 'Ḥāfiẓ. Printed Editions', *EIr*, Vol. 11, p. 479. *Cf.* Abū Ṭālib Khān, *Masīr-i Ṭālibī*, ed. Ḥusayn Khadiv-i Jam, *The Travels of Mīrzā Abū Ṭālib Khān, 1213/1796-1218/1801* (Tehran: Kitabhā-yi Jibī, 1352/1974), pp. 13-15. Mīrzā Abū Ṭālib Khān was an Iranian traveller who lived about 160 years ago and was known as 'Landanī'. Landanī is not famous amongst many Iranians. He travelled mostly to Asia, Africa and Europe. He compiled a travelogue entitled *Masīr-i Ṭālibi: The Travels of Mīrzā Abū Ṭālib Khān, 1213/1796-1218/1801*. Landanī resided in India. His father was born in Iṣfahān and died in Murshid Ābād in 1183/1766. In addition to his trav-

elogue, Landanī also published another book entitled *Khulāṣāt al-afkār* comprised of the anthologies of a number of Persian poets. Copies of this are currently kept at the British Library. Landanī's *Dīvān* of Ḥāfiẓ was published in 1791.

4 Abū Ṭālib Khān, *Masīr-i Ṭālibī*, p. 9. Cited in Khurramshāhī, *EIr*, Vol. 11, p. 479.

5 Abū Ṭālib Khān, *Masīr-i Ṭālibī*, p. 391. Landanī speaks of Muḥammad Pāshā in his travelogue, recording his good manners, honourable behaviour and hospitality; he asserts that Pāshā was a famous Ottoman minister.

6 Nīknām, *Kitāb shīnāsī-i Ḥāfiẓ*, Vol. 2, pp. 1-2. Cited in Khurramshāhī, *EIr*, Vol. 11, p. 479. According to Nīknām, this book was published in Calcutta in 1827. However, I have not had any success in obtaining a copy for further comparative studies; therefore, the accuracy of this claim relies heavily on Nīknām and Khurramshāhī's statement.

7 Ḥāfiẓ, *Diwan-i Hafiz: For The Degree of Honor Examination in Persian for Officers in the Military and Civil Services*, ed. M.H.S. Jarrett (Calcutta: Urdu Guide Press, 1881), English introduction. During the nineteenth century, a few editions were also published in Europe, including *Die Lieder des Hafis* (*The Songs of Ḥāfiẓ*), edited by H. Brockhaus (Leipzig, 1854-1856) and *Der Diwan des grossen lyrischen Dichters Hafis* (*The Dīvān of the Great Lyric Poet Ḥāfiẓ*), edited by Rosenzweig Schwannau. V.R. v. Rosenzweig Schwannau, *Der Diwan: des grossen lyrischen Dichters Hafis im persischen Original / herausgegeben ins Deutsche metrisch übersetzt und mit Anmerkungen vesehenvon* (Vienna: K.K. Hof-und Staatsdruckerei, 1858-1864). Cited in Khurramshāhī, *EIr*, Vol. 11, p. 479.

8 V.R. v. Rosenzweig Schwannau, *Der Diwan: des grossen lyrischen Dichters Hafis im persischen Original / herausgegeben ins Deutsche metrisch übersetzt und mit Anmerkungen vesehenvon*. Cited in Khurramshāhī, *EIr*, Vol. 11, p. 479.

9 H. Wilberforce Clarke, (trans.), *The Dīvān…Ḥāfiẓ-i-Shīrāzī* (Calcutta: Government of India Central Printing Office 1891), 2 vols. Reprinted as *Dīvān-i-Ḥāfiz* (Bethesda, MD.: Ibex Publishers 1998), 1 vol.

10 Ḥāfiẓ, *Dīvān-i Khawja Ḥāfiẓ Shīrāzī: Az rū-yi nuskhi-yi khaṭṭī ki dar tārīkh-i 827 Hijrī Qamarī 35 sāl ba'd az vafāt-i Khawja taḥrīr shuda ast*, ed. S. 'A.R. Khalkhālī (Tehran: Dunyā-i Kitāb, [n.d]). Cited in Khurramshāhī, *EIr*, Vol. 11, p. 480.

11 Ḥāfiẓ, *Ḥāfiẓ-nāma*, ed. S. 'A.R. Khalkhālī (Tehran: Majlis, 1320/1942), pp. 1-15.

12 S. Naysārī, *Muqadami'ī bar tadvīn-i ghazalhā-yi Ḥāfiẓ* (Tehran: Intishārāt-i 'Ilmī, 1376/1998), p. 43. *Cf.* Ḥāfiẓ, *Ḥāfiẓ-nāma*, ed. S. 'A.R. Khalkhālī, pp. 2-3.

13 Ḥāfiẓ, *Ḥāfiẓ-nāma*, ed. S. 'A.R. Khalkhālī, p. 80. Khalkhālī asserts that he collected various editions of Ḥāfiẓ's *Dīvān* over a period of thirty years. He emphasizes that he had neither the financial means, nor social connections to print and publish any valuable study in Iran. Moreover, most of the lithograph books were published and printed in India at that time.

14 Ibid., p. 2.

15 Ibid., p. 3.

16 Ḥāfiẓ, *Dīvān-i Ḥāfiẓ*, ed. H. Jāvid and B. Khurramshāhī (Tehran: Farzān, 1378/1999), p. 6.

17 Ḥāfiẓ, *Dīvān-i Ḥāfiẓ*, ed. P.N. Khānlarī (Tehran: Khārazmī, 1362/1984), Vol. 2, pp. 1125-1126.

18 Ḥāfiẓ, *Dīvān-i Ḥāfiẓ*, ed. Q. Ghanī and M. Qazvīnī, *muqadama-yi muṣṣa-ḥiḥ*, pp. *kab, kaj*. [n.p.ns]

19 Ḥāfiẓ, *Dīvān-i Ḥāfiẓ*, ed. B. Khurramshāhī (Tehran: Dūstān, 1385/2006), p. 36.

20 Ibid., *ghazal* 130, v. 1.

21 Avery, *Collected Lyrics*, p. 173; *ghazal* 126.

22 Ḥāfiẓ, *Dīvān-i Khawja Ḥāfiẓ Shīrāzī*, ed. Khalkhālī, *ghazal* 130, v. 1.

23 The word *Ṣabā* is a noun in Persian bearing two different meanings, one is 'the beginning' and the other is a name chosen for the eastern breeze; thus, in these verses edited by Khalkhālī, the more acceptable one would be 'the beginning'. It has been changed and corrected by Khurramshāhī because of the repetition of the word in the same hemistich, which I have underlined.

24 This translation follows that of Avery, with some modifications. Avery, *Collected Lyrics*, p. 173; *ghazal* 126.

25 Ḥāfiẓ, *Dīvān-i Ḥāfiẓ*, ed. Khānlarī, *ghazal* 126, v. 1.

26 Avery, *Collected Lyrics*, p. 173; *ghazal* 126.

27 Rādfar, *Majmu'a-yi zabān*, pp. 23-24.

28 Some of the facts and figures in the above statement are also cited in Khurramshāhī, *EIr*, Vol. 11, p. 480.

29 Ḥāfiẓ, *Dīvān-i Ḥāfiẓ Shīrāzī az rū-yi chāp-i Qudsī*, ed. 'A.A. Ḥikmat (Tehran: Ibn Sinā, 1342/1964), pp. 13-15.

30 'A.A. Ḥikmat, *Dīvān-i Ḥāfiẓ bi tashih-i Muḥammad Qudsī*, ed. 'A.A. Ḥikmat, Ḥ. Dhulfaqārī and A. 'A. Muḥammadī (Tehran: Nashr-i Chishmih, 1381/2002), p. 26.

31 Ibid., p. 1.

32 The total number of *ghazals* in Qazvīnī and Ghanī's edition are 495 and in Khānlarī, there are 486. However, the difference in Qudsī's edition exceeds one hundred *ghazals*, without any explanation as to why the editor believes they are authentic material.

33 Ḥāfiẓ, *Dīvān-i Khawja Shams al-Dīn Muḥammad Ḥāfiẓ Shīrāzī*, ed. Ḥ. P. Bakhtīyārī (Tehran: Birukhīm, 1315/1937). Cited in Khurramshāhī, *EIr*, Vol. 11, p. 480. Rādfar asserts that Ḥusayn Pizhmān Bakhtīyārī (d. 1352/1973) was the first to publish a critical edition of Ḥāfiẓ in Persia.

34 Rādfar, *Majmu'a-yi zabān*, p. 16. Cited in Khurramshāhī, *EIr*, Vol. 11, p. 480.

35 Ḥāfiẓ, *Dīvān-i Khawja Shams al-Dīn Muḥammad Ḥāfiẓ Shīrāzī*, ed. Bakhtīyārī, pp. 19-22.

36 Ibid., p. 19.

37 Personal communication from Dr. Julie Meisami, Berkeley, 24 October 2011.

38 Ḥāfiẓ, *Dīvān-i Ḥāfiẓ*, ed. H. Jāvid and B. Khurramshāhī, p. 7.

39 Ibid.

40 Ḥāfiẓ, *Dīvān-i Ḥāfiẓ*, ed. Q. Ghanī and M. Qazvīnī, introduction, p. 23, marked as (*kad*).

41 Khurramshāhī, 'Ḥāfiẓ', *EIr*, Vol. 11, p. 480. *Cf.* S. Naysārī (ed.), *Muqadama'ī bar tadvīn-i ghazalhā-yi Ḥāfiẓ* (Tehran: Intishārāt-i 'Ilmī, 1376/1998), pp. 44-142.

42 Ḥāfiẓ, *Dīvān-i Ḥāfiẓ*: *Qarā't quzīnī intiqādī*, ed. Khurramshāhī, pp. 7-8.

43 Ḥāfiẓ, *Dīvān-i Ḥāfiẓ*, ed. Khānlarī, Vol. 2, pp. 1126-1128.

44 Ḥāfiẓ, *Dīvān-i Ḥāfiẓ*, ed. H. Jāvid and B. Khurramshāhī, pp. 4-8.

45 Personal communication from Dr. Julie Meisami, Berkeley, 24 October 2011.

46 Ḥāfiẓ, *Dīvān-i Ḥāfiẓ*, ed. B. Khurramshāhī, p. 37.

47 Ḥāfiẓ, *Dīvān-i Khawja Ḥāfiẓ Shīrāzī*: *Kashf al-Abyyāt va kashf al-Lughāt*, ed. 'A.Q. Īnjavī Shīrāzī (Tehran: Jāvīdān, 1360/1982), pp. 10-18.

48 Ī. Ṣārimī, *Ḥāfiẓ az dīdgāh-i 'Allāma Muḥammad Qazvīnī* (Tehran: 'Ilmī, 1366/1988), pp. 53-55.

49 Ḥ. 'A. Hiravī, *Maqālāt-i Ḥāfiẓ* (Tehran: Kitābsarā, 1368/1990), pp. 204-208. Khurramshāhī, 'Printed Editions of the Dīvān of Ḥāfiẓ', *Elr*, Vol. 11, p. 481.

50 Hiravī, *Maqālāt-i Ḥāfiẓ*, p. 208.

51 Ḥāfiẓ, *Dīvān-i Ḥāfiẓ*, ed. S. 'A. Īnjavī Shīrāzī (Tehran: Ibn Sinā, 1346/1967), p. 2.

52 Ibid.

53 Ibid.

54 Ḥāfiẓ, *Dīvān-i Ḥāfiẓ*, ed. Khānlarī, Vol. 1, *ghazal* 22, v. 4.

55 Ḥāfiẓ, *Dīvān-i Ḥāfiẓ*, ed. Jāvid and Khurramshāhī, p. 7.
56 Ḥāfiẓ, *Dīvān-i Ḥāfiẓ*, ed. Khānlarī, Vol. 2, pp. 1130-1133.
57 Ḥāfiẓ, *Dīvān-i Ḥāfiẓ*, ed. J. Manṣūr (Tehran: Daurān, 1382/2003), p. 1. J. Manṣūr states in the introduction to his edition of the *Dīvān* that the basis for his research was the edition produced by Qazvīnī and Ghanī, as well as those by Khānlarī, Sāya, Naysārī, Khalkhālī, Nā'īnī and Nadhir Aḥmad. Kirmānī, *Ḥāfiẓ az dīdgāhhā-yi mukhtalif* (Tehran: Ādhar Ābādigān, 1364/1986), pp. 28-32. The above examples are not statements of preference; they are, however, indications of perceptible discrepancies in the two mentioned editions. Ḥāfiẓ, *Dīvān-i ghazalīyāt-i Muwlānā Shams al-Dīn Muḥammad Ḥāfiẓ Shīrāzī*, ed. Kh. Rahbar (Tehran: Ṣafī 'Alī Shāh, 1365/1987), p. 23.
58 S. Naysārī, *Muqadama'-i bar tadvīn-i ghazalhā-yi Ḥāfiẓ* (Tehran: Intishārāt-i 'Ilmī, 1376/1998), introduction.
59 Ḥāfiẓ, *Dīvān-i Ḥāfiẓ, Ḥāfiẓ bi sa'-yi Sāya*, ed. Hūshang Ibtihāj, known as Saya (Tehran: Nashr-i Kār-nāma, 1376/1997), pp. 706-716.
60 Ibid., p. 32.
61 Personal communication from Bahā' al-Dīn Khurramshāhī, Tehran, 18 May 2010.
62 Personal communication from Dr. Shahram Pazouki, Tehran, 20 May 2010.
63 M. Mu'īn, *Ḥāfiẓ-i shirīn sukhan* (Tehran: Sukhan, 1319/1941), Vol. 1, pp. 110-113.
64 Ibid., Vol. 2, pp. 527-569.
65 Ibid., Vol. 2, pp. 741-783.
66 Ibid., Vol. 2, p. 8.
67 Ibid., Vol. 1, p. 9.
68 J.M. Ṣahbā, *Sukhanī chand dar bāb-i aḥvāl va ash'ār-i Ḥāfiẓ* (Tehran: Ispāhān, 1321/1943).
69 Ibid., p. 103. Ḥāfiẓ, *Dīvān-i Ḥāfiẓ*, ed. M. Qazvīnī and Q. Ghanī, *ghazal* 274, v. 2.
70 Avery, *Collected Lyrics*, p. 338; *ghazal* 269.
71 Ṣahbā, *Sukhanī chand dar bāb-i aḥvāl va ash'ār-i Ḥāfiẓ*, p. 6. Strangely, there is no reference to such an important book by Ṣahbā; even the name of its author is not mentioned.
72 Ghanī, *Baḥth dar āthār va afkār va aḥvāl-i Ḥāfiẓ*, pp. 12-14.
73 Ibid., p. 19.
74 M. 'A Bāmdād, *Ḥāfiẓ-shīnāsī yā ilhāmāt-i Khawja* (Tehran: Ibn Sinā, 1338/1960), pp. 10-12.

75 Ibid., p. 18.

76 There is no publication date on this book; however, the John Rylands Library of the University of Manchester has registered this date in their catalogue.

77 M. ʿA. Muʿayyirī, *Ḥāfiẓ rā ham az Ḥāfiẓ bishnāsīm* (Tehran: Intishārāt-i Kitāb Furūshī-i Dihkhudā, 1354/1974).

78 Ibid., p. 1.

79 Ibid., pp. 7-8.

80 Ibid., p. 7. *Cf*, Ḥāfiẓ, *Dīvān-i Ḥāfiẓ Shīrāzī*, ed. M. Qazvīnī and Q. Ghanī, *ghazal* 281, v. 9.

81 Muʿayyirī, *Ḥāfiẓ rā ham az Ḥāfiẓ bishnāsīm*, pp. 14-24.

82 Ibid., p. 14, Ḥāfiẓ, *Dīvān-i Ḥāfiẓ Shīrāzī*, ed. M. Qazvīnī and Q. Ghanī, *ghazal* 158, v. 1.

83 M. Dārābī, *Laṭifa-yi Ghaybī: Ḥāfiẓ Shīrāzī bi zamima-yi bayān-i Iṣṭilāḥāt-i aḥl-i ʿirfān* (Shīrāz: Kitāb-Khāna- yi Aḥmadī, 1357/1979).

84 Personal communication from Dr. Shahram Pazouki, Tehran, 20 May 2010.

85 Personal communication from Dr. Mohammad Reza Movahedi, Tehran, 23 May 2010.

86 Personal communication from Dr. Shahram Pazouki, Tehran, 20 May 2010. The poems of Saʿdī and Rūmī are viewed in comparison with those of Ḥāfiẓ, providing illustrative evidence. Such verses are very similar to one another.

87 Personal communication from Dr. Shahram Pazouki, Tehran, 20 May 2010.

88 R.N. Niʿmatullāhī, *Nubūgh-i Ḥāfiẓ-i Shīrāz va nūr-i ashʿār-i aū* (Tehran: Zindagī, [n.d]).

89 Two verses of which merit citation here:

خاتمه در مرحله عشق نیست   خاتمه حد است، حد عشق چیست؟
عشق بود اول بی ابتدا   عشق بود آخر بی انتها !

There is no end to the degrees of love,
An end has a limit but love has no limit,

Love comes with a first that has no beginning;
Love is a last without any termination.

90 M. Murtaḍavī, *Maktab-i Ḥāfiẓ: Muqaddama bar Ḥāfiẓ shināsī* (Tehran: Ibn Sinā, 1344/1966), p. 4.

91 Ibid., pp. 12-18.
92 Ibid., p. 24.
93 Ibid., p. 72.
94 B. Khurramshāhī, *Ḥāfiẓ-nāma: Sharḥ-i alfāz, aʿlām, mafāhīm-i kilidī va abyāt-i dushvār-i Ḥāfiẓ* (Tehran: Intishārāt-i Surūsh, 1366/1988), p. 15.
95 Ibid., p. 29.
96 Ibid., pp. 40-90.
97 Ibid., pp. 91-100.
98 Personal communication from Dr. Mohammad Reza Movahedi, Tehran, 23 May 2010.
99 Ibid.
100 S.N. Kirmānī, *Dawlat-i pīr-i mughān* (Tehran: Pāzhang, 1374/1996), pp. 20-38.
101 Ibid., pp. 19-33.
102 S.Y. Yathrabī, *Āb-i Ṭarabnāk: Taḥlil-i muḍūʿī-yi Dīvān-i Ḥāfiẓ* (Tehran: Intishārāt-i Fikr-i Rūz, 1374/1996), pp. 13-15.
103 Ibid., p. 19.
104 Ibid., p. 35.
105 Ibid., p. 195.
106 Dhū'l-Nūr (ed.), *Dar justujū-yi Ḥāfiẓ*, p. 1.
107 Ibid., pp. 8-9.
108 Ibid., p. 8.
109 Ibid., p. 11.
110 M.B. Khāliqī, *Shākh-i Nabāt: Sharḥ-i ghazalhā* (Tehran: Zavvār, 1382/2004).
111 V.A. Durūdīyān, *In Kimīyā-yi hastī: Maqālihā va yāddāshthā-yi ustād Shafīʿī Kadkanī dar bārih-yi Ḥāfiẓ* (Tehran: Āydin, 1385/2007), pp. 5-7.
112 Ibid., p. 1.
113 Ibid., p. 33.
114 Ibid., p. 363.
115 Ibid., p. 362.
116 Ibid.
117 Ḥ. ʿA. Hiravī, *Sharḥ-i ghazalhā-yi Ḥāfiẓ* (Tehran: Nashr-i Naw, 1386/2008), Vol. 1, p. 5.
118 Ibid., Vol. 1, p. 49.
119 Ibid., Vol. 1, p. 7.
120 *zulf*, (tress), *ṭurra*, (lock of hair), *khāl*, (mole), *kamand*, (lasso), *kamān-i abrū* (the curve of the eyebrow).
121 Hiravī, *Sharḥ-i ghazalhā-yi Ḥāfiẓ*, Vol. 1, p. 14.

122 Ibid., Vol. 1, pp. 31-32.

123 M. Isti'lāmī, *Dars-i Ḥāfiẓ: Naqd va Sharḥ-i ghazalhā-yi Khawja Shams al-Dīn Muḥammad Ḥāfiẓ* (Tehran: Sukhan, 1388/2010), p. 1.

124 Ibid., p. 72.

125 'Ā. Nushāhī, '*Nakhustīn Sharḥ-i fārsī-yi Dīvān-i Ḥāfiẓ dar shibḥ-i qārriḥ*,' in *Sukhan-i aḥl-i dil, majmū'a-yi maqālāt* (Kungara-yi bayn ulmilalī-i buzurgdāsht-i Ḥāfiẓ, kumisiūn-i Unisco dar Iran, [n.d.]), pp. 761-771. *Cf.* A. 'A. Kh. Lāhūrī, B. Khurramshāhī, K. Manṣūrī, and Ḥ. M. Amīn (eds.), *Sharḥ-i 'irfānī-i ghazalhā-yi Ḥāfiẓ* (Tehran: Qatra, 1374/1996), Vol. 1, p. 2.

126 None of the above-mentioned commentaries, aside from those by Sūdī and Lāhūrī, have been published; because of the difficulty of accessing them in manuscript form, examination of their significance to Ḥāfiẓology must await a future study.

127 M.S. Bosnavī, *Sharḥ-i Sūdī bar Ḥāfiẓ*, trans. 'I. Sattārzāda (Tehran: Zarrīn, 1374/1966), Vol. 1, foreword.

128 Ibid., Vol. 1, p. 1.

129 Ibid.

130 Ibid., Vol. 1, p. 2.

131 Personal communication from Bahā' al-Dīn Khurramshāhī, Tehran, 18 May 2010, and personal communication from Dr. Shahram Pazouki, Tehran, 20 May 2010.

132 Lāhūrī, *Sharḥ-i 'irfānī-i ghazalhā-yi Ḥāfiẓ*.

133 The work contains all the *ghazals* of Ḥāfiẓ based on the editions of Qazvīnī/Ghanī and Khānlarī, an index on Qur'ānic verses, hadis, Arabic verses, a subject index, an index of proper names, an index of places, an index of all verses (*kashf al-abyāt*) in the commentary and finally a bibliography of reference works.

134 Lāhūrī, *Sharḥ-i 'irfānī-i ghazalhā-yi Ḥāfiẓ*, Vol. 1, pp. 1-15.

135 Ibid., Vol. 1, p. 159.

136 Personal communication from Bahā' al-Dīn Khurramshāhī, Tehran, 18 May 2010.

137 Lāhūrī, *Sharḥ-i 'irfānī-i ghazalhā-yi Ḥāfiẓ*, Vol. 1, p. 77.

138 B. Khurramshāhī, *Ḥāfiẓ* (Tehran: Nāhid, 1387/2008), p. 77.

Chapter VI – Conclusion

1 A. Dādbih, 'Mājirā-yi pāyān nāpazīr-i Ḥāfiẓ,' *Māh-nāma-yi Kilk*, No. 30 (Autumn 1371/1993), pp. 228-230.

2 Ḥāfiẓ, *Dīvān-i Ḥāfiẓ*, ed. Q. Ghanī and M. Qazvīnī (Tehran: Zavvār, 1381/2003), pp. 1-8.
3 The manuscripts published between the fifteenth century and the early sixteenth century were more reliable than those published during the early sixteenth to late eighteenth centuries.
4 Ibid.
5 Personal communication from Bahā' al-Dīn Khurramshāhī, Tehran, 18 May 2010.
6 Ḥāfiẓ, *Dīvān-i Ḥāfiẓ*, ed. Khānlarī, Vol. 1, *ghazal* 165, v. 1.
7 Avery, *Collected Lyrics*, p. 223; *ghazal* 165.
8 Ḥāfiẓ, *Dīvān-i Ḥāfiẓ*, ed. Q. Ghanī and M. Qazvīnī, *ghazal* 170, v. 1.
9 This translation follows that of Peter Avery, with some modifications.
10 Personal communication from Dr. Shahram Pazouki, Tehran, 20 May 2010.
11 Personal communication from Bahā' al-Dīn Khurramshāhī, Tehran, 18 May 2010.
12 Ibid.
13 Ibid.
14 D. Āshūrī, 'Ḥāfiẓ bi rivāyat-i 'Abbās Kīārustamī', *Iran shināsī*, No. 4 (Winter 1386/2008), p. 757.
15 Ṣ. Rāmsarī, 'Ḥāfiẓ-i Shirīn Sukhan va Muḥammad Mu'īn', *Māh-nāma-yi Kilk*, No. 5 (Summer 1369/1991), p. 165.
16 Personal communication from Bahā' al-Dīn Khurramshāhī, Tehran, 18 May 2010.
17 Jāvid's book is entitled *Ḥāfiẓ-i Jāvid* and was first published in 1375/1996, the book consists of 611 pages and primarily addresses the difficult phrases and verses in the *Dīvān* of Ḥāfiẓ. In his book, Jāvid explains the meanings of specific verses in detail, then interprets the selected verses by juxtaposing them with those of Nizāmī.
18 Personal communication from Bahā' al-Dīn Khurramshāhī, Tehran, 18 May 2010.
19 Personal communication from Dr. Julie Meisami, Berkeley, 24 October 2011.
20 Personal communication from Bahā' al-Dīn Khurramshāhī, Tehran, 18 May 2010.
21 Ferdowsi, 'The "Emblem"', p. 690. For further information about the above statement, see L. Lewisohn, 'Prolegomenon', *Ḥāfiẓ and the Religion of Love*, pp. 13-18.
22 Ibid.

23 Hazhīr, *Ḥāfiẓ-i tashrīḥ* (Tehran: Nashr-i ʿIlm, 1367/1988), pp. 44-45. Cited by Ferdowsi, 'The "Emblem"', p. 690.
24 Mijmar Shīrāzī, *Dīvān-i Mijmar*, ed. M. Ṭabāṭabā'ī (Tehran: Khayyām, 1345/1967), *ghazal* 30, v. 3.
25 Furūghī Basṭāmī, *Dīvān-i Furūghī Basṭāmī*, ed. Qilichkhānī, *ghazal* 9, v. 10.
26 Nishāṭ Iṣfahānī, *Dīvān-i Nishāṭ-i Iṣfahānī*, ed. Ḥ. Nakha'ī (Tehran: Sharq, 1362/1984), *ghazal* 49, v. 2.
27 Baraq, *Justujū dar aḥvāl va āthār-i Ṣafī ʿAlī Shāh*, p. 21.
28 Hādi Sabzivārī, *Dīvān-i Asrār*, ed. Amīn, *ghazal* 120, v. 4.
29 Ibid., *ghazal* 115.
30 Ḥāfiẓ, *Dīvān-i Ḥāfiẓ*, ed. M. Qazvīnī and Q. Ghanī, *ghazal* 193, v. 10.
31 Personal communication from Dr. Mohammad Reza Movahedi, Tehran, 23 May 2010.
32 Personal communication from Hushang Ibtehāj, Germany, 30 September 2012.
33 Personal communication from Bahā' al-Dīn Khurramshāhī, Tehran, 18 May 2010.
34 Ḥāfiẓ, *Dīvān-i Ḥāfiẓ*, ed. J. Manṣūr (Tehran: Duwrān, 1382/2004), p. 109. This particular verse has not been recorded in editions produced by Qazvīnī and Ghanī and Khānlarī.

Appendix – The Influence of Ḥāfiẓ on Eight Persian Poets of the Zand and Qājār Period

1 J. Perry, 'Ḥazin Lāhiji', *EIr*, Vol. 12, pp. 97-98.
2 Ibid.
3 M. Sālik (ed.), *Encyclopedia of Persian Language and Literature*, Vol. 2 (Tehran, 2007), p. 705.
4 Ibid.
5 Perry, 'Ḥazin Lāhiji', *EIr*, Vol. 12, pp. 97-98.
6 Ibid.
7 Ibid.
8 L. Richard, *Benares Seen from Within* (Washington: University Press, 1999), p. 3. It is also generally recognized as Benares or Banaras, a city situated on the left (west) bank of the River Ganga (Ganges) in the Indian state of Uttar Pradesh, considered as holy by Hindus, Buddhists and Jains. It is one of the oldest continually inhabited cities in the world. *Cf.* Ḥazīn, *Dīvān-i Ḥazīn Lāhījī*, ed. Tarraqī, p. 6; Subḥānī, *Tārīkh-i adabīyāt-i Iran*, p. 445; Sālik (ed.), *Encyclopedia of Persian Language and Literature*, p. 706.

9 Bahār, *Sabk shināsī*, vol. 3, p. 304. *Cf.* Ḥazīn, *Dīvān-i Ḥazīn Lāhījī*, ed. Tarraqī, pp. 3-6.
10 Sālik (ed.), *Encyclopedia of Persian Language and Literature*, p. 705.*Cf.* Hidāyat, *Majmaʿ al-fuṣaḥā*, ed. Furūhar, p. 136.
11 Khurram Ābād is a city in and capital of Luristān Province, Iran. Khurram Ābād is situated in the Zagros Mountains.
12 Ḥazīn Lāhījī, *Dīvān-i Ḥazīn Lāhījī*, ed. Tarraqī, p. 6.
13 Ibid., p. 19.
14 Ibid., p. 17.
15 Ibid., p. 125.
16 Ḥāfiẓ, *Dīvān-i Ḥāfiz*, ed. M. Qazvīnī and Q. Ghanī, *ghazal* 46, v. 3.
17 Ḥazīn, *Dīvān-i Ḥazīn Lāhījī*, ed. Tarraqī, p. 125.
18 Ḥāfiẓ, *Dīvān-i Ḥāfiz*, ed. M. Qazvīnī and Q. Ghanī, *ghazal* 46, v. 2.
19 Ḥazīn, *Dīvān-i Ḥazīn Lāhījī*, ed. Tarraqī, p. 126.
20 Ḥāfiẓ, *Dīvān-i Ḥāfiz*, ed. M. Qazvīnī and Q. Ghanī, *ghazal* 46, v. 8.
21 Ḥazīn, *Dīvān-i Ḥazīn Lāhījī*, ed. Tarraqī, p. 128. Similar rhyme (*Shibāhat-i radīf*).
22 Ḥāfiẓ, *Dīvān-i Ḥāfiz*, ed. M. Qazvīnī and Q. Ghanī, *ghazal* 36, v. 1.
23 Ḥazīn, *Dīvān-i Ḥazīn Lāhījī*, ed. Tarraqī, p. 128.
24 The forward-slash is the indication of a break in a word where the metre (*qāfīya*) is taken place.
25 Ḥāfiẓ, *Dīvān-i Ḥāfiz*, ed. M. Qazvīnī and Q. Ghanī, *rubāʿiyāt*, p. 376.
26 Ḥazīn, *Dīvān-i Ḥazīn Lāhījī*, ed. Tarraqī, p. 133.
27 Ḥāfiẓ, *Dīvān-i Ḥāfiz*, ed. M. Qazvīnī and Q. Ghanī, *ghazal* 46, v. 11.
28 This is a happy time following the month of Ramaḍān, during which Muslims celebrate the end of the fasting period.
29 Ḥazīn, *Dīvān-i Ḥazīn Lāhījī*, ed. Tarraqī, p. 139.
30 Ḥāfiẓ, *Dīvān-i Ḥāfiz*, ed. M. Qazvīnī and Q. Ghanī, *ghazal* 67, v. 3.
31 Ḥazīn, *Dīvān-i Ḥazīn Lāhījī*, ed. Tarraqī, p. 175.
32 Ḥāfiẓ, *Dīvān-i Ḥāfiz*, ed. M. Qazvīnī and Q. Ghanī, *ghazal* 74, v. 2.
33 Ibid., *ghazal* 74, v. 9.
34 Mijmar, *Dīvān-i Mijmar*, ed. M. Ṭabāṭabā'ī, p. 6.
35 Ibid., p. 10.
36 Āryānpūr, *Az Ṣabā tā Nīmā*, Vol. 1, p. 39.
37 Ibid., Vol. 1, p. 12.
38 Browne, *A Literary History of Persia: Modern Times (1500-1924)*, Vol. 4, p. 307.
39 Dihkhudā, *Lughat-nāma*, Vol. 7, p. 10734, s.v. 'Rafīq Iṣfahānī', Mullā Ḥusayn Rafīq Isfahanī (d. 1212/1795), was a well-known poet who had fluent literacy in poetry.

40 Hidāyat, *Majmaʿ al-fuṣaḥā*, ed. M. Muṣaffā, p. 452.
41 Rypka, *History of Iranian Literature*, p. 328.
42 Subḥānī, *Tārīkh-i adabīyāt-i Iran*, p. 487.
43 Ibid., p. 39.
44 Hidāyat, *Tadhkira-yi riyāḍ al-ʿārifīn*, Vol. 2, p. 538.
45 Mijmar, *Dīvān-i Mijmar*, ed. M. Ṭabāṭabāʾī, *ghazal* 21, v. 8.
46 Ḥāfiẓ, *Dīvān-i Ḥāfīz*, ed. M. Qazvīnī and Q. Ghanī, *ghazal* 217, v. 8.
47 Mijmar, *Dīvān-i Mijmar*, ed. M. Ṭabāṭabāʾī, *ghazal* 31, v. 6.
48 Ḥāfiẓ, *Dīvān-i Ḥāfīz*, ed. M. Qazvīnī and Q. Ghanī, *ghazal* 136, v. 8.
49 Mijmar, *Dīvān-i Mijmar*, ed. M. Ṭabāṭabāʾī, *ghazal* 35, v. 1.
50 Ḥāfiẓ, *Dīvān-i Ḥāfīz*, ed. M. Qazvīnī and Q. Ghanī, *ghazal* 217, v. 1.
51 Mijmar, *Dīvān-i Mijmar*, ed. Ṭabāṭabāʾī, *ghazal* 21, v. 1.
52 Ḥāfiẓ, *Dīvān-i Ḥāfīz*, ed. M. Qazvīnī and Q. Ghanī, *ghazal* 217, v. 3.
53 Dihkhudā, *Lughat-nāma*, Vol. 13, p. 19872, s.v. 'Nīshāt'.
54 Browne, *A Literary History of Persia*, Vol. 4, p. 311.
55 Browne, *A Literary History of Persia*, Vol. 4, p. 311. *Cf.* J. Rypka, *History of Iranian Literature*, pp. 326-328.
56 Fatḥ-ʿAlī Khān Ṣabā Kāshānī was born in 1179/1762 in Kāshān, and died at the age of 59/60 in Tehran. He was the first poet who followed the neoclassical school. Subḥānī, *Tārīkh-i adabīyāt-i Iran*, p. 483.
57 Rypka, *History of Iranian Literature*, pp. 326-328.
58 Hidāyat, *Ta zkira-yi riyāḍ al-ʿārifīn*, p. 552.
59 Razavī-Nizhād, *Chihār-ṣad shāʿir-i barguzidi-yi pārsī gui*, p. 1089.
60 Āryānpūr, *Az Ṣabā tā Nīmā*, Vol. 1, pp. 29-30.
61 Bahār, *Sabk shināsī*, Vol. 2, p. 2.
62 Nishāṭ Iṣfahānī, *Dīvān-i Nishāṭ-i Iṣfahānī*, p. 20.
63 Ibid., *ghazal* 48, v. 1.
64 Ḥāfiẓ, *Dīvān-i Ḥāfīz*, ed. M. Qazvīnī and Q. Ghanī, *ghazal* 42, v. 1.
65 This translation follows that of Peter Avery, with some modifications.
66 Nishāṭ Iṣfahānī, *Dīvān-i Nishāṭ-i Iṣfahānī*, *ghazal* 44, v. 5.
67 Ḥāfiẓ, *Dīvān-i Ḥāfīz*, ed. M. Qazvīnī and Q. Ghanī, *ghazal* 46, v. 8.
68 Nishāṭ Iṣfahānī, *Dīvān-i Nishāṭ-i Iṣfahānī*, *ghazal* 105, v. 1.
69 Ḥāfiẓ, *Dīvān-i Ḥāfīz*, ed. M. Qazvīnī and Q. Ghanī, *ghazal* 195, v. 9.
70 Nishāṭ Iṣfahānī, *Dīvān-i Nishāṭ-i Iṣfahānī*, *ghazal* 105, v. 8.
71 Ḥāfiẓ, *Dīvān-i Ḥāfīz*, ed. M. Qazvīnī and Q. Ghanī, *ghazal* 195, v. 7.
72 The Muslims' icon, the 'Guardian of the water of life', is located in a place of darkness to which only he knew the path.
73 Nishāṭ Iṣfahānī, *Dīvān-i Nishāṭ-i Iṣfahānī*, *ghazal* 105, v. 6.
74 Ḥāfiẓ, *Dīvān-i Ḥāfīz*, ed. M. Qazvīnī and Q. Ghanī, *ghazal* 195, v. 8.

75 Nishāṭ Iṣfahānī, *Dīvān-i Nishāṭ-i Iṣfahānī, ghazal* 130, v. 6.
76 Ḥāfiẓ, *Dīvān-i Ḥāfīz*, ed. M. Qazvīnī and Q. Ghanī, *ghazal* 173, v. 3.
77 Nishāṭ Iṣfahānī, *Dīvān-i Nishāṭ-i Iṣfahānī, ghazal* 205, v. 1.
78 Ḥāfiẓ, *Dīvān-i Ḥāfīz*, ed. M. Qazvīnī and Q. Ghanī, *ghazal* 345, v. 1.
79 Nishāṭ Iṣfahānī, *Dīvān-i Nishāṭ-i Iṣfahānī, ghazal* 245, v. 1.
80 Ḥāfiẓ, *Dīvān-i Ḥāfīz*, ed. M. Qazvīnī and Q. Ghanī, *ghazal* 457, v. 1.
81 Nishāṭ Iṣfahānī, *Dīvān-i Nishāṭ-i Iṣfahānī, ghazal* 245, v. 3.
82 Ḥāfiẓ, *Dīvān-i Ḥāfīz*, ed. M. Qazvīnī and Q. Ghanī, *ghazal* 457, v. 9.
83 Dihkhudā, *Lughat-nāma*, Vol. 9, p. 12767, s.v. 'Shams al-Shu'arā'.
84 H. Anvari, *Farhang-i buzurg-i sukhan* (Tehran: Sukhan, 1381/2003), Vol. 8.
85 Hidāyat, *Majma' al-fuṣaḥā*, Vol. 6, pp. 1336-1340.
86 Subḥānī, *Tārīkh-i adabīyāt-i Iran*, pp. 491-493.
87 Ibid., p. 492.
88 Surūsh Iṣfahānī, *Dīvān-i Shams al-Shu'arā', Muḥammad 'Alī Khān Surūsh Iṣfahānī*, ed. M.J. Maḥjūb (Tehran: Amīr Kabīr, 1339/1961), Vol. 1, p. 27.
89 Ibid., Vol. 1, p. 41.
90 Ibid., Vol. 1, p. 40.
91 Ibid., Vol. 1, p. 41.
92 Ibid., Vol. 1, p. 1.
93 Ibid., Vol. 1, p. 42.
94 Ḥāfiẓ, *Dīvān-i Ḥāfīz*, ed. M. Qazvīnī and Q. Ghanī, p. 374.
95 Surūsh Iṣfahānī, *Dīvān-i Shams al-Shu'arā'*, ed. M.J. Maḥjūb, Vol. 1, *ghazal* 8, v. 3.
96 Ḥāfiẓ, *Dīvān-i Ḥāfīz*, ed. M. Qazvīnī and Q. Ghanī, *ghazal* 480, v. 3.
97 Surūsh Iṣfahānī, *Dīvān-i Shams al-Shu'arā'*, ed. M.J. Maḥjūb, Vol. 1, p. 115.
98 Ḥāfiẓ, *Dīvān-i Ḥāfīz*, ed. M. Qazvīnī and Q. Ghanī, *ghazal* 28, v. 4.
99 This Riḍā Qulī Khān should not be mistaken with Riḍā Qulī Khān Hidāyat, who also lived during the same period as Humā.
100 Humā-yi Shīrāzī, *Dīvān-i Ṭarab*, ed. J. Humā'ī (Tehran: Furūghī, 1342/1925), pp. 4-7.
101 Humā-yi Shīrāzī, *Dīvān-i Humā-yi Shīrāzī: Shikkaristān*, ed. A. Karamī (Tehran: Nashriyyāt-i Mā, 1363/1946), p. 5.
102 Ibid.
103 Ibid., p. 5.
104 Ibid., p. 2.
105 Ibid., p. 579.
106 Ḥāfiẓ, *Dīvān-i Ḥāfīz*, ed. M. Qazvīnī and Q. Ghanī, *ghazal* 1, v. 6.
107 Humā-yi Shīrāzī, *Dīvān-i Humā-yi Shīrāzī: Shikkaristān*, ed. A. Karamī, p. 580.

108 Ḥāfiẓ, *Dīvān-i Ḥāfiz*, ed. M. Qazvīnī and Q. Ghanī, *ghazal* 1, v. 1.
109 Humā-yi Shīrāzī, *Dīvān-i Humā-yi Shīrāzī: Shikkaristān*, ed. A. Karamī, p. 585.
110 Ḥāfiẓ, *Dīvān-i Ḥāfiz*, ed. M. Qazvīnī and Q. Ghanī, *ghazal* 311, v. 2.
111 Humā-yi Shīrāzī, *Dīvān-i Humā-yi Shīrāzī: Shikkaristān*, ed. A. Karamī, p. 622.
112 Ḥāfiẓ, *Dīvān-i Ḥāfiz*, ed. M. Qazvīnī and Q. Ghanī, *ghazal* 46, v. 3.
113 Ḥāfiẓ, *Dīvān-i Ḥāfiz*, ed. M. Qazvīnī and Q. Ghanī, *ghazal* 34, v. 1.
114 This translation follows that of Peter Avery, with some modifications.
115 Furṣat al-Dawla Shirāzī, *Dīvān-i Furṣat al-Dawla Shirāzī*, ed. 'A. Zarrīn Qalam (Tehran: Kitābfurūshī Sīrūs, 1361/1982), p. 11.
116 Furṣat al-Dawla, *Dīvān-i Furṣat al-Dawla Shirāzī*, ed. Qalam, *ghazal* 22, v. 8.
117 Ḥāfiẓ, *Dīvān-i Ḥāfiz*, ed. M. Qazvīnī and Q. Ghanī, *ghazal* 51, v. 7.
118 Furṣat al-Dawla, *Dīvān-i Furṣat al-Dawla Shirāzī*, ed. Qalam, *ghazal* 22, v. 5.
119 Ḥāfiẓ, *Dīvān-i Ḥāfiz*, ed. M. Qazvīnī and Q. Ghanī, *ghazal* 51, v. 1.
120 Furṣat al-Dawla, *Dīvān-i Furṣat al-Dawla Shirāzī*, ed. Qalam, *ghazal* 96, v. 1.
121 Ḥāfiẓ, *Dīvān-i Ḥāfiz*, ed. M. Qazvīnī and Q. Ghanī, *ghazal* 347, v. 2.
122 Furṣat al-Dawla, *Dīvān-i Furṣat al-Dawla Shirāzī*, ed. Qalam, *ghazal* 96, v. 5.
123 Ḥāfiẓ, *Dīvān-i Ḥāfiz*, ed. M. Qazvīnī and Q. Ghanī, *ghazal* 347, v. 4.
124 Furṣat al-Dawla, *Dīvān-i Furṣat al-Dawla Shirāzī*, ed. Qalam, *ghazal* 96, v. 7.
125 Ḥāfiẓ, *Dīvān-i Ḥāfiz*, ed. M. Qazvīnī and Q. Ghanī, *ghazal* 347, v. 5.
126 The capital city of east Azerbaijan province in Iran. Dihkhudā, *Lughatnāma*, Vol. 4, p. 5575, s.v. 'Tabrīz.'
127 Subḥānī, *Tārīkh-i adabī-yi Iran*, pp. 617-621.
128 Anvarī, *Farhang-i buzurg-i sukhan*, Vol. 8.
129 Īraj Mīrzā, *Dīvān-i ash'ār-i Īraj Mīrzā*, ed. M.J. Maḥjūb (Tehran: Andisha, 1342/1963), pp. 1-20.
130 Ibid., p. 22.
131 A.K. Hakkak, '"Preservation and Presentation": Continuity and Creativity in the Contemporary Persian Qasida,' unpublished paper presented at the SOAS conference (14-16 July 1993), 'Qasida: The Literary Heritage on an Arab poetic form in Islamic Africa and Asia,' *Draft Conference Papers*, Appendix, p. 318.
132 Īraj Mīrzā, *Dīvān-i ash'ār-i Īraj Mīrzā*, ed. M.J. Maḥjūb, p. 22.

133 Bahār, *Sabk shināsī*, Vol. 3, pp. 600-610.
134 Ibid.
135 Dihkhudā, *Lughat-nāma*, Vol. 3, p. 3186, s.v. 'Īraj'.
136 S. Ḥā'irī (ed.), *Afkār va āthār-i Īraj* (Tehran: Intishārāt-i Jāvīdān, 1364/1947), p. 73.
137 Ḥāfiẓ, *Dīvān-i Ḥāfiz*, ed. M. Qazvīnī and Q. Ghanī, *ghazal* 55, v. 1.
138 Ḥā'irī (ed.), *Afkār va āthār-i Īraj*, p. 163.
139 Ḥāfiẓ, *Dīvān-i Ḥāfiz*, ed. M. Qazvīnī and Q. Ghanī, *ghazal* 178, v. 8.
140 Ḥā'irī (ed.), *Afkār va āthār-i Īraj*, p. 467.
141 Ḥāfiẓ, *Dīvān-i Ḥāfiz*, ed. M. Qazvīnī and Q. Ghanī, *ghazal* 168, v. 9.
142 Ḥā'irī (ed.), *Afkār va āthār-i Īraj*, p. 469.
143 Ḥāfiẓ, *Dīvān-i Ḥāfiz*, ed. M. Qazvīnī and Q. Ghanī, *ghazal* 199, v. 1.
144 Ḥā'irī (ed.), *Afkār va āthār-i Īraj*, p. 521.
145 Ḥāfiẓ, *Dīvān-i Ḥāfiz*, ed. M. Qazvīnī and Q. Ghanī, *ghazal* 137, v. 6.
146 Ḥā'irī (ed.), *Afkār va āthār-i Īraj*, p. 520.
147 Ḥāfiẓ, *Dīvān-i Ḥāfiz*, ed. M. Qazvīnī and Q. Ghanī, *ghazal* 208, v. 7.

Bibliography

Primary Sources

Abū Ṭālib Khān, *Masir-i Ṭālibī*, ed. Ḥusayn Khadiv-i Jam, *The Travels of Mīrzā Abū Ṭālib Khān, 1213/1796-1218/1801*, (Tehran: Kitabhā-yi Jibī, 1352/1974).

Anvari, H., *Farhang-i buzurg-i sukhan*, (Tehran: Sukhan, 1381), 8 vols.

'Ārif Qazvīnī, *Dīvān-i 'Ārif-i Qazvīnī*, ed. A.R. Āzād, (Tehran: Amīr Kabīr, 1342/1963).

———, *Dīvān-i 'Ārif Qazvīnī*, ed. M. 'A. Sipānlū, (Tehran: Nigāh, 1381/2002).

Āsif, M., *Rustam al-Tavārikh*, ed. M. Mushirī, (Tehran: Amīr Kabīr, 1348/1969).

Āyatī, 'A.M., *Tahrir-i Tārīkh-i Vaṣṣāf*, (Tehran: Bunyād-i Farhang-i Iran, 1349/1971).

———, *Tārikh-i Vaṣṣāf*, (Tehran: Intishārāt-i Bunyād-i Farhang-i Iran, 1346/1968).

Bābā Fighānī, *Dīvān-i 'ash'ār-i Bābā Fighānī*, ed. A.S. Khunsārī, (Tehran: Iqbāl, 1362/1984)

Bahār, M.T., *Dīvān-i 'ash'ār*, ed. C. Bahar, (Tehran: Intishārāt-i Ṭūs, 1380/2001), 2 vols.

Balkhī, Mawlānā Jalāl al-Dīn Muḥammad, *Mathnawī*, ed. M. Isti'lāmī, (Tehran: Mahārat, 1379/2001), 7 vols.

Bayhaqī-i Dabīr, Abū'l-Faḍl, *Tārīkh-i Bayhaqī*, ed. J.M. Ṣādiqī, (Tehran: Nashr-i Markaz, 1377/1999).

Bigdilī, Ādhar, *Ātashkada*, ed. Sādāt, (Tehran: Amīr Kabīr, 1339/1961), 4 vols.

———, *Dīvān-i Luṭf-'Alī Bayk Ādhar Bigdilī*, ed. N. Sādāt, (Tehran: Jāvīdān, 1366/1988).

Bukhārā'ī, Nāṣir, *Dīvān-i Nāṣir Bukhārā'ī, az sukhanvarān-i qarn-i hashtum-i hijrī*, ed. M. Dirakhshān, (Tehran: Nūryānī, 1353/1957)

Dihkhudā, 'A.A., *Amthāl va hikam*, (Tehran: Sipihr, 1352/1974), 4 vols.

———, *Lughat-nāma*, ed. M. Mu'īn and M. Ja'far Shahidi, (Tehran: Mu'assissi-yi Lughat-nāma Dihkhudā and Tehran University Press, 1373/1994), 14 vols.

Fasā'ī, Ḥājj Mīrzā Ḥasan Ḥusaynī, *Fārs-nāma-yi Nāṣirī*, (Tehran: Sanā'ī, 1304/1887), 2 vols.

Firdawsī, Abū'l Qāsim, *Shāh-nāma yi Firdawsī*, ed. R. Qazvin, (Tehran: Hermes, 1382/2003), 2 vols, (Based on the original printed edition in Moscow).

Furṣat al-Dawla Shīrāzī, *Āthār-i 'ajam*, (Bombay: Nāṣirī, 1313/1896).

———, *Dīvān-i Furṣat al-Dawla Shirāzī*, ed. 'A. Zarrīn Qalam, (Tehran: Kitāb-furūshī Sīrūs, 1361/1982).

Furūghī Basṭāmī, *Dīvān-i Furūghī Basṭāmī*, ed. H.R. Qilichkhānī, (Tehran: Intishārāt-i Rawzana, 1376/1998).

———, *Dīvān-i Furūghī Basṭāmī*, ed. H.R. Qilichkhānī, (Tehran: Ruznih, 1376/1998).

———, *Ghazalīyāt-i Furūghī Basṭāmī*, ed. M. Mushfiq, (Tehran: Ṣafī 'Alī Shāh, 1336/1958).

Furūghī, M. 'Alī Ẕakā' al-Mulk, *Maqālāt-i Furūghī*, (Tehran: Ṭūs, 1354/1976).

Ḥāfiẓ, Khawja Shams al-Dīn Muḥammad*

———, *Dīvān-i kuhna-yi Ḥāfiẓ*, ed. Ī. Afshār, (Tehran: Intishārāt-i Farhang-i Iran Zamīn, 1348/1969).

———, *Dīvān-i kuhna-yi Ḥāfiẓ: Az ruy-i nuskha-yi khaṭṭī-i nazdik bi zamān-i shā'ir*, ed. Ī. Afshār, (Tehran: Amīr Kabīr, 1366/1988).

———, *Dīvān-i Ḥāfiẓ bar asās-i nuskha-yi muvarikh-i 818 Hijri*, ed. N. Aḥmad, (New Delhi: Markaz-i Taḥqiqāt-i Zabān-i fārsī Jumhuri-yi Islamī-i Iran, 1367/1988).

———, *Dīvān-i Khawja Shams al-Dīn Muḥammad Ḥāfiẓ Shīrāzī: bi-inẓimām-i kashf al-ghazal, sharḥ-i ḥāl, farhang, tarjuma va tafsīr-i ash'ār va tasḥiḥ-i Dīvān*, ed. H.P. Bakhtīyārī, (Tehran: Birukhīm, 1315/1937).

———, *Dīvān-i Ḥāfiẓ bar asās-i nuskha-yi kuhan-i Naw yāfta*, ed. K. Bargnisi, (Tehran: [n.p.], 1379/2000).

———, *Dīvān-i Ḥāfiẓ*, trans. H. Wilberforce Clarke, *The Dīvān-i Ḥāfiẓ-i Shīrāzī*, (Calcutta: Government of India Central Printing Office 1981), 2 vols. Reprinted as *Dīvān-i Ḥāfiẓ*, (Bethesda, MD: Ibex Publishers, 1998).

———, *Diwan-i Ḥāfiẓ: For The Degree of Honor Examination in Persian for Officers in the Military & Civil Services*, ed. M.H.S. Jarrett, (Calcutta: Urdu Guide Press, 1881).

———, *Dīvān-i Ḥāfiẓ Shīrāzī az rū-yi chāp-i Qudsī*, ed. 'A.A. Hikmat, (Tehran: Ibn Sinā, 1342/1964).

———, *Dīvān-i Ḥāfiẓ bi tashih-i Muḥammad Qudsī*, ed. 'A.A. Hikmat, H. Ẕulfaqārī and A. 'A. Muḥammadī, (Tehran: Nashr-i Chishma, 1381/2002).

* The entry on Ḥāfiẓ is organized in alphabetical order.

———, *Dīvān-i Ḥāfiẓ: Ḥāfiẓ bi sa'-yi Sāyā*, ed. Hūshang Ibtihāj (Saya), (Tehran: Nashr-i Kārnāma, 1376/1997).

———, *Dīvān-i Ḥāfiẓ*, ed. H. Jāvid and B. Khurramshāhī, (Tehran: Farzān, 1378/1999).

———, *Dīvān-i Khawja Ḥāfiẓ Shīrāzī: Az rū-yi nuskha-yi khaṭṭī ki dar tārikh-i 827 Hijrī qamarī 35 sāl ba'd az vafāt-i Khawja taḥrir shuda ast*, ed. S. 'A.R. Khalkhālī, (Tehran: Bunyād-i Kitāb, 1306/1928).

———, *Dīvān-i Khawja Ḥāfiẓ Shīrāzī: Az rū-yi nuskha-yi khaṭṭī ki dar tārīkh-i 827 Hijrī Qamarī 35 sāl ba'd az vafāt-i Khawja taḥrīr shuda ast*, ed. S. 'A.R. Khalkhālī, (Tehran: Dunyā-i Kitāb, [n.d]).

———, *Ḥāfiẓ-nāma*, ed. S. 'A.R. Khalkhālī, (Tehran: Majlis, 1320/1942).

———, *Dīvān-i Khawja Shams al-Dīn Muḥammad: Mulhaqāt-i ghazalīyāt, qaṣā'id, Mathnawīyyāt, qaṭa'āt va rubā'īyāt*, ed. P.N. Khānlarī, (Tehran: Khārazmī, 1362/1984), 2 vols.

———, *Dīvān-i Khawja Ḥāfiẓ Shīrāzī: Az rū-yi nuskha-yi khaṭṭī ki dar tārīkh-i 827 Hijrī Qamarī 35 sāl ba'd az vafāt-i Khawja taḥrīr shuda ast; bā muqābala va taṣḥīḥ az rū-yi nuskha-yi Sayyid 'Abdul Raḥīm Khalkhālī*, ed. B. Khurramshāhī, (Tehran: Dunyā-i Kitāb, [n.d.]).

———, *Dīvān-i Ḥāfiẓ*, ed. B. Khurramshāhī, (Tehran: Dūstān, 1385/2006).

———, *Dīvān-i Ḥāfiẓ: Qarā't guzīnī intiqādī*, ed. B. Khurramshāhī, (Tehran: Farzān, 1378/2000).

———, *Dīvān-i Ḥāfiẓ*, ed. J. Manṣūr, (Tehran: Dawrān, 1382/2003).

———, *Dīvān-i Ḥāfiẓ mīrath-i girānqadr-i farhangi-i mā*, ed. J. Matinī, (Tehran: Iran-nāma Majala-yi Tahqīqāt-i Iran Shināsi, 1376/1998).

———, *Dīvān-i Khawja Shams al-Dīn Ḥāfiẓ Shīrāzī: Bar asās-i nuskha-yi muvarikh 812-817 AH*, ed. S.M. Naysārī, N. Aḥmad, (Tehran: Amīr Kabīr, 1350/1972).

———, *Dīvān-i Khawja Shams al-Dīn Muḥammad Ḥāfiẓ Shīrāzī*, ed. Muḥammad Qazvīnī and Qāsim Ghanī, (Tehran: Kitābkhāna Zavvār 1320/1941; 1381/2003).

———, *Dīvān-i ghazalīyāt-i Mawlānā Shams al-Dīn Muḥammad Ḥāfiẓ Shīrāzī*, ed. Kh. Rahbar, (Tehran: Ṣafī 'Alī Shāh, 1365/1987).

———, *Dīvān-i Khawja Ḥāfiẓ Shīrāzī*, ed. S.A.Q. Īnjavī Shīrāzī, (Tehran: Jāvidān, 1361/1982).

———, *Dīvān-i Khawja Ḥāfiẓ Shīrāzī: Kashf al-abyyāt va kashf al-lughāt*, ed. S. 'A.Q. Īnjavī Shīrāzī, (Tehran: Jāvīdān, 1360/1982).

———, *Dīvān-i Ḥāfiẓ*, ed. S. 'A. Īnjavī Shīrāzī, (Tehran: Ibn Sinā, 1346/1967).

———, *Dīvān-i Ḥāfiẓ*, ed. H. 'A. Yūsufī, (Tehran: Rūzigār, 1381/2003).

Ḥājj Mīrzā Habībullāh Khurāsānī, *Dīvān-i Ḥājj Mīrzā Habībullāh Khurāsānī*, ed. A. Habīb, (Tehran: Nashr-i Tābān, 1330/1951).

———, *Dīvān-i Ḥājj Mīrzā Habībullāh Khurāsānī*, ed. A. Habīb, (Tehran: Zavvār 1353/1933).

Hātif Iṣfahānī, *Dīvān-i Hātif Iṣfahānī*, ed. ʿA.I. Āshtīānī, (Tehran: Kitabfrushi-yi Adab, 1332/1953).

———, *Dīvān-i Hātif-i Iṣfahānī*, ed. Vahīd Dastgirdī, (Tehran: Nigāh, 1373/1995).

Hayātī Kirmānī, *Dīvān-i Hayātī Kirmānī*, ed. J. Nūrbakhsh, (Tehran: Yaldā Qalam, 1382/2003).

Ḥazīn Lāhījī, *Dīvān-i Ḥazīn Lāhījī*, ed. Bizhan Tarraqī, (Tehran: Chāp-i Pīrūz, 1350/1972).

Hidāyat, R.Q., *Khāṭirāt: Nivishta'i az tārikh-i shish pādishāh va gūshi'ī az dura-yi zindagī-yi man*, (Tehran: Rangīn, 1329/1951), 2 vols.

———, *Majmaʿ al-fusahā*, ed. M. Musaffā, (Tehran: Amīr Kabīr, 1339/1920; 1388/2009), 6 vols.

———, *Rīyāḍ al-ʿārifīn*, ed. N. Furūhar, (Tehran: Amīr Kabīr, 1388/2009).

———, *Rīyāḍ al-ʿārifīn*, (Tehran: Āftāb, 1316/1938).

———, *Tadhkira-yi Rīyāḍ al-ʿārifin*, (Tehran: Mahdīyya, 1316/1937), 2 vols.

Humā-yi Shīrāzī, *Dīvān-i Ṭarab*, ed. J. Humā'ī, (Tehran: Furūghī, 1342/1925).

———, *Dīvān-i Humā-yi Shīrāzī: Shikkaristān*, ed. A. Karamī, (Tehran: Nashriyyāt-i Mā, 1363/1946).

Ibn al-Balkhī, *Fārs-nāma*, ed. ʿAlī Naqī Bihrūzī, (Shīrāz: Sandikā-yi Intishārāt, 1342/1925).

Ibn Battūta, *Safar-nāma*, trans. M. ʿA. Muvvahid, (Tehran: Bungāh-i Tarjūma va Nashr-i Kitāb, 1337/1959).

Īraj Mīrzā, *Dīvān-i ʿashʿār-i Īraj Mīrzā*, ed. M.J. Maḥjūb, (Tehran: Intishārāt-i Andisha, 1342/1963).

———, *Taḥqiq dar aḥvāl va āthār va afkār va ʿashʿār-i Īraj Mīrzā va khāndān va nīyākān-i aū*, ed. M.J. Maḥjūb, (Tehran: Andisha, 1349/1970).

Jahān Malik Khātūn, *Dīvān-i kāmil-i Jahān Malik Khātūn qarn-i hashtum-i hijrī-yi qamarī*, ed. P. Kāshānirād, (Tehran: Zavvār, 1374/1996).

Jamālzāda, S.M. ʿA., *Āshnā'ī bā Ḥāfiẓ*, (Tehran: Sukhan, 1384/2005).

Jāmī, *Dīvān-i kāmil-i Jāmī*, ed. H. Razī, (Tehran: Pirūz, 1341/1963).

Kamāl Khujandī, *Dīvān-i Kamāl Khujandī*, ed. ʿA. Dulatābādī, (Tehran: Sāzimān-i Chāp va Intishārāt-i Islāmī, 1375/1997).

Kāshānī, M.M. Sh., *Vāqi'āt-i Ittfāqīya dar rūzigār-i Qājārīyi*, ed. M. Itiḥādīya, (Tehran: Nashr-i Tārikh-i Iran, 1362/1983), 3 vols.

Kirmānī, Khawja ʿImād al-Dīn ʿAlī Faqih-i, *Dīvān-i qaṣā'id va ghazalīyāt*, ed. R. Humāyūn-Farrukh, (Tehran: Ibn Sinā, 1348/1970).

Kirmānī, Khājū, *Dīvān-i Khājū Kirmānī*, ed. M. Burhānī, (Tehran: Zavvār, 1370/1992).

Mahastī Ganja'ī, *Dīvān-i ash'ār-i Mahastī-yi Ganja'ī*, ed. M. Mihrābī, (Tehran: Ṭūs, 1382/2003).

Marāgha'ī, *Sīyāḥat-nāma-yi Ibrāhīm Bayk*, ed. M. 'A. Sipāmlū, (Tehran: Asfār, 1364/1984), 3 vols.

———, *Sīyāḥat-nāma-yi Ibrāhīm Bayk: Yā balā-yi aū*, ed. Z.B. Mu'minī, (Tehran: Nashr-i Andīsha, 1353/1975), 3 vols.

Mathnawī of Mawlānā Jalāl al-Dīn Muḥammad Balkhī, ed. M. Isti'lāmī, (Tehran: Mahārat, 1379/2001), 7 vols.

Ma'ṣūm 'Alī Shāh, *Ṭarā'iq al-haqā'iq*, ed. M.J. Maḥjūb, (Tehran: Kitābkhāna-yi Bārānī, 1339/1960), 2 vols.

Ma'ṣūm, M, *Tārikh-i Ma'ṣūmī*, (Hyderabad, Pakistan: Sindhi Adabī Board, 1959).

Mijmar Shīrāzī, *Dīvān-i Mijmar*, ed. M. Ṭabātabā'ī, (Tehran: Chap-i Haydari, 1345/1966).

———, *Dīvān-i Mijmar*, ed. M. Ṭāvūsī, (Tehran: Khayyām, 1345/1967).

Mudarris, M.M. 'A., *Riḥānat al-adab fi tarjuma al-ma'rūfīn bil-kunīyat al-laqab, mushtamil bar tarjuma-yi ḥāl-i fuqahā va ḥukamā, va 'urafā va 'ulamā' va udabā va aṭibā va fuḍalā va shu'arā-yi buzurg-i Islāmī ki bā laqab va kunīya ishtihār dārand*, (Tabriz: Shafaq, [n.d.]), 2 vols.

Mu'īn, M., *Farhang-i Mu'īn*, (Tehran: Amīr Kabīr, 1373/1994), 6 vols.

Nāzir, M., *Nigārish bar ash'ār-i Parvin-i I'tisāmī: Some Observations on the Poetry of Parvin I'tisāmī*, (Tehran: Surūsh, 1360/1981).

Nimā Yūshij, *Majmū'a-yi kāmil-i ash'ār-i Nimā Yūshīj*, ed. S. Ṭāhbāzī, (Tehran: Nigāh, 1371/1993).

———, *Zindagī va shi'r-i Nimā Yūshij*, ed. S. Ṭāhbāz, (Tehran: Intishārāt-i Thālith, 1380/2001).

Nishāṭ Iṣfahānī, *Ganjina-yi Dīvān-i Nishāṭ Iṣfahānī*, ed. H. Nakha'ī, (Tehran: Sharq, 1362/1984).

Nizām Vafā, *Dīvān-i Nizām Vafā*, ed. A. Karīmi, (Tehran: Tālār-i Kitāb, 1362/1984).

Nūrbakhsh, J., *Farhang-i Nūrbakhsh, Istilāhāt-i taṣawwuf*, (Tehran: Marvī, 1372/1993), 5 vols.

Parvin-i I'tisāmī, *Dīvān-i Parvin-i I'tisāmī*, ed. V.A. Durūdīyān, (Tehran: Nashr-i Nay, 1382/2003).

Qā'ānī Shīrāzī, *Dīvān-i Hakīm Qā'ānī Shīrāzī*, ed. M.J. Maḥjūb, (Tehran: Amīr Kabīr, 1336/1957).

Qayyim, 'Abdulnabī, *Farhang-i Mu'āṣir-i 'Arabī bi fārsī*, (Tehran: Farhang-i Mu'āṣir, 1386/1966).

Qurrat al-'Ayn, *Shā'ira-yi āzādikhāh va milli-yi Iran*, ed. M.D. Mehrabi, (Koln, Germany: Nashr-i Rūyish, 1373/1994).

Rāzī, S.Q., *al-Maʿjam fi maʿāʾir ashʿār al-ʿajam*, ed. M. Qazvīnī, trans. E.G. Browne, (London: Luzac & Co, 1909).

Rūdakī Samarqandī, *Dīvān-i Rūdakī Samarqandī*, ed. S. Nafisī, (Tehran: Nigāh, 1376/1998).

Sabzivārī, Hādi, *Dīvān-i asrār: Kullīyyāt-i ʿashʿār-i fārsī-i Ḥājj Mullā Hādi-yi Sabzivārī*, ed. S.H. Amīn, (Tehran: Baʿthat, 1380/2001).

Safavī, S. Mīrzā, *Tādhkira-i Sāmī*, ed. Rukn al-Dīn Humāyūn Farrukh, (Tehran: ʿIlmī, 1967).

Ṣafī ʿAlī Shāh, *Dīvān-i Ṣafī ʿAlī Shāh*, (Tehran: Amīr Kabīr, 1336/1957).

———, *Dīvān-i Ṣafī ʿAlī Shāh*, (Tehran: Intishārāt-i Ṣafī ʿAlī Shāh, 1379/2000).

———, *ʿIrfān al-Ḥaqq*, (Tehran: Intishārāt-i Ṣafī ʿAlī Shāh, 1378/1999).

Ṣāʾib Tabrizī, *Dīvān-i Ṣāʾib*, ed. S. Betler and C.I. Djamili, (Tehran: Akhtar, 1381/2002).

———, *Dīvān-i Ṣāʾib*, ed. A. Firūzkūhī, (Tehran: Anjuman-i Āthār-i Millī, 1345/1966).

———, *Dīvān-i Ṣāʾib Tabrizī*, ed. J. Manṣūr, (Tehran: Nigāh, 1383/2004).

———, *Dīvān-i Ṣāʾib Tabrizī*, ed. M. Qahrimān, (Tehran: Shirkat-i Intishārāt-i ʿIlmī va Farhangī, 1363/1985).

———, *Dīvān-i Ṣāʾib Tabrizī*, ed. S. Shamīsā, (Tehran: Mustawfī, 1373/1995).

Salmān Sāvajī, *Dīvān-i Salmān Sāvajī*, ed. M. Mushfiq, (Tehran: Ṣafī ʿAlī Shāh, 1336/1958).

Shāh Niʿmatullāh Valī, *Kullīyāt-i ashʿār-i Shāh Niʿmatullāh Valī*, ed. J. Nūrbakhsh, (Tehran: Intishārāt-i Yaldā Qalam, 1382/2004 and 1385/2007).

Shahriyār, *Dīvān-i Shahriyār*, with biography by Zāhidī, (Tehran: Nigāristān-i Kitāb, 1388/2009), 2 vols.

———, *Kullīyāt-i Dīvān-i Shahriyār*, ed. M.H. Shahriyār, (Tabriz: Maṭbūʿāt-i Saʿdī, 1345/1967), 3 vols.

Shāmlū, A., *Āidā dar Āyana*, (Tehran: Nīl, 1343/1965).

———, *Bāgh-i Āyana*, (Tehran: Murvārīd, 1338/1960).

———, *Darhā va Dīvār-i Buzurg-i Chīn*, (Tehran: Nimūna, 1352/1974).

———, *Dashna dar Dīs*, (Tehran: Murvārīd, 1372/1994).

———, *Havā-yi Tāza*, (Tehran: Nigāh, 1363/1985).

———, *Lahzahā va Hamīshahā*, (Tehran: Nigāh, 1372/1994).

———, *Mafāhim-i rind va rindī dar ghazal-i Ḥāfiẓ*, (Sweden: Ārash, 1370/1992).

———, *Marthīyahā-yi Khāk va Shikuftan dar Mih*, (Tehran: Nigāh, 1372/1994).

———, *Qaqnūs dar Bārān*, (Tehran: Nīl, 1344/1966).

Shams Maghribī, *Dīvān-i Shamsi-i Maghribī*, ed. S.A. Mirʿābidinī, (Tehran: Amīr Kabīr, 1388/2009).

Sipihrī, S., *Hasht Kitāb*, (Tehran: Ṭahūrī, 1383/2004).

Surūsh Iṣfahānī, *Shams al-Shu'arā': Mīrzā Muḥammad 'Alī Khān Surūsh Iṣfahānī*, ed. A. Lāhūrī, (Tehran: Amīr Kabīr, 1382/1963), 2 vols.

———, *Dīvān-i Shams al-Shu'arā', Muḥammad 'Alī Khān Surūsh Iṣfahānī*, ed. M.J. Maḥjūb, (Tehran: Amīr Kabīr, 1339/1961).

Tabrizī, 'A.R.N. *Masālik al-muḥsinīn*, (Tehran: Shirkat-i Sahāmi-yi Kitābhā-yi Jibī, 1323/1906).

Tabrizī, M.H., *Burhān-i Qāṭi'*, ed. M. Mu'īn, (Tehran: Ibn Sinā, 1342/1964).

Ṭālibuf, 'A.R., *Masālik al-muḥsinīn*, (Tehran: Shabgīr, 1356/1978).

Taqizāda, S.H., *Kitābhā-yi āqā-yi Sayyīd Ḥasan Taqqīzāda must'amil bar shammā-ī az tārikh-i awā'il-i inqilāb va mashrūtīyyat-i Iran*, (Tehran: Amīr Kabīr, 1338/1959).

———, *Zindagī-yi Ṭūfānī: Khāṭirāt-i Siyyad Ḥasan Taqizāda*, ed. Ī. Afshār, (Tehran: Intishārāt-i 'Ilmī, 1369/1990).

'Ubiyd Zākānī, *Kullīyāt-i 'Ubayd Zākānī*, ed. 'A.I. Āshtīyānī, (Tehran: Iqbāl, 1334/1956).

'Urfī Shīrāzī, *Kullīyāt-i 'Urfī Shīrāzī*, ed. Gh. Javāhirī, (Tehran: Muḥammad 'Alī 'Ilmī, [n.d]).

Vāshingtun, Ḥājjī, *Tārikh-i ravābit-i Iran va Amrikā dar rūzigār-i Qājārīya va Pahlavi*, ed. Iskandar Dildim, (Tehran: Nashr-i Gul Fām, 1368/1989).

Viṣāl Shīrāzī, *Dīvān-i Viṣāl Shīrāzī*, ed. M. Ṭāvūsī, (Shīrāz: Navid Shīrāz, 1378/2000), 2 vols.

———, *Ganjina-i adab va 'irfān Iranī: Kullīyyāt-i Viṣāl Shīrāzī*, ed. 'A. Muḥammad, (Tehran: Fakhr Āzād, 1339/1960).

Yaghmā Jandaqī, *Dīvān-i ash'ār-i Yaghmā Jandaqī*, ed. S. 'A.A. Dāvūd, (Tehran: Intishārāt-i Ṭūs, 1369/1950).

———, *Majmu'ī-yi āthār-i Yaghmā Jandaqī*, ed. S. 'A. Āl-i Dāvūd, (Tehran: Intishārāt-i Ṭūs, 1357/1979 and 1369/1990).

———, *Majmu'i-yi āthār-i Yaghmā Jandaqī: Ghazalīyāt, Mathnawīhā*, ed. S. 'A.A. Dāvūd, (Tehran: Intishārāt-i Ṭūs, 1369/1990).

———, *Majmu'i-yi āthār-i Yaghmā Jandaqī: Makātīb va mansha'āt*, ed. S. 'A.A. Dāvūd, (Tehran: Intishārāt-i Ṭūs, 1362/1983).

Zarkūb, M., *Mu'īn al-Dīn Abūl 'Abbās Aḥmad ibn Abī al-Khayr Shīrāzī, Shīrāz-nāma*, ed. Ismā'īl Vā'iz Javādī, (Tehran: Bunyād-i Farhang-i Iran, 767/1350).

Secondary Sources

'Ābidī, K., *Az muṣāḥibat-i āftāb: Ta'amulāt va justujūhā'ī dar shi'r-i Suhrāb Sipihrī*, (Tehran: Rivāyat, 1996).

———, *Ta'amulāt va justijuhā'ī dar shi'r-i Suhrāb Sipihrī: az muṣāhibat-i āftāb*, (Tehran: Ravā, 1375/1996).

Abrahamian, E., *Iran Between Two Revolutions*, (Princeton, NJ: Princeton University Press, 1982).

———, *Khomeinism*, (London: I.B.Tauris, 1993).

Ādamīyat, F., *Amīr Kabīr va Iran*, (Tehran: Khārazmī, 1323/1944).

———, *Andishahā-yi Mīrzā Āqā Khān Kirmānī*, (Tehran: Amīr Kabīr, 1357/1978).

———, *Andishahā-yi Mīrzā Āqā Khān Kirmānī*, (Tehran: Ṭahūrī, 1364/1986).

———, *Andishahā-yi Ṭālibuf Tabrizī*, (Tehran: Damāvand, [n.d.]).

———, *Fikr-i Āzādī va Muqadama-i Nihḍat-i Mashrūṭīyyat-i Iran*, (Tehran: Intishārāt-i Sukhan, 1340/1961).

Afary, J., *The Iranian Constitutional Revolution, 1906-1911: Grassroots Democracy, Social Democracy & the Origins of Feminism*, (New York: Columbia University Press, 1996).

———, Anderson, K.B., *Foucault and the Iranian Revolution: Gender and the Seductions of Islamism*, (Chicago: University of Chicago Press, 2005).

Afshār, Ī., *'Abdul Raḥīm Ṭālibuf Tabrizī: Āzādī va Sīyāsat*, (Tehran: Sahar, 1357/1979).

———, *Fihrist-i Maqālāt-i fārsī: Ganjīna-yi fihrist va kitābshināsī, 1339-1345*, (Tehran: Tehran University Press, 1348/1929), 5 vols.

———, *Literature East & West* 20, Nos. 1-4, (Jan.-Dec. 1976).

——— (ed.), *Nathr-i fārsī-i mu'āṣir: muntakhabātī az bihtarīn āthār-i muvarrikhīn va muḥaqqiqīn-i nāmī-i Irān az ṣadr-i Mashrūṭīyat tā mu'āṣir*, introduction by Sa'īd Nafisī, (Tehran: Kānūn-i Ma'rifat, 1330/1951).

Aḥmad, N, 'Nazarī dar *Dīvān-i* Ḥāfiẓ', *Iran Nameh*, vol. 2, No. 1 (Summer 1367/1988), pp. 126-140.

Akbar, R., *Sharḥ-i aḥvāl va sabk-i ash'ār-i Bābā Fighānī*, (Hyderabad: Shālīmār, 1974).

Ākhūndzāda, F. 'A., *Maqālāt-i fārsī*, (Tehran: Āvā, 1350/1972).

Alam, M. and S. Subrahamanyan, *Indo-Persian Travels in the Age of Discoveries 1400-1800*, (Cambridge: Cambridge University Press, 2007).

Alexander, J.E., *Travels from India to England*, (London: Tauris, 1827).

Algar, H, 'Ākhūndzāda', *EIr*, Vol. 1, pp. 735-740.

——— (trans.), *Mirza Malkam Khan: A Study in the History of Iranian Modernism*, (Berkeley: University of California Press, 1977).

'Alī Zāda, J. (ed.), *Bi hamīn sādigī va zibā'ī: Yād-nāma-yi ustād Sayyid Muḥammad Ḥusayn Shahriyār 1285-1376*, (Tehran: Nashr-i Markaz, 1374/1995).

Amanat, A., *Pivot of the Universe: Nāṣir al-Dīn Qājār and the Iranian Monorchy 1830-1896*, (Berkeley: University of California Press, 1997).

———, *Resurrection and Renewal, the Making of the Babi Movement in Iran, 1844-1850*, (New York and London: Cornell University Press, 1989, 2005).

Amīn, S. (ed.), *Aḥvāl-i Mullā Hādī-yi Sabzivārī*, (Tehran: Intishārāt-i Ba'that, 1380/2001).

Amīrkhizī, I., *Qīyām-i Ādharbāyjān va Sattār Khān*, (Tehran: Tehran Press, 1960).

Ansari, A.M., *Man va Khandan-e Pahlavi* [The Pahlavi family and I], (San Jose, CA: Tooka Publishing, 1997).

———, *Modern Iran Since 1921, the Pahlavis and After*, (London: Pearson Education, 2003).

Anwār, 'A., 'Anjoman-e Okowwat', *EIr*, Vol. 2, pp. 88-89.

Arberry, A.J., *Classical Persian Literature*, (London: George Allen & Unwin Ltd, 1958).

———, *Shiraz: Persian City of Saints and Poets*, (Norman: University of Oklahoma Press, 1960).

Ardakānī, R.D., *Fārābī: Filsūf-i farhang*, (Tehran: Sāqī, 1382/2003).

Ardāqī, Khawsrū, 'Sādīq-i Hidāyat nivisanda-yi buzurg-i Mu'āṣir-i Iran darguzasht', *Rūz-nāma-yi parcham-i ṣulḥ*, Year 1, No. 2490 (1330/1950), p. 11.

Āryānpūr, Y., *Az Ṣabā tā Nimā*, (Tehran: Kitābhā-yi Jibī, 1972).

———, *Az Ṣabā tā Nimā: Tārikh-i 150 sāl adab-i fārsī*, (Tehran: Zavvār, 1372/1952), 2 vols.

Āsif, M.H., *Rustam al-hukamā/Rustam al-tavārikh*, (Tehran: Intishārāt-i Firdaws, 1382/2004).

Asīl, H., *Zindagī va andisha-yi Mīrzā Malkam Khān*, (Tehran: Nashr-i Nay, 1376/1998).

Āshtīyānī, 'A.I., *Shi'r va andisha*, (Tehran: Nashr-i Markaz, 1380/2001).

Āshtīyānī, S.J., *Sharḥ-i ḥāl va ārā-yi fal Ṣafī-yi Mullā Ṣadrā*, (Tehran: Bahār, 1378/1999).

———, 'Chand nukta dar Sharḥ-i *Dīvān-i* Ḥāfiẓ', *Iran Nameh* No. 4 (Summer 1368/1989), pp. 679-685.

———, *Shi'r va andisha*, (Teharn: Nashr-i Markaz, 1377/1998).

Āshūrī, D., K. Imāmī, Ḥ. M. Hamadānī (eds.), *Payāmī dar rāh: naẓarī bi shi'r va naqāshī-i Suhrāb Sipihrī*, (Tehran: Ṭahūrī, 1358/1980).

'Atā'ī, 'A.J. (ed.), *Nimā Yūshij: Zindagī va āthār-i aū*, (Tehran: Ṣafī 'Alī Shāh, 1346/1955).

Avery, P., *The Collected Lyrics of Ḥāfiẓ of Shiraz*, (Cambridge: Archetype, 2007).

———, *Modern Iran* (London: Benn, 1965).

———, 'Nadir Shāh and Afsharid Legacy', in Peter Avery, G.R.G. Humbly, and C.P. Melville (eds.), *The Cambridge History of Iran*, Vol. 7: *From Nadir Shah to the Islamic Republic*, (Cambridge: Cambridge University Press, 1986), pp. 3-63.

Awhadī, Taqī al-Dīn M., *Tadhkira-yi ʿarafāt al-ʿāshiqin va ʿarasāt al-ʿārifin*, (Tehran: Asāṭir, 1388/2010).

Axworthy, M., *A History of Iran: Empire of the Mind*, (New York: Basic Books Publications, 2008).

———, *Iran: Empire of the Mind, a History from Zoroaster to the Present Day*, (London: Penguin Books, 2007).

———, *Sword of Persia, Nader Shah from Tribal Warlord to Conquering Tyrant*, (London: I.B.Tauris, 2006).

ʿAyvazī, R., *Dīvān-i Ḥāfiẓ bar asās-i si nuskha-yi kāmil-i kuhan*, ed. A. Bihrūz, (Tehran: Sipihr, 1366/1987).

Āzhand, Y., *Tajadud-i adabī dar dawra-yi mashrūṭa*, (Tehran: Muʾasasa-yi Taḥqiqāt va ʿUlūm-i Insānī, 1384/2006).

Azimi, F., and I. Afshar, 'Forūgī, Mohammad-Alī Ḏokāʾ-Al-Molk', *EIr*, Vol. 10, pp. 108-111.

Bahādur, M., *Haftād u du millat*: *Mīrzā Āqā Khān Kirmānī*, (Berlin: Iranshahr, 1343/1965).

Bahār, C. (ed.), *Muḥammad Taqqī-i Bahār*, (Tehran: Intishārāt-i Ṭūs, 1380/2001), 2 vols.

Bahār, M.T., *Bahār va adab-i fārsi: Majmuʿī-yi yiksad maqāla az Malik al-Shuʿarā-yi Bahār*, (Tehran: Kitabhā-yi Jibī, 1351/1932), 2 vols.

———, *Dīvān-i ʿashʿār*, ed. C. Bahār, (Tehran: Intishārāt-i Ṭūs, 1380/2001), 2 vols.

———, *Malik al-Shuʿarāʾ: Sabk shināsī*, (Tehran: Amīr Kabīr, 1373/1994), 3 vols.

———, 'Saʿdī kist?', *Nawbahār*, No. 323 (January 1918), pp. 1-3.

———, *Tārīkh-i ahzāb-i sīyāsī-yi Iran*, (Tehran: Rangīn, 1323/1944).

———, *Tārikh-i mukhtasar-i ahzāb-i sīyāsī: Inqirāz-i saltanat-i Qājārīyi*, (Tehran: Nigāh, 1944).

Bāmdād, M. ʿA., *Ḥāfiẓ-shināsī: yā ilhāmāt-i Khawja*, (Tehran: Ibn Sinā, 1338/1960).

Banani, A. (ed.), *Tāhira: A Portrait in Poetry, Selected Poems of Qurrat al-ʿAyn*, (Los Angeles: Kalimat Press, 2004).

Banisard, ʿA.H., *Muqiʿīyat-i Iran va naqsh-i Muṣaddiq: Sayrī dar tārikh-i tahavul-i iqtisādī va sīyāsī va tabiʿī-yi Iran va andisha va akhlāq-i Muddaris*, ([n.p.]: [n.p.], 1356/1978).

Bast, O., 'Germany. I. German-Persian Diplomatic Relations', *EIr*, Vol. 10, pp. 509-519.

Bate, W.J., *The Burden of the Past and the English Poet*, (New York: W.W. Norton, 1970).

Bausani, A., *The Persians: From the Earliest Days to the Twentieth Century*, (London: Elek Inc., 1975).

———, *Religion in Iran: From Zoroaster to Bahā'llāh*, (New York: Eisenbrauns, 2000).

Bayat, M., 'Āqā Khan Kermānī', *EIr*, Vol. 2, pp. 175-177.

Bayza'ī, N., *Tadhkira-yi shu'arā-yi qarn-i avval-i Bahā'ī*, (Tehran: Bahā'ī Publishing Trust, 1361/1943).

Beelaert, A.L., 'Ḳāqāni Šervān', *EIr*, Vol. 15, pp. 521-529.

Bell, G.L., *The Earlier Letters*, ed. Elsa Richmond, (New York: Liveright, 1937).

———, *The Garden of Heaven: Poems of Ḥāfiẓ*, (Mineola, NY: Dover Publication, 2003).

Bihbahānī, S., *Yik rūz bā hasht kitāb*, (Tehran: [n.p.], 1376/1998).

Bly, R. and L. Lewisohn (trans.), *The Angels Knocking on the Tavern Door: Thirty Poems of Hafez*, (New York: Harper Collins, 2008).

Bosnavī, M.S., *Sharḥ-i Sūdī bar Ḥāfiẓ*, trans. 'I. Sattārzāda, (Tehran: Zarrīn, 1374/1966), 4 vols.

Bosworth, C.E., 'Ardabil', *EIr*, Vol. 2, pp. 357-360.

———, *The New Islamic Dynasties: A Chronological and Genealogical Manual*, (Edinburgh: Edinburgh University Press, 2004).

———, *Qājār Iran: Political, Social and Cultural Change 1800-1925*, (Costa Mesa, CA: Mazda Publication, 1992).

Browne, E.G., *A History of Persian Literature Under Tatar Dominion, (A.D. 1265-1502)* (Cambridge: Cambridge University Press, 1920).

———, *A Literary History of Persia*, (Cambridge: Cambridge University Press, 1906-1920), 4 vols. Reprinted Bethesda, MD: Iranbook, Inc. 1997.

———, *The Persian Revolution of 1905-1909*, (London: Cambridge University Press, 1910).

———, *The Press and Poetry of Modern Persia*, (Cambridge: Cambridge University Press, 1941).

Bruijn, J.T.P. de., 'Hafez's Poetic Art', *EIr*, Vol. 11, pp. 400-474.

———, 'Rind', *Encyclpaedia of Islam*, VIII, p. 531.

———, *Of Poetry and Piety: An Interaction of Religion and Literature in the Life and Works of Hakim Sana'i of Ghazna*, (Leiden: E.J. Brill, 1983).

———, *Persian Sufi Poetry: An Introduction to the Mystical Use of Classical Persian Poems*, (Surrey: Curzon, 1997).

———, 'Comparative Notes on Sana'i and 'Attar', in L. Lewisohn (ed.), *The Heritage of Sufism*, I: *The Legacy of Mediaeval Persian Sufism*, (Oxford: Oneworld, 1999), pp. 361-379.

———, 'The *Qalandariyyat* in Persian Mystical Poetry, from Sana'i Onwards', in L. Lewisohn (ed.), *The Heritage of Sufism*, II: *Classical Persian Sufism from its Origins to Rumi*, (Oxford: Oneworld, 1999), pp. 75-86.

Baraq, 'A.K. *Justujū dar ahwāl va āthār-i Ṣafī 'Alī Shāh*, (Tehran: Ibn Sinā, 1352/1973).

Burgel, C, 'Ambiguity: A Study in the Use of Religious Terminology in the Poems of Ḥāfiẓ', in Michael Glunz and J.C. Burgel (ed.), *Intoxication, Earthly and Heavenly: Seven Studies on the Poets of Ḥāfiẓ of Shiraz*, (Bern: Peter Lang 1991).

———, *The Feather of Simurgh: The 'Licit Magic' of the Arts in Medieval Islam*, (New York: New York University Press, 1988).

Burrell, R.M. and R.L. Jarman (eds.), *Iran Political Diaries 1881-1965*, (Oxford: Archive Editions Ltd 1997).

Buzurgmihr, J., *Risidigi-yi farjāmī dar Dīvān-i kishvar*, (Tehran: Shirkat-i Sahāmī-i Intishār, 1367/1989).

Chittick, W, 'Tasawwuf. 2. Ibn al-'Arabi and after in the Arabic and Persian lands, and beyond', *Encyclopaedia of Islam*, X, pp. 317-324.

Clinton, J.W., *The Divan of Manūchihrī Dāmghānī: A Critical Study*, (Minneapolis, MN: Bibliotheca Islamica, 1972).

Cooper, J., 'Mulla Sadra Shirazi', in E. Craig (ed.), *The Routledge Encyclopedia of Philosophy*, (London: Routledge, 1998), Vol. 6, pp. 595-599.

Corbin, H., *Mulla Sadrā*, (Tehran: Jāvīdān, 1980).

Corzon, G.N., *Persia and the Persian Questions*, (New York: Barnes and Noble Inc., 1966).

Culler, Jonathan, *Literary Theory*, (Oxford: Oxford University Press, 1997).

Cyrus, G., *Iran and the Rise of the Riḍā Shāh: From Qājār Collapse to Pahlavi Power*, (London: Tauris, 2000).

Dabāshī, H., 'Didgāhī bi afkār-i ijtimā'ī-i Mullā Sadrā', *Iran Nameh*, Vol. 3, No. 3 (Spring 1985), pp. 407-429.

———, 'Ta'birī bar ta'birāt-i Ḥāfiẓ', *Iran Nameh*, Vol. 6, No. 4 (Summer 1988), pp. 574-596.

Dādbih, A., 'Mājirā-yi Pāyān Nāpazīr-i Ḥāfiẓ', *Māh-nāma-yi Kilk*, No. 30 (Autumn 1371/1993), pp. 228-230.

Dalāl, G.A., *Ethics in Persian Poetry: With Special Reference to Timurid Period*, (New Delhi: Abhinav Publication, 1995).

Daniel, E.L., *Society and Culture in Qājār Iran*, (Costa Mesa, CA: Mazda Publication, 2002).

Danner, V, 'Arabic Literature in Iran', in R.N. Frye (eds.), *The Cambridge History of Iran*, Vol. 4: *The Period from the Arab Invasion to the Saljuqs*, (Cambridge: Cambridge University Press, 1986), pp. 566-594.

Dārābī, M., *Laṭifa Ghaybī: Ḥāfiẓ Shīrāzī bi zamima-yi bayān-i iṣṭilāḥāt-i ahl-i ʿirfān*, (Shīrāz: Kitāb-Khāna- yi Aḥmadī, 1357/1979).

Dashtī, ʻA., *Kākh-i ibdāʿ: Andishahā-yi gūnāgūn-i Ḥāfiẓ*, (Tehran: Shirkat-i Qalam, 1385/2007).

———, *Naqshī az Ḥāfiẓ*, (Tehran: Amīr Kabīr, 13812002).

Dastghayb, ʻA., *Naqd-i āthār-i Aḥmad Kasravī*, (Tehran: Pāzand, 1357/1979).

———, *Naqd-i āthār-i Aḥmad Kasravī*, (Tehran: IntishArAt-i Muʿin, 1378/1999).

———, *Naqd-i āthār-i Aḥmad Shāmlū* (Tehran: Āfarin, 1373/1995).

———, *Naqd-i āthār-i Aḥmad Shāmlū*, (Tehran: Chāpār, Shāhanshāhī 2537).

———, *Naqd-i āthār-i Ṣādiq Chūbak*, (Tehran: Kānūn-i Taḥqīqāt-i Iqtiṣādī va Ijtimāʿī-i Pāzhand, 1353/1974).

Dhū'l-Nūr, R. (ed.), *Dar justujū-yi Ḥāfiẓ*, (Tehran: Zavvār, 1362/1984).

Dickson, M.B. and S.C. Welch, *The Houghton Shahnameh*, (Cambridge, MA and London: Published for the Fogg Art Museum by Harvard University Press, 1981), 2 vols.

Dihbāshī, ʻA., *Yād-nāma-yi Sayyid Abū'l Qāsim Īnjavī Shīrāzī*, (Tehran: Sukhan, 1381/2003).

Dihkhudā, ʻA.A., *Charand u parand*, (Tehran: Afrāsīyāb, 1381/2002).

———, *Lughat-nāma: Muqadama*, (Tehran: Tehran University Press, 1336/1958).

Dunbulī, ʻAbdul Razzāq and H.Q. Ṭabātabā'ī (eds.), *Tajribāt al-aḥrār va taslīyat al-abrār*, (Tabriz: [n.p.], 1348/1970), 2 vols.

Durūdīyān, V.A., *In Kimīyā-yi hastī: Maqālihā va yāddāshthā-yi ustād Shafīʿī Kadkanī dar bāra-yi Ḥāfiẓ*, (Tehran: Āydin, 1385/2007).

Elliot, Robert C., *The Literary Persona*, (Chicago: University of Chicago Press, 1982).

Faghfoory, M.H., 'The Impact of Modernization on ʻUlamā in Iran, 1925-1941', *Iranian Studies*, Vol. 26, Nos. 3-4 (1993).

Falsafī, N., *Zindagi-i Shāh ʻAbbās-i avval*, (Tehran: ʻIlmī, 1985), 2 vols.

Fardūst, H., *Zuhūr va Suqūt-i Salṭanat-i Pahlavi*, (Tehran: Amīr Kabīr, 1371/1992).

Farmānfarmāyān, H. (ed.), *Khāṭirāt-i Amīn al-Dawla*, (Tehran: Amīr Kabīr, 1350/1971).

Farzād, M., 'Contemporary Poetry in Iran', in E. Yarshater (ed.), *Persian Literature*, (New York: Persian Heritage Foundation, 1988), pp. 336-366.

——— (ed.), *Ḥāfiẓ: Guzarishī az nīma rāh*, (Shīrāz: Intishārāt-i Dānishgāh-i Pahlavi, 1352/1974).

Farzāna, M.F., *Āshinā'i bā Ṣādiq-i Hidāyat*, (Tehran: Nashr-i Markaz, 1372/1993).

Fasā'ī, H., *History of Persia Under Qajar Rule*, trans. Herbert Busse, (New York: Columbia University Press, 1972).

Ferdowsi, 'A., 'The "Emblem of the Manifestation of the Iranian Spirit": Ḥāfiẓ and the Rise of the National Cult of Persian Poetry', *Iranian Studies*, Vol. 41, No. 5 (2008), pp. 665-691.

Fletcher, A., Allegory, *the theory of a symbolic mode* (Princeton and Oxford: Princeton University Press, 2012).

Floor, W., *A Fiscal History of Iran in the Ṣafavid and Qajar Periods 1500-1925*, (New York: Bibliotheca Persica Press, 1999).

Foran, J. *Fragile Resistance, Social Transformation in Iran from 1500 to the Revolution*, (Boulder, CO: Westview Press, 1930).

Fragner, B., 'Social and Internal Economic Affairs', in Peter Jackson and Laurence Lockhart (eds.), *The Cambridge History of Iran*, Vol. 6: *The Timurid and Ṣafavid Periods*, (Cambridge: Cambridge University Press, 1986), pp. 491-568.

Frye, R.N., *The Golden Age of Persia: The Arabs in the East*, (London: Weidenfeld and Nicolson, 1975).

Ghanī, C., *Iran and the Rise of the Reza Shāh: From Qajar Collapse to Pahlavi Power*, (London: I.B.Tauris, 2000).

Ghanī, Q., *Baḥth dar āthār va afkār va aḥvāl-i Ḥāfiẓ: Tārīkh-i 'aṣr-i Ḥāfiẓ yā tārikh-i fārs va muzāfāt va ayālāt-i mujāvirī dar qarn-i hashtum*, (Tehran: Zavvār, 1322/1944).

Ghanoonparvar, M.R., 'Chubak, Sadeq,' EIr online, www.iranicaonline.org/articles/chubak-sadeq, (accessed 27 September 2011).

———, *Prophets of Doom: Literature as a Socio-political Phenomenon in Modern Iran*, (New York: University Press of America, 1984).

Gibb, E.J.W., *A History of Ottoman Poetry*, (London: Luzac, 1900-1909), 5 vols.

Gray, E.T. (trans.), *Ḥāfiẓ the Green Sea of Heaven: Fifty Ghazals from the Dīwān of Ḥāfiẓ*, (Ashland, OR: White Cloud Press, 2002).

Groot, J., *Religion, Culture and Politics in Iran from the Qājārs to Khomeini*, (London: I.B.Tauris, 2007).

Gulbun, M., *Bahār va adab-i fārsi: Majmū'i-yi yikṣad maqāla az Malik al-Shu'arā-yi Bahār*, (Tehran: Kitābhā-yi Jibī, 1351/1972), 2 vols.

Gulshirī, H., *Jidāl-i naqsh bā naqqāsh dar āthār-i Simin-i Dānishvar*, (Tehran: Intishārāt-i Nilūfar, 1376/1998).

Hā'irī, M.H., *Maykhāna-yi Ārizū: Sharḥ-i aḥvāl, bar-risī-i āthār va guzida-yi ash'ār-i Ghālib Dihlavī, 1212/1285*, (Tehran: Nashr-i Markaz, 1371/1992).

Hā'irī, S.H. (ed.), *Afkār va āthār-i Īraj*, (Tehran: Intishārāt-i Jāvīdān, 1364/1947).

——— (ed.), *'Ārif Qazvīnī shā'ir-i milli-yi Iran*, (Tehran: Jāvīdān, 1364/1962).

Hakim-Ilāhī, H., *Zindagi-yi āqā-yi Sayyīd Ḍīyyā'*, (Tehran: Bahā, 1323/1944).

Hakkak, Aḥmad Karīmi-, *Modern Persian Literature Series: An Anthology of Modern Persian Poetry*, ed. E. Yarshater, (Boulder, CO: Westview Press, 1978).

———, 'Naqd-i adabī', *Iran Nameh*, Vol. 12, No. 1 (Winter 1994), pp. 3-34.

———, 'Nima Yushij: A Life,' in A. Karimi-Hakkak and K. Talattof (eds.), *Essays on Nima Yushij: Animating Modernism in Persian Poetry*, (Leiden and Boston: Brill, 2004)

———, 'Preservation and Presentation: Continuity and Creativity in the Contemporary Persian Qasida', Unpublished paper presented at the SOAS conference (14-16 July 1993), 'Qasida: The Literary Heritage on an Arab Poetic Form in Islamic Africa and Asia', *Draft Conference Papers*, Appendix, pp. 316-328.

———, *Recasting Persian Poetry: Senarios of Poetic Modernity in Iran*, (Salt Lake City: University of Utah Press, 1995).

Hamidī, M., *Daryā-yi guhar*, (Tehran: Sinā, 1320/1941).

Hanaway, W., 'Comments on Literature before the Ṣafavid Period, "Studies on Isfahan"', *Iranian Studies*, Vol. 7, (Winter-Spring 1974).

Haravī, N.M., *Jāmī*, (Tehran: Ṭarh-i Naw, 1377/1999).

Ḥasan, M., *Naqd va taḥlīl va guzīda-yi dāstānhā-yi Ṣādiq Chūbak*, (Tehran: Nashr-i Rūzgār, 1381/2002).

Ḥasanlī, K., *Chishma-i khurshid: Bāz khānī-i zindagī, andisha va sukhan-i Ḥāfiẓ-i Shīrāzī*, (Shīrāz: Navīd, 1385/2007).

Hāshimī, M.S., *Shi'r va shā'irī dar 'asr-i Ṣafavī*, (Tehran: Naqsh-i Jahān, 1323/1945).

Hazhīr, 'A. Ḥ. *Ḥāfiẓ-i tashrīḥ*, (Tehran: Nashr-i 'Ilm, 1367/1988).

Hillmann, M., *A Lonely Woman: Forough Farrokhzad and her Poetry*, (London: Mage Publishers, 1997).

Hiravī, H. 'A., *Majmū'i-yi maqālāt, Sukhan-i ahl-i dil*, (Tehran: Intishārāt-i Ufsit, 1371/1992).

———, *Maqālāt-i Ḥāfiẓ*, (Tehran: Kitābsarā, 1368/1990).

Hiravī-Khurāsānī, M., *Maqālāt-i Ḥāfiẓ*, (Tehran: Kitābsarā, 1368/1989).

———, *Sharḥ-i ghazalhā-yi Ḥāfiẓ*, (Tehran: Nashr-i Naw, 1386/2008), 4 vols.

———, *Tārīkh-i paydāyish-i mashrūtīyyat-i Iran*, (Tehran: Amīr Kabīr, 1332/1953).

Hujjatī, H., ''Urfī-i Shīrāzī', in Ḥasan Anūshā (ed.), Dānishnāma-i adab-i FARSI, IV, (Tehran, 2001), pp. 1760-1764.

Humā'ī, J. *Funūn-i balāghat va ṣanā'āt-i adabī*, (Tehran: Intishārāt-i Ṭūs, 1363/1985).

Hūman, M., *Ḥāfiẓ: Sukhanī chand dar bāra-yi tashiḥ-i Dīvān-i aū*, (Tehran: Firdawsī, 1325/1947).

Huqūqī, M., *Shiʿr-i zamān-i mā: Suhrāb Sipihrī*, (Tehran: Nigāh, 1371/1993).

Ḥusaynī, H. Bidil, Sipihrī va sabk-i Hindī, (Tehran: Surūsh, 1368/1989).

Ḥusaynī, S., Gulhā-yi niāyish: shiʿr va naqd-i Suhrāb Sipihrī, (Tehran: Nilūfar, 1996).

Imdād, H., *Shīrāz dar guzashta va hāl*, (Shīrāz: Itiḥādīya-yi Maṭbūʿātī-i -i Fārs, 1341/1963).

Inqitāʿ, N., *Ḥāfiẓ va Kish-i Mihr: Shaydā-yi shūrida-yi Shīrāz, dar kārgāh-i Kishī Kuhan*, (Tehran: Shirkat-i Kitāb, 1387/2008).

Istiʿlāmī, M., *Adabīyāt-i dawra-yi bidārī va Muʿāṣir*, (Tehran: Dānishgāh-i Sipāhīyān-i Inqilāb-i Iran, 1355/1976).

———, *Dars-i Ḥāfiẓ: Naqd va sharḥ-i ghazalhā-yi Khawja Shams al-Dīn Muḥammad Ḥāfiẓ*, (Tehran: Sukhan, 1388/2010).

———, 'Darvish-i bi rang', *Talāsh*, 54th series, Year 11, (Shāhanshāhī 2535, 1355/1976), pp. 42-45.

——— (ed.), *Maqālāt va Qataʿāt-i Ashʿār-i Parvin: Some Observation of the Poetry of Parvin Iʿtisāmī*, (Tehran: Surush, 1360/1981).

———, 'Shamāyil-i maʿshūq dar kalām-i Ḥāfiẓ', *Iran shināsī*, Vol. 19, No. 1 (Spring 1386/2007), pp. 25-32.

Itiḥād, H., *Pazhūhishgaran-i Muʿāṣir-i Iran*, (Tehran: Farhang-i Muʿāṣir, 1382/2004).

Ivanow, W., *Bibliotheca Indica: A Collection of Oriental Works: Concise Descriptive Catalogue of Persian Manuscripts in the Curzon Collection Asiatic Society of Bengal*, (Calcutta: Baptism Mission Press, 1926), 2 vols.

Jalālī, B. (ed.), *Furūgh Farrukhzād: Khāṭirāt-i Furūgh*, (Tehran: Murvārīd, 1372/1993).

Kadkanī, M.S., *Advār-i shiʿr-i fārsi*, (Tehran: Sukhan, 1380/2002).

———, *Mūsiqī-i shiʿr*, (Tehran: Āgāh, 1381/2002).

———, *Ṣuvar-i khīyāl dar shiʿr-i fārsi: Taḥqīq-i intiqādī dar tattavūr-i īmāzhīhā-yi shiʿr-i pārsī va sayr-i nazarīya-yi balāghat dar Islam va Iran*, (Tehran: Āgah, 1350/1971).

———, *Īn kīmiyā-yi hastī*, ed., V.A. Durūdīyān, (Tehran: Intishārāt-i Āyīn, 1385/2006).

Kasravī, A., *Dar pīrāmūn-i falsafa*, (Tehran: Pāydār, 1344/1966).

———, *Ḥāfiẓ chi migūyad*, (Tehran: Intishārāt-i Mihr, 1335/1956).

———, 'Shaykh Ṣafī va tabārash', *Iran Nameh*, Vol. 13, No. 3 (Summer 1995), pp. 377-386.

———, *Tārikh-i mashrūṭa-i Iran*, (Tehran: Zavvār, 1340/1961).

———, 'Vajeh: Saʿdī va bazgasht-i adabi', *Majala-i adabi va hunarī*, No. 7 (Tehran: 1386/2008), pp. 70-73.

———, *Zindagānī-yi man: Dah sāl dar ʿadlīya, va chirā az ʿadlīya bīrūn āmadam*, (Tehran: Pāzand, 1377/1960).

Katouzian, H., 'Hedayat,' *EIr*, Vol. 12, p. 121.

———, *Saʿdī: Shāʾir-i ishq va zindagī*, (Tehran: Nashr-i Markaz, 1385/2006).

———, *Ṣādiq Hidāyat: The Life and Literature of an Iranian Writer*, (London and New York: I.B.Tauris, 1991).

———, *State and Society in Iran: The Eclipse of the Qājār and the Emergence of the Pahlavis*, (London: I.B.Tauris, 2006).

Kausar, I.H., *Fighānī's Life and Work*, (Pakistan: Pakistan Historical Society, 1963).

Kāvīyānpūr, A., *Zindagi-yi adabī va ijtimāʿī-yi ustād Shahriyār*, (Tehran: Iqbāl, 1381/2001).

Kazāzī, M.J., *Maʿānī: Zibā shināsī-yi sukhan-i pārsī*, (Tehran: Nashr-i Markaz, 1368/1989), 2 vols.

Keddie, N.R. and Y. Richard, *Modern Iran: Roots and Results of Revolution*, (New Haven, CT: Yale University Press, 2006).

Kennedy, R.S., *A Biography of E.E. Cummings: Dreams in the Mirror*, (London: Norton & Co., 1980).

Keshavarz, Fatemah, *Reading Mystical Lyric: The Case of Jalāl al-Dīn Rumi*, (Columbia, SC: University of South Carolina Press, 1998).

Khāliqī, M.B., *Shākh-i Nabāt: Sharḥ-i ghazalhā*, (Tehran: Zavvār, 1382/2004).

Khalkhālī, S. ʿA., *Tadhkiri-yi shuʿarā-yi Muʿāṣir-i Iran*, (Tehran: Ṭahūrī, 1331/1953).

Khānlarī, P.N., *Haftād sukhan*, (Tehran: Ṭūs, 1369/1991).

———, 'Sukhan: Adabīyāt-i Muʿāṣir-i Iran', *Majala-i adabīyāt va dānish va hunar-i imrūz*, 4th Series, No. 6 (1332/1953), p. 637.

Khurramshāhī, B., 'Bi Munāsibat-i Tashihī az Dīvān-i Ḥāfiẓ', *Māh-nāma-yi Kilk*, No. 53 (Summer 1373/1995), pp. 50-53.

———, *Dhihn u zabān-i Hāfiz*, (Tehran: Intishārāt-i Khas, 1367/1988).

———, *Ḥāfiẓ*, (Tehran: Nāhid, 1387/2008).

———, 'Hafez's Life and Times', *EIr*, Vol. 11, pp. 465-469.

———, *Ḥāfiẓ-nāma: Sharḥ-i alfāz, aʿlām, mafāhim-i kilidī va abyāt-i dushvār-i Ḥāfiẓ*, (Tehran: Intishārāt-i Surūsh, 1366/1987).

———, 'Printed Editions of the Dīvān of Hafez', *EIr*, Vol. 11, p. 479.

———, *Qurʾān shinākht*, (Tehran: Nāhid, 1387/2008).

———, 'Mayl-i Ḥāfiẓ bi gunāh', *Iran Nameh*, Vol. 6, No. 4 (Summer 1988), pp. 662-695.

Khurūsh, K., *Satrnivisī tā kitābat: Majmūʿaʾī az khuṭūṭ-i nastaʿlīq dar aqlām-i mukhtalif: Rāhnamā-yi hunar jūyān-i khaṭṭ, shiva-yi Kay Khusru Khurūsh*, (Tehran: Intishārāt-i Yūsh, 1363/1985).

Kirmānī, Nazm al-Islām, *Tārikh-i bidārī-i Iranian*, ed. ʿAlī-Akbar Saʿīd Sirjānī, (Tehran: Bunyād-i Farhang-i Iran, 1345/1967).

Kirmānī, S.N., *Dawlat-i pīr-i mughān bād ki bāqī sahl as: Majmūʿa-yi maqālāt-i Ḥāfiẓ-shināsī*, (Tehran: Pāzhang, 1373/1995).

———, *Ḥāfiẓ az Dīdgāhhā-yi mukhtalif*, (Tehran: Ādhar Ābādigān, 1364/1986).

———, *Ḥāfiẓ Shināsī*, (Tehran: Intishārāt-i Pazhang, 1376/1997).

Kumisarov, D.S., *Ṣādiq Hidāyat muhaqiq va mutarjim: Haft maqala az Iranshināsān-i Shuravī*, trans. A. Āzmūda, (Tehran: Markaz-i Nashr-i Sipihr, [n.d.]).

Kutbī, M., *Tārikh-i Āl-i Muẓaffar*, ed. A.H. Navāʾī, (Tehran: Ibn Sinā, 1334/1956).

———, B. Khurramshāhī, K. Manṣūrī and H.M. Amīn (eds.), *Sharḥ-i ʿirfānī-i ghazalhā-yi Ḥāfiẓ*, (Tehran: Qatra, 1374/1996), 4 vols.

Langarūdī, S., *Tārikh-i Taḥlilī-yi Shiʿr-i naw: Az mashrūtīyyat tā kūditā. 1284-1332*, (Tehran: Saʿdī, 1370/1991).

Leaf, W., *Versions from Ḥāfiẓ: An Essay in Persian Metre*, (London: Grant Richards, 1898).

Lenczowski, G., *Iran under the Pahlavis*, (Los Angeles: Hoover Institution, 1978).

Lentz, T.W. and G.D. Lowry, *Timur and the Princely Vision: Persian Art and Culture in the Fifteenth Century*, (Los Angeles: Los Angeles County Museum of Art and Washington, D.C.: Arthur M. Sackler Gallery, 1989).

Levy, Reuben, *An Introduction to Persian Literature*, (New York: Columbia University Press, 1969).

Lewis, F., 'Hafez, VIII. Hafez and Rendi', *EIr*, Vol. 11, pp. 483-491.

———, *Rumi Past and Present, East and West: The Life, Teachings and Poetry of Jalālu'l-Dīn Rūmī*, (Oxford: Oneworld, 2000).

Lewisohn, Leonard, 'An Introduction to the History of Modern Persian Sufism, Part 1: The Niʿmatu'llāhī Order: Persecution, Revival and Schism', *Bulletin of the School of Oriental & African Studies*, Vol. 61, Pt. 3 (1998).

———, 'Prolegomenon', *Ḥāfiẓ and the Religion of Love*, (London and New York: I.B.Tauris, 2010).

———, 'Zindagī va dawrān-i Kamāl-i Khujandī', *Iran Nameh*, Vol. 10, No. 4 (Autumn 1992), pp. 689-706.

———, 'Ṭariq-i Sufiāna-yi maʿrifat', *Iran Nameh*, Vol. 11, No. 1 (Winter 1993), pp. 129-136.

Limbert, J., *Shiraz in the Age of Hafez: The Glory of a Medieval Persian City*, (Seattle: University of Washington Press, 2004).

Lockhart, L., Nadir Shah, (Ph.D. thesis, University of London, School of Oriental and African Studies, 1938).

———, *Nadir Shah: A Critical Study Based Mainly upon Contemporary Sources*, (London: Luzac, 1938).

———, 'European Contacts with Persia, 1350-1736', in P. Jackson and L. Lockhart (eds.), *The Cambridge History of Iran*, Vol. 6: *The Timurid and Ṣafavid Periods*, (Cambridge: University Press, 1986), pp. 373-412.

Loloi, P., *Hafez, Master of Persian Poetry: A Critical Bibliography*, (London: I.B.Tauris, 2004).

Loraine, M.B., 'Bahār, Malek al Šoʿarā', i. Life and Work', *EIr*, Vol. 3, pp. 476-479.

Losensky, P.E., 'Jāmī: Life and Works', *EIr* online, www.iranica.com/articles/jami, (accessed 18 April 2011).

———, 'Hedayat, Riḍāqolī Khān', *EIr*, Vol. 12, pp. 120-125.

———, *Welcoming Fighānī: Imitation and Poetic Individuality in the Safavīd-Mughal Ghazal*, (Costa Mesa, CA: Mazda, 1998).

Louis, H. and R. Borgomale, *Coins, medals and Seals of the Shāhs of Iran, 1500-1941*, (London: Iranian Numismatic Institute with cooperation of Amīr Kabīr Publications Organization, 1945).

Mackey, Sandra, *The Iranians: Persia, Islam and the Soul of Nation*, (New York: Penguin, 1998).

Maḥjūb, M.J., *Sabk-i Khurāsānī dar shiʿr-i fārsi: bar rasī-i mukhtassāt-i shiʿr-i fārsī, az āghāz-i ḍuhūr tā pāyān-i qarn-i panjum-i hijri*, (Tehran: Firdawsī, 1363/1985).

Makki, H., *Gulistān-i adab*, (Tehran: Kitābāfarin, 1370/1951).

———, *Muddaris qahrimān-i āzādī*, (Tehran: Bungāh-i Tarjuma va Nashr-i Kitāb, 1358/1980).

———, *Tārikh-i bist sāla-yi Iran*, (Tehran: Intishārāt-i Majlis, 1324/1945), 8 vols.

Malakī, M., 'Mashrūṭīyat va Riḍā Khān', *Iran shinasi*, Vol. 28, No. 1 (Spring 2006), p. 67.

Malikzāda, M., *Tārikh-i inqilāb-i mashrūṭīyyat-i Iran*, 5 vols (Tehran: Square Press, 1328/1949).

Mallāh, H. ʿA., *Manūchihrī Dāmghānī va mūsīqī*, (Tehran: Intishārāt-i Hunar va Farhang, 1363/1984).

Manz, Beatrice Forbes, *The Rise and Rule of Tamerlane*, (Cambridge: Cambridge University Press, 1989).

———, 'Temür and the Problem of a Conqueror's Legacy', *Journal of the Royal Asiatic Society*, Vol. 8, No. 1 (April 1998), p. 25.

Massignon, L., *Hallāj: Mystic and Martyr*, Herbert Mason (trans. and ed.), (Princeton, NJ: Princeton University Press, 1994).

Matin, F.P. 'Love: Nima's Dialogue with Hafez', in A.K. Hakkak and K. Talattof (eds.), *Essays on Nima Yushij: Animating Modernism in Persian Poetry*, (Leiden and Boston: Brill, 2004).

Matthee, R., 'Iran's Ottoman Diplomacy During the Reign of Shah Sulayman I. 1077-1105/1666-1694', in K. Eslami (ed.), *Iran and Iranian Studies, Essays in Honor of Iraj Afshar*, (Princeton, NJ: Zagros, 1998), pp. 148-177.

———, 'Transforming Dangerous Nomads into Useful Artisans, Technicians, Agriculturists: Education in Reza Shah Period', *Iranian Studies*, Vol. 26, Nos. 3-4 (1993).

Meisami, Julie S., 'Manuscripts of Hafez', *EIr*, Vol. 11, pp. 476-479.

———, *Medieval Persian Court Poetry*, (Princeton, NJ: Princeton University Press, 1987).

Melville, C., *History and Literature in Iran*, (Cambridge: Cambridge University Press, 1998).

Meskūb, S. *Iranian Nationality and the Persian Language*, (Washington, D.C.: Mage Publishers, 1992).

Mihrin, A., *Tārikh-i Zabān va adabīyāt-i Iran az zamān-i Qājār tā 'asr-i Pahlavi*, (Tehran: Mānī, 1353/1934).

Milani, A., *Eminent Persians: The Men and Women Who Made Modern Iran 1941-1979*, (Syracuse, NY: Syracuse University Press, 2008).

———, *Lost Wisdom: Rethinking Modernity in Iran*, (Washington, D.C.: Mage Publishers, 2004).

Milani, F., *Veils and Words: The Emerging Voices of Iranian Women Writers*, (Syracuse, NY: Syracuse University Press, 1992).

Mīnuvī, M., Naqd-i Hāl, (Tehran: [n. p.], 1351/1972).

Mirsepassi, A., *Intellectual Discourse and the Politics of Modernization, Negotiating Modernity in Iran*, (Cambridge: Cambridge University Press, 2000).

Mīrzā Safavī, S. and Rukn al-Dīn Humāyūn Farrukh (eds.), *TāẔkiri-i Sāmī*, (Tehran: 'Ilmī, 1967).

Mīrzā'ī, F., *Mafhūm-i rindī dar shi'r-i Ḥāfiẓ*, (Tehran: Kavīr, 1373/1995).

Moayyad, H., *Once a Dewdrop: Essays on Parvin E'tesami*, (Costa Mesa, CA: Mazda Publishers, 1994).

Molavi, A., *Soul of Iran: A Nation's Journey for Freedom*, (New York: Norton, 2005).

Mostofi, A., *The Administrative and Social History of the Qajar Period*, trans. N.M. Glenn, (Costa Mesa, CA: Mazda Publishers, 1993), 3 vols.

Mottahedeh, N., *Representing the Unpresentable: Historical Images of National Reform from the Qajars to the Islamic Republic of Iran*, (Syracuse, NY: Syracuse University Press, 2008).

Mozaffari, Nahid, 'Jamalzadeh, Mohammad-Ali', *Encyclopedia Iranica* online, www.iranica.com/articles/jamalzadeh-i.

Mu'ayyirī, M. 'A., *Ḥāfiẓ rā ham az Ḥāfiẓ bishnāsīm*, (Tehran: Intishārāt-i Kitāb Furūshī-i Dihkhudā, 1354/1974).

Muhājir, M., *Vāzhigān-i adabīyāt va guftimān-i adabī*, (Tehran: Āgāh, 1343/1964).

———, *Zabān shināsī-yi shi'r*, (Tehran: Nashr-i Markaz, 1376/1997).

Mu'īn, M. *Ḥāfiẓ-i shirīn-sukhan*, (Tehran: Sidā-yi Mu'āṣir, 1375/1966; 1389/2011).

———, *Ḥāfiẓ-i Shirīn sukhan*, (Tehran: Intishārāt-i Mu'īn, 1370/1991).

———, *Ḥāfiẓ-i shirīn sukhan*, (Tehran: Sukhan, 1319/1941).

Mu'minī, B., *Dīn va Dawlat dar 'asr-i Mashrūṭīyat*, (Sweden: Bārān, 1993).

Munibur, Rahman, 'Shihāb Iṣfahānī', *EI²*, Vol. 9, pp. 436-437.

Murtaḍavī, M., *Maktab-i Ḥāfiẓ: Muqadama bar Ḥāfiẓ shināsī*, (Tehran: Ibn Sinā, 1344/1966).

Mustafavī, R. *Bahth-i kūtāhī dar murad-i Ṣādiq Hidāyat va āthārash*, (Tehran: Amīr Kabīr, 1350/1972).

Mutlaq, J. Kh., 'Ḥāfiẓ va himāsa-yi milli-yi Iran', *Iran Nameh*, Vol. 6, No. 4 (Summer 1988), pp. 565-574.

Nādirpūr, N., *False Dawn: Persian Poems, 1951-1984*, trans. M.C. Hillman, (Austin: University of Texas Press, 1986).

Nafisī, S., *Dar pirāmūn-i ash'ār va aḥvāl-i Ḥāfiẓ*, (Tehran: [n.p.], 1381/2002).

———, *Tārikh-i ijtimā'ī va sīyāsī-i Iran dar dawra-yi Mu'āṣir*, (Tehran: Furūghī, 1956), 3 vols.

Najamī, N., *Tehran-i 'ahd-i Nāṣirī*, (Tehran: 'Attār, 1364/1986).

Nash, G., *From Empire to Orient, Travellers to the Middle East 1830-1926*, (London: I.B.Tauris, 2005).

Nāṣirī, H.S., *Ātashkada-yi Ādhar*, (Tehran: Amīr Kabīr, 1336/1958).

Nasr, S.H. 'Spiritual Movements, Philosophy and Theology in the Ṣafavid Period', in P. Jackson and L. Lockhart (eds.), *The Cambridge History of Iran*, Vol. 6: *The Timurid and Ṣafavid Periods*, (Cambridge: Cambridge University Press, 1986), pp. 656-698.

———, 'Sufism', in R.N. Frye (eds.), *The Cambridge History of Iran*, Vol. 4: *The Period from the Arab Invasion to the Saljuqs*, (Cambridge: Cambridge University Press, 1986), pp. 442-465.

———, 'The Religious Sciences', in R.N. Frye (eds.), *The Cambridge History of Iran*, Vol. 4: *The Period from the Arab Invasion to the Saljuqs*, (Cambridge: Cambridge University Press, 1986), pp. 465-481.

Navā'ī, A., 'The Budget in the First National Assembly', *Itila'āt-i māhāna* (1327/1948), pp. 8-19.

Navā'ī, Ḥusayn 'A. (ed.), *Asnād va mukātabāt-i sīyāsī-i Iran az sāl-i 1105 tā 1135 H.Q. hamrāh bā yāddāshthā-i tafṣīlī*, (Tehran: Mu'assisa-i 'Itilā'āt va Tahqīqāt-i Farhangī, 1362/1984).

——— (ed.), Nādir Shāh va Bāzmāndigānash: Hamrāh bā Nāmahā-i Saltanatī va Asnād-i Sīyāsī va Idārī, (Tehran: Intishārāt-i Zarrīn, 1367/1989).

Naysārī, S.M.J. (ed.), *Muqaddama'ī bar tadvīn-i ghazalhā-yi Ḥāfiẓ*, (Tehran: Markaz-i Pakhsh-i 'Ilmī, 1366/1988).

——— (ed.), *Muqaddama'ī bar tadvīn-i ghazalhā-yi Ḥāfiẓ*, (Tehran: Intishārāt-i 'Ilmī, 1376/1998).

———, *Tārikh-i adabīyāt-i Iran*, (Tehran: Shirkat-i H.M. Iqbāl va Shurakā', 1328/1950).

Newman, Andrew J., 'Dāmād, Mīr(-E), Sayyed Mohammad Bāqer', Encyclopedia Iranica, online www.iranicaonline.org/articles/damad-mir-e-sayyed-mohammad-baqer-b.

———, *Ṣafavid Iran: Rebirth of a Persian Empire*, (London: I.B.Tauris, 2006).

Nicolson, H., *Curzon: The Last Phase: 1919-1925*, (Boston: Boston University Press, 1934).

Niknām, M., *Kitāb shināsī-i Ḥāfiẓ*, (Shīrāz: Markaz-i Ḥāfiẓ Shināsī, 1381/2003), 2 vols.

Ni'matullāhī, R.N., *Nubūgh-i Ḥāfiẓ-i Shīrāz va nūr-i ash'ār-i aū*, (Tehran: Zindagī, [n.d.]).

Nudūshan, M. 'Alī Islāmī, 'Shīva-yi shā'irī-yi Ḥāfiẓ', *Iran Nameh*, Vol. 6, No. 4 (Summer 1988), pp. 521-558.

———, *Chihār sukhangu-yi vijdān-i Iran, Firdawsī, Mawlavī, Sa'dī va Ḥāfiẓ*, (Tehran: Nashr-i Qatra, 1381/2002).

Nu'mānī, M. Shiblī, *Shi'r al-'ajam*, (trans. and ed.), M.T. Fakhr-i Dā'ī Gilānī, (Tehran: Ibn Sinā, 1335/1956; 1339/1961).

Nuqabā'ī, H., *Tāhira: Qurrat al-'Ayn*, (Tehran: Bahā'ī Publishing Committee, 1972).

Nurbakhsh, Javād, *Bāyazid Basṭāmī*, (Tehran: Yaldā Qalam, 1373/1994).

———, *Dar kharābāt*, (Tehran: Yaldā Qalam, 1384/2005).

———, *Farhang Nūrbakhsh, Iṣṭilāḥāt-i taṣawwuf*, (London: Khaniqah-i Ni'matullahi, 1374/1995).

———, (ed.), *Gulshan-i rāz: Āthār-i Shaykh Maḥmūd Shabistarī*, (Tehran: Yaldā Qalam, 1382/2003).

———, *Kashkūl-i Nūr*, (Tehran: Yaldā Qalam, 1385/2006).

———, (ed.), *Risāla-yi Ḥaqq al-Yaqīn: Shaykh Maḥmūd Shabistarī*, (Tehran: Yaldā Qalam, 1382/2003).

———, (ed.), *Risāla-yi lama'āt va risāla-yi istilāhāt: Fakhr al-Dīn Ibrāhīm 'Irāqī*, (Tehran: Yaldā Qalam, 1382/2003).

———, (ed.), *Risālat al-quds va risāla-yi ghalatāt al-sākinin: Ruzbihān Baqlī Shīrāzī*, (Tehran: Yaldā Qalam, 1381/2002).

———, (ed.), *Risāla-yi savāna va risāla'ī dar mu'aza az āthār-i Shaykh Aḥmad Ghazālī* (Tehran: Yaldā Qalam, 1381/2002).

———, (ed.), *Shiblī*, (London: Khāniqāh-i Ni'matullāhī, 1376/1997).

Nūrbakhsh, M., *Bi surāgh-i man agar miā'īd: Sirr-i andisha-yi Suhrāb Sipihrī dar ā'ina-yi ash'ārash*, (Tehran: Murvārid, 1376/1998).

Palmer, E.H. *Oriental Mysticism*, (London: Octagon Press, 1974).

Parishānzāda, A.P., 'Irfān-i Iran: *Ta'amulī dar barkhī az abyyāt-i Ḥāfiẓ va qarā'at-i ān, majmū'i-yi maqālāt*', No. 15 (Spring 1382/2004), pp. 121-125.

Parsinejad, Ī., 'Aḥmad Kasravī va naqd-i adabī' *Iran Nameh*, Vol. 11, No. 3 (Summer 1993), pp. 481-504.

———, *A History of Literary Criticism in Iran, 1866-1915*, (Bethesda, MD: Ibex Publishers, 1382/2003).

———, 'Mīrzā Āqā Khān Kirmānī, Muntaqid-i adabī', *Iran Nameh*, Vol. 8, No. 4 (Autumn 1990), pp. 541-566.

———, 'Mīrzā Āqā Khān Kirmānī, Muntaqid-i adabī', *Iran Nameh*, Vol. 8, No. 3 (Summer 1995), pp. 301-320.

———, 'Zayn al-'Ābidin Marāqa'ī, muntaqid-i adabī', *Iran Nameh*, Vol. 9, No. 3 (Summer 1991), pp. 427-453.

———, 'Ṭālebof-e Tabrizī', *Iranshenasi*, Vol. 7, No. 3 (Autumn 1990), pp. 520-536.

———, *Mīrzā Fatḥ-'Alī Ākhūndzāda and Literary Criticism*, (Tokyo: Institute for the Study of Languages and Cultures of Asia and Africa, Tokyo University of Foreign Studies, 1988).

Perry, J.R., *Karīm Khān Zand: A History of Iran, 1774-1779*, (Chicago: University of Chicago Press, 1979).

Pizishkzād, Ī, *Ḥāfiẓ-i Nāshinida Pand*, (Tehran: Qatra, 1386/2007).

Preminger, Alex and T.V.F. Brogan, *The New Princeton Encyclopedia of Poetry and Poetics*, (Princeton, NJ: Princeton University Press, 1993).

Pūrjavādī, N., *Bū-yi jān: maqālahā'ī darbāra-yi sh'ir-i 'irfānī-yi fārsī*, (Tehran: Intishārāt-i Markaz-i Dānishgāhī, 1372/1993).

Qazvīnī, M., 'Ṭālibuf Tabrizī', *Majala-yi Yādigār*, Nos. 4/5 (1327/1949), p. 86.

Qesarim, A., *Iranian Intellectuals in the Twentieth Century*, (Austin: University of Texas Press, 1998).

Quinn, S.A., *Historical Writing During the Reign of Shah Abbas*, (Salt Lake City: University of Utah Press, 2000).

Rādfar, 'A.Q., *Majmu'a-yi zabān va adabīyāt-i fārsī: Ḥāfiẓ pazhūhān va Ḥāfiẓ pazhūhī*, (Tehran: Gustara, 1367/1989), 3 vols.

Rahbarān, Sh., *Jāygāh-i sukhan: Naqsh-i shā'ir va nivisanda dar Iran pas az inqilāb-i Islāmī*, (Kista, Sweden: Kitāba Arzā, 1383/2004).

Raḥīmpūr, H., 'Keyhān-i Farhangī', *Ghazalī az Ḥāfiẓ*, No. 3 (Summer 1364/1986).

Rahman, F. *Revival and Reform in Islam: A Study of Islamic Fundamentalism*, (Oxford: Oneworld, 2000).

Rahnema, A., *An Islamic Utopian: A Political Biography of Ali Shari'ati*, (London: I.B.Tauris, 1998).

Rāmsarī, S., 'Ḥāfiẓ-i Shirīn Sukhan va Muḥammad Mu'īn', *Māh-nāma-yi Kilk*, No. 5 (Summer 1369/1991), p. 165.

Rastigār, G.F., *Muntakhab-i shi'r-i Bahār va barrisi-i kūtāhī az ash'ār-i aū*, (Tehran: Bāstān, 1351/1973).

Ravāqī, 'A. 'Shab-i Tārik va Bim-i Mūj va…' *Māh-nāma-yi Kilk*, No. 21 (Autumn 1370/1992), pp. 70-81.

Razavī-Nizhād, M.A., *Chihār ṣad shā'ir-i barguzidi-yi pārsī gūī: Ḥikmat-i 'ilmi-yi zindagi-yi insānhā*, (Tehran: Intishārāt-i Tehran, 1369/1990).

Rāzī, 'A., *Tārikh-i Iran*, (Tehran: Sipihr, 1316/1938).

Rīyāḍ'l Islam, A Calendar of Documents on Indo-Persian Relations: 1500-1750, (Tehran and Karachi, 1979-1982).

Riḍā zāda-Shafaq, S. *Tārikh-i adabīyāt-i Iran*, (Tehran: Intishārāt-i Dānishgāh, 1320/1940).

Ridgeon, L. 'Aḥmad Kasravi's Criticisms of E.G. Browne', *Iran*, (London: Journal of the British Institute of Persian Studies, 2004).

———, *Religion and Politics in Modern Iran*, (London: I.B.Tauris, 2005).

———, *Sufi Castigator: Aḥmad Kasravi and the Iranian Mystical Tradition*, (London & New York: Routledge Taylor & Francis Group, 2006).

Rīyāhī, M.A. (ed.), *Guzārishā-i musāfirat va ma'mūrīyat-i sāfirān-i 'Othmānī dar Iran*, (Tehran: Intishārāt-i Zarrin, 1367/1989).

Rizvi, S., 'Molla Sadra Shirazi', *EIr Online*, www.iranica.com.

Roemer, H., 'The Jalayirids, Muẓaffarids and Sarbadārs', in P. Jackson and L. Lockhart (eds.), *The Cambridge History of Iran*, Vol. 6: *The Timurid and Ṣafavid Periods*, (Cambridge: Cambridge University Press, 1986), pp. 1-42.

———, 'The Ṣafavid Period', in P. Jackson and L. Lockhart (eds.), *The Cambridge History of Iran*, Vol. 6: *The Timurid and Ṣafavid Periods*, (Cambridge: Cambridge University Press, 1986), pp. 189-351.

———, 'Tīmūr in Iran', in P. Jackson and L. Lockhart (eds.), *The Cambridge History of Iran*, Vol. 6: *The Timurid and Ṣafavid Periods*, (Cambridge: Cambridge University Press, 1986), pp. 42-97.

———, 'The Successor of Tīmūr', in P. Jackson and L. Lockhart (eds.), *The Cambridge History of Iran*, Vol. 6: *The Timurid and Ṣafavid Periods*, (Cambridge: Cambridge University Press, 1986), pp. 98-146.

———, 'The Turkmen Dynasties', in P. Jackson and L. Lockhart (eds.), *The Cambridge History of Iran*, Vol. 6: *The Timurid and Ṣafavid Periods*, (Cambridge: Cambridge University Press, 1986), pp. 147-188.

Rushan, M., 'Ḥāfiẓ-i Sāya yā Sāya-yi Ḥāfiẓ', *Māh-nāma-yi Kilk*, Nos. 1-52 (Summer 1373/1995).

Rypka, J., *History of Iranian Literature*, ed. K. Jahn, (Dordrecht-Holland: D. Reidel Publishing Company, 1968).

Ṣādiqī, J.M., *Qiṣahā-yi Shaykh-i Ishrāq: Shahāb al-Dīn Yaḥyā Suhravardī*, (Tehran: Nashr-i Matkaz, 1375/1996).

Safā, Dh., *Ganj-i Sukhan: Shā'irān-i buzurg-i pārsī gūy va muntakhab-i āthār-i ānān*, (Tehran: Ibn Sinā, 1339/1961), 3 vols.

———, *Himāsa sarā'ī dar Iran az qadimtarīn 'ahd-i tārikhī tā qarn-i chāhārdahum-i hijrī*, (Tehran: Amīr Kabīr, 1333/1931).

———, *Tārīkh-i adabīyāt dar Iran*, (Tehran: Firdawsī 1370/1992), 4 vols.

———, *Tārikh-i adabīyāt-i Iran*, (Tehran: Firdawsī, 1378/2000).

Safa, Z., 'Persian Literature in the Ṣafavid Period', in P. Jackson and L. Lockhart (eds.), *The Cambridge History of Iran*, Vol. 6: *The Timurid and Ṣafavid Periods*, (Cambridge: Cambridge University Press, 1986), pp. 948-964.

———, 'Persian Literature in the Timurid and Turkmen Period', in P. Jackson and L. Lockhart (eds.), *The Cambridge History of Iran*, Vol. 6: *The Timurid and Ṣafavid Periods*, (Cambridge: Cambridge University Press, 1986), pp. 913-929.

Sahbā, J.M., *Sukhanī chand dar bāb-i aḥvāl va ash'ār-i Ḥāfiẓ*, (Tehran: Ispāhān, 1321/1943).

Sālik, M. (ed.), *Encyclopedia of Persian Language and Literature*, Vol. 2 (Tehran: Ḥazīn Lāhījī, 2007).

Sārimī, Ī., *Ḥāfiẓ az dīdgāh-i 'Allāma Muḥammad Qazvīnī*, (Tehran: 'Ilmī, 1366/1988).

Sarshar, H., 'Sepehri, Sohrab', *EIr Online*, www.iranicaonline.org/articles/sepehri-sohrab, (accessed May 2009).

Savory, R., ''Abbās I', *EIr*, Vol. 1, pp. 71-75.

———, *Iran under the Ṣafavids*, (Cambridge: Cambridge University Press, 1980).

———, 'The Ṣafavid Administrative System', in P. Jackson and L. Lockhart (eds.), *The Cambridge History of Iran*, Vol. 6: *The Timurid and Ṣafavid Periods*, (Cambridge: Cambridge University Press, 1986), pp. 351-372.

Schimmel, A. *A Two-Colored Brocade: The Imagery of Persian Poetry*, (Chapel Hill: North Carolina University Press, 1992).

———, 'Ḥāfiẓ and his Contemporaries', in P. Jackson and L. Lockhart (eds.), *The Cambridge History of Iran*, Vol. 6: *The Timurid and Ṣafavid Periods*, (Cambridge: Cambridge University Press, 1986), pp. 929-947.

Schwannau, Rosenzweig V.R. v., *Der Diwan: des grossen lyrischen Dichters Hafis im persischen Original/ herausgegeben ins Deutsche metrisch übersetzt und mit Anmerkungen vesehenvon*, (Vienna: K.K. Hof-und Staatsdruckerei, 1858-1864).

Shahidian, H., *Women in Iran: Gender Politics in the Islamic Republic*, (Westport, CT: Greenwood Press 2002).

Shakībāpūr, 'I., *'Itilā'āt-i 'umūmī*, (Tehran: Ishrāqī, 1384/2006).

Shamīsā, S., *Naqd-i adabī*, (Tehran: Firdawsī, 1383/2005).

———, *Nigāhī bi Sipihrī*, (Tehran: Murvārid, 1371/1993).

———, *Sabk shināsī-i shi'r*, (Tehran: Intishārāt-i Firdaws, 1374/1995).

Shari'at, M.J., *Jāvidāna Parvin: Immortal Parvin*, (Iṣfahān: Mash'al, 1356/1977).

Shari'atī, 'A., *Zan*, (Tehran: [n.p.], 1362/1983).

Shayegan, D., 'The Visionary Topography of Ḥāfiẓ', trans. Peter Russell, *Temenos: A Review Devoted to the Arts of Imagination*, Vol. 6 (1985), pp. 207-286.

Shīrāzī, S.A.A., *Firdawsī-nāma: Mardum va ahrimānān-i Shāh-nāma*, (Tehran: 'Ilmī 1369/1990), 3 vols.

Shuster, W.M., *The Strangling of Persia: A Personal Narrative*, (Washington, D.C.: Mage Publishers, 1987).

Sipanlu, M. (ed.), *Bāz āfarinī-yi vaqi'īyat: Bist u haft qiṣa az bist u haft nivisanda-yi Mu'āṣir-i Iran*, (Tehran: Nigāh, 1366/1988).

Storey, C.A., *Persian Literature: A Bio-Bibliographical Survey*, (London: Luzac & Co, 1972), 2 vols.

Subhānī, H., *Tārikh-i adabīyāt-i Iran*, (Tehran: Zavvar, 1386/2007).

Sūdī, D., *Sharḥ-i Sūdī bar Ḥāfiẓ*, (Tehran: Chāpkhāna-i Rangīn, 1341/1962).

Surūsh Iṣfahānī, *Dīvān-i Shams al-Shu'arā' Muḥammad 'Alī Khān Surūsh Iṣfahānī*, ed. M.J. Maḥjūb, (Tehran: Amīr Kabīr, 1339/1961), 2 vols.

Sutūda, Manūchihr, *Az Āstārā tā Istārbād*, (Tehran: Āgah, 1366/1987), 4 vols.

Sykes, P., *History of Persia*, (London: Macmillan, 1951), 2 vols.

———, *Ten Thousand Miles in Persia, or Eight Years in Iran*, (London: John Murray, 1902).

Ṭabātabā'ī, M.H., *Kernel of the Kernel*, (Albany: State University of New York Press, 2003).

Ṭāhbāz, S., *Kamāndār-i buzurg-i kuhistān: zindagi va sh'ir-i Nimā Yūshīj*, (Tehran: Thālith, 1380/2002).

——— (ed.) *Nāmahā-yi Nimā Yūshij*, (Tehran: Nashr-i Ābī, 1363/1972).

Tajrubikār, N., *Sabk-i shiʿr dar ʿaṣr-i Qājārīyā*, (Tehran: Maṣʿūd Saʿd Mihr, 1350/1972).

Talattof, K., *The Politics of Writing in Iran: A History of Modern Persian Literature*, (Syracuse, NY: Syracuse University Press, 2000).

Tamimdari, A., *ʿIrfān va adab dar ʿasr-i Safavī*, (Tehran: Hikmat, 1993).

Tapper, R., *Frontier Nomads of Iran: A Political and Social History of the Shahsevan*, (Cambridge: Cambridge University Press, 1997).

Taqipūr, N., *Taʾamulī dar shiʿr-i Aḥmad Shāmlū*, (Tehran: Ābān, Shāhanshāhī 2537).

Ṭarqī, M.T., 'Mīrzā Āqā Khān Kirmānī, Nāmaā-i Tabʿīd', *Iran Nameh*, Vol. 9, No. 3 (Summer 1991), pp. 478-487.

Thābitī, M., 'Khawja-yi Faqīr', *Majala-yi muḥīṭ*, No. 5 (Autumn 1321/1942), pp. 165-168.

Thackston, W.M., *A Millennium of Classical Persian Poetry: A Guide to the Reading and Understanding of Persian Poetry from the Tenth to the Twentieth Century*, (Bethesda, MD: Iranbooks, 1994).

Tucker, E., 'Explaining Nadir Shah: Kingship and Royal Legitimacy in Muḥammad Kazim Marvi's Tārīkh-i ālam-ārā-i Nādirī', Iranian Studies, *vol.* 26 (1993), pp. 95-117.

———, *Nadir Shah's Quest for Legitimacy in Post-Ṣafavid Iran*, (Gainesville: University Press of Florida, 1972).

Valī al-Ḥaqq Anṣārī, M. (ed.), *Kullīyāt-i ʿUrfī Shīrāzī*, (Tehran: Intishārāt-i Dānishgāh-i Tehran 1378/1999).

Varherām, Gh., *Tārikh-i sīyāsī va ijtimāʿ-yi Iran dar ʿaṣr-i Zand*, (Tehran: Muʿīn, 1366/1988).

Walcher, H.A., *In the Shadow of the King, Zill al-Sulṭān and Iṣfāhān under the Qājārs*, (London: I.B.Tauris, 2000).

Wellek, R. and A. Warren, *Theory of Literature*, (New York: Harcourt Brace Janovich, 1977).

Wilber, A., *Riza Shah Pahlavi: The Resurrection and Reconstruction of Iran*, (New York: Exposition Press, 1975).

Wilson, A.T., *Persia: The Modern World*, (London: Ernest Benn, 1932).

Wright, D., *The English amongst the Persians: Imperial Lives in Nineteenth-Century Iran*, (London and New York: I.B.Tauris, 1977).

Yarshater, Ehsan (ed.), 'The Constitutional Revolution', *EIr* online, www.iranica.com/newsite/, (accessed 19 July 2008).

———, 'ʿĪraj Mīrzā', *EIr*, Vol. 8, pp. 203-206.

———, *Iran Faces the Seventies*, (New York: Praeger, 1971).

———, 'Persian Poetry in the Timurid and Ṣafavid Period', in Peter Jackson and Laurence Lockhart (eds.), *The Cambridge History of Iran*, Vol. 6: *Persian Poetry in the Timurid and Ṣafavid Period*, (Cambridge: Cambridge University Press, 1986), pp. 965-994.

———, *Shi'r-i fārsī dar 'ahd-i Shāhrukh*, (Tehran: Chāpkhāna-yi Dānishgāh 1334/1956).

Yathrabī, S.Y., *Āb-i Ṭarabnāk: Taḥlil-i muḍū'ī-yi Dīvān-i Ḥāfiẓ*, (Tehran: Intishārāt-i Fikr-i Rūz, 1374/1996).

Yazdānfar, F., 'Taḥlilī az shiva-i nigārash-i Ākhūndzāda', *Iran Nameh*, Vol. 8, No. 1 (Winter 1990), pp. 95-105.

Yiktā'ī, M., *Ḥāfiẓ-i Yiktā'ī*, (Tehran: Intishārāt-i 'Alamī, 1328/1950).

Zarrinkūb, 'A.H., *Advār-i shi'r-i fārsī: Az Mashrūṭīyat tā suqūt-i saltanat*, (Tehran: Intishārāt-i Ṭūs, 1359/1980),

———, *Arastū va fann-i Shi'r*, (Tehran: Amīr Kabīr, 1382/2003).

———, *Arzish-i mirāth-i Sufīya*, (Tehran: Chāpkhāna-yi Sipihr, 1369/1990).

———, *Az kūcha-yi rindān*, (Tehran: Kitābhā-i Jibī, 1349/1971).

———, *Az kūcha-yi rindān: dar bāri-yi Zindagī va andisha-yi Ḥāfiẓ*, (Tehran: Mahārat, 1381/2003).

———, *Hadith-i khush-i Sa'dī: Dar bāra-yi zindagī va andisha-yi Sa'dī*, (Tehran: Intishārāt-i Nuvīn, 1379/2000).

———, *Justujū dar taṣawwuf-i Iran*, (Tehran: Chāpkhāna-yi Sipihr, 1367/1988).

———, *Naqd-i adabī: Justujū dar aṣūl va ravishhā va mabāḥith-i naqqādī bā bar risī dar tārikh-i naqd va naqādān*, (Tehran: Amīr Kabīr, 1354/1976), 2 vols.

———, *Sayrī dar shi'r-i fārsī*, (Tehran: Intishārāt-i Nuvīn, 1363/1984).

———, *Shu'la-yi Ṭūr: Dar bāra-yi zindagī va andisha-yi Ḥallāj*, (Tehran: Intishārāt-i Nuvīn, 1380/2001).

———, *Ṣidā-yi pā-yi Simurgh: Dar bāra-yi zindagī va andisha-yi 'Attār*, (Tehran: Sukhan, 1378/1999).

Personal Communications and Interviews

Dr. Humayoon Katouzian, Oxford, 4 June 2009.

Bahā' al-Dīn Khurramshāhī, Tehran, 18 May 2010.

Dr. Shahrām Pazouki, Tehran, 20 May 2010.

Dr. Muḥammad Riḍā Movahedi, Tehran, 23 May 2010.

Dr. Julie Meisami, Berkeley, 24 October 2011.

Dr. 'Alī Ferdowsi, Los Angeles, 26 October 2011/September 2012.

Hushang Ibtihāj *Sāya*, Germany, 30 September 2012.

General Index

Iranian Studies Series

J.C. Bürgel & C. van Ruymbeke (eds.)
Nizami: A Key to the Treasure of the Hakim
ISBN 978 90 8728 097 0

J. Coumans
The Rubáiyát of Omar Khayyám. An Updated Bibliography
ISBN 978 90 8728 096 3

F. Lewis & S. Sharma (eds.)
The Necklace of the Pleiades. 24 Essays on Persian Literature, Culture and Religion
ISBN 978 90 8728 091 8

Mahnia A. Nematollahi Mahani
The Holy Drama. Persian Passion Play in Modern Iran
ISBN 978 90 8728 115 1

C. Pérez González
Local Portraiture. Through the Lens of the 19th-Century Iranian Photographers
ISBN 978 90 8728 156 4

R. Rahmoni & G. van den Berg
The Epic of Barzu as Narrated by Jura Kamal
ISBN 978 90 8728 116 8

A. Sedighi
Agreement Restrictions in Persian
ISBN 978 90 8728 093 2

A.A. Seyed-Gohrab
Courtly Riddles. Enigmatic Embellishments in Early Persian Poetry
ISBN 978 90 8728 087 1

A.A. Seyed-Gohrab & S.R.M. McGlinn (eds.)
One Word – Yak Kaleme. 19th-Century Persian Treatise Introducing Western Codified Law
ISBN 978 90 8728 089 5

A.A. Seyed-Gohrab & S.R.M. McGlinn (eds.)
Safina Revealed. A Compendium of Persian Literature in 14th-Century Tabriz
ISBN 978 90 8728 088 8

A.A. Seyed-Gohrab, F. Doufikar-Aerts & S. McGlinn (eds.)
Embodiments of Evil: Gog and Magog. Interdisciplinary Studies of the 'Other' in Literature & Internet Texts
ISBN 978 90 8728 090 1

S. Tabatabai
Father of Persian Verse. Rudaki and his Poetry
ISBN 978 90 8728 092 5

K. Talattof & A.A. Seyed-Gohrab (eds.)
Conflict and Development in Iranian Film
ISBN 978 90 8728 169 4

Forthcoming titles in the *Iranian Studies Series*

J.T.P. de Bruijn, *The Journey of the Faithful to the Place of Return. A Persian Allegory on the Development of the Human Soul by Sanâ'i of Ghazna, Founding Father of Persian Sufism*

J.T.L. Cheung, *The Nartic Epic Tradition. Remnants of Iranian Lore from the Caucasus*

S.R.M. McGlinn, *Abdul-Baha's Sermon on the Art of Governance*